# ALL AROUND THE TOWN

## Second Edition

# ALL AROUND THE TOWN

## Amazing Manhattan Facts and Curiosities

## SECOND EDITION

### PATRICK BUNYAN

Empire State Editions

An imprint of Fordham University Press

New York   2011

Unless otherwise noted, all illustrations are credited to the Library of Congress, Prints and Photography Division.

Fordham University Press has no responsibility for the persistence or accuracy of URLs for external or third-party Internet websites referred to in this publication and does not guarantee that any content on such websites is, or will remain, accurate or appropriate.

Fordham University Press also publishes its books in a variety of electronic formats. Some content that appears in print may not be available in electronic books.

Library of Congress Cataloging-in-Publication Data

Bunyan, Patrick.
    All around the town : amazing Manhattan facts and curiosities / Patrick Bunyan.—2nd ed.
        p.   cm.
    Includes bibliographical references and indexes.
    ISBN 978-0-8232-3174-4 (pbk. : alk. paper)
    1. New York (N.Y.)—Miscellanea.   2. New York (N.Y.)—Guidebooks.   3. New York (N.Y.)—History.   I. Title.
F128.36.B86   2011
974.7'1—dc22
                                                2010026349

Printed in the United States of America

13 12 11   5 4 3 2 1

Second edition

To Scott Burns

# CONTENTS

# PREFACE

Since the publication of the first edition of *All Around the Town* more than ten years ago, much has happened in the city. The terrorist attacks on the World Trade Center are certainly the primary example. The city has just ended another one of its periodic building booms, and, as usual, the old has been torn down to make way for the new. But given Manhattan's layered past, some of these construction efforts have led to several archaeological discoveries.

This new edition of *All Around the Town* records the fascinating history that has happened on this island since the pre-colonial era—events that reflect not only the story of New York City but the story of the United States as well. These are as varied as the first exhibition of an elephant in the New World to the last-known sighting of the enigmatic Judge Joseph Crater.

This is a look back through the lenses of the city's modern landscape, by current street address. The book is an assortment of Manhattan sites, a compendium of facts, history, birthplaces, deaths, and "firsts" drawn from many sources—histories, biographies, newspapers, guidebooks, online sources, and maps. They include amusing anecdotes and familiar historical events that take readers from the Native American wilderness to the twenty-first-century super city.

The entries are arranged by today's street addresses. The book divides Manhattan into four sections:

- Lower Manhattan: south of and including Chambers Street and the Brooklyn Bridge.
- Chambers Street to 14th Street: north of Chambers Street up to and including 14th Street.
- Midtown: north of 14th Street up to and including 59th Street.
- Above 59th Street: the rest of Manhattan.

Within each of these sections, the named streets and places are listed first, alphabetically, followed by the numbered avenues and numbered streets in sequence. Last, the entries under each street or avenue are arranged by individual address or house number.

For example, 139 MacDougal Street is found in the "Chambers Street to 14th Street" section, listed alphabetically under the street name, MacDougal, then in order at No. 139. The entry for 4 West 54th Street is in the "Midtown" section, listed in numerical order under 54th Street, with East 54th Street before West 54th Street, then in order at No. 4.

The major parks are arranged by name in the alphabetical street sections. Streets are arranged by their most common usage. A street with several different names will be listed under each name. An address on East 59th Street will be listed with the numbered streets, while a Central Park South address will appear with the alphabetical streets.

A star (✦) marks what is currently at a site. A star at an address indicates that the structure is the same as referred to in the entry.

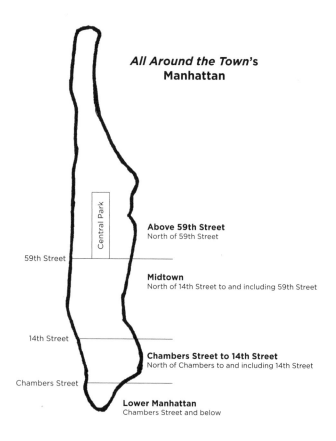

*All Around the Town*'s
**Manhattan**

Central Park

**Above 59th Street**
North of 59th Street

59th Street

**Midtown**
North of 14th Street to and including 59th Street

14th Street

**Chambers Street to 14th Street**
North of Chambers to and including 14th Street

Chambers Street

**Lower Manhattan**
Chambers Street and below

# ACKNOWLEDGMENTS

I thank the following friends for all their support and help on both editions of this book: Nava Atlas, Leonard Kniffel, Dale Neighbors, and Kelly Castro.

# ALL AROUND THE TOWN

## Second Edition

# LOWER MANHATTAN

## BARCLAY STREET

### 22 Barclay Street

*St. Peter's Roman Catholic Church* ✦ The serene Ionic-temple church on this site is the second St. Peter's. The first was consecrated on November 4, 1786, and was the first permanent Roman Catholic parish in New York state; the surrounding burial ground was the state's first Catholic cemetery. The current church was built in 1836 to replace the original, which was severely damaged in the Great Fire of 1835.

## BATTERY PARK

*Castle Clinton National Monument* ✦ The U.S. government built this one-time fort in 1807 on what was originally an artificial island about 300 feet from the shore. Constructed along with four other new fortifications in anticipation of the War of 1812, the West Battery, as it was called, never fired a shot in defense. Renamed Castle Clinton (for De-Witt Clinton, mayor and governor), it was vacated by the U.S. Army in 1823; the fort was turned over to the city, which used it as an official greeting site. The Marquis de Lafayette in 1824, President John Tyler in 1843, and Hungarian patriot Louis Kossuth in 1851 were all welcomed here. One rather unceremonious welcome was for President Andrew Jackson on June 12, 1833. The timber bridge from the fort to the Battery collapsed from the weight of the President's procession, dumping a number of men and horses into the harbor. The President, slightly ahead of the men and horses, was unhurt.

Jenny Lind, the "Swedish Nightingale," had her tumultuous American debut concert here in the now-roofed-over converted theater on September 11, 1850. More than 6,000 music lovers paid at least $3 a seat, a major coup for master showman P. T. Barnum, who had convinced Lind to perform.

From 1855 until Ellis Island opened in 1890, 7.5 million immigrants passed through this building while it served as the country's main immigration station.

The fort's penultimate incarnation was as the city's aquarium, from 1896 to 1941. It was the largest aquarium in the world when it opened, and its tanks were stocked with exotic fish from around the world.

Developer Robert Moses, who forced the aquarium to move to Coney Island, tried to have the old fort removed for his proposed Brooklyn–Battery Bridge. A public outcry stopped the bridge and the demolition of the fort. It was declared a National Historic Monument

Robert Moses proposed his Brooklyn–Battery Bridge in 1939. The plan was killed after objections from First Lady Eleanor Roosevelt and Secretary of War Harry Woodring, and the current Brooklyn–Battery Tunnel was built instead.

in 1946. After the terrorist attacks of September 11, 2001, the building housed National Guard troops for several weeks.

## BATTERY PLACE AT THE HARBOR

*Pier A* ✦ This pier has served as the gateway for many celebrities on their arrival in New York City. Charles A. Lindbergh, making his triumphal return after the first transatlantic flight on June 13, 1927; Douglas "Wrong Way" Corrigan, who made an off-course transatlantic flight on August 5, 1938; and Britain's King George VI on June 10, 1939, are among many.

But one visitor stands above all the rest: It was here that the legendary elephant Jumbo arrived on the *Assyrian Monarch* and first set his massive foot on American soil with all the fanfare P. T. Barnum could muster, on Easter Sunday, April 10, 1882. Barnum had recently purchased the elephant from the London Zoo for $10,000. Even after his death three years later in a train accident, Jumbo's fame lived on. No other animal's name has been so widely adopted into the English language.

There was a notable departure from Pier A on the evening of June 30, 1893, when President Grover Cleveland was secretly ferried to the yacht *Oneida* anchored in the East River. The purpose of the trip—five doctors and one dentist removed a large cancerous growth from Cleveland's upper jaw during a shipboard operation—was kept secret. The White House denied the rumors and insisted that the President had had a routine dental surgery. The truth was not revealed for more than 25 years, long after Cleveland's death.

P. T. Barnum's most famous circus attraction, Jumbo, paraded to the opening of "The Greatest Show on Earth" at Madison Square Garden. Jumbo arrived in America with Matthew Scott, his beloved keeper of 20 years. The pair became inseparable when Scott nursed the sick baby elephant back to health. (*Frank Leslie's Illustrated Newspaper*, April 22, 1882)

## BEEKMAN STREET

### Beekman Street at Nassau Street, southwest corner

*Beekman (Chapel) Street Theater* The earliest New York performance of *Hamlet* took place here on November 26, 1761, with 21-year-old Lewis Hallam Jr. playing the title role. Hallam was the first star known to colonial audiences and the first leading actor whose debut and early experiences were American. The theater was closed down by a riot over the Stamp Act controversy on May 5, 1766.

*Clinton Hall* On September 23, 1837, George Catlin opened his Indian Gallery here. A self-trained artist, Catlin spent several years living with Native Americans in the West, documenting their lives and customs. His sympathetic portraits and village scenes fascinated New Yorkers unfamiliar with Native American life. For almost a decade, the show traveled to other U.S. cities and to Europe. In 1852, Catlin ended up in a London debtors' prison and tried to sell his life's work to the U.S. Congress, which refused his already reduced price. Eventually the collection was donated to the Smithsonian Institution in Washington, D.C.

## BOWLING GREEN

### 1 Bowling Green between State and Whitehall streets

A small clearing in the primal forest, this area of lower Manhattan was likely the site of Peter Minuit's celebrated exchange with the natives in the late spring of 1626. The end of an age-old Indian trail that began in what is now Westchester County, north of the city, this is the beginning of today's Broadway, or *Breede Wegh* as the Dutch called it. Minuit, the French-born director-general of the Dutch colony of New Netherland, met with the natives and "bought" Manhattan island for 60 guilders or $24 worth of beads and tools.

*Fort Amsterdam* Early Dutch settlers built this fort, designed in 1626 by Kryn Frederycks. It was a four-bastioned compound that contained the governor's house, the officers' quarters, the barracks, the prison, and a church. The fort was the site of the first recorded murder in New Amsterdam, when Gerrit Jansen, a gunner, was stabbed to death in front of the gate in May 1638. The fort went through several name changes and additions with each succeeding tenant—the Dutch, the English, and the Americans—until it was torn down in 1790.

*Government House* An impressive two-story porticoed mansion was built here as a home for the President of the new nation, but by the

THE CUSTOM HOUSE, NEW YORK
1799-1815
ENGRAVED FOR THE SOCIETY OF ICONOPHILES, 1908

This imposing mansion, New York's version of the White House, stood at the foot of an unpaved Broadway. Never home to President George Washington, it was not completed until after the U.S. government moved to Philadelphia, the new capital.

time it was completed the newly formed federal government had left for Philadelphia. The house then served as New York's governor's mansion until Albany became the state capital in 1797. It was during this period that Governors George Clinton and John Jay lived here. The mansion was demolished in 1815 and replaced by smaller town houses. As business drove out residences in lower Manhattan in the mid-nineteenth century, these town houses eventually became headquarters for the leading shipping companies, and the block became known as Steamship Row.

*Alexander Hamilton United States Custom House* ✦ In 1907 this site was occupied by the country's largest and most profitable Custom House. The elaborate building was designed by Cass Gilbert and decorated with sculpture by Daniel Chester French, best known for his statue of the seated Abraham Lincoln in the sixteenth President's memorial in Washington, D.C. After the Customs Service moved to the newly opened World Trade Center in 1973, the building stood empty for more than 20 years. As a fitting memorial, this spot—long ago a meeting ground between the native population, the ancestors of the Delaware Nation, and the first European settlers—is now the New York branch of the National Museum of the American Indian.

## BOWLING GREEN PARK

A Dutch cattle market from 1638 to 1647, this spot was later the city's first park. In 1732, while the city was under British rule, it was fenced in and rented to local merchants Frederick Philipse, John Chamber, and John Roosevelt for use as a bowling area. The 10-year lease was for one peppercorn per year "for the recreation and delight of the inhabitants." It was here, also, that American patriots pulled down a gilded lead equestrian statue of King George III on July 9, 1776. They melted down the statue and used the lead for musket balls to shoot at the British.

## BROAD STREET

### 8 Broad Street

*New York Stock Exchange* ✦ This current home of the Exchange dates from 1903. All great booms and busts in the market will be measured against what happened on October 24, 1929. The great boom of the 1920s ended here on Black Thursday when 13 million shares were traded. Within a week, the losses totaled $26 billion. One of the reasons for the crash was that speculators had bought stock on margin, paying only a portion of the price, then borrowing the rest and using the stock as security for additional loans. This continued to fuel the boom as long as the market rose. But when prices fell, the borrowers needed more money to back up the drop in the value of their collateral, and panic selling followed. One resulting reform was to have the Federal Reserve Board set margin rates. The most recent bust occurred in the fall of 2008, after the collapse of the housing bubble and credit markets.

### 15 Broad Street

This was the law offices of Bangs, Stetson, Tracy and MacVeagh, where former President Grover Cleveland accepted a job after losing the 1888 election to Benjamin Harrison. Cleveland lived in New York until he returned to Washington after a successful rematch with President Harrison in 1892.

### 26 Broad Street

The first Latin school in New York was established here in the summer of 1659. Alexander Carolus Curtius, a professor from Lithuania, was hired as headmaster. He didn't last very long. He was unhappy about his salary, and parents complained that he was a poor disciplinarian. Dutch Governor Peter Stuyvesant closed the school two years later, and Curtius sailed back to Europe. The school reopened a year later with a new teacher.

## 38 Broad Street

When the fire of 1845 reached the warehouse of Crooker and Warren on the night of July 19, a tremendous explosion shook the city. The saltpeter stored here blew up with such force that the blast was felt as far away as Brooklyn and Jersey City and heard as far away as Sandy Hook, New Jersey.

## 44 Broad Street

*Woodhull, Claflin & Company*   On February 4, 1870, investors, traders, and the curious crowded the sidewalk at this address, straining to see something never before witnessed on Wall Street—the country's first

VIEW OF THE TERRIFIC EXPLOSION AT THE GREAT FIRE IN NEW YORK.
FROM BROAD ST. ...... JULY 19TH 1845.

The photojournalists of their day, the firm of Currier & Ives produced prints of news-worthy events. This lithograph depicts the July 19, 1845, explosion at a warehouse at 38 Broad Street that stored saltpeter.

brokerage firm operated by women. Victoria C. Woodhull and her sister, Tennessee Claflin, opened their business with the aid of their patron Commodore Cornelius Vanderbilt, a client from Victoria's earlier career as a clairvoyant. This office also served as campaign headquarters for Woodhull's 1872 candidacy for the U.S. presidency, 48 years before women gained the vote.

## 60 Broad Street +

This office building was once the headquarters of Drexel Burnham Lambert, one of the country's largest brokerage firms. On December 21, 1988, the company pleaded guilty in federal court to insider trading and stock manipulation and agreed to pay penalties of $650 million. The chairman of Drexel, Michael "Junk Bond King" Milken, and his friend and fellow trader Ivan Boesky both received jail terms for their involvement in the scandal. The firm, which closed in February 1990, came to symbolize the worst excesses of Wall Street wheeling and dealing during the Reagan years.

## Broad Street at Beaver Street

In the heady days leading to the Revolutionary War, this intersection marked a milestone on the road to war for American independence. On June 6, 1775, British soldiers garrisoned in the city were about to embark on the frigate *Asia* to join their fellow troops in a more receptive and safer Boston. They were stopped at this spot by Marinus Willett, an officer in the New York militia, who seized a cart full of their weapons. Willett, acting under local authority that had permitted the troops to depart but with only their own personal arms, insisted that the cart of weapons remain behind. The showdown ended with the British leaving peacefully without the additional weapons. These confiscated arms were later used by the first American troops raised in New York under the orders of Congress to fight the British. Willett served with distinction in the war and was later mayor of the city.

## Broad Street at South William Street

On the night of February 28, 1741, a chain of events began here that became known as the "Great Negro Plot," one of the saddest chapters in race relations in the city's history. On that winter night, someone broke into the shop of Robert Hogg at this corner. Some of Hogg's stolen linens later fell into the hands of John Hughson, the shady owner of a tavern that catered to slaves. Within the next few weeks, Fort George burned to the ground and there were several other mysterious fires. Determined to make a connection between the robbery and the fires, authorities arrested and questioned Hughson's young servant girl Mary Burton. Offered money and threatened with damnation, Mary spun a tale of a plot to burn the city and kill all the white people— except her boss, Hughson, who would then be crowned "king of New York." The rumored slave revolt inflamed the white colonists, whose resulting rampage ended with the execution of 31 African Americans, many of whom were burned at the stake. Another 154 were cast into prison, and 71 were deported to the West Indies. John Hughson and his wife were also executed.

## 101 Broad Street

The German-born C. T. Pachelbel, son of the renowned composer Johann, performed the first documented concert held in the city, at this site, the house of Robert Todd, a vintner, on January 21, 1736. The program consisted of instrumental music for harpsichord, flute, and violin.

*The Anglers' Club of New York* ✦ A lunchtime blast on January 24, 1975, rocked this club, an annex of next door's Fraunces Tavern, killing four people. The FALN, a Puerto Rican nationalist group, claimed responsibility for the bombing.

## Broad Street west of Water Street

*The Exchange Building* In addition to being the first capital of the United States, New York City was also the first capital of New York state. The state legislature's opening session took place in this building in January 1784. The senators and assemblymen continued to meet here until 1796, when the capital was moved to Albany. On November 3, 1789, the U.S. District Court convened here. Established under the Judiciary Act of 1789, it was the first federal court organized under the new Constitution. President George Washington appointed James Duane, former mayor of the city and the man for whom Duane Street is named, the first U.S. District judge. The highest court in the land, the U.S. Supreme Court, held its opening session here on February 17, 1790, presided over by Chief Justice John Jay. The building was demolished in 1799.

## BROADWAY

## 1 Broadway

*Kennedy Mansion* Built by Captain Archibald Kennedy of the Royal Navy in 1760, this elegant home, on the site of an earlier tavern, served as the Revolutionary War headquarters of General George Washington until the British occupied the city in September 1776 and used the house as their headquarters. It was converted into a hotel and lasted another 100 years before being replaced by the current Washington Building, the tallest office building in the world when it was built in 1884.

## 5 Broadway

This address was the home of Robert Livingston, chancellor of New York state and a member of the Continental Congress, famous for administering the presidential oath of office to George Washington in 1789. When he lived here in the early days of the republic, his garden extended down to the banks of the Hudson River.

## 9–11 Broadway

*Bowling Green Building* ✦ This Egyptian-style building once housed the offices of the White Star Line. For several days in April 1912, anxious relatives and friends of the passengers of the company's ship the *Titanic* crowded the sidewalk out front and overflowed into Bowling Green Park, hoping to receive word of the survivors of the doomed ship. Many famous New Yorkers lost their lives, including wealthy businessmen John Jacob Astor IV and Benjamin Guggenheim. Also lost were Isidor Straus, philanthropist and co-owner of R. H. Macy's department store, and his wife, Ida; their bravery and devotion to each other have become part of *Titanic* lore.

## Broadway at Beaver Street

The first time an elephant was exhibited in North America was near this intersection on April 29, 1796. The three-year-old female had arrived two weeks earlier from Bengal, India, the ship's captain, Jacob Crowninshield, having paid $450 for her. The elephant was a sensation. Crowninshield quickly resold his prize for $10,000 to a Philadelphian, who exhibited the pachyderm all over the East Coast.

## 26 Broadway

This corner was allegedly the site of the city's first documented play, perhaps so considered by biased theater historians because of the Broadway address. On December 6, 1732, *The Recruiting Officer* was performed in what was likely the barn of Mr. Rip Van Dam. The play, a farce written by George Farquhar, was performed by a company of English actors.

Both Alexander Hamilton and John Jay, at different times, had homes at this location.

The crowd outside 9 Broadway, the offices of the White Star Line, waits for a list of *Titanic* survivors after the ship sank on April 15, 1912. More than 1,493 passengers and crewmembers perished on the ship's maiden voyage to New York.

*Standard Oil Building* ✦ In 1886, the Standard Oil Trust, the world's largest and richest manufacturing concern, moved to this address from Cleveland, Ohio. That modest 10-story building was remodeled and expanded several times into the present building. Chairman John D. Rockefeller had his twenty-first-floor Tudor-style office here until the turn of the twentieth century. After he retired and turned to charitable work, the oilman-turned-philanthropist received up to 15,000 letters a week at this address asking for some of his money. One of Rockefeller's most trusted partners, Charles Pratt, who used his fortune to build the Pratt Institute and Pratt Institute Free Library, one of the first public libraries in the city, died here in his office on May 4, 1891. The Standard Oil Company moved uptown in 1956.

### 27–37 Broadway

This site is the first recorded location of a burial ground in Manhattan. In 1649, it was referred to as "the Old Church Yard" in early Dutch records. By 1676, all the lots were full. Within a few years, all the bodies were removed to a site farther north on Broadway, and this land was sold at auction.

## 39–41 Broadway

This is the legendary site of the first European dwellings on Manhattan island. Captain Adriaen Block (for whom Block Island in Rhode Island is named) and his crew were forced to spend the winter of 1613–14 here after their ship, the *Tiger*, anchored in the bay, burned that November. The Dutch sailors built four small crude huts in Native American fashion by bending over and joining the tops of two parallel rows of saplings. The following spring, the captain salvaged wood from the *Tiger* and built a new ship, which he named the *Restless*. Only 44.5 feet long, the *Restless* took Block and his crew back to Holland.

*Alexander McComb Mansion* President George Washington leased this mansion in February 1790 but lived here only several months before moving to the nation's new capital in Philadelphia. On August 30, 1790, Washington took his leave of New York City on a Hudson River wharf behind this house. The first President and the First Lady were given a 13-gun-farewell salute.

*Bunker's Mansion House* John Quincy Adams was a guest here at the old McComb Mansion, which had been converted into a hotel in 1821. The former President was in town for a dinner honoring the New-York Historical Society, on November 19, 1844.

## Broadway between Morris Street and Exchange Place, west side

At this site were the home and orchard of Hendrick Van Dyck. A Native American woman was trying to steal some peaches when Van Dyck spied her and killed her. Several days later, on September 15, 1655, Native Americans attacked the settlement in retaliation. Over a period of two days, 50 settlers were killed and many women and children were taken prisoner. This was the last major attack by native dwellers on the settlers.

## 50 Broadway

*Tower Building* A major advancement in the development of skyscrapers was skeleton-frame construction. The narrow 21.5-feet-wide, 13-story building that opened here on September 27, 1889, was the first to use this innovation. The walls were built with the new method, an iron armature supporting the weight of each floor. This key development allowed architects to build higher into the sky and not have to allocate valuable lower-floor space to thick exterior walls. One problem yet unsolved was how to reassure the public that these tall buildings wouldn't fall down. Bradford Lee Gilbert, the architect, addressed this issue by putting his own office on the top floor. This innovative monument was torn down in 1914 with little fanfare to make way for an even taller building.

## 57 Broadway

On September 7, 1879, two days after returning home from a trip abroad, Stanford White started his first day as a new partner here with fellow architects Charles McKim and William Mead. The three partners, who would create some of the most beautiful buildings in the country, mastered a classical style particularly suited to America's new wealthy class. They stayed at this address until 1894.

## 71 Broadway

*Empire Building*  Russell Sage, the wealthy financier and namesake of the philanthropic foundation, had a brokerage office on the second floor of an office building that once stood on this corner. On December 4, 1891, a madman named Henry W. Norcross entered the office and demanded $1.2 million from Sage. When Sage refused, Norcross set off a dynamite bomb, killing himself and a clerk and injuring seven others, including Sage. In addition to damaging the building, the explosion blew valuable securities out onto the street. The current Empire Building at this site was built in 1898.

## Broadway at the head of Wall Street

*Trinity Church* ✦ Richard Upjohn designed the present Gothic Revival church, the third on this spot, consecrated on May 21, 1846, Ascension Day. The ornate 281-foot stone spire made the church the highest structure in Manhattan for 30 years, until it was surpassed by the towers of the Brooklyn Bridge. During the nineteenth century, the church became a popular gathering place on New Year's Eve. The hushed crowd would listen for the lofty steeple's midnight chimes to welcome in the new year with hymns. This annual party moved uptown to the newly christened Times (formerly Longacre) Square in 1904. The first church, chartered by British King William III in 1697, was destroyed in the Great Fire of 1776.

Queen Elizabeth II visited here during the U.S. Bicentennial celebration, on July 9, 1976. The date of this visit was 200 years to the day

*The ruins of Trinity Church after the great fire in 1776.*

Like most of lower Manhattan, Trinity Church was destroyed in the fire of 1776. The British, who had recently occupied the city during the Revolutionary War, were accused of not effectively fighting the three-day blaze that destroyed 493 homes and a third of the city. (Author's collection)

American patriots had pulled down a statue of her great-great-great-great-grandfather King George III in Bowling Green Park. While here, the queen also collected 279 years' worth of "rent due the Monarchy"— 279 peppercorns—as the royal charter on the church had never expired.

The churchyard is the final resting place of several famous Trinity parishioners, including engineer and inventor Robert Fulton, Alexander Hamilton, and Francis Lewis, the only signer of the Declaration of Independence buried in Manhattan. The yard also contains the nation's first tomb to unknown soldiers, the Martyrs' Monument, honoring unidentified colonials who died in British prisons in the city during the American Revolution.

### Broadway at Wall Street

On March 24, 1987, two dozen pugnacious activists blocked traffic at this intersection until arrested and removed by the police. This protest to "crash the market" was the first by ACT-UP, the AIDS Coalition To Unleash Power. This determined, angry, and media-savvy group, founded by playwright Larry Kramer, focused attention on the AIDS epidemic, patients' rights, and the dearth of available medical treatment. They met here again 10 years later to mark the anniversary with another protest and to remind people that the AIDS fight was not over.

## 115 Broadway

*City Arm's Tavern*  An important event on the American road to independence from England took place here on October 31, 1765: a meeting of 200 merchants and the Sons of Liberty to protest the Stamp Act during which the participants decided on a non-importation agreement. Originally the mansion of Etienne De Lancey, built around 1700, the tavern went through several name and owner changes. It was the site of President George Washington's inaugural ball on May 5, 1789. Vice President John Adams, John Hancock, James Madison, Alexander Hamilton, and John Jay were guests. Because Martha Washington missed the party (she did not arrive until May 12), George danced with Mrs. Peter Livingston and Mrs. Alexander Hamilton.

*City Hotel*  This early example of a true hotel, rather than an inn, was erected in 1794. The five-story brick structure with 78 rooms was covered with the first slate roof in the city. The ground floor had fashionable shops along the Broadway side. Some 700 guests attended a grand military ball here on February 22, 1819, George Washington's birthday, in honor of General (later President) Andrew Jackson, a hero of the War of 1812.

## Broadway between Pine and Cedar streets

*The National Hotel*  Johann Maelzel and his invention The Turk, a fanciful chess machine, made their American debut on April 13, 1826, at this hotel. The Turk was a turbaned figure made of wood and filled with whirring gears, wheels, cogs, and metal parts that sat in front of a large box with a chess board on top. Maelzel and his mechanical marvel had recently amazed European audiences. The Turk had even played a chess game with Napoleon and won. Americans, too, were amazed, at least for a few years until the hoax was exposed. It was revealed that a small, skilled chess player was inside operating The Turk. This hidden assistant had managed to fool everyone by darting between inner compartments just before Maelzel opened a series of doors exposing The Turk's supposed mechanical workings.

*Equitable Building* ✦  An earlier Beaux Arts headquarters of the insurance company on this block was destroyed by a spectacular fire on January 9, 1912. The replacement and current structure with more than 1.2

Built in 1870, the Equitable Life Assurance Society headquarters at 120 Broadway was one of the first office buildings to incorporate elevators. Firefighters continued to hose down the building's shell in subzero weather during a fire on January 9, 1912.

million square feet of floor space was the world's largest office building when it was completed in 1915. The overwhelming bulk of this edifice, rising 40 stories straight up from the narrow streets, confirmed the need for long-proposed zoning laws. The city passed its first such law on July 25, 1916. The law restricted the total size of the building relative to the site and encouraged the use of setbacks on higher floors to allow more sunlight to reach the street.

One of the most enduring myths of the stock market crash of 1929 is that ruined investors were jumping out of windows en masse. The city's suicide rate was actually lower in October and November than earlier in the year when the market was still booming. What gave birth to this urban legend? Some of it can be attributed to the financial district's only suicide leap, off the roof of this building (not out of a window) on the morning of November 7, 1929. Hulda Browaski, a chief clerk in a brokerage firm, whose savings were safe, jumped, most likely as a result of stress from overwork.

### 165 Broadway

*Singer Building*   From 1908 to 1967, this location was home to the beautiful 47-story Singer Building. The rococo-style skyscraper, with innovative setbacks, was the world's tallest building for 18 months until the

The Singer Building that once stood at 165 Broadway was the first building to conform to the new zoning law regarding height and floor space. The narrow tower atop the block-long base allowed light and air to enter each floor. The innovative design proved to be its undoing. The limited space in each of the tower's floors proved too small for modern offices.

Metropolitan Life Tower at Madison Square Park was completed. The destruction of this landmark, the tallest building ever demolished until September 11, 2001, was a great loss to the city's architectural heritage.

### 176 Broadway
*Howard's Hotel*   President John Tyler stayed here on the night of June 25, 1844. The widowed President had secretly arrived earlier in the day by train from Washington, D.C., for his wedding to New Yorker Julia Gardiner. The clandestine ceremony at the Church of the Ascension the following day was kept from the public to ensure the newlyweds' privacy.

### 195 Broadway ✦
*American Telephone & Telegraph Company Building*   The first transcontinental telephone call, from the fifteenth-floor office of the president of AT&T to San Francisco over a 3,400-mile-long wire, was made on January 25, 1915. Alexander Graham Bell, from this address, spoke to his longtime assistant Thomas Watson on the West Coast. They reenacted the world's first spoken words on the telephone, the ones they had used in 1876. But this time, when Bell said, "Mr. Watson, come here, I need

you," Watson replied, "It would take me a week now." Shortly after their historic demonstration, President Woodrow Wilson called from Washington, D.C., with his congratulations.

## Broadway at Fulton Street, southwest corner

*Brady's National Gallery of Daguerreotypes* Mathew Brady opened his first daguerreotype studio on this corner in 1844. The new medium was a tremendous success in America. Within 10 years, there were more daguerreotype studios in Manhattan alone than in all of England, where legal restraints interfered with the commercialization of the process. Brady, who learned his craft from innovator Samuel F.B. Morse, was quick to see the commercial and documentary potential of photography. All the leading politicians of the day—among them Henry Clay, Daniel Webster, Martin Van Buren, and Millard Fillmore—had their photographs taken here.

## Broadway at Fulton Street

*Loew's Bridge* A lacy Gothic pedestrian bridge was built over this busy and dangerous intersection in 1867. Philip Genin, a hatter on the southwest corner, had encouraged the span's construction. A year later, his archrival, Knox the Hatter from the northeast corner, had the bridge removed by court order, claiming it blocked light and air to his store and attracted loiterers.

## Broadway between Fulton and Vesey streets

*St. Paul's Chapel* ✦ Completed in 1766, this is the oldest public building still in use in Manhattan. On April 30, 1789, almost the entire newly formed U.S. government—the Vice President, the Speaker of the House, and both houses of Congress—accompanied their newly inaugurated President of one hour, George Washington, on a walk to this chapel for a special thanksgiving service. The President worshiped here for most of the time he lived in New York. His pew, in the north aisle, is adorned with the first depiction in oil of the Great Seal of the United States. President George H.W. Bush used this same pew on April 30, 1989, while attending a special two-hundredth-anniversary service commemorating that first inauguration. Former President James Monroe's funeral was held here on July 7, 1831.

One day after its once-lofty neighbors the World Trade Center towers fell on September 11, 2001, this chapel became a tranquil refuge for the army of firefighters and rescue and construction workers. The undamaged chapel's volunteers provided meals, medical treatment, counseling, and even massages for the next eight months.

The Loew's Bridge, at Broadway and Fulton Street, enabled pedestrians to cross at all four corners of the intersection without encountering the street traffic below. (Author's collection)

### Broadway at Ann Street, southeast corner

Spring Garden   This corner was the location of the first pleasure garden in New York. Pleasure gardens, an idea imported from England, were outdoor restaurants in a landscaped setting. The Spring Garden, begun in the early 1700s, lasted until 1768.

*American Museum*   This site later became the home of P. T. Barnum's museum, a collection of natural history exhibits, "scientific" displays, and "freaks." It was here that the self-proclaimed "Prince of Humbugs" introduced the first "Siamese" (conjoined) twins, Chang and Eng, to the United States, along with General Tom Thumb, the famous little person. The building caught fire on July 13, 1865, killing most of the assembled menagerie. One Bengal tiger did manage to escape but was killed by a firefighter on Broadway. Barnum moved his new show uptown to 539 Broadway only to see that museum burn three years later.

New York Herald *Building*   Another version of nineteenth-century mass entertainment occupied this site in 1866: the *New York Herald* newspaper. It was from this building that editor James Gordon Bennett

Chang and Eng were a major attraction at P. T. Barnum's American Museum on Broadway at Ann Street. The conjoined twins from Siam, the original "Siamese Twins," later adopted the last name Bunker. The brothers saved their money, bought a plantation in North Carolina, and married two local sisters.

Jr. sent his correspondent Henry Morton Stanley on March 21, 1871, to find the missing missionary David Livingstone. Seven months later Stanley found the good doctor at Lake Tanganyika in Africa and greeted him with the words "Dr. Livingstone, I presume?" In 1896 this building was torn down, and the *Herald* moved uptown to 35th Street at Herald Square. The *Herald* ceased publication in 1924; the last vestige of the publication is the newspaper's elaborate clock in the triangular plot in front of R. H. Macy's department store.

### Broadway between Vesey and Barclay streets

*Astor House Hotel*  The Park Hotel—later renamed the Astor House Hotel—was built in 1834 on the site of a home once lived in by Rufus King, a member of the Continental Congress. John Jacob Astor, the hotel's builder, purchased the King home, lived in it for a while, and had it demolished along with the rest of the block to prepare for his innovative hotel. (It had running water in the rooms.) Opened two years later on June 1, 1836, it became the nation's favorite hotel. Andrew Jackson, Henry Clay, James Polk, Abraham Lincoln, Jefferson Davis,

The offices of the *New York Herald* are on the left in this view of Broadway looking south from Vesey Street in 1867. St. Paul's Chapel is on the right. The packed pedestrian bridge crossing busy Broadway is Loew's Bridge, an early effort at traffic control. (*Harper's Weekly,* June 8, 1867)

and Sam Houston all stayed here. William James, the psychologist, was born in the hotel on January 11, 1842. English author Charles Dickens stayed at this hotel on his first trip to New York, in 1842, and it was here 70 years later that his eldest surviving son, Alfred D'Orsay Tennyson Dickens, died suddenly on January 2, 1912. Alfred was in New York planning his father's centenary celebration.

### Broadway between Vesey and Murray streets
The city's first sidewalk lined these three blocks of Broadway in 1790. The narrow walkways were paved with stones and bricks.

### Broadway between Barclay Street and Park Place
This was once the site of Mayor Philip Hone's home. Mayor from 1826 to 1827, Hone was also a bank director, trustee of Columbia College, vice president of the New-York Historical Society, and founder of the Union Club. This Renaissance man is known today chiefly through his diary. His chronicle, kept from 1823 to 1851, has been a blessing to generations of historians eager to learn of New York City life in the mid–

President-elect Abraham Lincoln spoke from the balcony over the columned entrance of the Astor Hotel on February 19, 1861. He was visiting the city for two days while en route to his first inauguration in Washington. The hotel was torn down in 1914.

nineteenth century. In 1836, Hone recorded in his diary a now-familiar New York phenomenon: rising real estate values' prompting him to sell his home to the American Hotel next door and move uptown. The hotel was host to President Andrew Jackson, Daniel Webster, and other notables.

*Woolworth Building* ✦ This Gothic-style masterpiece is nicknamed "the Cathedral of Commerce." Opening celebrations on April 24, 1913, included a twenty-seventh-floor dinner for three U.S. senators and 78 congressmen. That night, President Woodrow Wilson, sitting in Washington, D.C., pushed a button that lit 80,000 light bulbs in what was then the world's tallest skyscraper. F. W. Woolworth realized the commercial and publicity value of having the tallest, as did his architect, Cass Gilbert, who wrote that the skyscraper is "a machine to make the land pay."

## 243 Broadway

Three small offices on the second floor of a building once at this address were the first home in 1863 of the National Union Life and Limb Insurance Company. It was chartered to insure Civil War soldiers in case of injury or death. After the war and several reorganizations, the company changed its name to Metropolitan Life, in honor of the "metropolitan" district of New York.

## Broadway at Warren Street, southwest corner

On September 21, 1837, Charles Lewis Tiffany and John B. Young opened a "fancy goods" and stationery shop at this address. Sales for the first day totaled $4.98, with a profit the first week of $334. The first Tiffany's remained at this location until 1841.

*Devlin & Company Clothing*   The basement of a later corner building was the hidden entrance to a subterranean room furnished with a grand piano, a fountain, and a goldfish tank. This sumptuous chamber served as the waiting room and ticket office for New York's earliest subway. The project, completed after 58 nights of tunneling, was built secretly to avoid the city corruption and graft kickbacks of the Tammany political bosses. The tunnel, 12 feet below Broadway, was designed for compressed-air propulsion and was only 9 feet in diameter and 312 feet long. This prototype, invented by the publisher of *Scientific American*, Alfred Ely Beach, was unveiled to the public on February 26, 1870. It was an immediate sensation. The *New York Herald* reported that the tunnel was an "Aladdin's cave" full of hidden magic. Over the next year, 400,000 people rode the fancy car at 25 cents a ride, the proceeds going to charity. But this type of subway system was never built on a larger scale. It was too expensive to produce the tremendous volume of air need to propel the train. Beach rented out his tunnel for a shooting gallery and as storage for wine, but he soon after had it sealed. The station and the tunnel were forgotten—until February 8, 1912, when subway workers, working on the current BMT (Brooklyn–Manhattan Transit) line, were astonished to discover it.

## 263 Broadway

The drugstore of Dr. James R. Chilton, a chemist and early photography buff, was once at this address. It was here that the first successful daguerreotype ever taken in the Western Hemisphere was displayed on September 16, 1839. The picture was taken on a sensitized copper plate by D. W. Seager, an Englishman living in New York. The subject matter

ENTRANCE TO TUNNEL, WITH PASSENGER-CAR COMING IN.

The capsule-shaped subway car is approaching the station beneath Broadway and Warren Street in this illustration from 1870. The experimental pneumatic tunnel system was powered with a huge helix fan. (*Frank Leslie's Illustrated Newspaper*, February 19, 1870)

was a faint image of St. Paul's Chapel, just down Broadway. The camera exposure for this picture was more than eight minutes long. This streetscape of the city has been lost, as have other early photographs of the city. The earliest-known photograph of New York City is an 1848 daguerreotype of a home on the Bloomingdale Road, what is now Broadway.

### Broadway at Chambers Street, southwest corner

*Chemical Bank Headquarters* An imposing classical-style bank here was the unofficial business address of Hetty Green, America's wealthiest woman and the bank's best customer. To circumvent the tax collector, she avoided having a permanent residence; for the same reason, she claimed never to have had a permanent business address. Beginning in the 1880s, she managed her mighty business empire from corner space she shared with the bank's clerks.

## BROOKLYN BRIDGE

A wonder of the nineteenth century, the East River Bridge, as it was first called, was a result of the engineering genius of its chief designer, John A. Roebling. He was one of the first to use steel cable on such a colossal scale in a suspension bridge. Roebling died while working on the project and was replaced by his son Washington. While working in the caissons on the riverbed, Washington was disabled by the pressure, what is now understood as "the bends." It took 14 years to complete what was then the world's longest suspension bridge, a proud symbol of the Industrial Age. Its Gothic towers strung with harp-like cables soared over the city. During opening-day ceremonies, on May 24, 1883, President Chester A. Arthur led a walk across the span from the nation's largest city, New York, to the nation's third-largest city, Brooklyn. (Brooklyn did not become part of New York City until 1898.) A week later, on Memorial Day weekend, a tragic stampede that killed 12 people, including two children, marred the celebrations.

A man named Steve Brodie claimed to have jumped from the bridge on July 23, 1886. Although no one saw him take the plunge, he was seen being pulled from the East River, and that was enough for him to become an actor, bar owner, and folk hero.

## CHAMBERS STREET

During one of the city's worst yellow fever epidemics—in August 1822—a fence was erected along Chambers Street, intended to prevent citizens from returning to their homes and businesses in lower Manhattan. Earlier, the authorities had forced the evacuation of much of the population in hopes of stemming the epidemic. A contemporary account recorded the scene: "Saturday the 24th August, our city presented the appearance of a town besieged. From daybreak till night one line of carts, containing boxes, merchandise and the effects, were seen moving towards Greenwich Village [from] the upper parts of the city." These summer outbreaks of yellow fever accelerated the development of the city northward up the island of Manhattan.

### Chambers and Centre streets, southwest corner

*The Rotunda*   This classical, domed, temple-like structure, erected in 1818 by painter John Vanderlyn with the help of his patron Aaron Burr,

On May 30, 1883, after hearing the screams of a woman who had fallen on a staircase, the crowd panicked, believing the new Brooklyn Bridge was collapsing. The resulting stampede killed a dozen people, including two children, and injured several more. (*Frank Leslie's Illustrated Newspaper*, June 9, 1883)

was intended as an art center for the new nation. The paintings of Thomas Cole, John Trumbull, Samuel F.B. Morse, and Asher Durand were exhibited along with Vanderlyn's own panorama of the Gardens of Versailles. The space beneath the dome served as a viewing room for the elaborate painted panorama. Guests, who stood in the center on an elevated platform, were surrounded by the painted garden. The venture was a financial failure. The city took over the building and it housed government offices until it was demolished in 1870.

## Chambers Street at Centre Street

Thousands of horrified pedestrians witnessed the electrocution here of Western Union lineman John Feeks on October 11, 1889. His smoking body hung in a tangle of overhead telegraph, telephone, and electrical wires for half an hour before his co-workers could safely cut him free. This graphic example of the dangers of overhead wires finally convinced the city to enforce a law requiring utilities to bury their lines underground. The law was prompted by the recent Blizzard of 1888, which downed so many wires that the city was cut off from the rest of the country.

## 31–33 Chambers Street

*Manhattan Company Reservoir*   An Egyptian-style reservoir topped with a reclining statue of Aquarius, the water bearer, stood at this spot. Future Vice President Aaron Burr founded this enterprise, called the Manhattan Company, in 1799. It supplied the growing city with fresh water from pine-wood pipes coated with tar for tightness and longevity. An unusual charter from the state legislature allowed the company to engage in banking activities. (The company was an early parent of the Chase Manhattan Bank.) One vocal critic of this reservoir company's being in the banking business was former U.S. Secretary of the Treasury Alexander Hamilton. This disagreement between Burr and Hamilton was the first of many that eventually led to their duel, which resulted in Hamilton's death, in 1804.

## 39–41 Chambers Street

*Palmo's Opera House*   Opened by Signor Ferdinando Palmo in 1844, this small theater was built to bring Italian opera to New York on a permanent basis. Palmo lost his opera house and all his money within two years. It later reopened as Burton's Chambers Street Theater. It was the first theater in the city to sell numbered seats, and tardy theatergoers were assured of an empty seat. This theater was one of many that staged risqué "artist model shows" in the middle of the nineteenth century. A contemporary account of the show described "living men and women in almost the same state in which Gabriel saw them in the Garden of Eden on the first morning of creation." Such shows were eventually outlawed.

## 52 Chambers Street

*New York Institution*   Originally the city's second almshouse in City Hall Park, this building was set aside for a variety of other benevolent purposes in 1816, when the poor were moved to Bellevue Hospital. It was an early home to the New-York Historical Society, the Society Library, and the American Academy of Fine Arts. Another early tenant located here was the Bank for Savings, the first savings bank in the United States. It opened for business on July 3, 1819, in the Institution's basement.

*Old New York Courthouse* ✦ The "Tweed" courthouse has come to symbolize the most corrupt era in the city's government. Legislation in 1858 set aside $250,000 for construction of this Victorian pile. But when it was completed in 1872, the total cost to the taxpayers came to more than $12 million. The difference ended up lining the pockets of "Boss" William Magear Tweed and his cronies. The eventual cost for New York's new courthouse was twice the price the United States had paid for the state of Alaska just five years earlier.

This courthouse served as a fitting stage for Judge Samuel Seabury's investigation into city corruption. On May 25, 1932, Mayor Jimmy Walker took the stand and confirmed what even his admirers suspected—that the popular "Night Mayor" wasn't very honest, even by New York standards. The mayor was summoned to Albany by Governor Franklin Roosevelt, a fellow Democrat, to face charges. Walker resigned on September 1, 1932, and promptly left for a European vacation.

In 2002, the courthouse was restored to its former glory; and, true to its legacy, the $85 million renovation project cost double the initial estimate. It was to become the new home of the Museum of the City of New York, but in a widely criticized decision, Mayor Michael R. Bloomberg decided that the space would become home to the Board of Education.

### 122 Chambers Street

In 1818, the wealthy Mr. Isaac Jones Jr. built his home at this address in what was then a very fashionable neighborhood. His socialite wife, Mary, was the inspiration for the character of Mrs. Mason Mingott in the novel *The Age of Innocence*, written by Jones's niece Edith Wharton. The house, which survived until 1858, was reputed to have had the city's first bathtub.

## CHERRY STREET

### 1 Cherry Street

From April 23, 1789, to February 23, 1790, President George Washington lived at this address in a red brick mansion owned by Walter Franklin.

DeWitt Clinton occupied the same house in 1817 before moving to Albany to become governor.

## 5 Cherry Street

This address was once the home of John Hancock. It later was the birthplace, on April 3, 1823, of New York City's most notorious politician, William Magear Tweed, whose middle name is often given incorrectly as Marcy. Tweed's father ran his chair-making business from his home at this address. This entire stretch of Cherry Street no longer exists; it was replaced by the Manhattan approach to the Brooklyn Bridge.

## 27 Cherry Street

New York City's answer to Betsy Ross, Samuel Chester Reid, lived in a house that once stood at this address. Reid, who was a naval officer in the War of 1812, is credited with designing the U.S. flag in its present modern form, with thirteen stripes and a varying number of stars. The first flag of his design, sewn by his wife, Mary, in their dining room, was raised over the U.S. Capitol on April 12, 1818.

## CHURCH STREET

### Church Street at Vesey Street

In 1859, this intersection was part of the wharf district where George Huntington Hartford and his partner George F. Gillman began their small tea company. This fledgling enterprise, which sold tea directly from ships arriving from Asia to their New York City customers, would grow to be one of the largest companies in the world, the Great Atlantic and Pacific Tea Company, commonly known as the A&P.

### 85 Church Street

This address was once the home of John Wesley Jarvis, an important early American portrait painter. Writer Thomas Paine, his friend, lived with him here for six months in 1806.

### Church Street between Park Place and Murray Street, west side

*King's College*   Here was the first permanent home of King's College, which was renamed Columbia College after the Revolutionary War. The school's first commencement exercises were held here on June 26, 1758. Alexander Hamilton, John Jay, Robert Livingston, Gouverneur

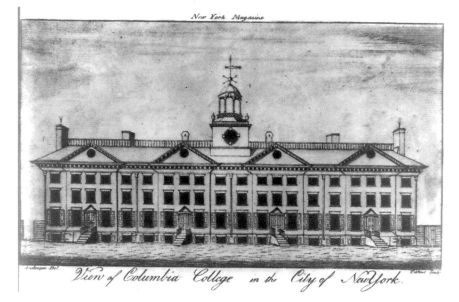

*View of Columbia College in the City of New York.*

This print shows the original Nassau Hall at King's College's, built in 1756, on Church Street. Classes were suspended during the American Revolution while the building was used as military hospital.

Morris, and DeWitt Clinton, all leaders of the newly independent nation, studied at this campus. Columbia was here from 1760 to 1857, when the school moved to East 49th Street and Madison Avenue.

## CITY HALL PARK

Once it was cleared of the forest, this *V*-shaped field between a Native American trail (now Broadway) and the High Road to Boston (now Park Row) was used as a communal pasture and the city commons. On the edge of town and undesirable, it was the site of the city's first almshouse, in 1735. An early attempt at social services, the almshouse provided housing and working quarters for "disorderly persons, parents of bastard children, beggars, servants running away or otherwise misbehaving themselves, trespassers, rogues and vagabonds." In May 1766, the Sons of Liberty erected their pole here to celebrate the repeal of the Stamp Act. British soldiers cut down this and subsequent Liberty Poles. The Bridewell Prison was built here in 1777 to house American patriots during the Revolution. On July 9, 1776, the fifth Liberty Pole served as a gathering point for a crowd, including General George Washington, to hear the Declaration of Independence read aloud.

**32** | **LOWER MANHATTAN**

*City Hall* ✦ This delicate French Renaissance–style structure has served as City Hall since its dedication just before the outbreak of the War of 1812; it is the oldest city hall in the United States still used for its original governmental function. For nearly 200 years it has been a focal point for the city's triumphs and tragedies, including the assassination on July 23, 2003, of Councilman James E. Davis. It has been a site for the mourning of fallen leaders and heroes who lay in state within its walls: Henry Clay on July 3, 1852; John Quincy Adams on March 8, 1858; and Ulysses S. Grant on August 5, 1885. Abraham Lincoln's body was placed on the circular staircase for his funeral on April 24, 1865. More than 120,000 mourners paid their respects to the Great Emancipator during the 24 hours the body was on view. The front steps have been a stage for mayoral inaugurations, protests, and speeches. These steps often serve as the finish line for Broadway ticker-tape parades honoring foreign dignitaries, winning athletes, politicians, and explorers.

*City Hall Subway Station* ✦ After an hour and a half of speeches above ground, the new mayor, George B. McClellan Jr., son of the Civil

The casket of President Abraham Lincoln is carried from City Hall to a horse-drawn hearse on April 25, 1865. Funeral services in New York City were one of many stops on the two-week 1,654-mile journey from Washington, D.C., to Springfield, Illinois. (*Harper's Weekly*, May 13, 1865)

War general, and other dignitaries made their way down to this station underneath the drive in front of City Hall to officially open the subway on October 27, 1904. This beautifully tiled station, unfortunately now closed to the public, was the start of that first ride at 2:35 P.M. With the words "I now, as Mayor, in the name of the people declare the subway open," McClellan pulled the Tiffany-made solid silver control handle, and the train lurched uptown. The enthusiastic mayor refused to relinquish the controls, as planned, and continued his role as conductor. He overshot several stations and jerked a few of his notable passengers out of their seats. In spite of the mayor's unsure hand, that first subway arrived at the last stop, at 145th Street, 26 minutes later. At 7:00, the Interborough Rapid Transit (IRT) line was opened to the public. By the end of the day, more than 110,000 passengers had entered the system.

## CLIFF STREET

### 65 Cliff Street
*African Free School*   On November 1, 1788, the first school for African Americans was opened by the Manumission Society, a group devoted to the abolition of slavery. The students, both boys and girls, were part of the first generation of black New Yorkers to be born in freedom.

## CORTLANDT STREET

### Cortlandt Street at West Street
This was the landing dock of the world's first steam ferryboat. On July 2, 1812, the *Jersey* carried the first passengers from here to New Jersey, just south of Hoboken. Designed and operated by Robert Fulton, the innovative all-wooden ship weighed 118 tons and was 30 feet wide and 80 feet long. The open, double-ended design made it unnecessary to come around 180 degrees before or after each landing, enabling wagons to disembark from the same direction from which they had boarded. This saved time and effort on every crossing and docking. Before the advent of steam-driven travel, ferries were powered by draft horses harnessed to treadmills connected to the paddle wheels.

### Cortlandt Street at Greenwich Street
On August 8, 1673, a band of Dutch sailors, cheered on by the local Dutch citizenry, landed here, at what was then the Hudson River shoreline, and marched down Broadway to Fort James. They were part of a Dutch fleet of 23 vessels in the harbor, and they easily recaptured the once-Dutch colony from the English. Their victory was short-lived. The

city reverted back to English control after the treaty of Westminster on February 19, 1674, which ended the third Anglo-Dutch War.

## DEY STREET

### Dey Street at Greenwich Street

During an excavation at this intersection in 1916, the earliest-known artifacts of Europeans in New York were discovered: the charred timbers of the Dutch ship *Tiger*. The ship's captain, Adriaen Block, and his men were forced to camp on Manhattan island during the winter of 1613–14 after the *Tiger* burned. The crew later built a new, smaller ship and returned to Holland.

## DOVER STREET

### Dover Street at Pearl Street

Cornelis Dircksen established the first ferry to Long Island around 1640 at this site, on what was then the East River shoreline. The passengers signaled Dircksen and his row boat by blowing on a conch shell horn hung on trees on each side of the shore. These passengers, the earliest recorded New York City commuters, were Dutch planters who farmed small plots in Brooklyn. The land, just recently purchased from the Native Americans, was still the property of the Dutch West Indian Company and leased to the planters until their debts were repaid.

## FRANKFORT STREET

### 39 Frankfort Street

George B. Smith, a member of Engine Company No. 12, placed the first modern fire hydrant in New York City at this address in 1817. Smith installed the hydrant, an octagon-shaped wooden enclosure held together with iron straps, in front of his own house at his own expense. Unfortunately, low pressure in the water main limited the effectiveness of the new device, and it wasn't until the 1840s that hydrants became widespread.

## FRANKLIN SQUARE

### 1 Franklin Square

Now replaced by the anchorage to the Brooklyn Bridge, this square was at the end of Cherry Street. It was the location for a public demonstration of the city's first gas street lamp on June 11, 1824. Two years later, these new gas-burning lamps were lighting up Broadway from the Battery to Grand Street.

## FULTON STREET

### Fulton Street at the East River
The Fulton Ferry Company, headed by engineer and businessman Robert Fulton, began the first steamboat ferry service to Brooklyn on Saturday, May 10, 1814. The ship, the *Nassau*, made the trip in about eight minutes at a speed of five miles per hour. Fulton's ferry hastened the development of Brooklyn as a residential community, the nation's first suburb. The ferry landings were later honored and renamed Fulton Street, one in New York and the other across the river in Brooklyn. The *Nassau*, after many years in service, was converted into a floating chapel tied to a New York wharf.

### 71 Fulton Street
Situated in a courtyard at the back of this lot was the city's first recorded permanent fire station. Built in the early 1820s, this "Fireman's Hall" served as both a headquarters and a social club for the volunteer firefighters. Prior to this structure, crude neighborhood sheds filled with ladders, hand engines, and buckets were the only means of defense against fire in the predominantly wooden city.

### 120 Fulton Street
Beginning in the early 1880s, José Martí, the revolutionary and poet, worked at the Uruguay consulate on the fourth floor of a building here, now gone. Martí, the editor of the nationalist newspaper *Patria* and founder of the Cuban Revolutionary Party, met here with other exiles and intellectuals to plan for Cuban independence. He left New York on January 31, 1895, to lead an expeditionary force to Cuba and was killed during the Battle of Dos Rios fighting the Spanish in May.

### 148 Fulton Street
On October 25, 1857, Joseph Wedemeyer, a friend of both Karl Marx and Friedrich Engels, founded the Communist Club of New York. His club, which met at this address, was the first Marxist organization in the Western Hemisphere.

### 168–172 Fulton Street
Opened in 1795, this was the warehouse, workshop, and showroom of America's leading furniture craftsman, Duncan Phyfe. He lived across the street at No. 169.

## 252 Fulton Street

*Jimmy the Priest's Saloon*   A ground-floor saloon with a flophouse above was once home to sailors in town between voyages. One of them was Eugene O'Neill. It was here, upstairs in his room, that the future playwright attempted suicide in December 1911. The saloon, complete with an old mahogany bar and sawdust on the floor, served as a model for the gin joints in his plays *The Iceman Cometh* and *Anna Christie*.

## GOLD STREET

### 55 Gold Street

At this address in the 1830s was a "soda fountain." John Matthews, the proprietor, invented a method of carbonating water by combining it with sulphuric acid and marble dust. During the construction of St. Patrick's Cathedral on Fifth Avenue, he purchased all the marble scraps to make his bubbly treat.

## GREENWICH STREET

### Greenwich Street between Battery Place and Cortlandt Street

This length of Greenwich Street was the test section of the world's first elevated railway. The inventor, Charles T. Harvey, rode the cable-driven car on its initial run on July 3, 1867. The line was built on a row of iron supports and consisted of a single track. Steam engines housed in underground vaults supplied the power to pull the continuously moving three-quarter-inch steel cable. The car edged forward when the driver engaged a clamp that extended below the wooden car and gripped the cable. Repeated cable breakdowns doomed the system until locomotive power replaced the cable system in 1871. Harvey's mass transit innovation evolved into the Ninth Avenue Elevated Line.

### 82–84 Greenwich Street

These two lots extending through to Washington Street were once the site of one of the earliest circuses in America. Showman John Bill Ricketts put together some equestrian acts, called his show a circus, and brought his troupe up from Philadelphia in 1793—first to a site on Broadway, then to this site in 1797. It was here that President John Adams watched the show on October 24th of that year.

### 250 Greenwich Street

*7 World Trade Center*   Learning of the terrorist attacks on September 11, 2001, Mayor Rudolph W. Giuliani hurried here to the city's Emergency Operations Center. Opened just two years earlier, the $13 million, twenty-third-floor EOC, created in response to the first World Trade Center attack, an underground bombing in 1993, was designed to coordinate the resources of the city, state, and federal governments in case of a disaster. It housed a sophisticated computer system, space for 87 agencies, and secure phone banks. The mayor was unable to enter; the police department had already ordered the building evacuated. Flaming debris from the twin towers and lack of water to fight the fires destroyed the building, which collapsed at 5:20 P.M., the last of the WTC complex to fall. The new "green" (environmentally friendly) 51-story skyscraper, the first at ground zero Zero to be rebuilt, opened in 2006.

## HANOVER SQUARE

Once along the East River shoreline, this square is one of the oldest public parks in the city. It was named for King George I, elector of the house of Hanover. On July 6, 2010, 84-year-old Queen Elizabeth II formally opened the revamped park as the British Memorial Garden in honor of the British subjects who died during the World Trade Center attack on September 11, 2001.

## HANOVER STREET

### Hanover Street at Exchange Street

*Mercantile Agency*   On August 1, 1841, Lewis Tappan offered his new service, credit rating, to the business community. The Mercantile Agency, which eventually became the giant Dun & Bradstreet, was a landmark in the development of credit and expansion of commerce. Tappan, an owner of a failed business, realized the need for reliable credit information. He collected and analyzed financial information on credit seekers and then sold it to his subscribers. A religious abolitionist, he used an existing network of trusted local community leaders, one of whom was a Springfield, Illinois, lawyer named Abraham Lincoln, to gather up-to-date information. Tappan eventually sold his company and devoted himself to anti-slavery causes.

### Hanover Street at Beaver Street

*Comstock and Adams Dry Goods Store*   The fire, caused by a gas pipe explosion, that started in this store on December 15, 1835, was the origin of the Great Fire of 1835. This conflagration burned for two days and engulfed the heart of the business district, everything south of Wall Street and east of Broad Street. More than 600 buildings were totally

THE GREAT FIRE OF THE CITY OF NEW-YORK, 16 DECEMBER 1835.

The greatest amount of property damage in the history of the city occurred during the Great Fire of 1835. The building with the cupola (*center*) was the recently completed Merchant's Exchange at 55 Wall Street.

consumed. In addition to the enormous loss to the financial community, nearly all the city's fire insurance companies were destroyed or bankrupted, leaving their clients with no hope of compensation. Yet for all the destruction, there was miraculously no loss of life.

## JOHN STREET

### 15–21 John Street

*John Street Theater*    One of the earliest theaters built in New York, the John Street Theater stood here from its opening on December 7, 1767, to 1798. The building was described as "principally of wood; an unsightly object, painted red." Royall Tyler's *The Contrast*, the first comedy in America produced by a native author, was performed here on April 16, 1787. It introduced the character of Jonathan, the stereotypical rustic

Yankee. Later, President and Mrs. George Washington, who had their own box, were welcomed at each performance with the "President's March," later known as "Hail Columbia." Washington's attendance helped mitigate local religious opposition to the theater.

## 44 John Street

*John Street United Methodist Church*   This is the site of the oldest Methodist Society in America. Philip Embury preached at the dedication service here at a small "Wesley Chapel" on October 30, 1768. The current church, the third on this site, was erected in 1840.

## John Street between Nassau and William streets

The Battle of Golden Hill was fought on this spot on January 19, 1770, shedding the first blood of the American Revolution, several weeks before the Boston Massacre. The Sons of Liberty and their sympathizers had rioted here on this site of a British Army barracks, outraged by the British removal of their Liberty Pole and over the issue of quartering

*Wesley Chapel in John Street, New York — the First Methodist Church in America*

Peter Williams Sr., pictured in the doorway of the John Street Methodist Church, was an African American slave purchased by the congregation. He became the chapel's sexton and undertaker. After he was given his freedom, he helped found the African Methodist Zion Church.

British soldiers in their homes. One patriot was killed and several were wounded.

### 81 John Street

This address was once the office of J. L. Haiger, who in 1877 became the first paid telephone subscriber in the city. A five-mile-long wire was laid across the half-finished Brooklyn Bridge connecting this office to his steel wire plant in Brooklyn.

## LIBERTY STREET

### 28–36 Liberty Street

*Livingston Sugar House*   A warehouse once on this spot served as a British military prison for American Revolutionary War soldiers from 1776 to 1783. Sugar houses were commonly used as jails by the British. Built of stone walls and having small windows and low ceilings, they were ideal for holding prisoners as well as sugar. This is now the site of Chase Manhattan Bank Plaza.

### 33 Liberty Street

*Federal Reserve Bank of New York* ✦ Bank President Timothy F. Geithner (later President Barack Obama's Treasury Secretary) called an emergency meeting here on Friday evening, September 12, 2008, to discuss the imminent collapse of Lehman Brothers and the subprime mortgage crisis. Those attending—Treasury Secretary Henry M. Paulson Jr., Federal Reserve Chairman Ben S. Bernanke, and Wall Street CEOs—hoped to find a buyer for the investment services firm by the time the markets opened the following Monday. But unlike Bear Stearns, which was taken over by J. P. Morgan in March, Lehman was forced to declare bankruptcy. The crisis reached a critical stage and only worsened the following week. The insurance giant American International Group (AIG) was given an $85 billion loan, the first of several, and failing Merrill Lynch was forced to merge with Bank of America. This was the beginning of the worst economic crisis since the Great Depression.

### 55 Liberty Street

Liberty Tower ✦ The current cooperative apartment house once housed the twenty-ninth-floor headquarters of the Sinclair Consolidated Oil Company, run by Harry Sinclair. In the early 1920s, U.S. Secretary of the Interior Albert B. Fall secretly transferred government oil lands to Sinclair's company. The deals, exposed by the end of the decade, became known as the Teapot Dome scandal and resulted in prison terms for both Sinclair and Fall. Franklin D. Roosevelt, then vice president and New York representative of the Fidelity and Deposit Insurance Company of Maryland, had a first-floor office here in the mid-1920s.

### 59 Liberty Street

In the early 1870s Charles Guiteau had a struggling law practice in a building that once stood at this address. Guiteau became infamous about 10 years later for shooting President James A. Garfield on July 2, 1881, in a Washington, D.C., train station. Garfield died two months later, and Guiteau was hanged for the assassination.

## MAIDEN LANE

### 19 Maiden Lane

James Madison was living in Elsworth's Boarding House, which once stood at this address, in 1787. It was here that the future President of the United States co-wrote *The Federalist Papers*, essays explaining the new Constitution and advocating its adoption.

### 57 Maiden Lane

After moving to the city on March 21, 1790, as the country's first Secretary of State, Thomas Jefferson wrote, "My first object was to look out a house on the Broadway as being the centre of my business. Finding none there vacant for the present, I have taken a small one in Maiden Lane, which may give me time to look about." Jefferson lived for three months in a house that stood at this address until 1929.

### Maiden Lane near William Street

It was near this spot, in an orchard owned by a Mr. Cook, long since replaced by modern office buildings, that a group of 25 African American and three Native American slaves met after midnight on April 7, 1712, to plan an insurrection against their white masters. They waited until the moon was setting at two o'clock and then their leader, a slave named Coffee, set fire to the outhouse of his owner, Peter Van Tilburgh. The plotters watched and waited as a crowd gathered, drawn by the blaze. The slaves attacked, killing nine people and wounding six others. The local militia caught and killed some of the revolutionaries within hours. The rest were rounded up and brutally executed—most burned alive—as an example to the colony's slaves.

## MURRAY STREET

### 24–26 Murray Street ✦

One of America's most-beloved Christmas presents, the Lionel toy train, was manufactured on the third floor of this building. Twenty-year-old founder and tinkerer Joshua Lionel Cowen took the motor out of an electric fan and placed it in a model railroad flatcar. He took his first toy engine and circle of brass track to a novelty shop, which quickly sold the set for $6 and ordered six more. On September 5, 1900, he moved here to make his trains and by 1921 he had sold more than a million sets.

## NASSAU STREET

### Nassau Street between Cedar and Liberty streets, east side

*Middle Dutch Church*   Dating from 1727, this gabled church was used as a prison and a riding school for the British during the Revolution. On April 29, 1839, the city celebrated at this church the fiftieth anniversary of the inauguration of President George Washington. The guest of honor was 69-year-old former President John Quincy Adams, who spoke for two hours. Adams shared the stage with a chair used by Washington at the 1789 inauguration. In 1845 the building was leased to the federal government as a post office. It was here, in a second-floor office, that the first U.S. stamps were issued on July 1, 1847. The stamps, a 5-cent issue with Benjamin Franklin's image and a 10-cent issue with George Washington's image, were a new innovation: prepaid postage. Prior to this, all letters were delivered with postage due.

### 82 Nassau Street

*New York Telephone Exchange*   The Bell Company opened the first telephone exchange here in March 1878. Later, in October, the city's first telephone directory, with 252 names, was issued on a small card. In the early days, there were no telephone numbers. Callers asked the operator for the name of the person they wanted to reach.

### 113 Nassau Street ✦

On September 18, 1851, the first issue of the *New York Times* was put to bed by candlelight. Henry J. Raymond and George Jones, founders of the newspaper, moved into the same five-story building that stands here today. Not yet finished, the new building lacked glass in the windows and gas for lighting.

## 115 Nassau Street

*Currier & Ives Shop*   The offices and salesroom of America's foremost lithographic team were at this address in the 1880s. Nathaniel Currier started his print shop in 1834. For the next 70 years he and James Merritt Ives, his partner after 1857, produced thousands of cherished prints. These scenes, whose subject matter ranged from domestic scenes to disasters, are an important visual record of nineteenth-century America.

## 126 Nassau Street

A boarding house at this address was once home to Mary Cecilia Rogers, a beautiful young woman who sold cigars and tobacco on Broadway near Duane Street. She was a familiar and beloved figure in the neighborhood. Her disappearance on July 25, 1841, and the finding of her strangled body floating in the Hudson River shocked the city. Her murder was never solved. Edgar Allan Poe, an admirer who frequented her shop, later based his "Mystery of Marie Rogêt" on this case.

## 135 Nassau Street

*Clinton Hall*   Built by the Mercantile Library Association as their circulating library, this building was the office of Lorenzo and Orson Fowler in 1835. The two brothers were the country's leading proponents and practitioners of phrenology, the art of analyzing character from the conformation of the skull. The "head reading" fad swept the nation in the mid–nineteenth century. As with many pseudo-sciences, phrenology had many unshakable devotees, including Walt Whitman and Edgar Allan Poe. This address served as the Fowlers' base of operations with examination rooms, a museum, a lecture hall, and a publishing center for their numerous books and journals.

## 140 Nassau Street ✦

*Morse Building*   This 10-story structure, now converted to an apartment house, was once home to one of the world's earliest film studios, the American Vitagraph Company. Founded by two English vaudeville performers, J. Stuart Blackton and Albert E. Smith, the company made silent motion pictures here from 1897 to 1903. The roof served as a studio to take full advantage of the sunlight needed for early cameras. Vitagraph's first feature, aptly titled *The Burglar on the Roof*, was a 60-second melodrama starring Blackton as the eponymous burglar.

## Nassau Street at Spruce Street, northeast corner

Tribune *Building*   It was from here in a rented office, in the building of a competing newspaper, that the young millionaire William Randolph

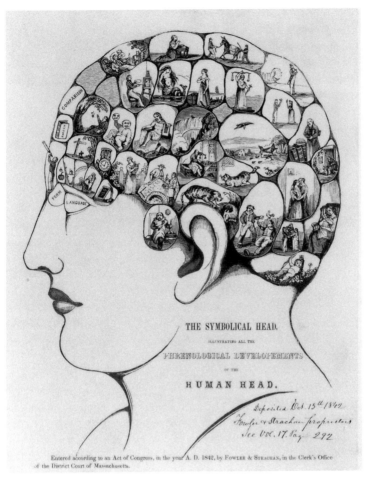

This fanciful chart from 1842 was just one of many items available for sale to phrenologists from the Fowler brothers' office at 135 Nassau Street. The pair became very wealthy from their lectures, journal and book sales, and skull "readings." Orson Fowler later became the chief proponent of another nineteenth-century fad, the octagon house.

Hearst set up shop after buying the *New York Journal* on October 7, 1895. He spent much of his own fortune to boost the readership of this paper. Hearst then launched a circulation war with the powerful Joseph Pulitzer's *New York World*. This rivalry spawned the era of yellow journalism in America. Both papers' sensational coverage of the conditions in Spain's colony of Cuba helped push the United States into the Spanish–American War.

### Nassau Street at Frankfort Street, southeast corner

This was the first home of Tammany Hall, which opened in 1812. Founded as a fraternal society in 1789, it became the Democratic Party organization in the city. It grew in political power with the arriving Irish immigrants. The party supplied the jobs and the Irish supplied the votes. By the 1880s, it had become completely corrupt.

## NEW STREET

### 7 New Street

Exchange Buffet   Opened on September 4, 1885, this was the world's first self-service restaurant.

### 34 New Street

On July 19, 1845, at 3:00 A.M., a fire began at this address, then the sperm whale oil shop of J. L. Van Doren. Before it was extinguished 12 hours later, 300 buildings had been destroyed and 30 people were dead. There was also more than $6 million in property loss, largely because of the destruction of the imported goods stored in the warehouses. The extent of the damage was almost as severe as that of the earlier Great Fire of 1835. These two blazes virtually destroyed every remaining Dutch colonial building from the seventeenth century.

### 58 New Street

*New York Gold Exchange*   The building that once stood at this address was the center of a financial whirlwind surrounded by anxious brokers on September 24, 1869, later to be known as Black Friday. It was here in the Gold Room, where gold was sold as a commodity, that traders began to feel the effects of Jay Gould and Jim Fisk's attempt to corner the market. Gould and his partner had hoped to buy all $15 million worth of gold then in circulation and thus drive up its price. President Ulysses S. Grant prevented this by allowing the U.S. Treasury's gold to be sold on the market. However, Gould's Washington spies, including Grant's brother-in-law, leaked him the news of Grant's decision, and Gould was still able to make an $11 million profit. Many brokerage firms and individual speculators were financially ruined.

## PARK ROW

### 21–25 Park Row

*Park Theater*   The theater that once stood on this site opened on January 29, 1798, with a performance of *As You Like It*. It was also the site of

Before federal government regulations, the nineteenth-century stock exchanges were susceptible to rogue traders. This was the case on Black Friday, September 24, 1869, in the Gold Room on New Street. Jay Gould and Jim Fisk financially ruined hundreds of investors by trying to corner the market on gold.

America's first grand opera ever presented in full in its original language, Rossini's *The Barber of Seville*, on November 29, 1825. On the night of February 14, 1842, some 2,500 guests attended the "Boz Ball" in honor of English author Charles Dickens's first visit to America. The stage and orchestra pit were covered over to accommodate the crowd. Between the cotillions and waltzes a curtain would rise, revealing a small stage with *tableaux vivants* from the storyteller's writings. Violinist virtuoso Ole Bull made his American debut on this same stage on November 25, 1843.

### 31 Park Row

New York World *newspaper offices*  A *World* reporter, Nellie Bly returned after her journey around the world to this address on January 26, 1890. Bly, who used a *nom de plume* (her actual name was Elizabeth Cochran), was hoping to beat the record set by Jules Verne's fictional character Phileas Fogg in *Around the World in 80 Days*. She did it in 72 days, 6 hours, 11 minutes, and 14 seconds—including a short detour to meet the author in Amiens, France. The front-page headline on the day

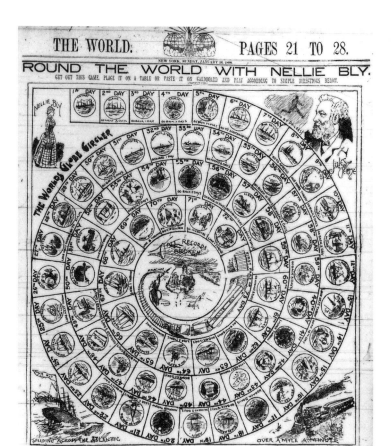

Players of board games could follow the path of "Girl Reporter" Nellie Bly on her trip around the world. This game was one of many *World* features that kept its readers involved in Bly's journey and helped increase its circulation.

of her return trumpeted "FATHER TIME OUTDONE." Later that year Joseph Pulitzer would move his paper into the new *World* Building down the block at the corner of Park Row and Frankfort.

### 37 Park Row

The first public demonstration of the phonograph took place here at the offices of *Scientific American* on December 7, 1877. Thomas Edison brought one of his two working models (the other was already at the patent office) to the magazine's editor, Alfred Ely Beach. The inventor set the machine down and turned the crank, and the machine promptly bid the editor a good morning. The modest talking machine was created with just a needle and a tin foil cylinder attached to a hand crank.

### Park Row at Frankfort Street, west side

On Friday, April 17, 1914, Mayor John Purroy Mitchel left City Hall to attend a luncheon and was approaching a waiting car when a man walked up and shot him point-blank. The mayor was only grazed and escaped serious injury, but an aide was hit in the mouth. The attacker, Michael Mahoney, was declared insane and sent to an asylum. Ironically, five years earlier, Mitchel, who was then the president of the board of aldermen, was made acting mayor during the recuperation of the previous mayor, William J. Gaynor, from an attempted assassination. Mayor Gaynor resumed his duties but died three years later as a result of his wound. Gaynor's death during the next mayoral campaign helped pave the way for Mitchel's election.

## PEARL STREET

### 6 Pearl Street

At 11:30 P.M. on August 1, 1819, author Herman Melville was born at this address. His mother, Maria, was the only daughter of Revolutionary War hero General Peter Gansevoort, and his father, Allan, was in the import business on the nearby docks. The future author of *Moby-Dick* lived here until 1824.

### Pearl Street at Whitehall Street

This was the site of the first market in the city where the townspeople could buy country produce. Peter Stuyvesant and the city council established the weekly Saturday market on September 12, 1656.

### 39 Pearl Street

Under the director-general of New Netherland, Wouter Van Twiller, the first building dedicated solely to religious purposes was built here in 1633. This wooden structure was abandoned in 1642 when a church was built inside Fort Amsterdam.

### 54 Pearl Street ✛

*Fraunces Tavern*   As was the case with many taverns of the colonial period, Fraunces Tavern was an important gathering place, particularly for early business meetings. The New York State Chamber of Commerce was founded here on April 5, 1768. But this tavern is best known for its connections to General George Washington. It served for 10 days as his last residence as a general of the American Revolutionary forces. He delivered his famous farewell speech to his officers here on December 4, 1783. The newly formed government's Departments of War, Treasury, and Foreign Affairs (later the State Department) were quartered here while the city served as the nation's capital. The current building, completed in 1907, is not the actual tavern but an educated guess as to what the building looked like. This reconstruction served as the locale for a special breakfast on April 30, 1989, celebrating the two hundredth anniversary of the inauguration of George Washington. The invited guests were all descendants or relatives of former U.S. presidents, from Lacey Washington, the first President's sixth great-niece, to Karen Denis, President Ronald Reagan's third cousin.

### 61 Pearl Street
The deed for this property was the first to be recorded in the Registrar's Office of New York County. Dated October 12, 1654, it documents that Cornelius Van Tienhoven sold this address and 26 Stone Street to Jacob Hendricks, one of the first surgeons in New Amsterdam. The doctor didn't own this real estate long; he resold it the same day to Jacob Steendam.

### 66 Pearl Street
This address sits on a portion of the city's earliest landfill project. In 1684, this property across from the Stadt Huys (City Hall) was created with earth and debris from nearby hills. Called "water lots," this landfill was the first of many devised by generations of Manhattan developers and city bureaucrats who sought to add more land to sell and tax. A small, gabled Dutch-style house that was the first built on this lot was owned by Peter and Mary Jay, who were most likely living here when their son John was born on December 12, 1745. John Jay went on to become the first Chief Justice of the United States.

### 71–73 Pearl Street
*Stadt Huys*  Rising above the neighboring gabled Dutch homes, this five-story stone building was a prominent landmark along the shoreline when it was built by Governor Willem Kieft. On New Year's Day 1642, it was leased for a *stadt herbergh* (public inn) to Philip Gerrisen for 300 guilders a year. For the next several years, outlying Dutch settlers sought refuge here from Native American raids during Governor Kieft's War. In 1653, the building became the Stadt Huys (City Hall), New York City's first. A cupola was added, and its entrance, which had faced

Fort Amsterdam, was changed to face the East River. It served as the seat of government until 1699. In 1979, excavations revealed the foundation, only 42 feet by 52 feet, of the old Stadt Huys. Archaeologists found many colonial artifacts, including fragments of Dutch and English pottery and even some Native American wampum.

### 77–79 Pearl Street
In 1665, Thomas Willett was appointed the first mayor of New York City by English Governor Richard Nicolls. Willett was living at this address in his small one-story house that he had bought 20 years earlier. For the next 150 years, the mayors were appointed first by the colonial governor and then by the governor of New York state. They were not elected by direct popular vote until 1834.

### 81 Pearl Street
This was the site of the first printing press in the New York colony. William Bradford was appointed the public printer on April 10, 1693. He was involved in several firsts in the history of printing in America: the first legislative proceedings published, the first New York paper money, and the first newspaper to appear in New York, the *New York Gazette*, on October 16, 1725. Bradford is buried in Trinity Churchyard.

### 119–121 Pearl Street
On May 16, 1691, ship owner and sea captain William Kidd married Mrs. Sarah Oort, who was probably the richest widow in New York at the time. The happy couple moved into her mansion, which once stood approximately at the rear of this lot. The captain lived here for eight years, then sailed for the Indian Ocean. It was at this point that Captain Kidd began his infamous career as a pirate. After he was hanged in London on May 12, 1701, rumors spread that he had buried his plunder along the coast of Long Island.

### 211 Pearl Street ✦
Only the façade of this rare 1832 Greek Revival building survives today. Built by William Colgate, the founder of the Colgate-Palmolive soap empire, it was used as a warehouse for Colgate's nearby candle, soap, and toothpaste shop.

### 218 Pearl Street
This site once held the home of Hercules Mulligan, a member of the Sons of Liberty and an Irish-born secret agent for the Americans during the Revolutionary War. On November 25, 1783, when the British left the

city, George Washington and four of his officers visited this house to pay their respects to Mulligan for helping the Patriot cause.

## 255–257 Pearl Street

The two dilapidated buildings that once stood at this site in what was then a run-down section of the waterfront were home to Thomas Edison's first commercial electric generators. At exactly 3:00 P.M. on September 4, 1882, the Pearl Street Station began supplying 59 downtown customers with electricity. Edison had chosen this location hoping to pay very little for the two buildings at a time when his capital was low and because he wanted to be near the financial district and potential investors.

## 326 Pearl Street

*Walton House*   Built in 1752, a four-story home on this site was considered the most beautiful home in America. The extravagant parties held here during colonial rule were referred to in the British Parliament as proof that the Americans could afford to pay higher taxes. By the end of the Revolutionary War, Pearl Street was turning more commercial. The building became the first home of the then–newly established Bank of New York, which opened on June 9, 1784. Alexander Hamilton, who bought a single share of stock, was elected one of the bank directors. It later became a boarding house before being torn down in 1881.

## 327 Pearl Street

In 1814 Martin Morrison owned a tavern—or porter house, in the vernacular of the day—that catered to the neighborhood sailors. Legend has it that late one night Morrison served a hungry ship's pilot the only beef left in his kitchen, a short loin normally used as a roast. The diner loved the broiled slice, and the porterhouse steak was born.

## 362 Pearl Street

Within a year of moving permanently to New York City and marrying Sarah Todd, John Jacob Astor moved in 1786 to a building at this address owned by his new mother-in-law. This was the first home and office of America's earliest self-made multimillionaires. At this address he sold musical instruments and sheet music as one of the first music dealers in the city before moving on to the more lucrative fur trade and real estate businesses with which he amassed his fortune.

## PECK'S SLIP

### Peck's Slip at South Street

During a blizzard on January 5, 1818, the packet ship *James Monroe* of the Black Ball shipping line set sail for Liverpool. The departure of this

424-ton vessel with two decks and three masts marked a high point in the economic development of New York City. What made this sailing noteworthy was that the ship sailed on the very day her owners had said she would sail. The *James Monroe* inaugurated the first regular dependable shipping service to Europe. Prior to this, ships left only when they were full and if the weather was good. Now, full or not, sun or snow, the Black Ball ships would guarantee merchants the delivery of their goods. The journey was also the first scheduled transatlantic departure for the eight pioneer passengers on the ship.

## PINE STREET

### 40 Pine Street
The country's oldest continuously published daily newspaper, the *New York Post*, was born at this address on November 16, 1801. Co-founded by Alexander Hamilton, the paper has included on its masthead some of America's greatest journalists: William Cullen Bryant, Lincoln Steffens, Franklin Pierce Adams, Heywood Broun, Pete Hamill, and Max Lerner. Feature writers included Walt Whitman, Sinclair Lewis, and two future Presidents, Martin Van Buren and Woodrow Wilson.

## POLICE PLAZA

*Rhinelander's Sugar House*   Part of this plaza was once the intersection of Duane and Rose streets, and it was here that a notorious Revolutionary War British prison once stood. Originally built as a warehouse in 1763, the building housed American prisoners, many of whom died of starvation and/or disease. A window from the building is encased in the current police headquarters and serves as a present-day memorial.

*Newsboys' Lodging House*   Another building now gone that stood in this vicinity at Duane and New Chambers streets was one of the most successful city charities of the ninteenth century, the Newsboys' Lodging House. Founded in 1853 for homeless boys, the home supplied reasonable meals and shelter for the thousands of homeless in the city. Horatio Alger, the author of the "industrious boy makes good, rags to riches" stories, was a guiding spirit and role model to the newsboys.

## RECTOR STREET

### 2 Rector Street ✦
*United Express Building*   Some 425 plate-glass windows were broken as a result of the Black Tom Island explosion on Sunday morning, July 30,

1916. The United Express Building, particularly the side facing the harbor, was the most severely damaged. Two tremendous explosions, heard as far away as Maryland, shook the entire tri-state area. Black Tom Island, an artificial peninsula along the New Jersey shore in New York harbor, was a storage facility for more than 2,138,000 pounds of munitions bound for England and France during World War I. The explosion was an act of German espionage, although this was at first only suspected, and not proved until 1939—before America's entry into the Great War. Remarkably, only seven people were killed, but the Allies suffered $50 million in damages.

## SOUTH STREET

### 174 South Street
This was the birthplace of Alfred E. Smith, governor of New York and the first Catholic major-party nominee for President (Democrat, 1928), on December 30, 1873. Here now are the Alfred E. Smith Houses, a housing development.

## SOUTH WILLIAM STREET

### 26 South William Street
The first synagogue in North America was built on this site. Congregation Shearith Israel, a Spanish and Portuguese synagogue, was dedicated on the seventh day of Passover, April 8, 1730. The one-story brick building remained in use for nearly a century.

## STATE STREET

### 7 State Street ✦
*Watson House*   This mansion is the lone survivor on a block once lined with the homes of wealthy New Yorkers. Attributed to John McComb Jr., the architect of City Hall, it was home to Elizabeth Ann Seton from 1801 to 1803. Mother Seton was canonized as the first American-born saint in 1975.

## STONE STREET

### 10 Stone Street
In the Dutch colonial period, this block was called Brouwers Straet, because of the breweries here between Whitehall Street and a canal along the present Broad Street. The West India Company brewery was

No. 7 State Street, the Shrine of St. Elizabeth Seton, was once one of the grand mansions on this block. By the time this photograph was taken, the neighborhood had become a commercial district—note the shipping barrels on the sidewalk. (Author's collection)

operating at this address in 1646. By 1656, Oloff Stevense Van Cortlandt, patriarch of the prominent New York family, had also opened his brewery on this block. One year later, this street was the first in the city to be paved—hence the name Stone Street.

## 59 Stone Street

Asser Levy, one of the original Jewish settlers in New Amsterdam in 1654, had a home at this address in 1663 and had also lived at No. 33 down the block. Levy fought and won an early discrimination battle with city authorities. Governor Peter Stuyvesant ordered all Jews exempt from military guard duty but imposed a special monthly tax in lieu of such service. Levy appealed to authorities in Holland, who then ordered Stuyvesant to allow Levy to stand guard. He became the first Jewish soldier in America.

## VESEY STREET

### 24 Vesey Street

George Washington's dentist, John Greenwood, had his office at this address in the 1790s. Dr. Greenwood, a former cabinetmaker and maker of nautical instruments, built a set of the President's false teeth. Not wooden, the dentures, made from human teeth attached to an ivory base, were held in place by Washington's lone remaining tooth. The renowned dentures are now in the collection of the New York Academy of Medicine.

### 62 Vesey Street

In the 1870s, this was the first factory of Adams' New York Gum No. 1. Thomas Adams, who ran a small glass shop near the Staten Island ferry dock, had met Mexican General Antonio López de Santa Anna, an exile living on Staten Island. The general was looking for an inventor to find a use for chicle, the juice from Mexican sapodilla trees. After experimenting, Adams realized it was a poor rubber substitute but a great "chewing gum." Renamed the American Chicle Company, Adams's company was the country's largest gum manufacturer.

## WALL STREET

Wall Street, now synonymous with high finance, was named after a wooden stockade fence with a 12-foot ditch on the northern side, built here at the northern boundary of the settlement in 1653. Governor Peter Stuyvesant ordered the barricade built by all male residents "without exception" as a defense against the British colonists of New England and not, as is widely believed, as protection against the indigenous people. The wall ran from the Hudson River to the East River and had one entrance, at Wall and Pearl streets. Called the Watergate, it was shut every night at nine o'clock under the Dutch rules. It stood until 1699, when it was taken down by the British.

## 7 Wall Street
At this address on October 15, 1915, Charles E. Merrill took on the first of many partners, Edmund C. Lynch, and changed his company's name to Merrill Lynch. In business for only a year himself, Merrill would go on to head the country's largest retail stock brokerage firm.

## 23 Wall Street
*Downing's Oyster House*   In the years before the Civil War, this corner restaurant was famous for its tasty menu. The owner, Thomas Downing, a black man, was a popular host to his Wall Street powerbroker costumers. The restaurant's basement also played host to runaway slaves as a station of the Underground Railroad.

*Morgan Guaranty Trust Company* ✦ An earlier Drexel, Morgan and Company bank building on this same site was the scene of one of the first commercial uses of electricity. On September 4, 1882, Thomas Edison personally connected the electric lamps in the office of his friend and enthusiastic support J. P. Morgan. The power was supplied from the inventor's Pearl Street generators. The current building, built in 1913, was the scene of a noontime bomb blast that killed 33 and injured 400 on the crowded sidewalk outside on September 16, 1920. Despite an $80,000 reward, the bomber or bombers were never caught, and their motive remained equally mysterious. The most common theory was that the blast was the work of foreign anarchists. A lasting reminder of the explosion is the damaged marble still visible on the façade. The building has been converted into apartments.

## Wall Street at Nassau Street, northwest corner
*Simmon's Tavern*   At a special meeting of the City Council, James Duane was sworn into office as the mayor of New York City at this tavern on February 7, 1784. Duane, the city's first American-born mayor, had been appointed by Governor DeWitt Clinton. The new mayor replaced the State Provisional Council, which had previously managed the city.

On the afternoon of September 16, 1920, a bomb destroyed this automobile and blew out the windows at the offices of Morgan Guaranty Trust at 23 Wall Street. The intense blast evaporated the horse-drawn wagon that delivered the explosives.

### 28 Wall Street

*Federal Hall*  This is one of the most important sites in the history of the United States. In 1703 it was location of New York City's second City Hall. The trial of John Peter Zenger, editor of the *New York Weekly Journal*, for libel against English colonial Governor William Cosby began here on August 4, 1735. Zenger's acquittal, with the help of his "Philadelphia lawyer," Andrew Hamilton, helped establish the principle of freedom of the press.

Another significant step toward American independence from England also took place here: The Stamp Act Congress met in the same building to draft a Declaration of Rights and Grievances on October 7, 1765. Twenty-eight delegates from the American colonies met to outline the 14 articles; chief among them was the protest against "taxation without representation" and the demand for the right to a trial by jury. After the Revolution, the building was remodeled by expatriate French architect Pierre L'Enfant as Federal Hall, and the government of the newly constituted United States began to function in a second-floor chamber. Outside this room on a balcony, on April 30, 1789, George

The only eyewitness rendering of the nation's first inauguration, Amos Doolittle's engraving depicted the April 30, 1789, event. George Washington, with his hand on a Bible, is being given the oath of office by Judge Robert Livingston.

Washington was inaugurated as the nation's first President and John Adams as the first Vice President. The new Congress adopted the Bill of Rights here on September 25, 1789.

*Federal Hall National Memorial* ✦ The current Greek Revival building was built in 1842 to house the first U.S. Custom House and served for a time as a subtreasury. John Quincy Adams Ward's statue of George

Washington, dedicated on November 26, 1883, by President Chester A. Arthur, stands on the approximate spot where Washington took the presidential oath in 1789. These steps have been a platform for speeches and rallies. On May 8, 1970, a peaceful noontime anti–Vietnam War rally was broken up by construction workers from the nearby World Trade Center site. The "hardhat" riot began here on the steps as the workers attacked the protestors, mainly students from local colleges. An hour later it ended at City Hall, where the workers forced city officials to return the American flag to full staff; it had been lowered to half-mast in mourning for the four Kent State University students killed by members of the Ohio National Guard four days earlier.

On September 6, 2002, Congress returned to commemorate the victims of the terrorist attacks of September 11, 2001. Some 300 members of the 107th Congress met here for a joint session, the first time in more than 212 years. Vice President Dick Cheney and House and Senate leaders spoke from a lectern made from the sandstone slab and balcony railing from George Washington's inauguration.

## 40 Wall Street +

A contender for the title of world's tallest building, this 1929 tower lost to the Chrysler Building when a 175-foot Art Deco spire was added to the Chrysler after 40 Wall Street was too far along to be changed. The tower proved too high, though, for a twin-engine Army Air Forces C-45 Beechcraft airplane. The doomed plane, flying at 650 feet, crashed into the fifty-eighth floor of what was then called the Manhattan Bank Building. Apparently lost, it hit the building on a foggy evening, May 20, 1946. The crash killed all five occupants of the plane but none of the 500 night workers in the building.

## 52 Wall Street

This was the first and longtime home of City Bank, now Citibank. The nation's first bank robbery took place here on Sunday, March 20, 1831, undiscovered until the following Monday morning when the bank opened. More than $200,000 in bank bills and 200 Spanish doubloons were missing. Edward Smith was caught within a week and sentenced to five years in Sing Sing for the crime.

## 55 Wall Street +

*Merchants' Exchange*  The first Exchange on this site was only eight years old when it was destroyed in the Great Fire of 1835. The present structure, a masterpiece of Greek Revival architecture, served as the Exchange until 1862, when it was converted into the U.S. Custom

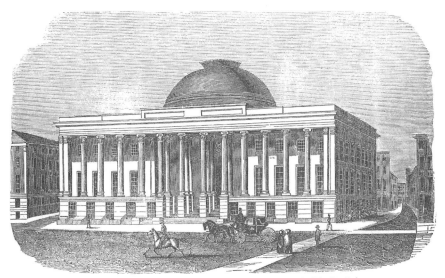

*589. Third Merchants' Exchange (built 1842: Isiah Rogers, architect), 55 Wall St., New York, N.Y., c. 1848. [38]*

Architect Isaiah Rogers designed the Merchants' Exchange at 55 Wall Street in 1842. This monumental building still stands as the base for the handsome and sympathetic Charles McKim addition of 1904. (Author's collection)

House. In 1871, Chester A. Arthur, a protégé of New York's powerful New York Senator Roscoe Conkling, was appointed Collector of the Port of New York. By a fortunate turn of events, Arthur's position here was his stepping stone to the White House. He served as collector for seven years until he was forced from office by corruption charges. As compensation and in exchange for Conkling's support of James A. Garfield as the Republican presidential nominee in 1880, Arthur was added to Garfield's ticket as his vice presidential nominee. The Republicans won and Arthur assumed the presidency on September 20, 1881, after Garfield died from an assassin's wounds.

In 1904 architect Charles McKim added five floors in his sensitive remodeling for the building's conversion to the headquarters of National City Bank, later renamed Citibank.

*Regent Wall Street Hotel* ✦ After 90 years the bank moved out, making way for the building's current incarnation as a luxury hotel in the 1904 addition and a ballroom in the grand hall. More than 300 members of Congress had lunch in this ballroom on September 6, 2002, after their historic meeting at Federal Hall to observe the first anniversary of the terrorist attacks on the World Trade Center.

## 56 Wall Street

The pirate Captain William Kidd owned but did not occupy this property in 1691. He sold the lot a year later for $35, making a $5 profit.

## Wall Street between William and Pearl streets

The legendary birthplace of the New York Stock Exchange is in the vicinity of the present No. 72. When the new Congress issued $80 million worth of bonds to pay for the Revolutionary War, traders began meeting here in the open air to trade the securities. On May 17, 1792, under a buttonwood tree, 24 of these merchants and auctioneers, future stockbrokers, established the new Exchange. They established rules of conduct and pledged themselves to give preference to the other members. That famous buttonwood tree (another name for a sycamore) survived until June 21, 1865, when it was felled by a storm.

## 74 Wall Street

Edward Livingston lived at this address in the early part of the nineteenth century. Livingston was mayor of the city and a member of the House of Representatives. He served with Andrew Jackson at the Battle of New Orleans in the War of 1812 and later became a U.S. senator from Louisiana.

## Wall Street at Water Street, southeast corner

*Merchants' Coffee House*   This was the second site of this tavern that earlier had stood on the opposite corner. Paul Revere, on one of his many rides, delivered a dispatch from the Boston Committee of Correspondence to the New York compatriots on May 17, 1774, encouraging them to protest a British order to close Boston harbor. On February 24, 1784, a meeting was held here to establish the Bank of New York, which has since become the oldest commercial bank in the country.

## Wall Street at Water Street, northwest corner

*Tontine Coffee House*   Opened in 1793 on the site of the first Merchants' Coffee House, this establishment was built with money raised by early brokers looking for a home for the new stock market. The first floor was used as a place for trading, and the rest of the building housed a ballroom, a dining room, and a bar.

## Wall Street at South Street

For much of the eighteenth century this was the foot of Wall Street. Landfills have since extended the shoreline. By 1709, this was the site of

TONTINE COFFEE HOUSE, WALL & WATER STREETS, ABOUT 1797
FROM A PAINTING OWNED BY THE NEW YORK HISTORICAL SOCIETY
SOCIETY OF ICONOPHILES
1910

Coffee houses were important commercial centers in colonial America, gathering places for merchants who traded imported goods, stocks, ships, and even slaves. Two of the most famous of these taverns appear in this print copied from a painting by Francis Guy in 1797. The Tontine Coffee House is on the left and the Merchants' Coffee House in on the far right.

a thriving slave market. The city was the second-largest slave-owning city in the British colonies, second only to Charleston, South Carolina. The auctioned slaves were not only blacks but whites, dependent women, orphaned children, and debtors. On the night of April 22, 1774, the New York equivalent of the Boston Tea Party took place here on Murray's Wharf.

Future first President George Washington arrived in New York at this spot on April 23, 1789, for his inaugural a week later. He stepped off an elaborately decorated barge manned by 13 oarsmen representing the first colonies. The journey had begun nine days earlier at his Mount Vernon home. Washington's landing was reenacted on April 29, 1889—somewhat farther east—by then-President Benjamin Harrison. The arrival was again reenacted here in 1989 by an actor who portrayed the first President on his journey all the way from Virginia. A retinue of reporters recorded every step of the reenacted journey.

## WARREN STREET

### 57 Warren Street
Master glassmaker and artist Louis Comfort Tiffany was born at this address on February 18, 1848. He was the son of Charles Lewis Tiffany, the founder of the famous jewelry store.

## WASHINGTON STREET

### Washington Street between Dey and Cortlandt streets
*Eli Hart and Company Warehouse*  Citizens protesting flour and grain prices broke into two warehouses here on February 13, 1837, then dumped flour and wheat into the streets. Mayor Cornelius W. Lawrence tried to quell the riot but was pelted with stones and forced to flee for his life.

### 229 Washington Street
*Smith & McNeill*  In 1850, newly arrived Englishman Fred Harvey started a job at this chophouse. He parlayed his skills here as a $2-a-week dishwasher into a restaurant and hotel empire. Dubbed the "Civilizer of the West," Harvey—along with his pretty "Harvey girls" employees—supplied the West with decent food and wives.

## WATER STREET

### 58 Water Street
James Hamlet, a freed African American man, was a porter working here at the store of Tilton and Mahone. He was the first person seized under the provisions of the Fugitive Slave Law. Within two weeks of Congress's passing the law, a warrant had been issued for Hamlet, and he was arrested here on September 30, 1850. Hamlet was forced to return to his former owner, Mary Brown of Baltimore. Hamlet was later ransomed back for $800 raised by the Union Safety Committee.

### 175 Water Street ✛
While excavating this building's foundation in January 1982, workers discovered the hull of a merchant frigate ship in what was once colonial-era landfill. Construction work was stopped for 34 days while nautical archaeologists were permitted to study this important find. Only a 20-foot section of the ship (dubbed the *Ronson*, after the developer who paid for the preservation) was saved and is now displayed at the Mariners' Museum in Newport News, Virginia.

### 273 Water Street +

*Captain Joseph Rose House*  From the 1840s to the 1860s, this small house was Kit Burns's Sportsman's Hall, a saloon. It was a popular hangout for the notorious gangs of the period, such as the Daybreak Boys, the Border Gang, the Patsy Conroys, and the Shirt Tails. The patrons were kept entertained in a first-floor amphitheater by bloody dog and rat fights. The building, which dates from before 1780, is the third oldest in Manhattan. For more than 200 years, this building has been a sea captain's home, an apothecary shop, a rooming house, a brothel, and later still a "home for fallen women." Life goes on at 273 Water Street, which was beautifully restored in 1997. It is now a four-unit apartment house.

### 286 Water Street

On April 22, 1824, this address was the site of the first house in the city to be lighted with gas. Directly behind this lot stood No. 7 Cherry Street, the home of Samuel Leggett, the first president of the New York Gas Company. Leggett had his own home illuminated with gas six months later.

### 304 Water Street

*John Allen's Dance Hall*  This was an infamous dance hall and brothel of the 1850s and '60s. The dancers/prostitutes who worked here were known for wearing red-topped black boots with sleighbells around their ankles—and often little else. Nicknamed "The Wickedest Man in New York" by a journalist, the proprietor, John Allen, proudly had the title printed on his business cards. About 1868, Allen, perhaps converted by one of his three brothers, all respectable clergymen, decided that he had found God and began giving sermons in his dance hall. His "conversion" did not last long, especially when business dropped off. But when he tried to reopen under the old policies, his regular customers abandoned him.

## WHITEHALL STREET

### 39 Whitehall Street +

*United States Army Building*  This former Army induction center was a popular target of the antiwar movement of the 1960s; activists Dr. Benjamin Spock and Allen Ginsberg were both arrested here. At one such rally on October 15, 1965, 22-year-old David Miller, a volunteer relief worker, stood atop a sound truck and used a cigarette lighter to burn his draft card. Several days later he was arrested in New Hampshire,

This engraving is of John Allen's Dance hall in 1868, probably depicted more rambunctiously than the small room could handle. The infamous dance hall was frequented by criminals, prostitutes, and sailors. (*Frank Leslie's Illustrated Newspaper*, August 8, 1868)

becoming the first person to be arrested under a federal law that prohibited the destruction of a draft card. Two months later, at another demonstration, 61 people were arrested for picketing and singing Christmas carols. The building was extensively remodeled in the mid-1980s.

## Whitehall Street at State Street

*Stuyvesant's Great House*   Peter Stuyvesant, the peg-legged Dutch governor of New Netherland, built a two-story stone house on this spot in 1655. After the British took control of New York, the house was used for the British governors. The street and the building were renamed Whitehall, in honor of the English seat of government in London. It was home to Sir Edmund Andros while he was in office between 1674 and 1681. The house was destroyed by fire in 1716. Robert Fulton died in a house on this same site on February 23, 1815. He had contracted a cold while inspecting his steamboats along the Hudson River.

GOV. STUYVESANT'S HOME,
"THE WHITEHALL," 1658.

Four years after Dutch governor of New Netherland Peter Stuyvesant built a country estate on the Bowery, he built this home at what is now Whitehall and State streets in 1655. In 1664, Stuyvesant surrendered the colony and the house to the British. Rather than return to the Netherlands, he retired to his Bowery farm.

## Whitehall Street near Water Street

This was the site of the city's first pier, a small wooden jetty, built in 1648–49 by Dutch Governor Peter Stuyvesant. Before landfills changed the shoreline, this spot was called Schreyer's Hook or Weepers' Point, so named because loved ones said their goodbyes here to travelers leaving on ships. By the time of the Revolutionary War the shoreline had moved another block south to just short of South Street. It was from this spot that George Washington boarded the Whitehall ferry to begin his journey home to Mount Vernon after bidding farewell to his officers at Fraunces Tavern on December 4, 1783. Six years later, he returned to the city—farther north, at Wall Street—for his first inauguration as President.

## Whitehall Street at Water Street

*Tavern of the Fighting Cocks*   Between one o'clock and two o'clock in the morning of September 21, 1776, this small tavern and brothel, near the original shoreline, was the likely origin of the Fire of 1776. Winds spread the blaze up Beaver and Broad streets, destroying everything west of Broadway to the Hudson River. The conflagration was ultimately checked when it reached Barclay Street and the open campus surrounding King's (later Columbia) College. This disaster happened only one week after the British began their occupation of the city during the Revolutionary War. Efforts to combat the fire were hampered by the animosity between citizens and the British authorities.

## WILLIAM STREET

### 21–23 William Street
*Delmonico's Restaurant*  This first home of the famous restaurant, considered by some the first American restaurant, opened in 1827. The two Swiss brothers John and Peter Delmonico introduced haute cuisine to America. Their chef, Charles Ranhofer, created Baked Alaska and Lobster Newburg. The building was destroyed, along with half the downtown area, in the Great Fire of 1835. Two years later, the brothers built a new restaurant, still standing today as an apartment house, nearby at 56 Beaver Street.

### 131 William Street
This was the birthplace of Washington Irving, on April 3, 1783. His childhood home was down the block at No. 128, where he began to write in 1802.

## WORLD TRADE CENTER

*World Trade Center*  September 11, 2001, a pivotal date in history, is now remembered the world over for the terrorist attacks on the World Trade Center and the Pentagon. These attacks occurred less than one year into what people hoped would be a peaceful new millennium. After the collapse of communism in the Soviet Union and its satellites, many hoped that a new era of democracy, freedom, and Western values was beginning. It was not to be. Unlike the previous century's Cold War with its superpower combatants, the enemy became small bands of Islamic extremists led by Osama bin Laden. Infuriated by modern society and what they viewed as the West's interference in the Middle East, they were determined to wage *jihad*, or holy war, and impose their fundamentalist version of Islam on the world. Though they are not averse to using new technology to further their ends, their weapon of choice against the West's vast military is the suicide bomber.

A "world trade center" or permanent trade exposition for lower Manhattan was proposed as early as 1946, but it was not until David Rockefeller, the president of Chase Manhattan Bank, promoted the project in the early 1960s that the World Trade Center was born. Under the guise of urban renewal and revitalization of the financial district, David, along with the help of his brother New York Governor (later Vice President) Nelson A. Rockefeller, was the catalyst for the enormous project. But the billion-dollar price tag and the complexity of the project proved too daunting for conventional developers. The planners turned to the Port Authority of New York and New Jersey. A quasi-government agency, the Port Authority was the ideal choice. It was self-supporting and able to raise tremendous capital, with the right of eminent domain and little public accountability.

In 1962, architect Minoru Yamasaki was chosen for his engineering skills. Masterfully, he solved several problems with the Hudson River site. He designed two oversized buildings with 10 million square feet of office space that could withstand hurricane winds, and then he placed them on landfill at the convergence of a major river and the ocean. Unlike conventional steel-skeleton construction, his tube-like towers were designed with strong load-bearing outside walls and an elevator core. Each of the 110 floors had almost an acre of column-free space, perfect for the modern office. His second innovation was the now-famous "bathtub," lining the seven-story-deep foundation. Actually, it was a bathtub in reverse, an underground slurry wall around the complex that held back the Hudson River.

By the time the first building opened in 1970, much of the oversized design was out of fashion. Two of the world's tallest buildings emerged from a huge barren plaza placed on a "super block" that eliminated any cross-street traffic or people. Criticized as being sterile, the complex stood apart from the activity of the city. The little street life left was diverted into the giant and banal underground shopping mall. Finding the complex difficult to love, New Yorkers remained indifferent at best.

But a surprising event on the morning of August 7, 1974, provoked a breakthrough in the public's acceptance. A French aerialist, Philippe Petit, secretly rigged a tightrope between the newly completed towers and then proceeded to dance on the wire before an audience of thousands of awestruck office workers. The sight of this seemingly tiny man walking through the air from one tower to the other helped humanize the huge, abstract buildings.

On Friday, February 26, 1993, at 12:18 P.M., a tremendous blast rocked the Vista Hotel in the complex with the force of an earthquake. The massive explosion created a crater 60 yards wide and several levels deep in the underground parking garage directly below the hotel. Six people died and more than 1,000 were injured in the blast. Most of the injured were overcome by smoke inhalation, as smoke permeated the complex and rose up more than 100 stories. All electric power was knocked out, and without the aid of elevators or instructions via the public address system, thousands of frightened office workers were forced to flee though the crowded, dark, smoky stairwells down to the safety of the street. Within a week, the first suspect, Mohammed A. Salameh, was arrested in New Jersey while trying to get his $200 deposit back on the rented van traced to the explosion. The FBI swiftly rounded up a small group of Islamic fundamentalists, followers of Brooklyn cleric Sheikh Omar Abdel-Rahman, and arrested them in connection with the explosion. Five of the conspirators were convicted, and each was sentenced to 240 years in prison. The 1993 bombing was a mere prelude to the catastrophe to come.

On September 11, 2001, American Airlines Flight 11 left Boston's Logan International Airport en route to Los Angeles. The Boeing 767 carried 92 passengers and crew, including five hijackers led by Mohamed Atta, the ringleader of an Islamic *jihad* sect. After the hijackers took control of the cockpit, they flew the jet to New York City and at 8:46 A.M. crashed it into Tower One (the north tower) on the north side between the ninety-fourth and ninety-eighth floors. It was the first of the four flights to crash that day. A second airliner, also originating in Boston, United Airlines Flight 175, with 65 passengers and crew, crashed into the south tower at 9:02 A.M., between the seventy-eighth and eighty-fourth floors.

Racing at more than 500 miles per hour, Flight 11 crashed with a massive fireball into the north tower and created a 156-foot gash. The strong framework of exterior columns, engineered to withstand only a crash from planes known in the 1960s, held as the building's load shifted to the undamaged columns. The collapse, 102 minutes after impact, was precipitated by the intense heat of thousands of gallons of burning jet fuel, pouring on the floors and down the staircases, igniting everything in its path. This heat softened the steel trusses, and eventually the weight of the floors above the impact pressed down until the surrounding framework buckled. Then each floor, in turn, slammed down on the floor beneath it. This phenomenon, called "pancaking," accelerated until both of the 110-story buildings were reduced to a 10-story pile of debris. What took more than five years to build evaporated in 10 seconds.

What happened in the north tower also happened in the south tower, only more quickly. Attacked second, it collapsed first. Flight 175, traveling even faster at more than 600 miles per hour, created more damage by hitting a lower area of floors. The tower remained standing for only 30 minutes. This critical time between impact and collapse in each building enabled as many as 10,000 people located below the carnage to escape to the street.

The finality and sudden destruction of the World Trade Center and the loss of life were almost incomprehensible: More than 2,700 people died as the result of the attacks. More than 400 heroic firefighters, police officers, and paramedics lost their lives trying to save others. In Virginia, just outside Washington, D.C., 184 people on the ground died when American Airlines Flight 77 crashed into the Pentagon, with 59 dead on the plane. The fourth hijacked jet, United Airlines Flight 93, crashed in Shanksville, Pennsylvania, killing all 40 aboard. Investigators have speculated that the ultimate target of Flight 93, which was headed in an easterly direction, was either the White House or the U.S. Capitol.

The destruction of the towers registered on an earthquake seismograph at the Lamont Observatory 21 miles north of Manhattan. A dust cloud, like that often associated with an apocalyptic nuclear winter, enveloped much of lower Manhattan. Debris rained down on nearby buildings, setting many on fire. By the end of the day, all the buildings with World Trade Center in their address, 1 through 7, had been destroyed.

All semblance of normal life stopped in Manhattan, as it would in the rest of the country. Power and phone lines were out in much of the financial district along with the PATH (Port Authority Trans-Hudson) trains and several subway lines. The loss of the giant antenna atop the north tower left the area without cellular phone service, broadcast television, and radio. All bridges and tunnels into Manhattan were closed. Thousands of shocked New Yorkers spilled into the streets trying to get home and fathom what had happened. Most walked, rode in vehicles locked in traffic, or took improvised ferry rides out of Manhattan. Once home, they watched the events being reported on television, along with the rest of the world.

For the rescuers, the immediate response was to find any possible survivors. This humane and hopeful reaction was virtually futile given the overwhelming destruction. Fewer than a dozen people survived the collapse of the towers and were rescued. The next concern was recovering and identifying the victims. More than 20,000 human remains were found. As of January 2010, the city's Office of the Chief Medical Examiner had identified 1,626 individuals with a variety of methods: DNA, dental records, personal belongings, and fingerprints.

An army of firefighters, police officers, rescue workers, and volunteers continued to converge on the site, as they had after the first crash. Their response was heartwarming but problematic. Ground Zero, as it became known, was a dangerous place with burning and smoking debris piles, some as high as 50 feet, all atop a destroyed substructure several levels deep. Dust, deemed safe at the time, filled the air and covered much of lower Manhattan. Within hours, disaster personnel from all levels of government took control of the massive repair and cleanup. Shoring up the original slurry wall along Liberty Street and the PATH train tunnels from New Jersey was a high priority to prevent flooding.

The cleanup operation continued around the clock, stopping only in respect for removal of a body. The debris was shipped by barge to the Fresh Kills Landfill site on Staten Island, where it was sorted by hand in search of personal items and human remains. More than 1.8 million tons of debris were removed during the next eight months—well below the original estimate of several years—at a cost of $750 million, also well below the estimated cost of $6 billion. On May 28, 2002, the last girder was removed, marking the end of the recovery and cleanup operation.

The past several years have witnessed tremendous healing and renewal marked with somber ceremonies on anniversaries and milestones. Thousands of people—survivors, families of the victims, dignitaries, and tourists—have come here to pay their respects and to try to comprehend the destruction and profound changes the attacks have wrought on American life. This deep emotional response was also reflected in the public's interest in the numerous design competitions for rebuilding the site and the future of the neighborhood.

Some progress has been relatively fast: the reopening of the Winter Garden, the subways, the PATH station, and the return of several companies to the repaired World Financial Center all within the first two years. On April 27, 2006, the foundation was laid for the 1,776-foot centerpiece of the redevelopment, first called the Freedom Tower and now known simply as One World Trade Center. A month later, the first building, Seven World Trade Center, was officially opened. The 52-story building was designed to be "green" (environmentally friendly), with improved safety standards reflecting post–September 11 building codes.

The rebuilding effort has also been marred by egos and politics. All the major players—two mayors, Rudolph W. Giuliani and Michael R. Bloomberg; two New York governors, George Pataki and Eliot Spitzer; the Port Authority; the leaseholder and developer, Larry Silverstein; the architects; the families of the victims; and the public—have contributed to and complicated every decision. Often the underlying debate is about finding a balance between the rebirth of a once-thriving commercial district and a memorial to tragedy.

The National September 11 Memorial is expected to be complete in time for the tenth anniversary of the attacks, on September 11, 2011.

Two huge pools containing waterfalls will mark the footprints of the two towers. An above-ground museum entrance will direct visitors to a cavernous space with exhibits and a wall containing the names of the victims of both the 1993 and 2001 attacks and of those lost in Pennsylvania and at the Pentagon.

The twin towers have become an icon in our anxious age. They will be remembered long beyond their 31-year life span. One hopes the towers will be remembered at their best, when viewed from across the Hudson River. On bright, cloudless days they appeared like a giant shimmering silver bridge between the sky and the water—just as they looked hours before they evaporated into a gray cloud on the morning of September 11, 2001.

# CHAMBERS STREET TO 14TH STREET

## ALLEN STREET

70 *Allen Street*   This was likely the birthplace, on November 20, 1859, of "Billy the Kid," who was born Michael Henry McCarty to Catherine McCarty, an Irish immigrant unwed mother. His legendary Western outlaw career also had its beginnings in New York. He committed his first murder on September 9, 1876, when he stabbed Thomas Moore in a knife fight on Pearl Street.

## ASTOR PLACE

### 13 Astor Place
*Astor Place Opera House*   On May 10, 1849, an angry crowd of more than 10,000 fans of American actor Edwin Forrest surrounded this building during a performance of *Macbeth* starring English tragedian William Charles Macready. The ensuing riot that night was the culmination of a bitter feud between the two rival actors and their fervent admirers. Macready had come to symbolize and magnify a deep-rooted anti-English resentment held by many of the city's poor. Thirty-one people died and 150 were injured in what became known as the Astor Place riots. The damaged hall, reconstructed and renamed Clinton Hall, was the second home of the Mercantile Library. It was also home to the Book Sales Room and Art Galleries, where on May 28, 1870, the first U.S. philatelic auction was held and more than 14,000 stamps were offered for sale.

## AVENUE B

151 Avenue B ✦ Jazz innovator and alto saxophonist Charlie "Bird" Parker lived in the basement apartment of this brownstone, now on the National Register of Historic Places. Parker and his family lived here from 1950 to late 1954.

## BANK STREET

### 63 Bank Street ✦
Sid Vicious, former punk-rock guitarist of the Sex Pistols, died of a heroin overdose at this address on February 2, 1979. Released from jail on bail only 13 hours earlier, he was here, at the apartment of an actress friend, to attend a party to celebrate his recent freedom. Vicious, whose real name was John Simon Ritchie, was awaiting trial for murdering his

The mob outside the Astor Place Opera House refused to disperse even after the besieged British actor William Charles Macready finished his performance and retreated to safety. This Currier & Ives print depicts the militia and police shooting into the crowd.

girlfriend and acting manager, Nancy Spungen, four months earlier at the Chelsea Hotel.

### 105 Bank Street ✚

After moving to the United States in 1971, John Lennon and Yoko Ono sublet an apartment from Lovin' Spoonful musician Joe Butler. It was here that Lennon entertained his left-wing friends, including Abbie Hoffman and Jerry Rubin, and began his involvement in the antiwar movement. These same activities prompted the Nixon administration and the FBI to spy on Lennon and attempt to have him deported.

### Bank Street near Hudson Street

On Halloween night 1974, Ralph Lee, a mask designer and theater director, with a group of friends wearing masks and carrying large puppets all made by Lee, began a lively and meandering procession to Washington Square Park. This ragtag band has evolved over the years into the celebrated and uninhibited Greenwich Village Halloween Parade. The event is now attended by more than a million costumed and uncostumed revelers annually.

## 155 Bank Street

*Westbeth* ✦ This building was once the home of the famous Bell Telephone/Western Electric Laboratories in 1897. Several important inventions were developed here, including the vacuum tube; the electrical, digital, and analog computers; and sound movies. Dr. Herbert E. Ives gave one the first demonstrations of television here, on April 7, 1927. A tapdancer on the roof, to take advantage of full sunlight, performed before an early camera, while the image was broadcast to a tiny screen in Dr. Ives's office below. In 1969 the complex, remodeled by architect Richard Meier, was converted into the nation's biggest federally subsidized artist colony. The Merce Cunningham dance company moved here in 1970. Diane Arbus, photographer of the bizarre, committed suicide in her apartment here in July 1971.

## BAXTER STREET

### 153 Baxter Street
The Reverend Charles B. Ray, pastor of Bethesda Congregational Church and editor of *The Colored American*, lived at this address in the years before the Civil War. His home served as a station on the Underground Railroad, helping slaves to freedom.

## BAYARD STREET

### 33 Bayard Street
Nineteenth-century American composer of German birth Anthony Philip Heinrich, called the "Beethoven of America," died at this address—the home of his friend Dr. Wolf—on May 3, 1861. His funeral was held here two days later.

## BEACH STREET

### 3 Beach Street
James Fenimore Cooper wrote *The Pilot* here in 1823. The novel, whose main character was based on John Paul Jones, is credited with creating the genre of the sea novel.

### 36 Beach Street
This stretch of Beach Street, Ericsson Place, was named after naval engineer John Ericsson, who lived in an elegant town house (now gone)

between 1864 and 1889. After years as a recluse, the 85-year-old engineer of the *Monitor*, the first ironclad battleship, died here on March 8, 1889.

### Beach Street at the Hudson River

*West Point Foundry Works*   In the early part of the nineteenth century, Beach Street extended to the Hudson River. On this site the first steam locomotive in America, the *Stourbridge Lion*, arrived from England in May 1829. The train was then sent on to Pennsylvania, where it had a successful test run on August 8, 1829.

## BEDFORD STREET

### 75½ Bedford Street ✚

Renowned as an architectural oddity, "the narrowest house in New York City," this address was home for a short time to poet Edna St. Vincent Millay (who was named after St. Vincent's Hospital) and her new husband, Eugen Jan Boissevain, in 1923. Another famous tenant of this house was anthropologist Margaret Mead, who lived here in the 1930s. She was staying with her sister Elizabeth and Elizabeth's husband, the cartoonist William Steig. Often overlooked, the house next door at 77 Bedford carries the distinction of being the oldest house in Greenwich Village.

### 86 Bedford Street

*Chumley's Restaurant* ✚ This former speakeasy with another discreet entrance on Barrow Street was a literary hangout in the 1920s for writers John Dos Passos, Upton Sinclair, Theodore Dreiser, and Edna St. Vincent Millay. The bar has yet to reopen after a fire and a wall collapse on April 5, 2007.

## BLEECKER STREET

### 4 Bleecker Street

*Washington Square Village*   This stretch of Bleecker Street, now called Washington Square Village South, was once named Leroy Place. And it was here, at a house at No. 13, on the morning of October 3, 1839, that John Lloyd Stephens left on a journey that would transform modern archaeology. Stephens, the owner of the house, a lawyer and amateur archaeologist, left along with his friend and artist Fredric Catherwood on a voyage of discovery to Central America. In the next few years, these early explorers "discovered" the Mayan empire and challenged the prevailing history of pre-Columbian history of the Americas.

## 33 Bleecker Street

From the age of five to nine, Herman Melville lived at this address with his family. The family moved one more time, to 675 Broadway, the site of the Central Hotel, before his father's business failed and they left New York City to live in Albany.

## Bleecker Street at Broadway

This intersection marked the beginning of the end for the last horse-drawn trolley in the city. On the morning of July 26, 1917, several railroad officials and dignitaries boarded the last trolley for a final trip to the horse barn and into history. The Interborough Rapid Transit Company (IRT) was retiring the old-fashioned trolley because of a lack of revenue and passengers.

## Bleecker Street at Mercer Street, Southeast Corner

*African Grove Theater* The first African American theater in the United States opened in 1821. The theater's location, still debated, was most likely at this corner in what was then an established African American neighborhood. The theater advertised, "Neither time nor expense has been spared in rendering this entertainment agreeable to the ladies and gentlemen of color." The company performed *Othello* and other Shakespearean dramas. The proprietor, William Brown, wrote and staged the first African American play, *King Shotaway*. Ira Aldridge and James Hewlett, two early prominent African American actors, performed here. The theater lasted only two seasons. The reasons for the closing have been lost to history, but a popular version places the blame on a segregated seating policy requiring whites to sit in the rear of the theater.

## 152 Bleecker Street +

*Café Au Go Go* Dirty-talking standup comic Lenny Bruce's most publicized arrest was made at this basement coffee house on April 3, 1964, even before he appeared on stage. Two plainclothes police officers had attended the show two days earlier, on April Fool's Day, and determined the show was obscene by New York City standards. In November, a criminal court convicted Bruce of giving an obscene performance. Bruce died in 1966 of a drug overdose; two years later, his conviction was reversed by the New York Appellate Court. The club was also the scene of Bruce Springsteen's New York City debut in 1966. He appeared here with his high school band, the Castilles.

### 157 Bleecker Street ✚

*The Slide*  This dance hall, named after the slang term for male prostitutes in drag, was one of the first widely known gay clubs in the city. The Slide, along with exotic Chinatown and the city's bordellos, became a late-night stop for urban sophisticates out "slumming" in the 1890s. In addition to amusing the tourist trade, these early gay clubs served as a safe haven and meeting place for gay men drawn to America's cities as the country changed from a rural society to an urban one. The club's notoriety was its undoing; the police closed it after a few years of operation.

### 160 Bleecker Street ✚

*The Greenwich*  In 1897 this was the first New York City address of author Theodore Dreiser. At that time, this building was a "hotel for gentlemen," and a bed for the night cost 25 cents. Originally called the Mills House, the hotel was built a year earlier by philanthropist Darius O. Mills as a cheap but "moral" lodging for unmarried working men. There were 1,500 units surrounding an enclosed courtyard. In 1976, the building was converted into a private residence called the Atrium.

### 172 Bleecker Street ✚

Author, playwright, and critic James Agee lived on the top floor of this building from 1941 to 1951. It was here that he wrote the screenplay for *The African Queen.*

### 337 Bleecker Street ✚

This was the home of Lorraine Hansberry, playwright of *A Raisin in the Sun.* The play, the first by an African American woman to appear on Broadway, was based on her own experience at the age of eight, when her family moved into a white neighborhood.

## BOND STREET

### 5 Bond Street

This address was the home of Albert Gallatin—financier, U.S. Secretary of the Treasury, and statesman—from 1820 to 1833. He was also a founding trustee of New York University. It was also home to Major General Winfield Scott.

### 31 Bond Street

The sensational stabbing murder of Dr. Harvey Burdell, a well-known dentist, took place here in his home on the night of January 30, 1857.

The curious, gathering outside the home of Dr. Harvey Burdell at 31 Bond Street on January 31, 1857. His murder the night before was only the beginning of a long and tawdry melodrama. (*Frank Leslie's Illustrated Newspaper*)

Emma Cunningham, his one-time tempestuous lover and boarder, quickly declared she was the doctor's secret wife and was entitled to his estate. Her surprising claim aroused suspicion, and she was arrested. The prosecution lacking a murder weapon or an eyewitness, she was acquitted for insufficient evidence. A later court declared she had married an imposter, not Burdell, and the marriage was declared illegal. Cunningham's final attempt to inherit the murdered victim's money was to pretend she was pregnant with his child. The police exposed this deception, too, catching her trying to buy a newborn baby.

## BOWERY

### Bowery at Bayard Street, northwest corner

*New England Hotel*   Stephen Foster, the composer of many of America's favorite songs, was found in this run-down hotel when he suffered a fatal accident on January 10, 1864. He was found on the floor of his room, naked and bleeding, after gashing his neck on a porcelain washbasin. He was taken to Bellevue Hospital, where he died, alone and unrecognized, three days later. The near-destitute songwriter had long been battling alcoholism. "Beautiful Dreamer," another one of his popular songs, was published posthumously.

## 37-39 Bowery

*Zoological Institute*  More a menagerie than a zoo, the Institute was the first permanent display of imported "exotic" animals for the paying public in the 1830s. America's first lion tamer, Isaac A. Van Amburgh, got his start here as a cage cleaner.

*Bowery Amphitheater*  The Virginia Minstrels appeared at this theater on January 31, 1843, and forever changed the image of African Americans in popular American culture. Four unemployed white actors—Billy Whitlock, Dan Emmett, Frank Pelham, and Frank Brower—originated a variety troupe done entirely in blackface. Whites in blackface had already become a theatrical standard by the early nineteenth century, but the minstrel shows created a sensation by portraying African Americans as happy simpletons. These cruel characterizations, written with a romantic misconception of plantation life, appealed to unsophisticated audiences in the years around the Civil War. It reinforced their idea that African Americans, whether enslaved or free, were inferior, and, more insidiously, it etched this racist image on the American consciousness to this day.

## 40-42 Bowery

A saloon that once stood at this address was the headquarters of the Bowery Boys, a tough gang that allied itself with the Native American Party on the basis of a common hatred of the poor immigrant Irish population. The Bowery Boys' rivals were the Dead Rabbits, a gang of Irish Democrats. This longstanding political animosity came to a head in a riot on July 4, 1857. The violence lasted for two days and spread over several blocks, including Bayard, Mulberry, and Baxter streets. There were many deaths and injuries on both sides.

## 46-48 Bowery

*Bull's Head Tavern*  General George Washington and Governor DeWitt Clinton stopped here on their triumphal public entry into the city on November 25, 1783, after the final British troops withdrew after the Revolution.

*Bowery Theater*  When it opened in 1826, this theater was the largest in the country. It can claim two "firsts" in theater history. It was the

On July 4, 1857, a riot broke out between the Dead Rabbits, a gang of Irish immigrants, and their archrivals, the nativist Bowery Boys. The riot was prompted in part by two measures passed by the state legislature to check Tammany Hall's power: a new Metropolitan Police to replace the city's force and Sunday liquor laws at selected saloons.

first to be lighted with gas and the first in the United States to present a ballet performance. The ballet, *The Deserter*, opened on February 7, 1827. Seven years later, on July 9, 1834, the theater was the target of an anti-abolitionist mob, which sacked the auditorium in search of English actor George Percy Farren. The actor's allegedly anti-American comments were interpreted as being against slavery, an unpopular stand with many New Yorkers at the time. A later, rebuilt theater was the scene of a serious accident on the night of June 18, 1868. The fire department had just extinguished a blaze across the street when the boiler of their steam engine exploded, hurling scalding water into a crowd outside the theater during an intermission.

### 49 Bowery
*Café Logeling*   On November 24, 1877, the Manhattan Chess Club was founded in a room behind this restaurant. The club was the oldest in the country and survived until 2001. Members have included Wilhelm Steninitz, José Raúl Capablanca, and Bobby Fischer.

### 114 Bowery ✦
Steve Brodie, one of the most colorful characters of the Bowery, owned a saloon here in the late 1880s. Steve's claim to fame was his presumed

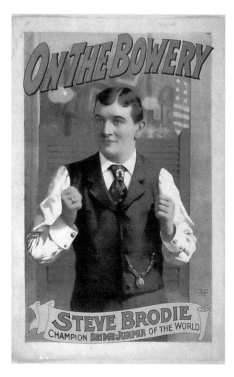

Steve Brodie, pictured in front of his bar, appears in an 1894 poster for the play "On the Bowery." More a series of skits than a play, the show was created to capitalize on Brodie's new-found fame. He sang, danced, and, of course, saved the heroine by jumping off the Brooklyn Bridge.

jump off the Brooklyn Bridge in 1886, three years after the bridge opened. He was also an actor, a singer, a bartender, and a tireless self-promoter. He also became part of the language. *Webster's* defines a "brodie" as "a suicidal leap, hence a fall or flop." Brodie's was one of many bars along the turn-of-the-twentieth-century Bowery where a teenage Izzy Baline—the future Irving Berlin—eked out a living singing for tips.

### Bowery at Grand Street

A field just east of this present-day intersection was the site of the hanging of Thomas Hickey on June 28, 1776. An 18-year-old private and member of George Washington's personal guard, Hickey was convicted of mutiny and sedition. Washington, who signed the death warrant, ordered all his soldiers not on duty to be present in the hope that Hickey's "unhappy fate" would serve as an example. It was the first execution by the American Army.

### 165 Bowery

*Miner's Bowery Theater*   Giving a performer "the hook" originated at a vaudeville theater that once stood at this address. Beginning about

1899, members of the audience were permitted to perform on amateur night. Naturally this led to the question of how to remove the untalented from the stage. A clever stage manager tied a handy shepherd's crook prop to a long pole and yanked such would-be entertainers off stage.

### 201 Bowery

*Tony Pastor's Opera House*   Tony Pastor, a comic singer and former P. T. Barnum employee, opened his concert saloon in 1865. Called "the father of American vaudeville," he helped transform the bawdy music-hall tradition of the mid–nineteenth century into an acceptable form of entertainment for the middle class and women. He banned smoking and alcohol and instructed his performers to keep their acts "clean" of offensive language and behavior. He even offered door prizes of dress patterns and kitchenware to entice women into the theater. Lillian Russell made her debut here on November 22, 1880, and a year later Pastor moved his playhouse uptown to Tammany Hall on East 14th Street in the Union Square theater district.

### 222 BOWERY ✦

When built in 1884, this structure was the first branch of the Young Men's Christian Association (YMCA) in New York City. Over the years, it was home to writer William Burroughs and painters Fernand Léger and Mark Rothko. The Queen Anne–style building designed by Bradford Lee Gilbert was designated a New York City landmark in 1998.

### Bowery between Prince Street and Union Square

On November 14, 1832, the world's first streetcar carried Mayor Walter Bowne and other dignitaries up this section of the Bowery. John Stephenson was the 23-year-old inventor and patent holder of this "horse-drawn carriage running on rails." That first car, built at Stephenson's Elizabeth Street workshop, was christened the *John Mason* after the president of the New York and Harlem Railroad. The car, equipped with padded seats and glass windows, was pulled by a team of two horses. The fare was less than a nickel.

### 315 Bowery ✦

*CBGB & OMFUG*   The initials stand for "Country Bluegrass Blues and Other Music For Uplifting Gormandizers," and the club was the American birthplace of punk and New Wave music. Famous alumni like Blondie, Talking Heads, the Ramones, and Sonic Youth performed here, along with an estimated 10,000 not-so-famous bands over the years. The club opened in December 1973, and Patti Smith played the final show on October 15, 2006.

## BROADWAY

### Broadway at Chambers Street, northwest corner

*Irving House*   Before dawn on May 14, 1851, President Millard Fillmore awoke and prepared for a momentous railroad journey. The President; members of his cabinet, including Secretary of State Daniel Webster; and other notables stayed overnight in the city before embarking on the first train to travel from the Atlantic seaboard to the Great Lakes. The longest trunk line in the world, the New York and Eric Railroad crossed southern New York, linking Piermont on the Hudson River with Dunkirk on Lake Erie. In spite of a pouring rain and the early hour, the streets were lined with well-wishers cheering the departing dignitaries, who first took a steamboat to Piermont to board their train. Six months later, Louis Kossuth, the leader of the short-lived rebellion against the Habsburgs, made this same hotel his headquarters while in exile. The Hungarian patriot was in the United States to help further the cause of independence for his native land.

### Broadway at Reade Street, southeast corner +

*Washington Hotel*   Completed in 1812, this hotel was a gathering place for many important figures of the early nineteenth century. It served as the Federalist Party headquarters in the city. The hotel's most regal guest was Prince Louis Napoleon, the nephew of Napoleon Bonaparte, who stayed here while he was in exile in America for several months in the spring of 1837. The future Napoleon III, emperor of France, spent his time being entertained by New York society. The building was destroyed by a fire in 1844 and replaced by the A. T. Stewart department store, which eventually covered the entire block front.

*A. T. Stewart Dry Goods Store*   This building housed the first true department store, and at the time it opened in 1846 it was the largest in the world. A glorious commercial monument to the emerging American consumer, it was nicknamed the "Marble Palace." The store was decorated with mahogany counters, frescoes, and chandeliers and was served by an all-male army of 300 salesmen and clerks. The building is still here. It was home to the *New York Sun* from 1919 to 1952 and now houses the city's Buildings Department.

In the 1820s New York's first literary club, the Bread & Cheese, met at the Washington Hotel on Broadway and Reade Street. Founded by James Fenimore Cooper, the club included William Cullen Bryant, Fitz-Greene Halleck, and Samuel F.B. Morse as members. (Author's collection)

## Broadway at Thomas Street, west side

*New York Hospital*  It was here at the hospital's first home that the Doctors' Riot began on April 13, 1788, after some boys observed medical students in Dr. Richard Bayley's anatomy class working on cadavers. Word of this discovery and rumors of body snatching inflamed a crowd that set out for the hospital. Mayor James Duane managed to calm and disperse the crowd. The next day, the jail where the doctors and students had taken refuge was stormed. This time the militia fired into the rioters and five were killed. The following year a law was passed allowing only the corpses of executed murders, arsonists, and burglars to be used for medical study.

## 340–344 Broadway

*Broadway Tabernacle*  A two-day Women's Rights Movement Convention attended by Lucretia Mott, Susan B. Anthony, Elizabeth Cady

Stanton, and Lucy Stone was held here beginning on September 7, 1853. The participants had gathered to discuss prosperity and political power for women, especially the right to vote. Preacher William Lloyd Garrison and former slave Sojourner Truth spoke on the evils of slavery. In this same hall in 1856, former President Millard Fillmore was nominated as candidate for the presidency of the American, or Know-Nothing, Party.

## Broadway at Leonard Street, southeast corner

*New York Society Library*   This was the second home of the library, and in the 1840s it was also the home of the National Academy of Design. It was here in September 1847 that the Academy held the first public exhibition of the statue *The Greek Slave* by Hiram Powers. The first public display of a nude female statue in America caused a sensation. Normally a life-size statue of a female nude would have horrified puritan American tastes, but the sculptor shrewdly justified the subject's nudity by explaining it was beyond her control, taken, as she was, a slave by the Turks. Moreover, he wrote in the exhibition program, his subject represented the triumph of Christian virtue over her humiliating fate. Powers became the most popular sculptor in America, and reproductions of *The Greek Slave* became a fixture of every well-appointed parlor.

## 402 Broadway

*Allen Dodworth Dancing Academy*   Nineteenth-century commentator Thomas I. Nichols reported, "If there is anything New Yorkers are more given to than making money, it is dancing." And where were they learning to dance? Why, here at Allen Dodworth's first academy, which opened in 1842. Dodworth was a violinist with the New York Philharmonic and an influential social arbiter. He operated an exclusive school for the sons and daughters of the upper crust; letters of introduction were required if one was to attend. At the end of his long career he wrote a dance/etiquette manual called *Dancing and Its Relation to Education and Social Life* in 1855.

## 412 Broadway

*Apollo Hall*   On December 7, 1842, at 8:00 P.M., the New York Philharmonic (then called the Philharmonic Society of New York) gave its first concert, to about 600 music lovers. Three conductors took turns leading the 63-piece orchestra, including the orchestra's founder, Ureli Corelli Hill, a German-trained musician from Connecticut, who led

Beethoven's "Fifth Symphony." The Society has the distinction of being the oldest permanent orchestra in the English-speaking world.

This same hall was the historic site of the National Radical Reformers' Convention on May 10, 1872. They formed the Equal Rights Party, the first political party in American history to nominate a woman, Victoria C. Woodhull, for the presidency of the United States. In another equally radical move, they nominated an African American man, Frederick Douglass, for the vice presidency. The party, led by one-time spiritualist and Wall Street broker Woodhull, advocated free love, birth control, vegetarianism, easier divorce laws, and the abolition of capital punishment.

## 434 Broadway

*Barnum's Hotel*   Margaret Fox and her sister Kate, who launched the modern spiritualism movement in America, amazed New York with their mysterious "rapping" séances at this hotel in the summer of 1850. Mystically minded Victorians flocked to attend these performances for $1 per person. *New York Tribune* editor Horace Greeley, one of many influential people thoroughly convinced of the Foxes' powers, regaled his readers with their exploits. Almost 40 years later, on October 21, 1888, Margaret confessed her longtime deception at an Academy of Music meeting of spiritualists. Rather than messages from the "other side," Margaret admitted that she produced the rappings by cracking her joints.

## 472 Broadway

*Mechanics Hall*   This was home to the famous E. P. Christy's Minstrels, whose blackface musical show set an American-stage longevity record of a decade of continuous run. Also on this stage the song "I Wish I Was in Dixie," also known as "Dixie's Land," now known simply as "Dixie," by Dan Emmett, was introduced on April 4, 1859, by a later group called the Bryant's Minstrels. Emmett, an originating member of the first true blackface minstrel troupe, the Virginia Minstrels, was a Northerner who never intended his song to become the battle cry of the Confederacy.

## 488–492 Broadway

*Haughwout Building* ✦ Elisha Otis installed the first practical passenger elevator in this cast-iron gem in April 1857. It made the five-story trip in less than a minute. Not only was it considered fast, it was also secure, coming fully equipped with an automatic safety device. Haughwout, a

The demure Fox sisters, Margaret, Catherine (Kate), and Leah, performed their lucrative spirit readings for more than 30 years. Their careers came to an end after Margaret confessed their deception and they quarreled with Leah, who also claimed to be a medium.

prototype for the larger modern department stores, sold china, porcelains, and silverware on the first three floors and used the upper floors for manufacturing. The building had fallen on hard times by the 1960s and was slated for destruction, as was a huge stretch across Manhattan, for developer Robert Moses's plan for what would have been the Lower Manhattan Expressway. Fortunately, the expressway proposal was killed, but it wasn't until 1995 that this architectural masterpiece was restored.

### 509 Broadway
The first giraffes in America were exhibited in a vacant lot at this address in July 1838. The two giraffes were the only survivors of a total of 11 that made the trip from southern Africa.

### 513–527 Broadway
*St. Nicholas Hotel (The Middle Portion, 521–523, Remains)* ✦ Opened on January 6, 1853, this white marble hotel cost more than a million dollars to build. It included the novelty of a central heating plant that piped

This is an 1847 poster of the Christy's Minstrels troupe, one of the most famous minstrel shows. Originally just blackface sketches, their performances grew into a formulaic full program in New York City by the 1830s. Minstrel shows were replaced by vaudeville by the end of the nineteenth century.

warm air, through registers, into every guest room. Mayor George Opdyke used a suite here as headquarters for the city government during the Draft Riots of July 1863. The mayor met here with Governor Horatio Seymour and the city police, the Union Army, and National Guard commanders to plan a strategy to stop the insurrection.

Another Civil War episode in the city's history also took place at this hotel. On November 25, 1864, the St. Nicholas was seriously damaged in a Confederate sabotage plot to burn down the city. More than 11 hotels and Barnum's American Museum were set ablaze in a desperate attempt by Southern spies who hoped to stave off defeat in the waning months of the war. The fire in this hotel was set in room 175 with "Greek fire," the same flammable mixture used to start the fires in the other hotels. No lives were lost and the fires were quickly extinguished. Only one of the conspirators was ever caught. He was Captain Robert Kennedy, a veteran of the Battle of Shiloh. Kennedy, found guilty of spying and arson, was hanged at Fort Lafayette on March 25, 1865, two weeks before the surrender at Appomattox.

## Broadway at Prince Street, northeast corner

*Niblo's Garden*   Dating from the 1820s, this celebrated pleasure garden and theater was at this location until the 1890s. In 1837, Daniel Webster, the great orator and statesman, spoke on political issues, as did the leading actors of their day, such as Edwin Forrest and Joseph Jefferson.

*Metropolitan Hotel*   The Metropolitan Hotel opened in 1852 and shared this site with Niblo's. The hotel's most famous guest was Japan's Crown Prince Tateish Onojero, quickly dubbed "Tommy" by the American press, on June 16, 1860. The first Japanese royal to visit the United States, the teenage "Tommy" was the object of intense public curiosity and affection. Another famous Tom is also associated with this hotel—its bartender, Professor Jerry Thomas. In 1862, Thomas was the author of *The Bon-Vivant's Companion or How to Mix Drinks*, the first authoritative bar manual. He was also the inventor of the "Tom and Jerry" and "Blue Blazer" cocktails. Another invention had its birthplace here. What is considered the first American musical production, *The Black Crook*, opened on September 12, 1866. By all accounts, it was a disjointed variety show that included ballet dancers, music, and melodrama. But it was a big hit and ran for a record 475 continuous performances.

## 579 Broadway ✦

*Stanwix Hall*   Bill "the Butcher" Poole was a notorious thug, xenophobe, and champion of the Nativist Party. On February 25, 1855, he was fatally shot here in this newly opened saloon, the result of his feud with rival gang leader and prizefighter John Morrissey. On his deathbed 12 days later, he allegedly said, "Good-bye, boys, I die a true American." Poole was later immortalized in the book *Gangs of New York* by Herbert Asbury and the 2002 movie of the same name.

## 585 Broadway

This was the final address of John Jacob Astor. When he died at the age of 84, on March 29, 1848, in a brick house that stood on this spot, he was the wealthiest man in America. Much of his fortune had been made in real estate. Shortly before his death, he was quoted as saying, "Could I begin my life again, knowing what I know now, and I had the money to invest, I would buy every foot of land on the island of Manhattan."

## Broadway at West Houston Street, northwest corner

*St. Thomas Episcopal Church*   The funeral for John Jacob Astor was held here on March 31, 1848. Honorary pallbearers were friends Washington Irving and former Mayor Philip Hone. After the service, Astor was buried in the family vault at the back of the church. By 1866, the once-fashionable neighborhood had changed dramatically, and the church shared the street with bawdy dance halls and saloons. Consequently,

Crowds line both sides of Broadway outside John Jacob Astor's home at 585 Broadway on March 31, 1848. His funeral and burial in the church's vault was held down the street at St. Thomas' Episcopal Church. (*Frank Leslie's Illustrated Newspaper*)

the congregation moved the church to its present location on Fifth Avenue at West 53rd Street. John Jacob Astor and what remained of his family left even sooner, in 1851, for a better neighborhood, the Upper West Side's Trinity Church Cemetery on Broadway and West 155th Street.

### 624 Broadway

*Laura Keene's Varieties Theater*   Keene, the actress and impresario, opened this theater on November 18, 1856. She later became well known for performing in the play *Our American Cousin* at Ford's Theatre in Washington, D.C., the night President Abraham Lincoln was assassinated there. This theater went though various names changes before being demolished in 1881.

### 643 Broadway

The third daguerreotype gallery of Mathew Brady was in a building that once stood at this address. It was here that Brady took his most famous photograph, a portrait of Abraham Lincoln. While campaigning

Mathew Brady's influential photograph of Abraham Lincoln helped convince voters that he was not a country-bumpkin lawyer but a respectable leader. Still in the suit he wore for his Cooper Union speech, Lincoln had his portrait taken in a building that once stood at 643 Broadway on February 27, 1860.

for the Republican nomination for President, Lincoln had his photo taken at this studio on February 27, 1860, the day of his famous speech at Cooper Union. Lincoln credited the widely distributed Brady photo with helping him win the election. Another famous sitter was the future king of England; the Prince of Wales, later Edward VII, had his portrait made here on October 16, 1860.

## 647 Broadway ✦

*Pfaff's*  The basement of this same building was the site of the rathskeller restaurant Charlie Pfaff's, a hotbed of the early Greenwich Village bohemians in the years before the Civil War. Nonconformist writers and hacks, thespians, and intellectuals gathered here for lively debates with regulars such as free-love champion Henry Clapp, satirist George Farrar Browne (pseudonym of Artemis Ward), and the scandalous actress Ada Clare, the "Queen of Bohemia." Clapp's weekly *Saturday Press*, founded in 1858, was a forum for another Pfaff's favorite, Walt Whitman, the great poet.

## 663 Broadway

*National Academy of Design*    Opened in 1850, this was the first building of the Academy that had been founded in 1826 by artist and inventor Samuel F.B. Morse and 30 other artists. Louis Comfort Tiffany and Augustus Saint-Gaudens were students here in the years before the Civil War.

## 667–677 Broadway

*Metropolitan Hall*    This auditorium was the site of the World's Temperance Convention on September 1, 1853. Delegates included Susan B. Anthony, Horace Greeley, Lucretia Mott, and P. T. Barnum, who approved resolutions pledging to work for total abstinence, to label drunkenness a crime, and to "end the reign of Satan among Christians." The meeting helped bring together several expanding nineteenth-century social movements: temperance, women's rights, vegetarianism, and nativism.

*Winter Garden Theater*    This theater replaced the burned Metropolitan in 1859. All three Booth brothers—Junius Jr., Edwin, and John Wilkes—performed only once together during their careers, appearing on this stage in *Julius Caesar* on November 25, 1864, in a benefit performance to raise money for a statue of William Shakespeare in Central Park to commemorate the Bard's three hundredth birthday. Less than five months later the youngest brother, John Wilkes Booth, assassinated President Abraham Lincoln in Washington, D.C. It was at this same theater that Edwin made his return to the stage in January 1866. After the assassination he had vowed never to act again, but financial necessity forced him to return. The forgiving audience welcomed him back with wild applause.

*Grand Central Hotel*    In turn, this hotel replaced the Winter Garden. Jim Fisk, the stock market speculator and partner of Jay Gould, was shot on a main staircase here on January 6, 1872. Edward S. Stokes, the killer, and Fisk were in love with the same woman, Josie Mansfield, an actress the press nicknamed "Twenty-third Street Cleopatra." The building lasted another 100 years and collapsed on August 3, 1973, killing four people who were living in the then–welfare hotel.

## Broadway at Bond Street, northeast corner

Samuel Ward's mansion and the adjacent art gallery, said to have been the first private gallery in America, once stood on this corner. Known

On November 25, 1864, the three famous Booth brothers appeared together for the only time, in a benefit performance of *Julius Caesar*: John Wilkes (*left*) as Marc Antony, Edwin (*center*) as Brutus, and Junius as Cassius. That same night, the La Farge next door was among the city's hotels set ablaze in a Confederate plot. Edwin Booth stepped out of character to calm the audience alarmed by the fire engines.

as "The Corner," the handsome square building was topped with a delicate cupola. Ward was a patron of the arts, a civic leader, and a trustee of Columbia College in the first half of the nineteenth century. He was also the father of Julia Ward Howe, the composer of "The Battle Hymn of the Republic." The current building was home to the Brooks Brothers men's store from 1874 to 1884.

## 683 Broadway

*Children's Aid Society*   This charitable organization, still active today, was founded by Reverend Charles Brace in March 1853 and had it first offices at this corner address. Over a span of 75 years, the society sent more than 150,000 poor and homeless New York City children to live with families in the West. The first of these "orphan trains" left on September 20, 1854, with 46 boys and girls bound for a new life in Dowagiac, Michigan.

## 721 Broadway

*New York Hotel*   Opened in 1844, this innovative hotel was the first to introduce room service and an "à la carte" menu. August Brentano began his bookselling business with a small newsstand in the lobby in 1853. Because of the hotel's popularity with Southerners at the time of the Civil War, it was widely believed to be a hotbed of Confederate spies and blockade runners. The fact that it was spared during the Confederate plot to burn down several hotels in November 1864 only seemed to confirm these suspicions.

## Broadway between East 8th and East 23rd Streets

This stretch of Broadway, only recently labeled "the Ladies' Mile," was the city's major shopping artery in the second half of the nineteenth century. Middle-class prosperity, the availability of mass-produced consumer goods, changing roles for women, and increasingly sophisticated advertising helped create a shopper's paradise. The clever displays of goods and plate-glass windows gave birth to "window shopping." These remaining grand shopping emporiums were designated part of a historic district in 1989, and today the area is again a flourishing shopping district.

## 764 Broadway

*Descombe Rooms*   The first chess tournament of importance won by an American-born player, 20-year-old Paul Charles Morphy, was held at this address from October 6 to November 10, 1857. The American Chess Congress, sponsored in part by the New York Chess Club, sent invitations to the world's best-known players, including James Thompson and C. H. Stanley. The brilliant Morphy defeated the 16 other participants and won the $300 first prize. He became a somewhat reluctant popular native hero, having a cigar and a hat named after him. Sales of chess sets skyrocketed, and Morphy was asked to write a column for *Chess Monthly* and the *New York Ledger*. Within a few years, the fad passed and Morphy gladly faded into oblivion.

Paul Charles Morphy's decisive chess wins made him a national hero. This print, picturing one of Morphy's matches at the first American Chess Congress, was a popular souvenir of the 1857 event. He was also a brilliant student who spoke several languages and earned a law degree at age 20.

## Broadway at East 9th Street, northwest corner

This corner was the approximate site of the home of Captain Robert Richard Randall, a wealthy shipmaster and merchant. In 1801, he bequeathed his house and the surrounding 21 acres, from roughly Waverly Place to 10th Street and from Fifth Avenue to Fourth Avenue, for the founding of Sailors' Snug Harbor, for "the purpose of maintaining and supporting aged, decrepit, and worn-out sailors." The Harbor home moved to Staten Island in 1833, and then on to North Carolina in 1976, but it continues to lease its 21 acres of prime real estate in the Village to this day.

## Broadway at East 9th Street to East 10th Street, east side

*A. T. Stewart's Department Store*   Opened as A. T. Stewart's second department store in 1862, this huge cast-iron building covered 2.5 acres and, like the flagship store on lower Broadway, was a tremendous success. By this time Stewart's business, both retail and wholesale, was so vast that it generated 10 percent of the imports into the port of New York. Purchased by John Wanamaker in 1896, it became Wanamaker's Department Store and was expanded into an annex built in 1907, still standing one block south. The store survived until 1954, long after most of the retail trade had moved north to Herald Square and Fifth Avenue. On July 15, 1956, some 208 firefighters were injured fighting a 25-hour blaze that engulfed the empty, legendary store.

### Broadway at East 10th Street, northeast corner

*Fleischmann's Vienna Model Bakery*   Now a leafy churchyard, this was once a bake shop popular with women shoppers in the heyday of "the Ladies' Mile." The term "breadline" originated on this corner as the needy lined up after hours to receive free baked goods from the charitable owners.

### 800 Broadway

*Grace Church* ✚ This Gothic Revival masterpiece was the scene for the wedding of General Tom Thumb, the country's most popular sideshow performer, and Lavinia Warren on February 10, 1863. More than 1,200 guests, described by the *New York Times* as "the elite, the crème de la crème, the upper ten, the bonton, the select few, the very first families of the city—nay of the country" witnessed the vows of the happy couple, whose combined height was only five feet, six inches. The newly-weds traveled to Washington, D.C., where they were received by America's tallest president, Abraham Lincoln, who remarked on their respective heights, "God likes to do funny things, here you have the long and the short of it."

### 818 Broadway

One of the city's most popular and palatial gambling casinos was located at this address in the years after the Civil War. It was operated by John "Old Smoke" Morrissey, a gang leader, championship prizefighter, and U.S. congressman.

### Broadway at East 11th Street, southwest corner

*St. Denis Hotel* ✚ Mary Todd Lincoln, the wife of assassinated President Abraham Lincoln, was a guest at this hotel on September 17, 1867. Mrs. Lincoln had stayed here before with the President, but this time she was traveling incognito and registered under the pseudonym "Mrs. Clark." The former First Lady and her African American servant, a former slave named Lizzie Keckley, were forced to stay in the hotel's only integrated quarters, an attic room. They were in New York on a desperate scheme to raise money by selling Mrs. Lincoln's old clothes and jewelry. The whole affair ended badly a few days later when they were taken in by hucksters interested only in capitalizing on the Lincoln name. Mrs. Lincoln also created a political uproar after her unflattering

Charles Sherwood Stratton and Lavinia Warren—Mr. and Mrs. Tom Thumb—posing in their wedding clothes. The celebrated pair were happily married for 20 years until Tom's death in 1883. Lavinia married another little person and continued her show business career.

correspondence to the slain President's allies, in which she tried to enlist them in her old-clothes sale, appeared in the newspapers. This incident was the one of the first public signs of Mrs. Lincoln's mental instability, which eventually led to her son Robert's request for a hearing to determine her sanity. In 1875, she was formally committed to an Illinois institution for the insane. She was released after four months, but the public was never convinced of her stability.

On May 11, 1877, the St. Denis's second-floor "gentlemen's parlor" was the scene of Alexander Graham Bell's first public demonstration of the telephone. This call was the first to use wire invented for the telephone and not telegraph wire, which Bell had used earlier. Some 200 invited guests watched Bell as he called an assistant in Brooklyn.

## 839 Broadway

*Roosevelt Building* ✦ The rooftop of this building served as the first movie studio of the American Mutoscope and Biograph Company in the 1890s. William Kennedy Laurie Dickson, a pioneer film maker who first worked with Thomas Edison, designed a rotating stage on tracks to keep the sun at the best lighting angle for filming. Dickson, the company's chief cameraman, became a part owner of the studio by 1896. The company moved to an indoor studio at 11 East 14th Street in May 1906.

## 851 Broadway

Cornelius van Schaack Roosevelt, a wealthy real estate broker, played host here to society and literary figures of the mid–nineteenth century. Some of his guests included James Fenimore Cooper, Washington Irving, and Louis Napoleon. One of Roosevelt's grandsons, Theodore Roosevelt, became the twenty-sixth President of the United States. It was from a second-story window of this house that six-year-old "Teedie" watched the funeral procession of another President, Abraham Lincoln, pass by on April 25, 1865.

## BROOME STREET

### 211 Broome Street

*New Irving Hall* Two groups not normally involved in labor disputes, newspaper boys and housewives, held separate meetings in this hall, known for its raucous mass meetings at the turn of the twentieth century. More than 5,000 "newsies" gathered on here July 24, 1899, to form a union during their strike against Joseph Pulitzer's *New York World* and William Randolph Hearst's *New York Journal*. The boys won concessions from the newspapers, and the Ladies' Anti–Beef Trust Association won its struggle against the powerful Beef Trust. Their association, which met here on May 15, 1902, was formed after meat wholesalers raised the price of kosher beef from 12 to 18 cents a pound. When boycotts and riots on the Lower East Side spread to Brooklyn, the Bronx, and as far away as Boston, the suppliers dropped the price to 14 cents.

On April 25, 1865, the funeral procession for President Abraham Lincoln passed the house of Cornelius van Schaack Roosevelt on Broadway south of Union Square Park. The two small children in the second-story window are believed to be Theodore Roosevelt and his younger brother, Elliott. (Theodore Roosevelt Collection, Harvard College Library)

## CANAL STREET

### 54–58 Canal Street
*S. Jarmulovsky's Bank Building* ✦ This private bank, founded in 1873, grew with the hard-earned savings of new immigrants living on the Lower East Side. But as political instability in Europe grew before World War I, depositors withdrew savings to send to their families overseas. Rumors and runs on this bank forced it to close on August 4, 1914, financially ruining the lives of thousands of trusting immigrants.

## CATHERINE STREET

### 47 Catherine Street
In 1826, Samuel Lord, a recent immigrant from England, and George W. Taylor, his wife's cousin, opened their dry-goods store at this address. The Lord & Taylor store prospered and outgrew this and several other uptown addresses before settling in 1914 at its present location on Fifth Avenue at West 38th Street.

### 90 Catherine Street
This address was the birthplace of Jimmy Durante, on February 10, 1893. The famous comedian was the fourth and youngest child born to Rosa and Bartolomeo Durante.

## CENTRE STREET

### 12 Centre Street
Although he spent much of his time in Brooklyn, Walt Whitman did live at several boarding houses in Manhattan. The poet lived at one at this address—run by a Mrs. Chipman—in 1842. His stay here was documented for posterity in an amusing story he wrote for the *New York Aurora*. It relates his getting home late one night, being locked out, and being forced to spend the night in a city shelter.

### 40 Centre Street
*Foley Square—United States Courthouse* ✦ The 1949 Communist Party conspiracy trial; the 1951 Julius and Ethel Rosenberg espionage trial; and two 1984 libel cases, that of General William Westmoreland versus CBS and that of Ariel Sharon versus *Time* magazine, are among the celebrated that have taken place here. Defendants faced with dodging an army of reporters on these 17 front steps have included alleged spy Alger Hiss, mob boss Paul Castellano, Philippines First Lady Imelda Marcos, former Miss America Bess Myerson, hotelier Leona Helmsley, and style guru Martha Stewart.

### Centre Street at Leonard Street
*Collect Pond*   In the long geological history of the island of Manhattan, the site of this present-day intersection was the island's largest source of natural fresh water. The pond was about the size of three city blocks and surrounded by pristine wilderness. Archaeological studies have confirmed the existence of an early Native American settlement along

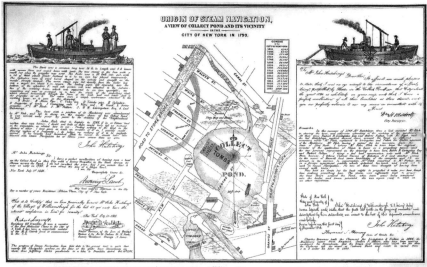

A map of Collect Pond superimposed over the current street grid. This pond was the location of John Fitch's experiments with steam-powered screw-propeller vessels in 1796. Less than 15 years later, slaughterhouses and tanneries on the southern shore polluted the water, and the pond was filled. (Author's collection)

the western shore. By the colonial period the pond provided the locals an abundant supply of fish, oysters, and fresh water. It drained into the Hudson River by way of a ditch that became Canal Street. In 1796, inventor John Fitch used the pond to experiment with his steamboat almost 10 years before Robert Fulton launched the *North River* or the *Clermont*, as the ship has been recorded in history. Fitch's ships were successful, but he was unable to obtain financial backing. In despair he killed himself two years later. By 1811, the pond, which had become polluted as the city grew around it, was filled in.

### Centre Street at Franklin Street, northwest corner

*Halls of Justice*   This prison, named the Tombs because of its exotic Egyptian Revival–style architecture, was built in 1839. One of its most famous inmates, John C. Colt, the brother of Samuel Colt, inventor of the revolver, was convicted of the murder of his printer, Samuel Adams. He was to be hanged here on November 18, 1842. On that day two strange events took place: Colt was allowed to marry his common-law wife, Caroline Henshaw, and a mysterious fire broke out. Once the fire

On February 21, 1862, in the courtyard of the Tombs prison on Centre Street, Captain Nathaniel Gordon was hanged for slave trading. Gordon was active in the trade for more than 40 years and transported slaves as young as six months old. (*Harper's Weekly*, March 8, 1862)

was extinguished, it was discovered that several prisoners had escaped, and a body was found in Colt's cell with a knife in its heart. Officials had the body buried within three hours and announced Colt's suicide. Within days his bride disappeared, never to be seen again. It was widely speculated that Colt had faked his own "suicide" and escaped with the aid of his wealthy brother.

Another infamous Tombs prisoner who did not escape the hangman was Captain Nathaniel Gordon. On February 21, 1862, Gordon became the only person executed in the United States for engaging in the slave trade. Active for years, he was eventually convicted of transporting 897 blacks, half of whom were children, from the west coast of Africa to the United States to sell as slaves. President Abraham Lincoln, as a statement to the Confederate States, refused to pardon the prisoner. A second prison was erected on this site in 1902. The current incarnation of the Tombs, built in 1939, is across the street.

### Centre Street at Grand Street
*Bayard's Mount* Once a natural hill, this spot was fortified by American rebels before the British occupation during the Revolutionary War.

On July 23, 1788, the city's first great parade ended here, at the home of merchant William Bayard, with a huge picnic. The parade, which had started at the commons (present-day City Hall Park) at eight o'clock that morning, was held to demonstrate local support for the ratification of the new federal Constitution. Major Pierre L'Enfant, the future designer of Washington, D.C., designed the parade, along with the picnic pavilions. The procession was composed of all the city's major trade groups: merchants, carpenters, printers, and doctors. Elaborate floats, including a model of the federal ship *Hamilton* under full sail carried by sailors, were interspersed between the marchers. The parade was a great success. Three days later, in Poughkeepsie, the New York State Convention ratified the Constitution of the United States.

## 240 Centre Street

*Old Police Headquarters* ✦ After World War I at the height of the "Red Terror," the public was near hysteria over supposed communist, socialist, and revolutionary influence in America. On November 7–8, 1919, there were nationwide raids to round up people who were considered Bolsheviks and subversives. These raids were called "Palmer raids," after the then–Attorney General of the United States, A. Mitchell Palmer. In New York City, more than 2,000 people were brought here to be questioned. All noncitizens were deported. The building is still a bastion of capitalist power, only now it is a luxury cooperative apartment house.

## CHARLTON STREET

### Charlton Street near Hudson Street

*Richmond Hill* A beautiful Georgian mansion sat atop what was once a high hill that covered several blocks of this neighborhood. The mansion, built in 1767, overlooked the Hudson River, a brook, and a pond. It served briefly as George Washington's headquarters during the American Revolution, and it was also home to the country's first Vice President, John Adams. It was also the home of another Vice President, Aaron Burr, who lived here from 1797 until his killing Alexander Hamilton in a duel forced him to leave New York in 1804. John Jacob Astor purchased the estate and developed the property. He moved the mansion down the hill, cut through present-day Charlton Street, leveled the hill, and laid out building lots. Many of the houses, built in the mid-1820s as a result of Astor's development, are still standing today on the nearby blocks. The Richmond Hill mansion didn't fare as well. Moved yet again, it was converted into a theater in 1831, and later a circus.

A View of the present Seat of his Excel. the Vice President of the United States.

The Society of Iconophiles
Re-engraved on copper    NEW YORK.    by Sidney L. Smith
1901

The Greenwich Village country estate Richmond Hill was home to Vice President John Adams. The Vice President wrote of his stay here, "Never did I live in so delightful a spot."

During this period, on its stage here Isaac A. Van Amburgh in 1833 presented the first wild-animal act in America on its stage. American-born animal trainer Van Amburgh is reputed to have been the first man to put his head in the mouth of a lion. Finally a tavern, the Richmond Hill mansion was demolished in 1849.

## CHATHAM SQUARE

### 5 Chatham Square
This address was the barber shop of Samuel F. O'Reilly in 1899, and it was here that modern mechanical tattooing was invented. O'Reilly, who adapted the ink tube and tip of Thomas Edison's new electric engraving pen, changed his shop into the country's first tattoo parlor.

## CHERRY STREET

### Cherry Street at Catherine Street, northeast corner
*Brooks Brothers Clothing Store*   Henry Sands Brooks founded his menswear firm here on April 7, 1818. His two elder brothers, Henry and

Brooks Brothers Clothing was at the northwest corner of Cherry and Catherine streets, for 56 years, until 1874. The firm outfitted Civil War Generals Ulysses S. Grant, William T. Sherman, and Philip Sheridan. President Abraham Lincoln was wearing a Brooks Brothers suit when he was assassinated. (Author's collection)

Daniel, joined him, and they became known as Brooks Brothers. Because the firm supplied uniforms for the Union Army during the Civil War, looters sacked the store during the Draft Riots of 1863. The store stayed in the neighborhood long after it was no longer fashionable, finally moving uptown in 1874.

## Cherry Street between Clinton and Montgomery streets to Monroe Street

*Belvedere House*  The tavern that once stood on this site and surrounding land is considered the first "country club" in America, opened in 1793. Membership was limited to just 33 "gentlemen." In 1804, Jerome Bonaparte, Napoleon's brother and the future king of Westphalia, rented the property for the summer and fall seasons while in New York seeking refuge from the British. The building was razed in 1830.

## 330 Cherry Street

In 1893, the newly immigrated (from Russia) Baline family, including their son Israel, the future Irving Berlin, moved into a third-floor apartment over a grocery store at this address. In 1901, a year after his father's death, 14-year-old Israel left home to lessen the financial burden on his mother and siblings. He survived on the streets by singing in bars for tips. After he became successful, he bought a "country" home for his mother in the Bronx.

## CHRISTOPHER STREET

### 51 Christopher Street*

*The Stonewall Inn*   A routine police raid on this gay bar gave birth to the gay-rights movement. On June 28, 1969, at 1:20 A.M., deputy inspector Seymour Pine and seven other policemen from the Public Morals Section closed the bar, alleging that liquor was being sold without a license, and announced that all the employees would be arrested. In addition to the employees, customers without proper identification and likely cross-dressers were detained for questioning. As these suspects were being loaded into a paddy wagon, their friends and fellow patrons surprised the police and began throwing pennies, cans, bottles, and bricks at the officers, who retreated into the bar. The fight escalated when the mob broke the front window and set the bar on fire. What started as just another example of police harassment of gay people sparked a revolution. This act of defiance and the four days of rioting that followed marked a turning point in the quest for equal rights for gays and lesbians. The Stonewall Rebellion victory is commemorated each year in the Gay Pride Parade in June in New York and throughout the world.

### 59 Christopher Street ✦

*Lion's Head Tavern*   For 30 years this bar was a storyteller's paradise, populated with writers, journalists, and politicians. Here, journalist Pete Hamill and Robert F. Kennedy debated the prospect of Kennedy's entering the 1964 New York Senate race. Norman Mailer campaigned for his 1969 New York City mayoral race here, and here Frank McCourt met his wife, who convinced him to write *Angela's Ashes*.

## CHURCH STREET

### 236 Church Street, between Worth and Leonard streets, west side

The first newspaper in the United States owned and published by African Americans, *Freedom's Journal*, was launched at this site in 1827, the same year slavery was abolished in New York state. The paper was edited by the Reverend Samuel Cornish and John Russwurm, the first

African American to receive a college education in the United States. The paper's goal was printed in the first issue: "We wish to plead our own cause. Too long have others have spoken for us."

## Church Street at Leonard Street, southwest corner

*Mother African Methodist Episcopal Zion Church*  In 1796, this was the site of the first church built by and for African Americans in New York City. Before this time, African Americans were unable to be full members of the city's churches. They were banished to balconies or back pews and not allowed to bury their dead in sanctified churchyards. One of the founders of this new church was Peter Williams Sr., a slave purchased by the trustees of the John Street Methodist Episcopal Church. Williams— who later purchased his freedom—became a wealthy tobacconist and donated the land and much of the money to build the church. It was, later, here that Sojourner Truth renounced her slave name. The church was ransacked during an anti-abolitionist riot on July 9, 1834. The congregation is now located on West 137th Street near Lenox Avenue.

## Church Street at Leonard Street, northwest corner

*Italian Opera House*  On November 18, 1833, Rossini's *La Gazza Ladra* was performed here in the first theater in the United States designed exclusively for opera. Lorenzo da Ponte, a librettist for Mozart and professor of Italian at Columbia College, financed and built the theater. This cultural beachhead closed within two years, mostly likely because of its poor location and limited Italian opera repertoire. The building became the National Theater, burned to the ground on September 23, 1839, was rebuilt, and burned again.

## CLINTON STREET

### 79 Clinton Street

A little frame house that once stood on this spot was the home and headquarters of "Mother" Frederica Mandelbaum, reputedly the most successful "fence" (receiver of stolen property) in the annals of New York City crime. Beginning in 1862 and for the next 20 years, she was believed to have handled almost $10 million in stolen goods. "Mother," who weighed more than 250 pounds, also gave lessons in pickpocketing and burglary to eager students. When the police finally closed down her profitable operation, she fled to Canada.

The promise of that glorious first night at the Italian Opera House was unfulfilled. The ambitious cultural enterprise at Church and Leonard streets failed after two seasons. Renamed the National Theater, it burned along with three neighboring churches— Northwest Reform Dutch, Eglise du St. Esprit, and Mother African Methodist Episcopal Zion—in a spectacular fire on September 23, 1839. (Author's collection)

## COOPER SQUARE

### 41 Cooper Square

*Cooper Union for the Advancement of Science and Art* ✦ Built by inventor and industrialist Peter Cooper in 1859, this school was the first free nonsectarian coeducational college in the nation. Cooper, a great social reformer who never received a formal education, wanted to help educated, gifted students from the working class. Cooper Union is still free to all students who qualify.

Abraham Lincoln delivered his first and only campaign speech in New York in the Great Hall of this building on February 27, 1860. Introduced by William Cullen Bryant and sponsored by the Young Men's Republican Union, this appearance before an audience of 1,500 New Yorkers launched Lincoln's presidential candidacy. The speech included the famous passage "Let us have faith that right makes might, and in that faith let us to the end dare to do our duty as we understand it." Three sitting Presidents—Woodrow Wilson, Bill Clinton, and Barack Obama—as well as others have also used this forum for great causes:

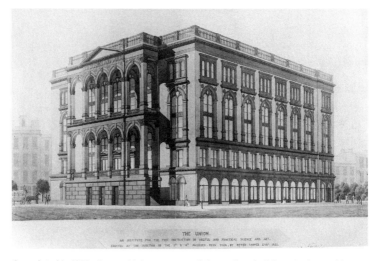

Completed in 1859, Cooper Union was one of the earliest buildings in the world to use wrought-iron beams. This innovative structure was equipped with a floor-to-roof circular shaft anticipating improvements in the newly invented elevator. For more than a century a square cab rode up and down the shaft, but in 1972 a round elevator cab was specially designed to fit.

Victoria C. Woodhull on women's rights, Jacob Riis on the plight of the poor, and Booker T. Washington on African American rights.

## DELANCEY STREET

### Delancey Street at Chrystie Street, northwest corner

The country home of James de Lancey once stood near this corner on a street now named for him. He was both the chief justice of New York Colony and lieutenant governor. He died suddenly here on July 30, 1760. Delancey Street marks the northern boundary of what was the family's estate, which extended from the Bowery to the East River and from Stanton to Division streets. Consisting of more than 120 blocks, it was the largest estate then owned by a single family on Manhattan island.

## DESBROSSES STREET

### Desbrosses Street at the Hudson River

On the morning of April 24, 1865, the body of slain President Abraham Lincoln arrived at this spot at what was then a ferry landing. This was the beginning of the two-day New York City portion of Lincoln's final journey from Washington, D.C., to Springfield, Illinois, for burial. Six gray horses covered in black pulled the coffin in a hearse with glass sides and topped with huge plumes of black and white feathers. The procession, which moved down Hudson Street to Canal Street and then on to Broadway, was escorted by the city's own 7th Regiment to City Hall, where the body lay in state. The almost complete silence of the spectacle was broken only by the muffled drums in various bands and the slow tolling of church bells.

## DOYERS STREET

### 5–7 Doyers Street
*Chinese Opera House*   A basement theater at this address was once a home away from home for thousands of Chinese immigrants living in the city at the turn of the twentieth century. On August 6, 1905, it was the site of one of the deadliest battles of the tong wars. The tongs were secret protective societies in Chinatown. Four theatergoers were killed and many injured after the Hip Sing tong opened fire on their archrivals the On Leong tong during the Sunday night performance.

## EAST BROADWAY

### 165 East Broadway ✦
*Garden Cafeteria*   An earlier restaurant on this site was a popular gathering place for Yiddish intellectuals, many of whom worked at the nearby *Jewish Daily Forward*. It was also a place for spirited discussions among Russian anarchists Alexander Berkman, Emma Goldman, and Leon Trotsky in the years before World War I. Writer Issac Bashevis Singer was a frequent diner.

### 173–175 East Broadway ✦
The Jewish Daily Forward   Part of what was once called the "Yiddish Publishers' Row," the *Forward* was founded by Abraham Cahan in 1897. The beloved advice column, "Bintel Brief" or "bundle of letters," helped educate, amuse, and assimilate the new Jewish immigrants on the rocky road to their American dream. The building was a Chinese church for many years and is now a condominium apartment house.

### 197 East Broadway
*The Education Alliance* ✦ Wealthy German Jews established this Jewish community center, originally known as the Hebrew Institute, in 1889.

It has helped Americanize three generations of later eastern European Jewish immigrants. The Alliance offered day and evening classes in English and citizenship. A free library was available before there were public libraries in New York City. This is where David Sarnoff learned English, Arthur Murray learned to dance, and Sir Jacob Epstein took art classes. On May 15, 1916, it was the site of the funeral service for beloved Yiddish author and humorist Sholem Aleichem. Second Avenue was lined with more than 100,000 mourners en route to the Alliance.

## EAST HOUSTON STREET

### 26 East Houston Street

*Harry Hill's Concert Saloon*   Hill's was a bawdy dance hall that also staged special diversions for its lowlife customers and "slumming" tourists, such as weekly poetry readings by the owner or Punch and Judy shows. Another specialty of the house was impromptu boxing matches, at a time when they were illegal in New York state. At a "testimonial benefit" for John L. Sullivan on March 31, 1881, the future champ offered $50 to anyone who could stay in the ring with him for four three-minute rounds. Steve Taylor, a boxer from New Jersey, tried and admitted defeat after two rounds. Sullivan gave Taylor $25 for his trouble.

## ELIZABETH STREET

### 206 Elizabeth Street

On June 5, 1900, a tenement at this address was one of the first stops on an unannounced tour of sweatshops by New York Governor Theodore Roosevelt. The progressive governor was accompanied by his personal friend Jacob A. Riis, who was a social reformer, photographer, journalist, and author of *How the Other Half Lives*. They also visited about 20 other tenements on this street and Mulberry Street to investigate apartments that served as factories for the immigrants of the neighborhood. They found many violations, including overcrowding, unlicensed manufacturing, and filthy conditions. Roosevelt's interest in housing and sweatshop reform helped focus public attention on the appalling living conditions of the poor.

## ESSEX STREET

### 64–66 Essex Street

*Sinsheimer Café*   The long-ago restaurant at this address was the birthplace of the B'nai B'rith on October 13, 1843. This secular fraternal society was one of the nation's first service organizations. B'nai B'rith, which translates to "Sons of the Covenant," was founded by German Jews in reaction to the potent anti-immigrant movement of the time.

## GANSEVOORT STREET

### Gansevoort Street at Little West 12th Street
The area from here to the Hudson River was once the location of a Sapokanickan ("farm in the woods") Indian trading site. This native tribe traded with the Dutch settlers in the 1600s.

## GAY STREET

### 12 Gay Street
Betty Compton lived in a two-story house here in the 1920s. In addition to being an actress, she was the girlfriend of Mayor Jimmy Walker. Their scandalous extramarital affair was a further embarrassment for the already embattled mayor, who was fighting corruption charges. After the mayor resigned from office and obtained a divorce, he married Compton in 1936 while in France. Another, later resident was the creator of Howdy Doody, puppeteer Frank Paris.

### 14 Gay Street ✝
Writer Ruth McKenney and her sister Eileen lived in the basement apartment of this house in the 1920s. Her "My Sister Eileen" stories of their adventures in the big city were first published in *The New Yorker* and were later made into a book, a play, a musical, and a movie.

## GRAND STREET

### 504 Grand Street
*R. Hoe and Company*   The most violent antisemitic riot in U.S. history took place at this location. On July 30, 1902, the employees of R. Hoe, a printing press company at this address, during their lunch break began jeering at the 50,000 Jewish mourners following the hearse carrying the body of their leader Rabbi Jacob Joseph. The taunting escalated to throwing printing paraphernalia, bits of iron, and wood from the upper floors of the factory. The Jews ran for cover and began throwing back the projectiles. When the police reserves arrived, they sided with the predominantly Irish workers and set upon the Jews. By the time the assault ended, more than 300 Jews required medical attention. The police arrested 11 Jews and one Hoe employee. Mayor Seth Low appointed

an investigative commission, which placed much of the blame on Irish and police antisemitism.

## GREAT JONES STREET

### 17 Great Jones Street

In 1868, the spirit of the ancient Greek Demosthenes supposedly appeared to Victoria C. Woodhull, told her that "[her] work is about to begin," and instructed her to "go to New York City, to 17 Great Jones Street." Answering this call from beyond the grave, Woodhull packed up her family, took a train to New York, and came directly to this address. In later retellings, a friendly landlady answers the door and asks if they have come about the rooms for rent. All Woodhull's doubts about her vision and the impulsive move vanished after seeing a book of Demosthenes' writings in the parlor. Within two years, Woodhull, who had become a successful newspaper publisher and stockbroker, moved on to fancier lodgings at 15 East 38th Street.

### 57 Great Jones Street ✦

This building was the home and studio of 27-year-old artist Jean-Michel Basquiat, found dead here on August 12, 1988, of a heroin overdose. He had rented this space from his friend and mentor, and owner of the building, Andy Warhol, who had died a year earlier.

## GREENWICH AVENUE

### 10 Greenwich Avenue

*Women's House of Detention*   In October 1970 a prison once on this block held Angela Davis, the 1960s radical. Davis, who had made the FBI's Ten Most Wanted Fugitives list, was eventually extradited to California for her involvement with the attempt to free the Soledad Brothers, a group of Marxist prison inmates. Social activist Dorothy Day, Soviet spy Ethel Rosenberg, and anti–Vietnam War protestors Judith Malina and Andrea Dworkin were also held here. Always unwelcome and out of place with the neighborhood, the jail was torn down in 1974, and this area is now the site of a lush community garden.

### 48 Greenwich Avenue

Author William Styron moved here to a one-bedroom sublet apartment in the fall of 1951 for several months. While he lived here his first novel, *Lie Down in Darkness*, was published. He won the Prix de Rome Prize and left for Europe the following spring.

## 86 Greenwich Avenue

A triangular tenement that once stood here was the address of James and Susan Light. Their spacious 17-room apartment served as home and gathering place for many Greenwich Village intellectuals around the time of World War I. Some residents included photographer Berenice Abbott, writers Djuna Barnes and Matthew Josephson, and critics Malcolm Cowley and Kenneth Burke. Suffragist Dorothy Day lived downstairs. The Greenwich Theater now stands on this site.

## GREENWICH STREET

### 666 Greenwich Street ✦

*The Customs Court of Appeals*   An apartment complex is here now, but on October 21, 1927, this was the site of a legal victory important to the nation's cultural history. The landmark ruling *Brâncuși vs. United States* answered the questions: what was art? who defines it? and what is abstract art? Photographer Edward Steichen appealed a U.S. Customs Service decision that *Bird in Space*, an abstract bronze sculpture he had purchased in Paris from artist Constantin Brâncuși, was not a work of art. Upon his return home, a New York Customs agent declared it was "an object of manufactured metal" and therefore subject to duty at 40 percent of the French purchase price. After hearing testimony from artists and critics, the judge sided with Steichen. "IT'S A BIRD," headlined the newspapers.

## GROVE STREET

### 45 Grove Street ✦

This one-time private home had become a boarding house by the time of the Civil War. It was home to actor Samuel Chester. His friend and fellow actor John Wilkes Booth visited him here on Christmas night 1864 to persuade him to join in a plot to assassinate President Abraham Lincoln. Chester resisted, even after Booth sent him $50. Later he was a key government witnesses in the investigation.

Hart Crane was living on the second floor in 1923 when he wrote "The Bridge," his love poem to New York.

### 59 Grove Street

Thomas Paine died on this site in the farmhouse of his friend Marguerite de Bonneville on June 8, 1809. The current structure, from about 1850, houses a restaurant, Marie's Crisis Café, named after Paine's *Crisis Papers.*

## HAGUE STREET

### 3–5 Hague Street

Neither this address nor this street exists today. The entire street was eradicated to build the Alfred E. Smith Houses, a housing project now occupying several former blocks just north of the Brooklyn Bridge to Catherine Street. On the morning of February 4, 1850, this was the site of the city's greatest loss of life up to that time. Sixty-seven people died and 50 were injured in a steam boiler explosion which destroyed the two tenement buildings that stood here. One of the tenants, lucky enough not to have been here at the time of the explosion, was Isaac Merritt Singer, who lost his working model of the practical sewing machine. The struggling Singer found a new investor and rebuilt his invention.

## HORATIO STREET

### Blocks bounded by Greenwich, Jane, and Washington streets

*William Bayard's Home*   The dying Alexander Hamilton was brought to a house at this site on July 11, 1804, after being shot during his duel with Vice President Aaron Burr in Weehawken, New Jersey. Dr. David Hosack, the physician who attended the duel, did what he could for the mortally wounded patriot at the scene. Semiconscious, Hamilton was placed in a boat and rowed across the Hudson River. On the Manhattan shore, he was met by his friend William Bayard, who had him taken to his home. Hamilton died the next day, surrounded by this family. On July 14, 1804, he was buried in Trinity Churchyard. Burr fled to Philadelphia but was never prosecuted for the murder of his political enemy.

## HUDSON STREET

### 555 Hudson Street +

The unassuming apartment house on this tree-lined street epitomizes the urban-planning philosophy advocated by its one-time occupant Jane Jacobs. While raising a family here in the 1950s, she wrote her seminal book *Life and Death of Great American Cities*. Dismissed by postwar mega-builders of the time, her commonsense ideas about healthy small-scale neighborhoods are now standard planning principles. Jacobs's writings and activism helped kill the proposed Lower Manhattan

Neighborhood advocate Jane Jacobs was chair of the Committee to Save the West Village, a group that blocked a 14-block urban-renewal project with 16 high-rise buildings. She appeared at press conference at a neighborhood hangout in December 1961.

Expressway and the extension of Fifth Avenue through Washington Square Park.

### 567 Hudson Street

*White Horse Tavern* ✦ Poet Dylan Thomas spent the afternoon of November 4, 1953, here, drinking at his favorite bar. Popular with the neighborhood crowd and longshoremen, it reminded the poet of an English pub. He staggered home to the Chelsea Hotel and announced, "I've had 18 straight whiskeys. I think that's the record." He promptly collapsed and was taken to St. Vincent's Hospital, where he died five days later.

### 633 Hudson Street

In the summer of 1934, author John Cheever moved into a $3-a-week rented room here. The building, now gone, was home to the well-groomed Bostonian and his bemused dock worker neighbors. His neatly made bed was immortalized by his friend Walker Evans in a photograph now in the collection of the Museum of Modern Art.

## JAMES STREET

### 32 James Street

*St. James Church* ✦ The heart of the Irish immigrant community in the nineteenth century, this church was where the Ancient Order of the Hibernians, a fraternal organization, was founded in May 1836. The order was created to protect the members of the Roman Catholic clergy and church at a time of extreme anti-Catholic bigotry in the United States. The nativism movement, formed in reaction to increased immigration, favored the interests of "native" Americans over those of recent immigrants. Proponents suggested laws that required 21 years to become a citizen and denied public office to Roman Catholics.

## JEFFERSON STREET

### Jefferson Street at Henry Street

The area surrounding this present-day intersection was once the site of the Native American village of Recktauck in the early seventeenth century. After midnight on February 25, 1643, Dutch soldiers under the command of Maryn Adrianesen massacred 40 tribesmen in their sleep. Another 80 natives were also killed in the village of Pavonia, the site of present-day Jersey City, the same night. Governor Willem Kieft ordered these raids in retaliation for earlier Native American attacks on Dutch settlements. Called Governor Kieft's War, these attacks were the most violent in the long-running tension caused by the European settlement of North America. The Dutch settlers and the Native Americans kept fighting for two more years, until August 30, 1645, when peace was agreed upon at a meeting in Fort Amsterdam. The fighting began again in September 1655.

### Jefferson Street at South Street

*Pier 46* Unlike today, on July 29, 1897, the East River was busy with boat traffic and lined with piers. It was here that the bedeviled battleship *USS Maine* rammed Pier 46 to avoid an excursion boat named the *Isabel*. The *USS Maine*'s Captain Charles Dwight Sigsbee was fully exonerated by a naval board of inquiry that termed the crash unavoidable. A year and a half later, on February 15, 1898, the *Maine* mysteriously exploded in Havana harbor, with a loss of 260 sailors. The incident helped spark the Spanish–American War.

## KING STREET

### 17 King Street ✦

On May 16, 1955, writer James Agee left his home here for a doctor's appointment and died of a massive heart attack while in a taxi. His best-known work, *A Death in the Family*, was published posthumously and won the 1957 Pulitzer Prize for fiction. A central theme in the novel was the death of his father, who died May 18, 1916.

## LA GUARDIA PLACE

### 542 La Guardia Place ✚
Artist Keith Haring had a home in this building. Initially a subway graffiti artist, Haring was welcomed into the New York art gallery scene of the 1980s. His lively cartoons, instantly recognizable, were a tremendous commercial success. He died here on February 16, 1990, of complications resulting from AIDS.

## LAFAYETTE STREET

*142 Lafayette Street*   On February 2, 1860, a tragic tenement fire at this address prompted the widespread installation of fire escapes. The blaze started in a ground-floor bakery and spread throughout the six-story building. Twenty people either died in the flames or perished by trying to leap to safety. Less than four months later, the city passed a much-needed law requiring all residences housing more than eight families to have either interior fireproof stairwells or outside fireproof balconies and stairs, later known as fire escapes.

### 425 Lafayette Street ✚
*Astor Library*   Opened on January 9, 1854, with $400,000 bequeathed by John Jacob Astor, this handsome Romanesque structure became the city's first free library. Washington Irving, the first librarian, cared for its 1,000 volumes, the country's largest collection at the time. The famous library attracted other eminent writers, such as William Thackeray, Henry Wadsworth Longfellow, and Ralph Waldo Emerson. The expanded building later became home to the Hebrew Immigrant Aid Society, responsible for sheltering and relocating thousands of Jewish refugees. The city's recently enacted Landmarks Preservation law and theater producer Joseph Papp saved the library from demolition in 1965, and the building interiors were renovated and became the Public Theater. The company's premier production, *Hair*, the archetypal '60s musical, opened on October 17, 1967. This theater also served as the site for Papp's funeral on November 11, 1991.

### 428–434 Lafayette Street
*Colonnade Row* ✚ These four surviving town houses were originally part of a group of nine houses that extended farther south along the

The Astor Library, now the Public Theater at 425 Lafayette Street, was the principal charity of the Astor family. Both John Jacob Astor and his eldest son, William B. Astor, gave financial support to this library, which helped educate the city's poor and immigrant populations. Brooke Astor continued the legacy by giving millions to the New York Public Library. (*Harper's Weekly*, October 2, 1875)

street and were once named La Grange Terrace after Marquis de Lafayette's country home in France. The 1833 design is attributed to Seth Geer and not, as was often thought, to Alexander Jackson Davis. These gracious homes were the first row house development in the city unified behind one façade, a common first-floor façade topped with two-story-high slender Corinthian columns. Considered too far north of downtown for some, the complex nevertheless proved popular with the city's affluent. Warren Delano, grandfather of Franklin Delano Roosevelt; New York Governor Edwin Morgan; and John Jacob Astor II all

All nine original Greek Revival houses are pictured in this print of the unified Colonnade Row. The five houses on the left-hand side, once part of the Colonnade Hotel, were torn down in 1901 and replaced by the current warehouse. (Author's collection)

lived here. A small wedding reception for President John Tyler and Julia Gardiner took place at No. 430, the home of the bride, on June 26, 1844.

## LEROY STREET

### 110 Leroy Street
New York City's Roaring Twenties mayor, James "Jimmy" Walker, was born at this address on June 19, 1881. Jimmy's father, William, was an Irish immigrant who, like his son, was a Tammany Hall politician.

## LISPENARD STREET

### 36 Lispenard Street at Church Street
The home of David Ruggles once stood here. A free African American sailor, he was an author and publisher of anti-slavery magazines and pamphlets. His 1838 *Mirror of Liberty* was the first African American magazine in the United States. He opened a bookstore down the block at No. 67, but a racist mob destroyed it after a year. An early promoter of the Underground Railroad, he helped more than 600 fugitive slaves

escape to freedom. One of those slaves was Frederick Douglass, who hid in this house in 1838.

## LITTLE WEST 12TH STREET

### Little West 12th Street at the Hudson River

The *Seneca Chief*, the first boat to travel through the Erie Canal, anchored here near Fort Gansevoort. The canal boat arrived on November 4, 1825, at 6:00 A.M. after the nine-day trip from Buffalo. The 500-mile journey culminated in a ceremony in the harbor, where Governor DeWitt Clinton performed the "marriage of the waters" by pouring a keg of Lake Erie water into the Atlantic Ocean. Once here at the dock, the *Seneca Chief*'s cargo—flour, whitefish, butter, potash, maple, and red cedar from western New York, Pennsylvania, Ohio, and Michigan—was unloaded. This was only the beginning of a cornucopia of goods that could now be cheaply transported to and from the city. The canal was a tremendous economic boom to New York City, which subsequently became the nation's dominant seaport for goods traveling to the West.

## LUDLOW STREET

### 55 Ludlow Street

Buried deep beneath Ludlow Street, south of Grand Street, the police uncovered the body of Isaac Finkelstein on January 7, 1910. Finkelstein suffocated after his hand-dug tunnel caved in. His brother-in-law and cohort, who tipped off the police, confessed that they were planning to rob the jewelry store at the corner by digging the tunnel from the empty basement of 55 Ludlow. Finkelstein, a painter, lived with his wife and five children next door at 53 Ludlow.

### Ludlow Street between Grand and Broome streets, east side

*Ludlow Street Jail*   On November 5, 1872, election day, candidate Victoria C. Woodhull, the first woman to run for the presidency, was housed in cell number eleven. She had been arrested for publishing in her *Woodhull & Claflin's Weekly* the first account of the affair between the Reverend Henry Ward Beecher and one of his parishioners. She lost the election to President Ulysses S. Grant, but she was acquitted of the obscenity charges and released. On and off for the next five years, this jail would be home to William Magear Tweed. Boss Tweed, the leader of Tammany Hall—the most powerful and corrupt political machine in nineteenth-century America—spent his time here in a two-room "suite"

Still in his Ludlow Street Jail cell, the ghost of Boss Tweed continues to haunt honest city government in this Thomas Nast cartoon titled "The spirit of Tweed is still mighty." (*Harper's Weekly*, December 18, 1886)

complete with servant and piano. During his 20-year career, he and his cronies may have embezzled as much as $75 million in various schemes to loot the city's treasury. The beginning of the end for the Tweed Ring was on July 8, 1871, when the *New York Times* began publishing an exposé. The *Times* articles and Thomas Nast's scathing cartoons in *Harper's Weekly* ultimately led to Tweed's 1873 conviction on misappropriation of public funds. Several trials, an escape to Spain, and failing health took their toll on the overweight, once-powerful boss. He died on April 12, 1878, here in the jail, the building of which he as a member of the Board of Supervisors had authorized in 1859.

## MACDOUGAL ALLEY

### 19 MacDougal Alley ✦

In 1907, Gertrude Vanderbilt Whitney, heiress *cum* sculptor, converted this vacant stable into her artist's studio. Whitney was a late convert to this artist's enclave. Frederick Triebel had moved into No. 6 in 1902 and was soon followed by three additional sculptors, Henry Kirke Bush-Brown, Daniel Chester French, and James D. Fraser. By 1917, people in the art world were calling the block "Art Alley de Luxe." In later years, Gaston Lachaise lived here, as well as Filipino muralist Alfonso Ossorio, with whom Jackson Pollock and Lee Krasner often stayed during 1949 and 1950.

## MACDOUGAL STREET

### 93 MacDougal Street +
*San Remo Bar*   This corner bar was the epicenter of the Beat Generation in the late 1940s and early '50s. The regulars were Larry Rivers, Merce Cunningham, Paul Goodman, and James Agee. Allan Ginsberg referred to the patrons as the "subterraneans," the term Jack Kerouac used as the title of his novel about the scene. After the uptown gawkers discovered the place, the Beats moved on to other quarters.

### 113 MacDougal Street +
This building was the birthplace of *Reader's Digest* in February 1922. DeWitt Wallace founded and worked on early issues of the popular magazine while in the basement of a speakeasy.

### 133 MacDougal Street
*Provincetown Playhouse*   Eugene O'Neill's play *The Emperor Jones* was first produced in this theater in 1920. The production was considered radical for the time because an African American actor played a leading role. A 21-year-old Bette Davis made her New York acting debut at this theater in 1929. The first home of the playhouse in 1916–17 was down the block at 139 MacDougal.

### 139 MacDougal Street
*Liberal Club*   In 1913, this site was an influential meeting ground for Village left-wingers and intellectuals. Members like Lincoln Steffens, Margaret Sanger, Sherwood Anderson, Max Eastman, and Emma Goldman passionately discussed all possible topics, including eugenics, women's rights, free love, free verse, and Sigmund Freud. A year later the club gave birth to the Washington Square Players, a group of theater amateurs, including Lawrence Langer and Helen Westley. The Players, who later changed their name to the Theater Guild, helped encourage more intellectual and artistic theatrical productions in the city. Polly's Restaurant on the ground floor was the like-minded eatery

where the participants would go to continue their discussions. The club lasted until 1919, when Polly's moved around the block.

## MERCER STREET

### 251 Mercer Street
*Courant Institute, New York University* ✦ As a protest against the killing of four student by members of the Ohio National Guard at Kent State University the day before, about 100 students took over this NYU building on May 5, 1970. They demanded that the university pay a $100,000 ransom (to be used as bail for a jailed member of the Black Panthers), or a second-floor computer jointly used by the university and the Atomic Energy Commission would be destroyed. Just as the 48-hour deadline passed, two assistant mathematics professors risked their lives to extinguish the burning bomb fuses.

### 300 Mercer Street ✦
On September 8, 1985, artist Ana Mendieta fell to her death here from the thirty-fourth floor. Mendieta and her husband since January, renowned minimalist sculptor Carl Andre, were having the last of their many heated arguments. Andre was arrested on suspicion of murder and, after a lengthy trial, was acquitted.

## MONROE STREET

### 10 Monroe Street ✦
*Knickerbocker Village* While in his top-floor apartment here, Julius Rosenberg was arrested by the FBI on July 17, 1950. Rosenberg and his wife, Ethel, were later convicted for their alleged part in passing atomic secrets to the Soviet Union. In spite of massive protests, they were both put to death in the electric chair in Sing Sing prison on June 19, 1953. The couple were the only American civilians ever to be executed for espionage.

### 32 Monroe Street
A tenement at this address, replaced by Knickerbocker Village, was the first American home to Annie Moore on January 1, 1892, her fifteenth birthday. Moore has the distinction of having been the first immigrant to arrive earlier that day at the opening of Ellis Island Immigration Station. After years of confusion and much research, it was determined that this Annie Moore, and not a Texan Annie Moore, was indeed the

first. Moore is immortalized in two statues, one in Cobh, Ireland, and another at Ellis Island.

## MOTT STREET

### 4 Mott Street

A tenement at this address was one of best-known opium dens in the city in the 1880s. One of the first to cater to non-Chinese patrons, it was popular with bohemians rebelling against Victorian-era restraints. Poppy, the owner, moved through the smoky room serving opium in little seashells to his customers lounging on low, cushioned platforms.

### 22 Mott Street ✦

*Peking Duck House*   While dining here at one of his favorite Chinese restaurants on July 26, 1981, Mayor Ed Koch began choking on a piece of watercress. His dinner companion used the newly developed Heimlich maneuver and saved the mayor's life. A grateful convert to this simple yet effective lifesaver, the mayor pressed for an ordinance requiring that the now-familiar choking sign be posted in every New York

A *Harper's Weekly* illustration of an opium den on October 8, 1881, reflected the public's fascination and concerns with the growing opium addiction in the country, particularly among the non-Chinese immigrant population. (*Harper's Weekly*, October 8, 1881)

City restaurant. The incident was memorably headlined in the *New York Post* as "how'm i chewin'," a play on the mayor's catchphrase "How'm I doin'?"

### 141 Mott Street

*People's Bathing and Washing Establishment*   In 1849 the Association for Improving the Condition of the Poor—with the help of the state legislature—opened the city's first public bathhouse. Built to "promote cleanliness and comfort among the poor," it offered bathing and clothes-washing facilities. The cost, 5 to 10 cents a bath, proved to be too expensive, and the bathhouse closed in 1861.

## MULBERRY STREET

### 129 Mulberry Street ✦

*Umberto's Clam House*   Joseph "Crazy Joe" Gallo was celebrating his forty-third birthday here early on the morning of April 7, 1972, when he was shot and killed by a rival gangster. The Brooklyn crime boss was here with Sina, his bride of less than a month. The restaurant has since moved to a new location on Broome Street.

### 247 Mulberry Street ✦

*Ravenite Social Club*   Long a hangout for the mob, this was where Charlie "Lucky" Luciano ran his bootleg operations from during Prohibition. In the late 1980s, the FBI secretly bugged the back room of the club and the apartment two floors above. The taped conversations became the basis of the government's evidence used to finally convict the country's leading Mafia head, John Gotti, during his fourth racketeering trial. It was here in the clubhouse that John Gotti and his underboss Salvatore "Sammy the Bull" Gravano, who later turned government key witness, were arrested on December 11, 1990. The U.S. Marshals Service seized the property and sold it in 1998.

### 260–264 Mulberry Street

*Old St. Patrick's Cathedral* ✦ Begun one year after the Catholic diocese of New York was established by Pope Pius VII in 1809, the original building was one of the earliest Gothic Revival churches in America. It served as the Roman Catholic cathedral for the archdiocese until it was destroyed by a fire and was replaced by the larger uptown St. Patrick's. Rebuilt and remodeled, the building was demoted to a neighborhood parish church. It was here on April 27, 1875, that John McCloskey was invested as the first American cardinal. A year later, on April 16, 1876,

Emperor Dom Pedro II of Brazil attended Mass here while on a visit to the United States to attend the Centennial Exposition.

In the fall of 1990, the body of Pierre Toussaint, a one-time black Haitian slave, was carefully removed from the graveyard here and interred in a place of honor in the crypt at the midtown St. Patrick's. His removal and Pope John Paul II's 1996 proclamation of "venerable" have marked Toussaint's passage to sainthood—a far cry from the days when he was turned away from this church because of his race. In 1787, he came to New York with his master's family. Freed 10 years later, Toussaint became a successful hairdresser. Some historians have suggested that one of his famous clients might have been Martha Washington. A kind, generous, and religious man, he gave to many charities and helped other slaves buy their freedom.

### 300 Mulberry Street

*Police Headquarters* While Theodore Roosevelt was the president of the Board of Police Commissioners from 1895 to 1897, he had an office in this building, the department's first headquarters. Roosevelt introduced several innovations to the force: training for new recruits, the bicycle squad, and his policy that every officer be polite to the public.

## NORTH MOORE STREET

### 20 North Moore Street +

Flowers and memorials began appearing on the doorstep of this building on July 17, 1999, the day after John F. Kennedy Jr. was reported missing after taking off from a New Jersey airport in a private plane to attend a family wedding in Massachusetts. Kennedy and his wife, Carolyn Bessette Kennedy, lived in a top-floor loft apartment. The makeshift shrine became a converging spot for the anxious, the curious, and the media in the days that followed. The bodies of the couple and Lauren Bessette, Carolyn's sister, were recovered a few days later and on July 23 were buried at sea near the spot where the plane had crashed.

## OLIVER STREET

### 25 Oliver Street +

Now a National Historic Landmark, this Greek Revival house was the home of Alfred E. Smith from 1909 to 1923. While living here he rose from member of the New York State Assembly to governor of the state.

President of the New York City Board of Police Commissioners Theodore Roosevelt in his office at 300 Mulberry Street. One of the changes Roosevelt initiated during his two-year tenure was to redesign the police uniform to resemble that of the London bobby. (Theodore Roosevelt Collection, Harvard College Library)

## ORCHARD STREET

### 97 Orchard Street

*Orchard Street Tenement Museum* ✦ This museum is now a living memorial to the 7,000 immigrants who lived here from 1863 to 1939. Reconditioned to look very much as it did during the earlier period, the tenement helps illustrate how several generations of newcomers lived, contributed to, and assimilated into the American experience. Actor Sam Jaffe was born here on March 10, 1891.

## PARK ROW

### Park Row at Pearl Street

On Sunday, July 16, 1854, Elizabeth Jennings, an African American schoolteacher, stepped aboard a Third Avenue horse-drawn streetcar reserved for whites. She was on her way to the First Colored American Congregational Church, where she was the organist. After the conductor demanded she get off and she refused, he ejected her with force. Jennings, with the support of the African American community and Frederick Douglass, who printed an account of the episode in the African American newspaper the *North Star*, sued the privately owned streetcar company and won. Her 24-year-old attorney was Chester A. Arthur, a recent law school graduate and future President of the United States. Jennings was awarded a settlement of $250, and as a result of her case, all New York City streetcars were desegregated.

### Park Row near Worth Street

*Tea Water Pump*   The freshwater spring that once flowed near this present-day intersection was prominent in the colonial history and growth of the city. The water from this pump, considered the best for making tea, was carted around the city in casks and sold. This and other neighborhood pumps plus backyard cisterns supplied the city's population, then about 10,000 people, with water until the development of the Manhattan Company Reservoir on Chambers Street in 1799.

### 201–205 Park Row

*Chatham Theater*   In 1844 one of three "dance matches" was held here. What is noteworthy was that it was the first instance in which a black performer was permitted to appear on the same stage as a white one. The African American dancer, "Master Juba," born William Henry Lane, was matching his skills against those of Jack Diamond, the famous Irish jig dancer. Lane, who is credited with inventing tapdancing, became famous and performed for Queen Victoria.

It was later known as the National Theater, and the first New York performance of *Uncle Tom's Cabin* opened here on August 24, 1852. The play, hastily written by Charley Taylor and minus the characters Topsy and Eva, was put into production to take advantage of the uproar caused by Harriet Beecher Stowe's novel. The play was very popular and ran almost continuously until May 1853.

## PARK STREET

### 61 Park Street
*The Old Brewery*  This one-time brewery was a notorious flophouse, cache for stolen goods, and gang hangout that even the police shunned. It was a five-story dilapidated eighteenth-century building with a dirt basement sometimes used for sudden and secretive burials. The upper floors were a labyrinth of many chambers, the largest one called the "Den of Thieves," where more than 75 men, women, and children lived in appalling squalor. As early as the 1820s it had the reputation of being the most dangerous spot in the city. Out of sheer frustration, the Ladies' Home Missionary Society had the building razed and replaced by a mission in 1853. Abraham Lincoln on a visit spoke to a Sunday school class on March 11, 1860. The 118 boys in that class sent him a thank you for his inspiring talk, a prized possession of the President. The mission survived well into the twentieth century and was then leveled for the present New York Courthouse.

## PATCHIN PLACE

### 4 Patchin Place ✛
The poet e. e. cummings lived here, a cul-de-sac hidden off West 10th Street, for more than 40 years until his death in 1962. He first lived on the top floor of this three-story 1848 house in 1923 with his new wife, fashion model Marion Morehouse.

## PELL STREET

### 12 Pell Street
*Pelham Café*  In 1904, Chuck Connors, the self-proclaimed "Mayor of Chinatown," helped Izzy Baline get a $7-a-week job here as a singing waiter. It was a productive three years for the fledging teenage singer and songwriter. While here he taught himself how to play the piano; received his first press notice; wrote his first song, titled "Marie from Sunny Italy"; and changed his name to Irving Berlin.

## PERRY STREET

### 4 Perry Street ✛
Margaret Sanger was living in this town house in 1914 when she founded the National Birth Control League. She opened America's first birth-control clinic in Brooklyn on October 16, 1916.

## Perry Street and the block bounded by Charles, West 4th, and Bleecker Streets

*Sir Peter Warren's Mansion*   One of the largest landowners in Greenwich Village, Sir Peter Warren owned property extending from present-day Fifth Avenue to the old Hudson River shore, today's Washington Street, north to West 21st Street, and south to Christopher Street. Warren, who arrived in the city in 1728, was a vice admiral of the British Navy and commander of its fleet in the colony. He was also a pirate, which, in addition to his 1731 marriage to Susannah de Lancey of an old New York family, accounted for his ability to buy so much land. After his return to England in 1747, he was knighted and served in Parliament. He is buried in Westminster Abbey. His house, complete with widow's walk, survived until 1865, when it was replaced by the current town houses.

## PRINCE STREET

### Prince Street at Lafayette Street, northwest corner

In a small two-story brick house that once stood on this corner, former President James Monroe died on July 4, 1831. After his wife died the year before, the ailing 73-year-old Monroe had moved here from Virginia to live with his daughter, Maria, and her husband, Samuel L. Gouverneur, postmaster of New York City.

### 113 Prince Street ✛

This address was the home of six-year-old Etan Patz. On May 25, 1979, Etan left his home to catch a school bus and has not been seen since. The publicity surrounding his haunting disappearance helped create a national awareness of the missing-children problem.

## READE STREET

### Reade Street between Broadway and Centre Street

*African Burial Ground*   Present-day Reade Street runs roughly through the middle of a graveyard that occupied this site from 1712 to 1795 on land that was then on the outskirts of the city. A burial ground for slaves and free African Americans, it was also a potter's field for paupers, criminals, and American prisoners of the British who died during the Revolutionary War. Uncovered in September 1991 during construction of the Foley Square Federal Office Building, the hundreds of graves and skeletons proved a great find to archaeologists and historians hoping to learn more about the lives and conditions of African Americans during the colonial period. What they did not find was interesting too: almost no worldly goods, leading the archaeologists to believe these were very poor people, indeed. David N. Dinkins, the city's first African American mayor, observed that, "Two centuries ago, not only could African Americans not hope to govern New York City, they could not even hope to be buried within its boundaries." On October 4, 2003, some 419 sets of remains uncovered 12 years earlier were re-interred in a solemn ceremony attended by Mayor Michael R. Bloomberg. The African Burial Ground National Memorial visitor center opened on February 27, 2010.

## ST. JAMES PLACE

### 55–57 St. James Place
*First Shearith Israel Graveyard* ✦ Members of Shearith Israel, the first Jewish congregation in North America, arrived in New York City in 1654. They were Spanish and Portuguese Jews who had fled from Recife, Brazil, during the Inquisition. Not permitted to worship freely by the Dutch, they were nonetheless given a small plot of consecrated burial ground outside the city limits in 1656. The site of this original graveyard has been lost to history. What today is known as the First Shearith Israel Graveyard dates from 1683. This triangular graveyard, which once covered the entire square, is the oldest Jewish cemetery in the United States and has the distinction of being the oldest remaining European landmark in Manhattan. The renowned Rabbi Gershom Mendez Seixas, a leader of Shearith Israel and a clergyman at George Washington's inauguration, is buried here, along with 18 Revolutionary patriots, all members of the congregation.

## ST. LUKE'S PLACE

### 6 St. Luke's Place ✦
This address was the childhood home of Mayor James J. Walker and became the mayor's official residence in 1925. "Jimmy" Walker, a successful songwriter, was stylish, urbane, and perfectly suited to the extravagance and follies of the Jazz Age. His Honor loved the Broadway nightlife and often didn't arrive at City Hall until late in the afternoon and only a couple a days a week at that. The demands of the job finally did catch up to the mayor, though. In 1932, he was forced to resign after Judge Samuel Seabury's investigation discovered citywide corruption in his administration. This town house is still adorned with a pair of ornamental lanterns marking it as a mayor's residence.

Dating from 1683, this is the Shearith Israel cemetery at 55 St. James Place. The only Jewish congregation until 1825, Shearith Israel was important in gaining religious and civil freedoms for the city's Jewish population. The congregation is still active today; their current synagogue is at Central Park West and West 70th Street.

## 14 St. Luke's Place ✦

Poet Marianne Moore lived in the basement apartment of this town house with her mother from 1918 to 1929. For one year, 1922, she had literary neighbors on both sides: Sherwood Anderson lived at No. 12, and Theodore Dreiser lived at No. 16.

## ST. MARK'S PLACE

### 8 St. Mark's Place

Innovative teacher and reformer Juliet Corson opened the first cooking school in the United States, the New York Cooking School, here in her home in November 1876. Tuition was based on one's ability to pay. She often held her classes at public markets to teach about quality, freshness, and price. In addition to writing food columns for both *Harper's Bazaar* and the *New York Tribune*, she was the author of several cookbooks and handbooks on household management.

### 30 St. Mark's Place ✚

The counterculture political organization the Youth International Party, whose adherents were called Yippies, was born in Abbie Hoffman's basement apartment here on New Year's Day 1968. Hoffman, Jerry Rubin, and a couple of friends were smoking dope and dreaming of creative political protests, particularly at the upcoming Democratic Convention in Chicago. The result was the YIP.

### 77 St. Mark's Place ✚

This building was home to poet W. H. Auden, who lived in a four-room apartment on the second floor from 1953 to 1972. Another famous tenant, revolutionary Leon Trotsky, lived in the basement in 1917.

## SOUTH STREET

### South Street between Rutgers and Jackson streets

The ship *Mary Celeste* sailed off into maritime lore on November 5, 1872, from what was once Pier 50. A month later, the abandoned ship was found drifting under full sail west of the Azores. Captain Benjamin Briggs, his wife and child, and a crew of seven were never seen again. No one knows what happened. There have been many theories, including pirates, earthquakes, alien abduction, and even a solution in a story written by Arthur Conan Doyle.

## SPRING STREET

### 29–31 Spring Street ✚

Once a private sanatorium, this 20-room building was home and studio to sculptor Louise Nevelson. The Ukrainian-born artist, who used the space to create her large-scale wooden sculptures, lived here from 1959 until her death on April 17, 1988.

### 53 Spring Street ✚

The first pizzeria in New York City, perhaps the country, opened at this address in 1905. The restaurant was a combination Italian social club, grocery, and bakery run by Gennaro Lombardi, an immigrant from Naples.

### 91 Spring Street

Eighty-nine-year-old Lorenzo da Ponte died here in his home on August 17, 1838. Da Ponte, the librettist of Mozart's *Marriage of Figaro, così fan tutte*, and *Don Giovanni*, was a man of many talents: an ordained Catholic priest, a poet, a scholar, and a scoundrel who left many debts and lovers behind in Europe. He was also the guiding force in building the city's first opera house.

## STUYVESANT STREET

### 21 Stuyvesant Street

*Stuyvesant–Fish Home* ✦ Seemingly out of sync with Manhattan's mostly right-angled streets, Stuyvesant Street is the only true east–west street in Manhattan. It served as the approach to Dutch Governor Peter Stuyvesant's country home from the old Bowery road. The house at No. 21 Stuyvesant Street was built in 1804. It was a wedding present for Governor Stuyvesant's great-great-granddaughter Elizabeth Stuyvesant and her husband, Nicholas Fish, from the bride's father. Nicholas Fish was a colonel during the American Revolutionary War. Their son, Hamilton, born here on August 3, 1808, served as governor of New York and as a U.S. senator. General Marquis de Lafayette, a friend of the family, visited this house on September 10, 1824, during his second trip to the United States.

### Stuyvesant Street at East 10th Street

The country home of the last Dutch governor, Peter Stuyvesant, stood just south of this intersection until it burned down in 1778. Here were signed the Articles of Capitulation that delivered New Amsterdam to the British on September 6, 1664. The story of the end of Dutch rule began earlier, when King Charles II of England gave his brother, James, the Duke of York, a grant in America covering the Dutch holdings. Shortly after, Colonel Richard Nicolls, the first deputy-governor of the duke's territories, quickly set sail with four warships for the city and forced the Dutch to surrender. Colonel Nicolls immediately renamed the city and the province New York, in honor of the duke.

## SULLIVAN STREET

### 177 Sullivan Street

This address was the birthplace of Mayor Fiorello La Guardia on December 11, 1882. The colorful future mayor spent the first three years of his life here. The building collapsed while undergoing renovation on November 11, 1987, and a 13-month-old child was killed.

## 181 Sullivan Street

*Sullivan Street Playhouse* ✦ On January 13, 2002, the final curtain came down on *The Fantasticks*. This enduring two-act fable, known for its catchy tune "Try to Remember," is the world's longest-running musical. Premiering here on May 3, 1960, the play has been performed in every state and 67 countries and made into a television special and a feature film.

## THOMAS STREET

### 41 Thomas Street

A brothel at this address on April 10, 1836, was the scene of the grisly axe murder of beautiful and renowned prostitute Helen Jewett. Her lover, Richard Robinson, the last person to see her alive, was arrested. The "penny press," the new mass-circulation daily newspapers competing for readership, extensively covered Robinson's murder trial. He was acquitted by a jury which felt, as did the press, that he did the community a service by killing the celebrated sinner.

## TOMPKINS SQUARE PARK

On the subzero morning of January 13, 1874, about 7,000 unemployed workers and their families filled this park to demonstrate for jobs in the midst of a financial panic. They were waiting to hear Mayor William F. Havemeyer, who never appeared. The police declared the rally illegal, and a melee broke out. The mounted officers charged the crowd and clubbed the protesters. The park has continued to be a lightning rod for opposing forces: the hippies versus the establishment in the 1960s and the homeless versus those who would "gentrify" the neighborhood in the 1980s.

## UNIVERSITY PLACE

### 24 University Place

*Cedar Tavern* Once the epicenter of the "New York School" of painting, this bar was a popular 1950s watering hole for painters Jackson Pollock, Willem de Kooning, and Franz Kline. The bar was as famous for its marathon boozing and brawling as it was for its intense discussions on the nature of art. It was also popular with the literary crowd of the period, including Frank O'Hara, Allen Ginsberg, Gregory Corso, and Jack Kerouac. The regulars discouraged the management from remodeling the rather drab decor, hoping to prevent "uptown types" from dropping in. The bar left this address in 1963 and moved up the street.

## University Place at East 11th Street, southeast corner

*Albert Hotel* ✦ Now an apartment house, this one-time hotel was owned by the brother of artist Albert Ryder and named in his honor. The romantic painter had a studio here for a short time. The hotel room of Robert Louis Stevenson also as served as an artist's studio. It was here that the ailing and bed-ridden author sat for his portrait medallion, created by sculptor Augustus Saint-Gaudens. Two other famous writers, Leo Tolstoy and Thomas Wolfe, also stayed here.

## VARICK STREET

### 85 Varick Street

A rear building at this address was the first home of Steinway & Sons, the world-famous piano makers. In this rented loft space on March 5, 1853, the recent German immigrant Heinrich Steinway and his three sons began their musical enterprise. Their first piano was sold to a Brooklyn family named Griswold for $500. Today, that piano is part of the collections of the Metropolitan Museum of Art and is considered priceless.

## WASHINGTON PLACE

### 10 Washington Place

The last home of Cornelius Vanderbilt once stood at this address. A modest town house, it hid an extensive stable and a small racing track in the back. The "Commodore" died here on January 4, 1877. At the age of 16, he had bought a sailing ship and started a ferryboat service between Staten Island and Manhattan. At his death at age 82 he was the richest man in the United States, worth more than $100 million. His death, like that of other American millionaires of the period, was well publicized and held up as an example of how hard work is rewarded.

### 14 Washington Place ✦

A twelfth-floor apartment, with bulletproof windows, in this building was home to Ed Koch from 1965 to 1989. Even while he was mayor for 12 years and had the use of Gracie Mansion, he refused to give up his lease on this $479.49-a-month rent-controlled one-bedroom apartment. He did give up his lease after losing the Democratic primary to David

Dinkins in 1989. He spent his last night in office at Gracie Mansion on December 31, 1989, and then moved to his new home at 2 Fifth Avenue.

### 23 Washington Place ✦

On March 25, 1911, a fire at this location killed 146 workers, most of whom were poor Italian and Jewish women and girls. The Triangle Shirtwaist Company was located on the top three floors of this building. Trapped because many of the exits were locked and the rear fire escape had collapsed, some of the victims choose to jump to their deaths rather than be burned alive. The company ran an all-too-common garment-worker sweatshop. The immigrant laborers worked long hours under horrendous conditions for low wages, not only here but in more than 10,000 similar shops mainly in the Village and on the Lower East Side, sewing mass-produced clothing for the thriving fashion industry. The company owners were acquitted of any wrongdoing, but the tragedy increased support for the International Ladies' Garment Workers' Union. In addition, the New York state legislature passed 36 laws improving regulations on safety in the workplace.

### 27 Washington Place

This address was the birthplace of author Henry James on April 15, 1843. James, a great chronicler of the Washington Square social scene, lived at this address only six months before his family visited Europe. But the author and his brother, future psychologist William, did spend time visiting their grandmother Elizabeth Walsh's home at 18 Washington Square North, the setting for Henry's *Washington Square*.

## WASHINGTON SQUARE EAST

### 80 Washington Square East ✦

*The Benedick*   Completed in 1879, this studio-style building was designed and built especially for bachelors, unwelcome tenants to most Victorian-era landlords. The management supplied cleaning service, breakfast, and all-night elevator service. Painters Winslow Homer, John LaFarge, and Albert Pinkham Ryder; sculptor Olin Levi Warner; and architect William R. Mead were among the many resident artists.

### 100 Washington Square East ✦

*New York University Old Main*   Construction of this building, considered a replica of King's College Chapel in Cambridge, England, prompted New York's first labor demonstration, which escalated into the four-day Stonecutters' Riot in August 1834. The building contractor

This is the front page of the March 26, 1911, *World* the day after the Triangle Shirtwaist fire. The building is still here at the northwest corner of Washington Place and Greene Street.

had hoped to save costs by using convicts from Sing Sing prison as labor. The stonecutters' guild protested, and eventually the National Guard had to be called in to keep the peace. Old Main also supplied housing for NYU faculty and others. It was here that professor of fine arts Samuel F.B. Morse invented the telegraph, Samuel Colt developed the "six-shooter" revolver, and John William Draper experimented with the daguerreotype photography process. Draper, a chemistry professor, "snapped" one of the earliest photos of a human face by sunlight while on the roof. The March 1840 portrait is of his sister Dorothy Catherine Draper in a flowered bonnet. Other famous lodgers were poet Walt

Whitman, architects Alexander Jackson Davis and Richard Morris Hunt, and painters Eastman Johnson and Winslow Homer. Old Main was demolished in 1894 and replaced by the current building. The first museum in the United States devoted to modern art opened here on December 13, 1927. Free to the public, the Gallery of Living Art held the collection of Albert Eugene Gallatin, the great-grandson of diplomat and NYU founder Albert Gallatin.

## WASHINGTON SQUARE NORTH

### 2 Washington Square North ✦
One of his generation's finest architects, Richard Morris Hunt lived here between 1887 and 1895. Hunt was the first American architect trained at the Ecole des Beaux-Arts in Paris and the founding president of the American Institute of Architects.

### 3 Washington Square North ✦
For more than 50 years, this was the home and studio of artist Edward Hopper, who died here while working in his fourth-floor studio on May 15, 1967. Other artists who lived here were Thomas W. Dewing, William Glackens, Ernest Lawson, and Rockwell Kent. The building now houses New York University's School of Social Work.

## WASHINGTON SQUARE PARK

Originally a marsh fed by the Minetta Brook, which still flows below ground, this area was a favored colonial hunting ground. Purchased by the city in 1793, it was drained and filled for a much-needed potter's field. More than 22,000 victims of the yellow fever epidemics that afflicted lower Manhattan in the early years of the nineteenth century were buried here. The cemetery also served as a public hanging ground. The Revolutionary War hero General Marquis de Lafayette was reported to have been a guest at the execution of 20 highwaymen during his American tour in 1824. On the Fourth of July 1828, the anniversary of the signing of the Declaration of Independence, the Washington Military Parade Ground was officially opened as a public park. Governor DeWitt Clinton hosted the celebration with a public barbecue. The pastoral setting attracted the wealthy, who built homes on the streets that lined the park. The city grew around Greenwich Village and the park, leaving the Village's street pattern intact—which helped keep passing traffic out and ensured the quiet village atmosphere. The eight-acre rectangle of green is the heart of Greenwich Village and the unofficial campus of New York University.

ARTOTYPE COPY OF THE EARLIEST SUNLIGHT
PICTURE OF A HUMAN FACE.

Miss DOROTHY CATHERINE DRAPER, TAKEN BY HER
BROTHER, PROFESSOR JOHN WILLIAM DRAPER, M. D., LL. D.,
OF THE UNIVERSITY OF THE CITY OF NEW YORK EARLY IN 1840.
THE ORIGINAL DAGUERREOTYPE IS THE PROPERTY OF SIR WILLIAM
JOHN HERSCHEL OF ENGLAND.

Frozen in time, Dorothy Catherine Draper sat still for 15 minutes in front of her brother's early camera for an 1840 portrait. Professor Draper also used the roof of New York University Old Main on Washington Square East to capture the first photographic image of the moon.

## WASHINGTON SQUARE SOUTH

### 42 Washington Square South

Once a rooming house, this site was home to muckraking journalist Lincoln Steffens in 1912. His friend and fellow writer John Reed (whose life was depicted in the 1981 film *Reds*) lived in the room one floor below. Reed made the house famous in his farcical poem "A Day in Bohemia: Or, Life Among the Artists." This address was also home to Eugene O'Neill in 1916 and to sculptor Jacques Lipchitz, who lived here in the early 1940s after fleeing France during World War II.

### 55 Washington Square South

*Judson Memorial Baptist Church* ✦ This church was devoted to improving the lives of the large immigrant population south of Washington Square at the end of the nineteenth century. Always progressive, the church took an even sharper philosophical left turn in 1956 when Howard Moody was appointed minister. A self-proclaimed "Christian atheist," he led the congregation in reform politics and support for civil rights. In 1961, the church won the hearts of the neighborhood by helping to overturn the police ban on folk singing in the park. It was a center of early-1960s avant-garde art, particularly in theater and dance. The church has continued its activist role to the present day, fighting to protect the environment and protesting against indifference to the AIDS epidemic.

### 58 Washington Square South

A small wooden house that once stood on this corner was the home of Daniel Megie. He was the hangman for the state prison on Washington Street and didn't have far to walk to work. The public hangings were performed on the large elm tree (no longer here), one of the city's oldest, in the northwest corner of Washington Square Park.

In 1913, Guido Bruno moved into the second floor of this house. An original and true Greenwich Village bohemian, he was a native of Czechoslovakia and a patron of the arts. He promoted and published Hart Crane and Djuna Barnes.

### 61 Washington Square South

Until its demolition in 1948, the "House of Genius" stood at this location. The four-story boarding house was run by Swiss-born Marie Branchard, who favored writers as tenants. As the nickname implies, several illustrious boarders lodged here: Stephen Crane, Frank Norris, and poet Alan Seeger. Artistic license and time have added numerous artists to the roster, but most were just visitors.

## WASHINGTON SQUARE WEST

29 Washington Square West ✦ After President Franklin D. Roosevelt's death in office in 1945, his widow, Eleanor, moved to an apartment in this building. She and the President had planned to retire to New York City after the completion of his third presidential term in 1941, but he won an unprecedented fourth term (the third term was also unprecedented) and died in office the following year. The former First Lady lived here until 1953.

## WASHINGTON STREET

### Washington Street between Christopher and Perry streets
*State Prison*   New York state's first prison opened on this once-bucolic site along the shore on November 28, 1797. The prison, one of the first reform penitentiaries in the country, was viewed as a model of rehabilitation with separate quarters for women, bathing areas, and workshops for teaching the inmates a trade. As the neighborhood grew more residential and security became more of a concern, the prison was relocated "up the river" to the town of Ossining in Westchester County as Sing Sing prison in 1829.

### Washington Street at Little West 12th Street
*Fort Gansevoort*   A small fort, nicknamed the White Fort, was erected near this corner in 1811. The fort was designed to help protect the city against the British in the War of 1812. It was leveled in 1849 as part of a landfill project to extend the shoreline one block west.

### 835 Washington Street ✦
*The Mineshaft*   An earlier gay dance club, called the Fawn, was here in the early 1960s, but later this location was home to the notorious gay bar and sex club The Mineshaft. The club opened in September 1976 and flourished along with the sexual revolution. But by the mid-1980s this club, along with others, became the center of a heated debate over the spread of AIDS. The city shut down The Mineshaft in 1985.

## WATER STREET

### 616 Water Street
This address was listed in the 1825 city directory as a "Fresh Provision Store." It was also home to Ezra Daggett and his son-in-law Thomas

Kensett, who introduced canning to America. On January 19, 1825, they were the first to obtain a patent to "preserve animal substances in tin." Salmon, lobster meat, and oysters were the first such substances to be packed in tin cans.

## WAVERLY PLACE

### 112 Waverly Place ✦
In 1911, this was the home and studio of artist Everett Shinn. A realist painter and member of "The Eight," Shinn was also an amateur playwright. His Waverly Place Players performed their humorous satires on a backyard stage.

### 116 Waverly Place
In 1845, a house at this address was the setting for America's earliest literary salon. Hosted by Anne Charlotte Lynch, these weekly gatherings were attended by the leading writers of the time: William Cullen Bryant, Herman Melville, Horace Greeley, Margaret Fuller, and Bayard Taylor. It was here that Edgar Allan Poe gave the first public reading of his best-known poem, "The Raven." Later the wife of Professor Vincenzo Botta, Lynch moved her home several times farther uptown, each time faithfully followed by her *literati* friends and guests.

### 137 Waverly Place ✦
This house was once the home of artist John Trumbull. Later, in 1837, it was home to Edgar Allan Poe and his bride and cousin, Virginia Clemm, who was only 14 years old.

## WEST STREET

### 507 West Street
In December 1866 author Herman Melville began work here as a Customs agent for the Port of New York. For 19 dull years, despite administration changes, blatant corruption, and cronyism, Melville toiled honestly and faithfully as Inspector 75. He was often assigned duties on the nearby wharves at the foot of Gansevoort Street, named for his maternal grandfather, Revolutionary War General Peter Gansevoort.

## WEST SIDE HIGHWAY

### West Side Highway between Little West 12th and Gansevoort streets
On December 15, 1973, a dump truck and a passenger car fell through the northbound lane of the elevated highway. The truck was carrying

10 tons of asphalt to repair this part of the decrepit artery. Both drivers suffered only minor injuries, but the consequences were to last more than 20 years. The accident was a prelude for the ill-fated $1.1 billion boondoggle project called Westway, a totally new roadway from the Battery to West 42nd Street, half to be tunneled through new landfill. Every politician up to and including President Ronald Reagan took a stand, sometimes several over the years, on Westway, but the mega-scheme died a slow death from local opposition, largely based on environmental concerns.

## WOOSTER STREET

### 22 Wooster Street ✦

On January 10, 2004, actor and playwright Spalding Gray was last seen leaving his apartment in this building. For two months, his worried family and friends hoped the often depressed Gray would return. His body was discovered in the East River on March 7.

### 80 Wooster Street ✦

Before SoHo became a neighborhood of high-priced boutiques and luxury lofts, it was a Victorian-era manufacturing zone of factories with cast-iron façades. A turning point in its transformation was the conversion of this 1895 warehouse to artist's studios. In 1967, the "father of SoHo," George Maciunas; film maker Jonas Mekas; and other artists including Yoko Ono organized a communal purchase of the building. Their pioneering effort, which didn't always go smoothly, was crucial in the city's decision to rezone SoHo as residential in 1971.

## WORTH STREET

### Worth Street at Baxter and Park streets

This intersection, now gone, was once the infamous Five Points, so named because of the meeting of these three streets. This was the heart of the nation's most notorious slum for much of the nineteenth century. The run-down buildings were homes to newly arrived and destitute immigrants, the poorest of the poor, and the city's toughest gangs. The slum became a daytime tourist stop for Victorians eager to learn about the plight of the urban poor. During a visit, Davy Crockett said, "I would rather risk myself in an Indian fight than venture among these creatures after night." Today much of the neighborhood is gone; it was leveled to build the U.S. courthouse on Foley Square.

This is a typical Five Points lodging cellar from the 1872 book *Lights and Shadows of New York Life*. Thousands of New York's poorest citizens rented a space to sleep on the dirt floors of windowless cellars.

## EAST 1ST STREET

### 50 East 1st Street
*Justus Schwab's Saloon*   A saloon once at this address was the favored hangout where anarchists and *literati* mixed and argued during the last decade of the nineteenth century. Stocked with books, it was frequented by Johann Most and Emma Goldman.

## SECOND AVENUE

### Second Avenue between East 2nd and East 3rd streets
*New York Marble Cemetery* ✚ This spot marks the entrance to the cemetery centered in the block bounded by Second Avenue and the Bowery and East 2nd and East 3rd streets. Opened on July 13, 1830, this cemetery was Manhattan's first nonsectarian burial ground open to the public. Among those buried here are bibliophile and philanthropist James Lenox (for whom Lenox Avenue is named) and members of the Kips family of Kips Bay.

### 87 Second Avenue ✚

*Binibon's Restaurant*   Career criminal Jack Henry Abbott killed waiter Richard Adan outside this coffee shop on July 18, 1981. A tormented but gifted writer, he had been pardoned only six weeks earlier with the help of his literary mentor, Norman Mailer. Abbott, a literary celebrity, had been promoting his bestselling gritty prison memoir, *In the Belly of the Beast.* He was returned to jail, where he committed suicide on February 10, 2002. A jury awarded Adan's widow all the royalties from Abbott's book under New York state's so-called Son of Sam law, which prevents criminals from profiting from their crimes.

### Second Avenue at East 6th Street, northwest corner

*Fillmore East*   On June 27, 1971, this one-time movie palace was the site of the "last" rock 'n' roll concert. This swan song show was performed by the Allman Brothers, Edgar Winter, the Beach Boys, and Country Joe McDonald. Music promoter Bill Graham had created this concert hall shrine to rock only three years earlier. In the early 1980s, the interior was remodeled into the Saint, a disco and center of gay nightlife. Famous for its "Black and White" parties, the club's dance floor was covered with a huge dome. Much of the structure was torn down in 1997 and replaced by an apartment house. The old lobby was converted into a bank.

### 149 Second Avenue

*Le Metro Café*   This coffee shop was a popular hangout with the Beat poets of the 1950s. Poets Allen Ginsberg and Jack Kerouac gave readings here. The cover charge was 25 cents, for a cup of coffee.

### Second Avenue at East 10th Street, northwest corner

*St. Mark's-in-the-Bowery Church* ✚   This location has been used continuously for houses of worship for more than 300 years—longer than any other church site in the city. The present church, which dates from 1799, was erected on the site of a 1660 Dutch chapel built by Peter Stuyvesant on his estate. Grave robbers took the remains of A. T. Stewart, the "Merchant Prince," from the family vault in the churchyard. The body, stolen on November 7, 1878, was returned two years later after Stewart's widow paid a $20,000 ransom, and the remains were reburied in Westchester County. Two famous New Yorkers still buried here are Peter Stuyvesant and former Mayor Philip Hone.

### Second Avenue at East 12th Street, southeast corner

*New York Medical College for Women*   Dr. Elizabeth Blackwell and her sister Emily, also a doctor, opened this medical college for women in

Women medical students listening to a lecture at the New York Medical College for Women, at Second Avenue and East 12th Street. Dr. Elizabeth Blackwell, the first woman graduate from an American medical school, founded the school. (*Frank Leslie's Illustrated Newspaper*, April 16, 1870)

1868. Elizabeth, who had been rejected by 29 medical colleges before being accepted, wanted to help other women enter the medical field. She had also earlier established the nation's first nursing school, to train nurses for the Union Army during the Civil War.

## EAST 2ND STREET

### 52–74 East 2nd Street

*New York City Marble Cemetery* ✦ In 1831, former President James Monroe was one of the first persons to be interred in this cemetery, which was then on the outskirts of town. But in 1858 his remains were exhumed and moved to his native Virginia. Another famous man once buried here and then exhumed was John Ericsson, the builder of the ironclad *Monitor*, who died in 1889. His remains were returned to Sweden the following year. Still here are members of the Kip, Fish, and Roosevelt families.

At dawn on July 2, 1858, former President James Monroe's body began its journey to Richmond, Virginia, for reburial. New York City Marble Cemetery, entered from East 2nd Street, is now surrounded by neighboring buildings. (Author's collection)

## THIRD AVENUE

### Third Avenue between 6th and 7th streets, east side
*Seventh Regimental Armory*  On April 19, 1861, just five days after the shots were fired at Fort Sumter in South Carolina, beginning the Civil War, the men of the Seventh Regiment, NYSM (New York State Militia), were given a rousing farewell as they marched down Broadway on their way to defend Washington, D.C., for the Union. The regiment, established for the War of 1812 and famous for its service during the nearby Astor Place riots in 1849, was the first regiment selected from New York for Civil War duty. Their arrival six days later in Washington earned them the sobriquet "The regiment that saved the capital." The armory, with a market on street level and drilling rooms on the floor above, was home to the Seventh before it moved uptown to its present location on Park Avenue at 69th Street in 1881.

### 97 Third Avenue
Maxwell Bodenheim, a successful poet and novelist of the 1920s, and his third wife were discovered murdered at this address on February 7, 1954. The couple was staying in an unheated furnished room belonging

SEVENTH REGIMENT ARMORY.

A far cry from the current modernist Cooper Union building now on the site, this was the Seventh Regiment Armory on Third Avenue at East 6th Street in 1868. Urban militias were essential to keeping the peace in nineteenth-century America.

to an acquaintance, Harold Weinberg, who confessed to killing them and was declared insane.

### Third Avenue at East 13th Street, northeast corner
From 1647 to 1867, a pear tree that had been planted by Governor Peter Stuyvesant grew at this corner, which was once his orchard. Originally imported from Holland, the tree flourished, bearing fruit for more than 200 years before becoming a victim of a traffic accident involving two wagons.

## EAST 3RD STREET

### 46 East 3rd Street ✦
This was the home of Quentin Crisp, the unapologetic, flamboyant gay author. Known for his 1968 memoir, *The Naked Civil Servant*, describing his life in an intolerant Britain in the 1930s, he became a gay icon for a new generation. He lived here from 1981 until his death in 1999.

## 55 East 3rd Street

*Mary House* ✦ Dorothy Day died on November 29, 1980, here, at this Catholic settlement house, one of the "Houses of Hospitality" she founded. The 83-year-old Day, the co-founder of the Catholic Worker movement, was a revered radical activist devoted to helping the poor.

## 112–138 East 3rd Street

*First Houses* ✦ This block of tenements was remodeled during the depths of the Great Depression, as the first municipal housing project of the New York City Housing Authority. Inaugurated on December 3, 1935, by Governor Herbert Lehman, Mayor Fiorello La Guardia, and First Lady Eleanor Roosevelt, this venture was also the nation's first public low-income housing project. After advertisements touting one-bedroom apartments with private bathrooms for only $4.40 per week appeared, 4,000 families applied for the 122 available apartments.

## East 3rd Street at the East River

*3rd Street Pier* The *General Slocum*, a triple-decked paddle-wheeler, left for an outing to Locust Grove on Long Island Sound at 9:40 A.M. on June 15, 1904, from this site. Filled with more than 1,330 happy picnickers, mainly mothers and children, the boat headed upriver in a brisk wind. Less than a half hour later, the *Slocum* caught fire. Captain William Van Schaick increased the boat's speed, hoping to reach North Brothers Island, but succeeded only in fanning the flames. The charred wreck came to rest on a sand bar opposite 145th Street in the Bronx. The final death toll was 1,021 people.

## FOURTH AVENUE

### 61 Fourth Avenue between East 9th and East 10th streets

*The Reuben Gallery* A venue for new and experimental work, this art gallery is regarded as the birthplace of "Happenings." Happenings of the 1960s were part art show and part performance art with audience participation. The first was Allan Kaprow's "18 Happenings in 6 Parts," held on October 4 and 6–10, 1959, when the gallery was arranged into three rooms with transparent partitions and multicolored lights. Tape recorders and slide projectors were also used along with the hundred guests, who were part of the action.

### 145 Fourth Avenue

Once called "Bookseller's Row," this portion of Fourth Avenue was part of the city's used-bookstore district in the early decades of the twentieth century. The shop at No. 145, owned by Jacob Abrahams, also

On the left, a fireboat continues to pump water on the ruins of the *General Slocum*. Thirty minutes after the fire was discovered by a small boy, the wooden side-wheeler ship was almost completely consumed. The fire was the worst disaster in the city's history until September 11, 2001.

traded in secrets. It was used by German spies during World War I to pass messages.

## EAST 4TH STREET

### 64 East 4th Street ✛

*Labor Lyceum* It was here, in this building, that the International Ladies' Garment Workers' Union was founded on June 3, 1900.

### 66–68 East 4th Street ✛

*Turn Hall* On August 18, 1882, the German fraternal and gymnastic society housed here was the site of the first professional performance of a Yiddish play in the United States. Boris Thomasshefsy, a choir singer in an East Side synagogue, presented Avrom Goldfaden's play *The Witch*. Nearby Second Avenue would later become known as "the Jewish Rialto" in the early years of the twentieth century, when the avenue was lined with close to 20 theaters staging Yiddish plays.

## WEST 4TH STREET

### 11 West 4th Street ✛

*Gerde's Folk City* This popular cabaret was an essential stop for all folksingers hoping to make a name for themselves. On April 11, 1961,

Bob Dylan, opening for John Lee Hooker, made his debut as a paid performer. The club also hosted the debut of Simon & Garfunkel.

## 147 West 4th Street ✦

Finding this setting more conducive than his nearby Patchin Place home, John Reed in 1918 completed the articles that became *Ten Days That Shook the World*, his personal account of the Bolshevik Revolution. This diminutive house was also the home of the Whitney Studio Club, which offered art classes and exhibitions and was for a time the second home to the popular eatery Polly's Restaurant.

## 171 West 4th Street ✦

*Allan Block's Sandal Shop* Opened in 1950, a small leather store at this address was a gathering place for the flourishing folk music movement in the postwar years. Allan Block, a self-taught leather worker and fiddle player from Wisconsin, owned the shop, which was famous for its Saturday night jam sessions and sandals, the scene's required footwear.

## 238 West 4th Street ✦

After years of false starts and struggle, Edward Albee was determined to write his first play by his thirtieth birthday, only a month away, on March 12, 1958. He quit his Western Union messenger job and started writing full time. The result, *The Zoo Story*, a one-act play, was critically acclaimed and the start of his exceptional career as a playwright.

## FIFTH AVENUE

### Fifth Avenue at Washington Square North

*Washington Arch* ✦ A wooden arch covered with plaster spanning Fifth Avenue was built at this site in 1889 to commemorate the centennial of George Washington's inauguration as President. The arch was popular with Village residents, who asked Stanford White to design a permanent marble monument. Set back into the park, it was completed in 1895. The arch has long been a symbol of Greenwich Village and the subject of countless paintings. As such, it was fitting that the roof of the arch was the place to declare Greenwich Village a free and independent state. This act of rebellion was performed in January 1917 by Gertrude Drick and several other artistic types, including John Sloan and Marcel Duchamp.

### 3 Fifth Avenue

*"A Club"* A fundraising banquet for the Russian revolutionary movement sponsored by Mark Twain, William Dean Howells, and Jane Addams was held at this literary club on the night of April 11, 1906. The

The original wooden and plaster Washington Arch spanned Fifth Avenue between 8th Street and Washington Square North. (Author's collection)

guest of honor was writer Maxim Gorky, who was touring America speaking out against the czarist government. In an effort to discredit Gorky, the Russian embassy leaked to the press that his female companion was not his wife. Within days, the scandalized management at the Hotel Belleclaire on Broadway at 77th Street, where he was staying, asked the writer to leave. Refused at several other hotels, Gorky and his companion were forced to take refuge back here at the club.

### Fifth Avenue at East 8th Street, northeast corner

*Hotel Brevoort* The first female of royal lineage to visit the United States, Emma, dowager queen of the Sandwich Islands, was a guest here on August 8, 1866. The hotel, the first to be built on Fifth Avenue, was a Village landmark well into the 1920s. Its basement café was popular with avant-garde personalities in the arts, including Charles Demuth, Isadora Duncan, Eugene O'Neill, and John Reed. The Brevoort was also a landmark in the history of fashion. Henri Gretchen, the hotel's barber, is credited with inventing the daring and liberating "bob" haircut for dancer Irene Castle and her flapper followers. Another celebrity of the 1920s, Charles A. Lindbergh, was honored here for his solo nonstop flight to Paris. A breakfast was held on June 17, 1927, to present the Lone Eagle with a $25,000 prize, offered by Raymond Orteig, the owner of the hotel.

### Fifth Avenue at West 8th Street, southwest corner
John Taylor Johnston built the first marble house in the city at this corner in 1856. He converted the stables behind the house into an art gallery, which he opened to the public every Thursday. Johnston later became a founder and the first president of the Metropolitan Museum of Art.

*Brevoort Apartments* ✦ The entire block was razed in 1954 and replaced by the current white brick building. The corner apartment 4-H was home for several months to pioneer rock 'n' roll star Buddy Holly and his bride. While staying here, he recorded his legendary "apartment tapes," with six songs, including "Peggy Sue Got Married" and "Crying, Waiting, Hoping." On January 20, 1959, Holly left New York to join Ritchie Valens and "Big Bopper" Jiles P. Richardson on their ill-fated Winter Dance Party tour. All three died in a plane crash on February 3, 1959.

### 14 Fifth Avenue
On August 7, 1860, Mary Ann Sponsler spotted her common-law husband, Isaac Merritt Singer, with another woman on Fifth Avenue and began screaming hysterically. That night, in their mansion, Singer, the inventor of the famed sewing machine, beat Mary Ann unconscious. It was not the first time. The public scandal and the subsequent discovery that Singer had two other wives and families living in New York prompted him to leave the country for England. Singer fathered at least 19 children by five women.

### Fifth Avenue at East 9th Street, southeast corner
In 1851 architect James Renwick Jr., a cousin of Henry Brevoort, his neighbor across the street, designed a three-story Italianate house for his own home. He created a special study for his friend Washington Irving, who wrote here while visiting the city. Another author, Mark Twain, lived in this house from 1904 to 1908. He wrote *The Mysterious Stranger* while at this address. The house, too, was torn down to build the Brevoort Apartments.

## 23 Fifth Avenue

No longer here, a town house at this address was the home of the extraordinary Daniel Sickles. A U.S. congressman, he shot and killed Philip Barton Key, the son of Francis Scott Key, because of Key's attentions to Mrs. Sickles. At his trial, he was the first person in the United States acquitted on a plea of temporary insanity. He subsequently became a major general during the Civil War and lost a leg at the Battle of Gettysburg. In 1912, he rented his second floor to the equally colorful Mabel Dodge and her estranged second husband, architect Edwin Dodge. Mrs. Dodge's famous weekly soirées attracted intellectuals, artists, and celebrities of the period. Her involvement with radical causes led to her meeting John Reed, who later became her lover. Rounding out this cast of characters was William Sulzer, who lived on the top floor. He was governor of New York for about a year until he was impeached and removed from office in 1913. Sickles died here at the ripe old age of 91 on May 3, 1914.

## Fifth Avenue at East 9th Street, northwest corner

This corner was once the home of Henry Brevoort. Completed in 1834, his was the first great mansion built on Fifth Avenue. The Greek Revival home, attributed to architect Alexander Jackson Davis, was the enchanted scene of one of the city's first costume balls, on February 24, 1840. One of the guests, Matilda Barclay, the daughter of the British consul to New York, used her disguise as a Persian princess in order to meet her American boyfriend, Captain Burgwyne, of whom her parents did not approve. At four o'clock in the morning, the lovers slipped out of the party, found a preacher, and were married before dawn, all the while in costume. Society was aghast and blamed the scandal on the masquerade party. No New York hostess dared give another costume ball for 14 years.

## 36-38 Fifth Avenue

*Church of the Ascension* ✝ Erected in 1840, this was the first church on Fifth Avenue. President John Tyler, a widower with seven children, married Julia Gardiner here in a secret ceremony on June 26, 1844. The country's new First Lady was a local beauty who was 30 years younger than the President. The President had met his bride only four months earlier under tragic circumstances. Julia and her father, David Gardiner, were aboard the warship *USS Princeton* as guests of the President on a Potomac River cruise. One of the ship's guns exploded and several passengers, including Mr. Gardiner, were killed. The President was very

A dignified Daniel Sickles posed for this portrait around 1902. As a New York state senator, Sickles was a major sponsor of the legislation to purchase the land for Central Park.

kind to Julia in her grief. They fell in love and decided to wed. She bore him seven more children, the last when Tyler was 70 years old.

### 40 Fifth Avenue ✦
New York Supreme Court Judge Joseph F. Crater, "the missingest man in New York," once lived in a fourth-floor two-bedroom apartment in this building at the corner of 11th Street. In January 1931, almost five

months after he vanished and after several police searches, three envelopes with cash, insurance policies, and the judge's will mysteriously turned up in the bedroom. These items, most likely placed after his disappearance, offered no clues to his whereabouts. Judge Crater was declared legally dead in 1937.

## Fifth Avenue at East 12th Street, northeast corner

In 1845, William Lenox built a 20-room Gothic Revival mansion on this corner. His son James Lenox inherited the house and lived here as a

The mystery man himself, Judge Joseph F. Crater in the photograph that was used on his missing-person flyers circulated throughout the country and the world. Crater lived with his wife at 40 Fifth Avenue.

wealthy, eccentric bibliophile until his death. James gave land and his book collection to establish the Lenox Library, which later became part of the New York Public Library. The house was the first home of the Institute of Musical Art, later renamed the Juillard School. Woodrow Wilson, then president of Princeton University, spoke at the opening ceremonies on October 31, 1905. The school moved uptown in 1910. Illustrious students have included Richard Rodgers, Yo-Yo Ma, Itzhak Perlman, and Van Cliburn.

### 65 Fifth Avenue

*Edison Electric Light Company*  Thomas Edison leased this four-story brownstone early in 1881 as headquarters and showplace for his new company. On April 4, 1881, some 100 lights came on, making this building the first anywhere to be lighted exclusively by electricity.

### 66 Fifth Avenue ✦

After leaving her first dance studio at Carnegie Hall, Martha Graham moved to the fourth floor of this building in the late 1920s. Always short of money for her struggling school, she often couldn't pay the rent. But her landlord, who became a lifelong friend, permitted her to stay and even replaced a worn dance floor.

## EAST 5TH STREET

### 210 East 5th Street ✦

*Beethoven Hall*  Now beautifully restored, this 1860 building was once a concert hall and television studio. On September 9, 1895, the American Bowling Congress (ABC) was formed to revive declining interest in the game, stigmatized as a betting sport. The organization established the modern game by standardizing rules and equipment and in 1901 sponsored the first national championship games.

## SIXTH AVENUE

### 145 Sixth Avenue

On January 16, 1901, Murray Hall, a powerful member of the General Committee of Tammany Hall, died here. The next day, the city coroner reported that "Mr." Hall was a woman. Hall's political cronies were shocked that one of their own, a cigar-smoking, poker-playing deal maker, had died of untreated breast cancer. Born Mary Anderson, Hall had lived the past 25 years as a man, married twice, adopted a daughter, and even voted at a time when women were disenfranchised.

## Sixth Avenue at West 4th Street, southeast corner

*The Golden Swan*   The Irish saloon that once stood here was always called "The Hell-Hole" by the regulars. The nickname fit, in spite of such pretensions as a 4th Street "family entrance" and a front room restricted to men. One of those regulars was playwright Eugene O'Neill, who used the bar patrons as inspiration for his play *The Iceman Cometh*. It was also subject matter for artists John Sloan and Charles Demuth. The building was demolished to make way for the subway in 1928.

## Sixth Avenue at Washington Place

On June 28, 1970, one year to the day after the Stonewall Rebellion, a group of several thousand proud marchers gathered here to begin the first New York Gay Pride March. The march up Sixth Avenue grew in number and strength as normally indifferent New Yorkers offered restrained support to the column of gay men and lesbians who were marching into the mainstream of American consciousness. The parade was only one of several events that week to celebrate the historic riot at the Stonewall bar, where gay patrons had refused to be harassed by the police. The parade ended in typical 1960s fashion in Central Park's Sheep Meadow with a "Gay-In."

## 425 Sixth Avenue

*Jefferson Market Library* ✦ This exuberant example of Victorian Gothic architecture was built in 1877 as a combination police and civil court-house, produce market, and volunteer fire station, complete with fire lookout. The courtroom on the second floor was the site of the Harry K. Thaw murder trial, which opened on January 23, 1907. Thaw, a men-tally unstable millionaire, shot and killed architect Stanford White, who had had a torrid affair years earlier with Thaw's wife, Evelyn Nesbit, before her marriage to Thaw. The trial ended in a hung jury. A second jury found Thaw not guilty by reason of insanity, and he was sent to an asylum until his release in 1915.

By the 1950s, the courthouse was considered an architectural mon-strosity and was threatened with demolition. A tenacious group of ad-mirers, in the days before any Landmarks Preservation Commission, convinced the city in 1967 to save the building and turn it into a branch library.

## 522–524 Sixth Avenue

This was the first address of Macy's "fancy dry goods store," in 1858. Former Nantucket sea captain Rowland Hussey Macy opened his small shop selling ribbons, laces, and handkerchiefs. On opening day, October

On April 29, 1878, the first train on the Sixth Avenue elevated railroad line passed the Jefferson Market Courthouse at Greenwich Avenue. The world's first session of night court was held here on September 1, 1907. (*Frank Leslie's Illustrated Newspaper*)

27, 1858, the proceeds were a modest $11.06, but the business grew and by the 1870s the store occupied the entire block from 13th to 14th streets.

## EAST 6TH STREET

### 325 East 6th Street
*St. Mark's Lutheran Church* ✛ This Lutheran congregation was the spiritual heart of "Kleindeutschland," or Little Germany, an immigrant neighborhood. On Wednesday morning, June 15, 1904, the Reverend George Haas and his parishioners from this church left for a Sunday school outing. They boarded the ill-fated *General Slocum*, chartered for the church's annual excursion, and set off for Long Island Sound. By nightfall, more than 1,000 people, including the reverend's wife and daughter, were dead as result of the fire that swept the ship. The disaster was also the death knell for the German community here as many families moved uptown to Yorkville and other sections of the city to escape painful memories. As more Jews moved into the area, the church became a synagogue in 1940.

## 742 East 6th Street ✦

Once a fire-damaged hulk, this tenement was rehabilitated in part by former President Jimmy Carter and his wife, Rosalynn, along with other volunteers from Habitat for Humanity in September 1984. After their 24-hour Trailways bus ride from Americus, Georgia, the Carters, well known for their humanitarian and charitable work, spent the next week as construction workers. The couple's hard work and invaluable publicity were a boon to the charity that rehabilitates and builds affordable housing.

## EAST 7TH STREET

### 15 East 7th Street

*McSorley's Old Ale House* ✦ One of the city's oldest saloons still in operation, McSorley's was opened in 1854 by John McSorley, an Irish immigrant. The bar was open to Presidents Franklin D. Roosevelt and John F. Kennedy, but not to women. Not until August 10, 1970, 116 years after the opening, were women permitted entrance, and then only after a court order. In 1912, the bar was immortalized in a painting by John Sloan that now hangs in the Detroit Institute of Arts.

### 206 East 7th Street ✦

A fifth-floor walk-up apartment in this building was the longtime home of poet Allen Ginsberg. He shared his apartment in 1953 with another Beat writer, William Burroughs. Ginsberg lived here until 1996 and then moved to a loft on East 13th Street, where he died on April 5, 1997.

## EAST 8TH STREET

### 35 and 39 East 8th Street

Friday night symposia on modern art were held at No. 35 in 1948. The group included artists Robert Motherwell, Mark Rothko, Adolph Gottlieb, and Willem de Kooning. By 1949 some of this group spilled over to No. 39, a small rented loft, and became known as "The Club." Lectures and panel discussions on a wide range of aesthetic topics were presented, especially abstract expressionism. Membership grew to include the major artists of the period, such as Franz Kline, Helen Frankenthaler, and Robert Rauschenberg.

### 46 East 8th Street

Artist Jackson Pollock lived and worked here beginning in 1933, joined by his future wife, Lee Krasner, in the early 1940s. Peggy Guggenheim, his patron, commissioned a work for her town house. The mural, more than 19 feet long, was the largest work Pollock ever painted and required knocking out a wall here to complete it. Pollock and Krasner stayed until 1945 and then moved to East Hampton, on Long Island.

## WEST 8TH STREET

### 5 West 8th Street ✦
*Marlton House Hotel*   The future president of Ecuador, Galo Plaza, was born in this building on February 17, 1906. His father was a minister to the United States at the time.

### 8 West 8th Street ✦
*Whitney Museum of American Art*   Gertrude Vanderbilt Whitney leased this address, once the studio of sculptor Daniel Chester French, for additional space because it was directly behind her studio at 19 MacDougal Alley. Whitney, a prominent sculptor herself, was the granddaughter of Cornelius Vanderbilt and the wife of financier Harry Payne Whitney. In 1929 she decided to donate her collection of American art to the Metropolitan Museum of Art. The Metropolitan's director, Dr. Edward Robinson, declined the offer, saying "What will we do with them, my dear lady? We have a cellar of those things already." That refusal precipitated the opening at this address and the three adjoining town houses of the Whitney Museum of American Art on November 18, 1931.

### 17 West 8th Street
"Queen of the Night Clubs" Mary Louise Cecilia "Texas" Guinan lived here during much of the 1920s, a decade she helped define with her party-girl antics, which were duly recorded in all the tabloid newspapers. The exotic and dimly lit decor was conducive to sleeping during the day.

### 18 West 8th Street
Philosopher and critic Randolph Bourne died at this address on December 22, 1918. Severely handicapped by a birth defect and childhood spinal tuberculosis, the gifted writer was only 32 years old when he succumbed to the flu epidemic of 1918.

### 52 West 8th Street
*Electric Lady Studios* ✦   Hans Hofmann, the German-born abstract-expressionist painter and teacher, had his art school on the floor above

an avant-garde movie theater in this building from 1938 to 1958. Considered a major figure in the development of modern and abstract art, Hofmann inspired a new generation of American artists. Some of his students were Helen Frankenthaler, Lee Krasner, Red Grooms, Allan Kaprow, and Larry Rivers.

In 1970 rock musician Jimi Hendrix converted the theater space into his Electric Lady recording studio. He left America for the last time on the day it formally opened. He died soon after in Europe, but the space has continued to be used by many renowned musicians, including Stevie Wonder, Diana Ross, Led Zepplin, and the Rolling Stones.

## EAST 9TH STREET

### 60 East 9th Street
Once a vacant barber shop, this storefront was transformed into an art gallery for an early showing of the abstract-expressionists. The "Ninth Street Show," which began on May 21, 1951, was the public's early exposure to this emotional nonfigurative movement. Some 61 artists, including Robert Rauschenberg, Jackson Pollock, Robert Motherwell, and Franz Kline, were permitted to submit one work each.

## WEST 9TH STREET

### 10 West 9th Street ✦
In 1919 "Ashcan" painter William Glackens bought this house and lived here until his death in 1938. He had a studio built on the roof. The studio was bathed in soft northern light, blocked when the Fifth Avenue Hotel was built across the street.

### 12 West 9th Street ✦
Henry Jarvis Raymond lived here from 1860 to 1867. Raymond was a founder and first editor of the *New York Times* and the first editor of *Harper's Magazine*. He later was a lieutenant governor of New York and a member of the U.S. House of Representatives.

### 35 West 9th Street ✦
Poet Marianne Moore died here at the age of 84 on February 5, 1972. She had lived here in apartment 7B since 1966.

### 56 West 9th Street ✦
Based on his fame as a Western explorer, "the Pathfinder," John Charles Frémont, was nominated in 1856 as the first presidential candidate of

the newly founded Republican Party. Frémont stayed close to home here and avoided active campaigning, as was the political custom at the time. "Free soil, free men, Frémont" lost to James Buchanan, the Democrat, but his campaign laid the groundwork for Republican Abraham Lincoln's win in 1860.

## 62 West 9th Street ✦

*The Lion*  In the early summer of 1960, Barbara (before she became Barbra) Streisand sang at a nightclub here in a talent contest. She sang "A Sleeping Bee" and "When Sunny Gets Blue." The 18-year-old from Brooklyn won and signed a two-week engagement at the gay club.

## EAST 10TH STREET

### 90 East 10th Street

*Tanager Gallery*  When this address was the second home of the Tanager Gallery, this was an important stepping stone to public recognition for artists of the 1950s. This once low-rent block and surrounding area, collectively referred to as "Tenth Street," was the place to see daring and innovative American art. By 1956, this block between Third and Fourth avenues was home to the studios of more than a dozen artists, including Michael Goldberg, Philip Guston, Willem de Kooning, Milton Resnick, and Esteban Vicente. It was also home to the Camino, Brata, Area, and March galleries.

### 118 East 10th Street

Stanford White, the Gilded Age's most famous architect, was born at this address on November 9, 1853. His father was Richard Grant White, the music and drama critic.

### 127 East 10th Street

This was the last home of photographer Mathew Brady. Largely forgotten by the public, he spent the last months of his life organizing an exhibition of his work. He died in poverty at Presbyterian Hospital on January 15, 1896. The exhibition, which helped confirm his stature as America's greatest nineteenth-century photographer, was held two weeks later at Carnegie Hall.

### 269 East 10th Street

In late 1883 this was the home of Edward H. Johnson, an associate of Thomas Edison. The holiday trimmings were very special this year, as the Johnson Christmas tree was the first in the world to be decorated with electric lights.

## WEST 10TH STREET

### 14 West 10th Street ✦
Mark Twain lived in this house shortly after returning from Europe in 1900. Sadly, this house also has a tragic history; it was here that Joel Steinberg fatally beat his six-year-old illegally adopted daughter, Lisa. Steinberg was found guilty of first-degree manslaughter on January 30, 1989. Damaging testimony by Hedda Nussbaum, Steinberg's lover, helped convict him. The shocking details of the couple's life in this building drew nationwide attention to the problem of child abuse.

### 20 West 10th Street ✦
Sculptor Frederick MacMonnies had his studio here in the 1930s. He created several public works in the city, among them the controversial statue *Civic Virtue*, which once stood in front of City Hall. *Civic Virtue*, a male chauvinist allegory of "good" government pictured as a male figure standing atop female "evil" forces, was banished to Queens Borough Hall in the 1940s. Later, painter Louis Bouche also lived here.

### 23 West 10th Street
*Marshall Chess Club* ✦ In 1915, Frank J. Marshall, the U.S. champion between 1909 and 1936, founded this chess club. The club's most famous member was Marcel Duchamp, the Dadaist artist. In 1949, he won every game in the Class A Section of the New York State Chess Association Tournament. A lifetime aficionado of the game, in the late 1950s, he lived down the block at 28 West 10th Street just to be near this club. He was quoted as saying chess had "all the beauty of art—and much more."

### 51–55 West 10th Street
*Studio Building* No longer here, the Studio Building, designed by architect Richard Morris Hunt, was built especially for artist's studios. When opened in 1858, it soon became the center of late-nineteenth-century artistic activity in the city. Painters Frederick Church, Emanuel Leutze, William Merritt Chase, Winslow Homer, Albert Bierstadt, and Eastman Johnson all had studios here, as did sculptors Augustus Saint-Gaudens and A. Stirling Calder, father of mobile creator Alexander Calder. Each studio was connected to its neighbor by large doors, which were kept open during receptions and art shows. Hunt was justifiably

The first Christmas tree lighted with incandescent bulbs in December 1882. This was the home of Edward H. Johnson, vice president of the Edison Electric Light Company on East 10th Street. (Edison National Historic Site)

proud of his building—his first large commission in New York—and established his own studio and office here. Poet Kahlil Gibran, who was also a painter, had an apartment here for 20 years beginning in 1911. The building was razed in 1956.

### 58½ West 10th Street ✦

The small building at the back of this lot on a courtyard was the home of artist Francis Hopkinson Smith. It also served as the headquarters for the celebrated Tile Club in the 1880s. Among the members of this supper/artist club were Stanford White, Sanford Gifford, Winslow Homer, William Merritt Chase, and Augustus Saint-Gaudens.

### West 10th Street at the Hudson River
Robert Fulton invited 40 guests to witness the first public trial of his steamboat on August 17, 1807. After a false start and a slight embarrassing delay, the ship lurched forward to the cheers of the crowd and the passengers. The ship was most likely called the *North River Steam Boat* or simply the *North River*. It wasn't generally called the *Clermont* until 1810. The historic journey up the Hudson to Albany took about 30 hours at five miles per hour. The *North River* was not the first steamboat, but it was the first one built and operated at a cost that promised fair profits to its investors.

## EAST 11TH STREET

### 125 East 11th Street
*Webster Hall* ✦ Nicknamed "The Devil's Playhouse," this building, still operating as a club, was a popular place for many avant-garde parties as well as left-wing political rallies. On the night of May 25, 1917, it was the site of the fancy dress "Blind Man's Ball," attended by artists Marcel Duchamp, Joseph Stella, Man Ray, and Francis Picabia. Inspired by the Dada art movement balls in Paris, this party was a protest against the Society of Independent Artists' recent exhibition, which had refused to display Duchamp's entry, *Fountain*. Submitted as a test of the Society's rather lax rules, Duchamp's "ready-made" porcelain urinal was signed with the pseudonym "R. Mutt." Branded as "non-art" by the show judges, it has since become an icon in the history of modern art.

### 318 East 11th Street ✦
Abraham Goldfaden, the "father of Yiddish theater," died here in his home on January 9, 1908. More than 75,000 mourners lined the route of his funeral cortege to his burial in Brooklyn.

## WEST 11TH STREET

### 18 West 11th Street
A powerful explosion destroyed a Greek Revival–style town house, once occupied by novelist Walter D. Edmonds, here on March 6, 1970. The 1960s revolutionary group the Weather Underground was using the building's basement as a bomb factory. Three died in the blast.

Cathlyn Wilkerson, a daughter of the owner and one of the survivors, fled the scene and went into hiding for 10 years. At her trial in 1980, she was sentenced to and spent several months in jail for illegal possession of dynamite.

## EAST 12TH STREET

### 234 East 12th Street
According to a detailed Pinkerton National Detective memorandum recording the whereabouts of Butch Cassidy and the Sundance Kid, the two outlaws were living at this address in early 1901. Robert Parker (aka Butch Cassidy) and Harry Longabaugh (aka Sundance) were staying here at the boarding house of a Mrs. Taylor.

## WEST 12TH STREET

### 24 West 12th Street ✦
Built in 1851, this brownstone was a gift to "Old Fuss and Feathers," Winfield Scott, from a group of admirers headed by U.S. Senator Hamilton Fish. Another admirer, the Prince of Wales, the future King Edward VII, visited the war hero here on October 13, 1860.

### 31 West 12th Street
*Ardea Apartments* ✦ The world's most eminent female scientist, Marie Curie, was greeted at the entrance to this apartment house with a sea of flowers, a gift from an admirer whose cancer had been treated successfully with radium. Curie was staying here during her only visit to the United States, in May 1921. Frail and unhealthy after years of experimenting with radioactive materials, she was honored at several ceremonies, including one at the White House, where she was given an ounce of radium by President Warren G. Harding.

### 37 West 12th Street
*Butterfield House* This address was the home of Daniel E. Butterfield, the Union general and composer of "Taps," the bugle call. The current apartment house was named for him.

### 212 West 12th Street
Georges Clemenceau, the future prime minister of France, lived in the United States from 1865 to 1869. Trained as a physician, he taught French and was a Civil War correspondent for the French newspaper *Paris Temps*. While in New York City he lived at this address.

### 247 West 12th Street ✦

*Manufacturers Transit Company*   This building, once a warehouse for flammable chemicals and whiskey, exploded on July 18, 1922. Nicknamed the "Greenwich Village Volcano," the fire smoldered and burned for four days. Some 70 people were hurt and 2,000 neighbors were forced to evacuate their homes. The building is now condominium apartments.

## EAST 13TH STREET

### 128 East 13th Street ✦

Originally built in 1904 as a stable for polo ponies and racehorses for auction to the horsey set, this building became a training center for women factory workers during World War II. Its most recent incarnation was as the studio for artist Frank Stella from 1978 to 2005.

### 208 East 13th Street ✦

Political radical Emma Goldman lived in a two-room apartment in this tenement from 1903 to 1912. In 1906 her longtime lover and fellow revolutionary Alexander Berkman was released from prison for his attempted assassination of industrialist Henry Clay Frick. He often joined her here, writing together for her anarchist journal, *Mother Earth*. They were both deported to the Soviet Union in 1919.

## WEST 13TH STREET

### 8 West 13th Street ✦

Two famous muralists lived in this apartment house in the 1930s. Diego Rivera, along with his wife, Frida Kahlo, moved here for several months in 1933 shortly after he was dismissed from his controversial murals commission at Rockefeller Center. The other muralist, Thomas Hart Benton, lived here while he worked on his mural at the New School.

### 421 West 13th Street

*Delamater Iron Works*   The boilers and engine for the famed Civil War ironclad the *Monitor* were made here in the 1860s. A hundred years later this address was the site of one of the earliest gay "members only" after-hours bar, called the Zoo.

### West 13th Street at the Hudson River

*Cunard Piers*   On April 18, 1912, at 9:00 A.M., the *Carpathia* docked here at Pier 54 with survivors from the "unsinkable" *Titanic*. The newest luxury liner of Britain's White Star line, the *Titanic* had hit an iceberg on her maiden voyage to New York and sunk, killing 1,493 passengers and crew. The rescue ship, the *Carpathia*, picked up the SOS signal and rushed to the scene, but she didn't arrive until about two hours after the magnificent ship had slipped beneath the waves. The *Carpathia* took on board as many dazed survivors from the too-few lifeboats as it could find and headed for New York. More than 700 of the survivors arrived here, where many were taken to St. Vincent's Hospital in the Village for treatment.

The Cunard Line piers were also the scene of the last sailing for the *Lusitania*, on Saturday, May 1, 1915, at 12:28 P.M. Another ill-fated British luxury liner, this ship was sunk by a German submarine a week later on May 7, while en route to Liverpool during World War I; 1,198 passengers and crew, including 128 Americans, lost their lives. American indignation over the sinking contributed to U.S. entry into the war against Germany two years later.

## EAST 14TH STREET

### 11 East 14th Street

*Cunard Mansion*   In 1906 a Victorian brownstone once at this address was the second home to one of the earliest motion picture studios, the American Mutoscope and Biograph Company. The old ballroom served as a studio for many of the fledgling silent films that were first made in New York City. D. W. Griffith directed his first movie, *The Adventures of Dollie*, here in 1908. Many of the silent screen's greatest stars—Mary Pickford, Lionel Barrymore, Lillian and Dorothy Gish, Mabel Normand, and Mack Sennett—began their careers here.

### 109–111 East 14th Street

*Steinway Hall*   Opened after the Civil War, the hall was the site of performances by renowned pianists Anton Rubinstein, Rafael Joseffy, and Moriz Rosenthal. On Year's Eve 1867, Charles Dickens gave a reading of *David Copperfield*. In the audience was Mark Twain with his future wife, Olivia, whom he had met for the first time that evening. She was the sister of his friend Charley Langdon. Forty years later, Twain wrote, "from that day to this the sister has never been out of my mind nor heart." Operatic soprano Adelina Patti also gave a series of concerts here in 1881.

### 110 East 14th Street

*Luchow's*   This famed German eatery, established in 1882, was popular with writers H. L. Mencken, George Jean Nathan, and Theodore Dreiser. Luchow's had the distinction of receiving the first restaurant liquor

The *Lusitania* docked at the West 13th Street pier soon after her maiden voyage to New York. When the *Lusitania* left this pier for the last time on May 1, 1915, the German embassy ran ads in the morning newspapers, warning passengers of a "war zone." Six days later, a German submarine torpedoed and sank the ship off the coast of Ireland.

license after the repeal of Prohibition on December 1, 1933. This was four days before the Utah state legislature voted for repeal, officially ending Prohibition. The site is now student housing for New York University.

### 116 East 14th Street

*Gramercy Gym*   Cus D'Amato, one of the greatest boxing trainers, ran this gym for more than 40 years. D'Amato, who died in 1985, trained three world champions here. Both Floyd Patterson, the youngest heavyweight champion ever, and José Torres, the light-heavyweight champ in 1965, were his pupils. His greatest student and virtually adopted son was Mike Tyson.

### East 14th Street at Irving Place, northeast corner

*Academy of Music*   On the night of October 12, 1860, the imposing theater that once stood on this corner was converted into a huge ballroom

The highlight of the Prince of Wales' New York City visit in October 1860 was a gala at the Academy of Music on East 14th Street. The teenage son of Queen Victoria and future king of England reportedly had a grand time dancing and didn't leave until 4:30 in the morning. (*Harper's Weekly*, October 20, 1860)

for a party in honor of the Prince of Wales. The 19-year-old prince, later King Edward VII, was given the royal treatment by New York City society eager to impress the first member of British royalty to visit this former colony. Even the collapse of the temporary dance floor—dumping 200 well-heeled guests—was unable to diminish the excitement.

A few months later, on February 20, 1861, Abraham Lincoln saw his first and only opera, Verdi's *Masked Ball*, here. The President-elect was in the city on a stop-over visit on his way to his inauguration in Washington. Another opera, *Aida*, had its U.S. premiere at this theater on November 26, 1873.

### 145–147 East 14th Street

*Tammany Hall*  The once-powerful Tammany organization was built here, on the former site of the first New York University Medical School, in 1866. The hall officially opened for the Democratic National Convention on the Fourth of July in 1868. Delegates from all 37 states

This 1914 photograph of East 14th Street shows Tammany Hall with the statue of Tamanend, the Delaware chief and their symbol, in the roof-top niche. Next door is the Academy of Music covered with a fire escape, and barely discernible in the middle of the next block is Steinway Hall.

nominated a reluctant Horatio Seymour, a former governor of New York, for President on the twenty-second ballot. For his running mate, they chose Civil War hero and former Republican Congressman Francis P. Blair Jr. of Missouri. This mismatched ticket lost in November to Ulysses S. Grant and the Republicans. Tony Pastor moved his successful vaudeville theater into the building in 1881.

## WEST 14TH STREET

### 142 West 14th Street

*Church of the Annunciation*  On July 2, 1858, the body of former President James Monroe lay in state at a church that once stood on this site. The President had died 27 years earlier, on July 4, 1831, and had been buried in the New York City Marble Cemetery at 52–74 East 2nd Street. The body was taken to Monroe's native Virginia for reburial.

## 210 West 14th Street ✦

Dadaist artist Marcel Duchamp rented a fourth-floor walk-up studio here in early 1943. His rent was only $25 a month, but he was still unable to afford a telephone. His friends had to reach him by letter or telegram.

# MIDTOWN

## BEEKMAN PLACE

### 17 Beekman Place ✦
This town house was the last home of Irving Berlin. The 101-year-old dean of American popular music died here on September 22, 1989. In 1911, he wrote his first hit, "Alexander's Ragtime Band," and continued writing songs well into the 1960s. Some of his best known were "Always," "White Christmas," and "There's No Business Like Show Business."

## BROADWAY

### Broadway between West 14th and West 26th streets
". . . the bright white jets along Broadway began to flame out like stars emerging from the darkness." This poetic line from a *New York Times* article described the moment, at 5:27 P.M. on December 20, 1880, when the first electric street lights were turned on in New York City. The invention of Charles Francis Brush, the electric arc lights stood on tall poles marching uptown from Union Square.

### 1107 Broadway
*Albemarle Hotel*   Sarah Bernhardt, a guest at this hotel while on her first visit to the United States on October 27, 1880, stayed in a second-story suite with a balcony over the main entrance. Henry Abbey, her New York producer, had it redecorated to remind her of her Parisian home. Two years later, on October 23, 1882, Abbey booked the same suite for another foreign theatrical star making her U.S. debut, Lillie Langtry. The arrival of the "Divine Sarah" in New York may have been as tumultuous as Langtry's, but only the "Jersey Lily" was welcomed to the United States by a brass band playing "God Save the Queen" and by her friend and compatriot Oscar Wilde dressed in a cowboy hat, direct from his tour of the American West.

### 1115–1117 Broadway
*Hoffman House*   This popular Victorian hotel was home to the kitschy nude painting *Nymphs and Satyr* by Adolphe Bouguereau, which hung in the male-only hotel bar. Widely advertised by savvy management, this painting became a must-see tourist attraction at the turn of the twentieth century. So great was the demand from art lovers that one day a week was set aside for ladies to view to the masterpiece. This was also the first New York City home of publisher William Randolph Hearst, in 1895.

### 1133 Broadway
*St. James Building* ✦ Future Israeli prime minister Golda Meir worked for the Pioneer Women's Organization for Palestine for two years at this

Patrons of this males-only bastion enjoy a drink in the Hoffman House hotel bar at 1115 Broadway. The large canopied painting on the right is the establishment's prized possession *Nymphs and Satyr* by Adolphe Bouguereau.

address in the early 1930s. This Zionist group was concerned with female participation in the building of Palestine.

## 1155 Broadway

The ground floor of a corner building here was once the Holland Brothers' Kinetoscope Parlor. This first home of Thomas Edison's new invention, the kinetoscope, was opened on April 6, 1894. The hand-cranked

The Kinetoscope was a short-lived one-person machine used for viewing motion pictures. Thomas Edison named his invention by joining two Greek words—"kineto," meaning "movement," and "scopos," meaning "to watch." (Edison National Historic Site)

machine allowed the viewer to see true moving pictures. One of these short clips exhibited the rippling muscles of Eugen Sandow, the celebrated strongman. The kinetoscope and the many parlors opened all over the country were made obsolete just two years later by another Edison invention, the Vitascope, the first motion picture projector. Earlier, at this same address had been the studio of John Rogers, who was best known for his statuette groups that he successfully marketed to the American middle class hungry for culture. Called "Rogers Groups," these reasonably priced, massed-produced plaster reproductions depicted Civil War scenes, literary figures, and sentimental genre scenes.

### 1186 Broadway +

*Hotel Breslin*   Now an apartment building, this was once a fashionable hotel and the site of Mrs. Cassie Chadwick's arrest on December 7, 1904, by seven federal agents. Chadwick was the most notorious con artist of her day, famous for her charade as the illegitimate daughter of Andrew Carnegie. She fooled bankers into lending her millions of dollars before being convicted of fraud and embezzlement. Sentenced to 10 years, she died in prison.

### 1200 Broadway at West 29th Street, northeast corner +

*Gilsey House Hotel*   This hotel replaced the Anderson cottage, the last surviving farmhouse in midtown off Broadway. It was also the first

Looking very much as it does today, the Gilsey House Hotel is now a cooperative apartment house. When this photograph was taken in 1916, Broadway was being excavated for the construction of the West Side IRT subway.

hotel in the United States to offer telephone service to guests. Originally painted white when it opened on April 15, 1871, this cast-iron creation looked like a giant tiered wedding cake. It closed in December 1904 and was converted into offices. In the 1970s it was again converted, this time into a cooperative apartment house.

### Broadway between West 29th and West 30th streets, west side

*Wood's Museum*   In spite of the highbrow name, this theater was one of the earliest homes to burlesque or the "girlie show." In 1868, it was on this stage that Lydia Thompson and her British Blondes appeared. The act was a song-and-dance skit performed in form-fitting tights, a common Victorian guise to reveal women's figures.

### 1300 Broadway ✦

*McAlpin Hotel*   On March 26, 1926, the ballroom in this one-time hotel was the setting for a match made in tabloid heaven. Edward Browning, a 51-year-old real estate developer, met 15-year-old schoolgirl Frances

Heenan. The threesome, which included her mother, were virtually inseparable up to the couple's wedding 15 days later. An inordinate amount of newsprint was devoted to "Peaches and Daddy's" antics, including their appearances in child and divorce courts.

## 1410 Broadway

*Casino Theater*   This corner lot was the site of the renowned Casino Theater, the first theater illuminated entirely with electricity and the first with a roof garden. On January 18, 1896, the first X-ray machine was publicly exhibited here. The machine's medical benefits remained undeveloped and it was regarded as just a sideshow attraction. It was billed as the "Parisian Sensation" and the curious were charged 25 cents to see it. Another revealing innovation introduced at this theater four years later was the Floradora Girls, the earliest Broadway chorus line.

## Broadway between West 39th and West 40th streets, west side

*Metropolitan Opera House*   This block of Manhattan real estate marked the final battleground between old New York society and the robber barons. The robber barons won. By the Gilded Age of the 1880s, the Academy of Music on East 14th Street had become too small to accommodate the growing number of rich businessmen eager to flaunt their new wealth and status. After the old guard had refused to vacate or allow any new boxes to be built at the Academy, William K. Vanderbilt and other members of the nouveau riche decided to build their own larger, more opulent opera house. The Metropolitan Opera Company was formed. It was not long before owning a plush red box here became the ultimate symbol of social success. The new company's opening night was on October 22, 1883. *Faust* was performed, starring Italo Campanili. Many more momentous nights at the opera followed: November 23, 1903, Enrico Caruso's American debut; December 10, 1910, the world premiere of Giacomo Puccini's *La Fanciulla del West* with the composer seated in the audience; and April 12, 1916, dancer Vaslav Nijinsky's American debut. On its final night, April 16, 1966, conductor Leopold Stokowski said to the audience, "I beg you to help save this magnificent house." But it was not to be. Efforts to preserve the grand dame failed, and the building was razed the following year. The opera moved to its new home at Lincoln Center.

## 1466 Broadway +

*Knickerbocker Hotel*   Opening in 1906, the Beaux Arts Knickerbocker was a fashionable hotel for the theater crowd attracted to the burgeoning and recently renamed (from Longacre Square) Times Square. In

The Metropolitan Opera House on Broadway at West 39th Street about 1912. The Times Tower is the tall building at the right, at West 42nd Street. (Author's collection)

addition to 556 guest rooms, it had multiple dining rooms and bars that seated more than 2,000 people a night. It was also home to opera great Enrico Caruso from 1908 to 1920. In 1919, his daughter, Gloria, was born here in his 14-room suite on the ninth floor. Also a favorite with George M. Cohan (of "Give My Regards to Broadway" fame), the hotel was converted into an office building in the 1920s. It was home to *Newsweek* for 20 years.

### Broadway at West 42nd Street, northwest corner +

Times *Tower*   Once home to the *New York Times*, namesake of Times Square, this tower was stripped of its frilly terra cotta ornamentation during a 1966 renovation. The building's opening on December 31, 1904, began the tradition of celebrating New Year's Eve en masse in Times Square. Midnight fireworks marked the evening's first observance. When the city later tightened the regulations on fireworks above crowds, the *Times* ushered in the annual celebration, with the lowering of the familiar rooftop lighted ball. The ball was copied from nineteenth-century "time balls" used in seaports to set ships' chronometers.

Enrico Caruso was one of the earliest singers to realize the potential of records. His first American recording in 1904 was "Questa o quella" from *Rigoletto*, the same opera he performed for his debut at the Metropolitan Opera the year before.

The ball has dropped right on time every year since then, except for 1943 and 1944, when it was feared the lights might attract an Axis air attack during World War II. The tower, now called One Times Square, is still home to the world's first "moving sign." This wraparound sign began on November 6, 1928, by flashing the results of the presidential

One of the largest crowds in history came to Times Square to celebrate the end of World War II on V-J Day, Victory in Japan, on August 14, 1945. These happy revelers are standing on Broadway at West 44th Street. Hector's Cafeteria, in the upper right, was a favorite hangout of the Beat poets in the 1950s.

election: Herbert Hoover over New York Governor Alfred E. Smith. This same sign touched off one the city's largest and most joyous celebrations at 7:03 P.M. on August 14, 1945. The message, "OFFICIAL— TRUMAN ANNOUNCES JAPANESE SURRENDER," was a godsend to the thousands of New Yorkers crowding nearby streets, signaling the end of World War II. The *New York Times* reported the next day that a thunderous roar from the crowd lasted for 20 minutes after the announcement. On December 31, 1999, more than 2 million revelers, the largest crowd since V-E Day, filled the streets from 42nd Street to Columbus Circle.

## Broadway at West 43rd Street

The fabled "New York to Paris" automobile race began at this intersection on February 12, 1908. A huge holiday crowd watched as Mayor George B. McClellan Jr. fired the starting pistol. Six primitive automobiles began the grueling trek over 20,000 miles on three continents, including a steamship ride over the Pacific Ocean. The four-cylinder

Lined up on Broadway at West 42nd Street, these automobiles are waiting for the starting pistol to signal the start of the "New York to Paris" automobile race on February 12, 1908. George Schuster Sr., the American driver, crossed the finish line in Paris after 169 days.

60-horsepower *Thomas Flyer*, the American entry, was declared the winner in Paris on July 30.

### Broadway at West 43rd Street, northeast corner

*Barrett House Hotel*   This hotel, now gone, in the heart of the theater district was a fitting birthplace for America's greatest playwright. Eugene O'Neill was born in room 236 on October, 16, 1888, while his actor father was in town on tour in *The Count of Monte Cristo*.

### Broadway between West 43rd and West 44th streets, east side

*Rector's*   The famous "lobster palace" restaurant that once occupied the middle of this block was a favorite with Gay Nineties society and the theatrical crowd. Bon vivant James Buchanan "Diamond Jim" Brady with his legendary appetite was a favored diner. Charles Rector referred to him as "the best 25 customers I have." The front entrance had New York's first revolving door installed, about 1899. The restaurant was torn down in 1910 to build the Hotel Rector, which later became the Claridge.

## Broadway at West 44th Street, southeast corner

*Hotel Claridge*   ASCAP, the American Society of Composers, Authors and Publishers, was born here on February 13, 1914. The group was founded to ensure that songwriters and music publishers would be fairly compensated for public performances of their works. Music publisher George Maxwell was elected president of the new organization, whose first members included composers Irving Berlin, John Philip Sousa, and Victor Herbert.

The hotel also served as the home for the fondly remembered Camel cigarette sign that blew giant smoke rings. Put up in 1941, the smoking billboard was an imaginative answer to the World War II blackout ban on outdoor lights. The sign blew its last puff in 1966.

In 1943, the Camel smoker was still dressed in uniform for the duration of World War II. The tireless chainsmoker on the side of the Hotel Claridge blew smoke rings into Times Square for 25 years.

## 1505 Broadway

*Paramount Building* ✦ Built in 1926 as the New York headquarters of Paramount Motion Pictures, this office building was also home to the Paramount Theater, a 3,900-seat movie palace famous for its live stage shows, featuring many of the studio's greatest stars, such as Rudy Vallee, Gloria Swanson, Fred Astaire, Jack Benny, Bob Hope, and Bing Crosby. It was a favorite with the Big Bands of the 1930s and '40s. Frank "The Voice" Sinatra, the first of the teenage idols, made a solo appearance on this stage on December 30, 1942, in a program with Benny Goodman and his orchestra. Sinatra's concerts were the scenes of near-riots and mass hysteria among his "bobbysoxer" fans. At another frenzied return engagement, on October 12, 1944, more than 30,000 of Sinatra's fans mobbed Times Square. These public exhibitions of devotion helped launch the singer's career but provoked outcries from authorities and parents worried about wartime frivolousness and truancy.

## Broadway between East 44th and East 45th streets, east side

*Olympia Theater* Oscar Hammerstein, grandfather of Broadway lyricist Oscar Hammerstein II and unofficial "grandfather of Times Square,"

The Paramount Theater at 1505 Broadway in the fall of 1942. The theater was converted into additional office space in 1964, the same year the marquee was removed. The current one is an electronic replica added in 1996.

Oscar Hammerstein's Olympia Theater stood on the east side of Broadway between East 44th and East 45th streets. The Olympia was too large, too soon, and was never very successful this far uptown. Hammerstein was forced to sell and it was divided into three separately managed theaters. The building was demolished in 1935.

opened here on November 25, 1895, the first theater above 42nd Street on what was then called Longacre Square. The block-long complex was actually three theaters seating 6,000 patrons, all under one glass-enclosed roof garden. One of them, the New York Theater, was the birthplace of the Foxtrot in the summer of 1914. Vaudeville actor Harry Fox and his wife, Yansci Dolly of the famous Dolly Sisters vaudeville act, used trotting steps to ragtime music. It was an immediate sensation, and the new dance was called "Fox's trot." The rooftop Jardin de Paris was the first home of Florenz Ziegfeld's "Follies" in 1907.

### 1515 Broadway

*Hotel Astor*  The hotel that once stood on this site was the 1916 election-night headquarters for the Republican presidential candidate, Charles Evans Hughes. Believing he had won the election, he went to bed, but while he was asleep, late returns from California gave the election to President Woodrow Wilson. When pressed by a reporter from the *New York World* for Hughes's reaction, a valet told him, "The President has retired." "When he wakes up," the reporter replied, "tell him he is no longer the President."

## 1557 Broadway ✚

Joseph Horn and Frank Hardart, collectively known as Horn & Hardart, opened their first New York City "automat" at this location in 1913. The automat, a modern marvel thoroughly identified with New York, was not a native. The proprietors were from Philadelphia, where the first coin-operated automatic restaurant had opened 11 years earlier. This restaurant with a seemingly endless supply of tempting food behind little glass doors was a hit. The novelty eateries peaked by the 1920s and eventually succumbed to the fast-food chains. The last automat closed on April 9, 1991, at 200 East 42nd Street.

## 1564 Broadway

*Palace Theater* ✚ The Palace was built in 1913 and quickly became the career destination of every vaudevillian, whose dream it was "to play the Palace." American's most celebrated performers have played this stage: Eddie Cantor, Fanny Brice, Kate Smith, W. C. Fields, Will Rogers, and the Marx Brothers. Sophie Tucker, another popular alumna, prevented panic during her act after a fire broke out backstage. Her cool reaction saved lives and earned her the next day's tabloid headline tribute, "RED-HOT MAMA BURNS UP PALACE THEATER."

When vaudeville started to fade, the theater reluctantly turned to movies to fill the house. One of those movies was Orson Welles's *Citizen Kane*, believed by many to be the greatest movie ever made, which premiered here on May 1, 1944. The director had been unable to find any theater willing to show his classic because the RKO studio and William Randolph Hearst, the thinly disguised subject of the picture, had tried to block the film. It was only after Welles threatened to sue RKO that the studio agreed to release his masterpiece.

On November 28, 1947, the funeral procession for Bill "Bojangles" Robinson stopped here for a final tribute. The crowd of mourners for the "King of Tap" along Broadway and the rest of the route to Evergreen Cemetery in Brooklyn numbered more than half a million.

The Palace is forever linked in many people's minds with Judy Garland's triumphal engagement beginning on October 16, 1951. Garland's 19-week run broke the theater's all-time long-run record. Today's Palace, once again presenting Broadway shows, is entirely encased in a slick skyscraper.

## Broadway to Seventh Avenue at West 47th to West 48th streets

This small trapezoidal block, now home to the Ramada Renaissance Times Square Hotel, has been the site of some of Manhattan's greatest

The Palace Theater at 1564 Broadway is the tall building on the right in this photograph from about 1920. The exterior has changed dramatically, but the interior theater, encased in a new building, was New York City–landmarked and remains the same.

nightclubs, starting in the 1920s, when the Palais Royal, where bandleader Paul Whiteman made his debut, was here. From 1936 to 1940, it was the legendary Cotton Club, transplanted from Harlem. The club's headliners were Duke Ellington, Cab Calloway, Ethel Waters, Lena Horne, and Louis Armstrong. Next Lou Walters, father of Barbara Walters, opened the Latin Quarter in 1942, where the entertainment was supplied by stars like Ted Lewis, Sophie Tucker, Frank Sinatra, and Milton Berle. The Latin Quarter lasted until 1969. Changing tastes and a changing neighborhood contributed to a slow decline of this showplace block.

### 1600 Broadway

*Studebaker Building*　Torn down in 2004 for luxury condominiums, this building was the home of Fleischer Studios, the biggest film animation company outside of Hollywood, from 1923 to 1938. The studio was the birthplace of cartoon flapper Betty Boop and Popeye along with the "follow the bouncing ball" screen songs. Another 1920s celebrity, jazz great Bix Beiderbecke, had his New York debut here at the second-floor Cinderella Dance Palace, on September 12, 1924.

### 1645 Broadway at West 51st Street, southwest corner

*Capitol Theater*   A lavish movie theater, the Capitol was used for early radio broadcasts such as "Major Bowes' Original Amateur Hour." This show, first broadcast coast to coast on March 24, 1935, was a cultural phenomenon. "Around and around she [the Wheel of Fortune] goes, and where she stops, nobody knows," the show's opening line, was a siren call for Depression-weary listeners and hopeful contestants. The amateurs, with varying degrees of talent—including one New Jersey singer, Frank Sinatra—flocked to New York to appear on the show and be discovered. Travelers Aid and the Salvation Army had to care for the overflow of hopefuls, who often used the last of their savings to get here. *Newsweek* reported that in only one month in 1935, 1,200 would-be contestants had applied for emergency food and shelter.

### 1650 Broadway ✦

*Havana-Madrid*   In March 1946 this popular Latin-themed nightclub was the scene of a chance meeting that is now show business legend. Hyperactive adenoidal comic Jerry Lewis and laconic lounge singer Dean Martin were each booked separately here. But they soon joined forces after realizing that audiences loved them together. The mismatched duo were wildly successful with a radio and television show, live appearances, and 16 motion pictures.

### 1658 Broadway

*Roseland Ballroom*   This was one of the largest ballrooms in the city from the 1920s through the 1940s. The expression "taxi dancing" is said to have originated here. Male patrons bought their 10-cent tickets allowing them to dance with a hostess, whose income depended on the tickets she earned. The hostess was likened to a taxi driver who worked for hire. A later, 1956 incarnation of Roseland is on West 52nd Street.

### 1662 Broadway

*Warner's Theater*   The first feature-length "talking" picture, *The Jazz Singer*, staring Al Jolson, premiered at this theater on October 6, 1927. This picture was the first to feature singing and a few lines of dialogue. In addition to being a milestone in the history of the movies, *The Jazz Singer* also introduced some great songs: "Waiting for the Robert E. Lee," "Blue Skies," and "Toot, Toot, Tootsie (Goo' Bye)." The first "all-talking" picture also premiered at this same theater a year later, on July

7, 1928. *The Lights of New York* was advertised by Warner Bros. as "100% Talking." The review in *Variety* was far less kind; it called the picture "100% Crude."

## 1678 Broadway ✦

*Birdland*   Headliner and namesake Charlie "Bird" Parker opened this legendary jazz cabaret on December 15, 1949. Also appearing were several caged parakeets who within weeks succumbed to all the smoke and the air conditioning. Parker made his final public appearance here on March 4, 1955; he died eight days later. Revered by jazz lovers, the club had its own theme song, "Lullaby of Birdland," composed by George Shearing.

## 1685 Broadway ✦

*Colony Theater*   Now a stage theater called the Broadway, this was originally built as a motion picture theater in 1924. It was here on November 18, 1928, that the world's first talking cartoon with sound, Walt Disney's *Steamboat Willie*, debuted with Walt himself providing the voice of the film's star, Mickey Mouse.

## 1697 Broadway

*The Ed Sullivan Theater* ✦ Originally named Hammerstein's Theater, this playhouse was built in 1927 by Arthur Hammerstein as a monument to his father, Oscar, the opera impresario. The versatile auditorium has been used for film, radio, and Broadway productions. In the 1930s, it even served as a mob-connected nightclub. Beginning in the late 1940s and lasting until today, the theater has been home to several television shows, including "The Honeymooners" and "The Merv Griffin Show." In 1967 it was renamed in honor of television variety host Ed Sullivan, whose eponymous long-running show was broadcast from here. His most famous guests, the Beatles, appeared live on this stage and on millions of American television screens on February 9, 1964. The theater welcomed Paul McCartney to "Late Night with David Letterman" as a return guest on July 15, 2009. He and his band performed atop the theater's marquee.

## 1701 Broadway

*Hotel Cumberland* ✦ The tabloid headline "WIFE SHOT DEAD IN HER SLEEP" could have been written about the murder here of Nellie Chapin on December 16, 1918. It could have also been written by the murderer, her husband, Charles, the dictatorial editor of the *New York Evening World* and model for the editor in the stage play and movie

*The Front Page.* Charles Chapin was deeply in debt and shot his wife rather than reveal that they were broke. Sentenced to life in prison, he began a second career as a master gardener and earned the moniker "Rose man of Sing Sing."

## 1721 Broadway
*Hotsy Totsy Club* Gangster Jack "Legs" Diamond was a silent partner at this notorious second-floor speakeasy, in a building long since replaced. It was from here that he directed his illegal activities and rackets. It was also the murder site of a hoodlum named Red Cassidy on Friday, July 13, 1929. Legs and his crony Charles Entratta were the police's prime suspects. However, the case against the two was eventually dropped when all the known witnesses, by some counts eight people, died or mysteriously disappeared.

## Broadway at West 55th Street, northwest corner
The small IRT subway exit on this corner was the primary escape route for injured riders in one of the city's worst transit accidents, on January 6, 1915. During the morning rush hour, three downtown subway cars stalled because of a short circuit between the Columbus Circle and 50th Street stations. Heavy smoke resulting from the electrical fire slowly filled the tunnel. Stranded and in the dark, the passengers panicked at the smell of smoke. It took rescuers hours to get almost 2,500 terrified passengers to street level. Two people died and 172 were injured. Many of the injured suffered from smoke inhalation, but most of those who were hurt were injured during the panic.

## 1790 Broadway ✝
*National Headquarters of The National Association for the Advancement of Colored People* An emotional press conference with Clarence Norris, the sole surviving member of the "Scottsboro Boys," was held here to announce that Norris had been given a "full and unconditional" pardon by Alabama Governor George C. Wallace on October 25, 1976. In 1931 Norris and eight other African American youths were ordered off a train and accused of raping two white women. At a trial the following year they were found guilty, and eight were sentenced to death. The celebrated case, a symbol of racial injustice before the modern civil rights movement, eventually reached the U.S. Supreme Court and became an international cause. Norris spent 15 years in prison, five on death row, and 30 years as a fugitive for violating an earlier Alabama parole and leaving the state to ultimately live in New York City.

On January 6, 1915, Broadway at West 55th Street was the scene of a subway fire. The sidewalk grates have been removed to fight the fire and help survivors escape at the IRT Station.

## BRYANT PARK

Cleared by the city with convict labor, this land was used as a potter's field in 1823. It was the site of America's first world's fair, the "Exhibition of the Industry of All Nations," which was opened on July 14, 1853, by President Franklin Pierce and Secretary of War Jefferson Davis. The centerpiece of the fair was an enormous yet delicate iron and glass hall, the Crystal Palace, which held 4,000 exhibitors from around the world. More than a million visitors came to marvel at the displays of machinery and the new consumer goods available as America entered the Industrial Age. The Crystal Palace remained as a showplace for exhibits and fine art after the fair, but it burned to the ground in about an hour on the night of October 5, 1858. A few years later, Union troops used the site as a camp during the Civil War.

Declared a park in 1871, it was later named for poet William Cullen Bryant, a major advocate for public parks in the city. On August 26, 1970, the park was the site of an early and enthusiastic rally for women's liberation. Some 10,000 demonstrators marched down Fifth Avenue to

Designed for the Exhibition of 1853 in today's Bryant Park, the Crystal Palace was a marvel of modern architecture. New technological advances, such as the iron frame and prefabricated parts, enabled the engineers to cover a vast space. (Author's collection)

the park to celebrate the fiftieth anniversary of American women's being given the right to vote and to mark "Women's Strike for Equality Day." Gloria Steinem, Kate Millett, and Betty Friedan spoke to the crowd. After work on the huge storage area for the New York Public Library's book stacks beneath the park was finished in the early 1990s, the park was beautifully restored and reclaimed from the drug dealers who often considered it their own turf.

## CENTRAL PARK SOUTH

### 36 Central Park South

*Park Lane Hotel* ✦ Shortly after midnight on April 15, 1992, Leona Helmsley tried to sneak out of her duplex penthouse apartment atop this hotel, which she owned, hoping to avoid the reporters waiting for her out front. The self-proclaimed hotel "queen" was off to federal prison near Lexington, Kentucky, having been convicted of tax evasion and fraud. Helmsley, who according to the testimony of a housekeeper had said, "We don't pay taxes. Only the little people pay taxes," was ordered to begin serving her four-year sentence on that fateful day, April 15, when Americans file their income tax returns. She returned here on November 26, 1993, to finish the remainder of her reduced sentence in "house confinement." Helmsley, known as "the Queen of Mean," achieved some measure of redemption when after the terrorist attacks of September 11, 2001, she donated $5 million to help families of New York City firefighters. She died on August 20, 2007.

## 50 Central Park South

*St. Moritz* + This hotel was the first U.S. home of Marc Chagall. The painter, who had been living in France, arrived in the United States on June 23, 1941, the same day the Nazis invaded his native Russia. It was also the longtime home of gossip columnist Walter Winchell and baseball star Mickey Mantle.

## 240 Central Park South +

This address was home to author and aviator Antoine de Saint-Exupéry beginning in early 1941. The exiled Frenchman lived here during the German occupation of France. He used the upper-floor apartment as a laboratory to ponder some possible military options for the Allied invasion of France. The airman sailed paper helicopters out the windows into Central Park to simulate an airborne attack and the bathtub was used for wave studies for a water attack. He wrote *The Little Prince* here and in a summer house on Long Island.

## GRAMERCY PARK

This handsome two-acre private park was once part of a farm owned by James Duane, the city's first mayor and the man for whom Duane Street is named, after the American Revolution. He had purchased the land from the descendants of Peter Stuyvesant. The land was already called Gramercy Seat—from the original Dutch *krom moerasje*, meaning, roughly, "crooked little swamp." In 1831 the park was created by Samuel B. Ruggles, a lawyer and developer, as an added attraction to selling the surrounding 66 property lots.

## GRAMERCY PARK EAST

## 34 Gramercy Park East +

Built in 1883, this Queen Anne–style apartment building is one of the earliest cooperatives in the city. The nine-story structure had the distinction of having one of the oldest direct plunger elevators, installed by Otis Elevator, when the building was constructed. Two large water tanks, one on the roof and one in the basement, contained the water that drove the five-story-high piston assembly up and down. The 111-year-old elevator was replaced in 1994. The building was popular with actors; owners have included Margaret Hamilton and James Cagney.

## GRAMERCY PARK NORTH

### 52 Gramercy Park North +

*Gramercy Park Hotel*   The current hotel, built in 1923, replaced the corner town house of Stanford White, the Beaux Arts architect, and the town house, two doors west, of Robert G. Ingersoll, noted agnostic lecturer. The hotel was home to 11-year-old John F. Kennedy, who lived on the second floor for a few months in 1928. The Kennedy family was living here temporarily before moving to London where father Joseph had recently been appointed U.S. ambassador. The humorist S. J. Perelman also lived here from 1972 until his death in 1979.

### 60 Gramercy Park North

This address, replaced in 1929 by the Gramercy Park Hotel Annex, was home to George Templeton Strong. Strong, a great chronicler of mid-nineteenth-century New York City life, was married to Ellen Ruggles, the daughter of Gramercy Park developer Samuel B. Ruggles. Strong was one of the leading supporters and treasurer of the Civil War Sanitation Commission, created to aid the Union cause. Shortly after the war, the man of the hour, General Ulysses S. Grant, showed his appreciation by accepting a dinner invitation to this house on November 18, 1865.

## GRAMERCY PARK SOUTH

### 10 Gramercy Park South +

From 1909 to 1919, this was the home and studio of Robert Henri. It was here on the top floor that Tuesday evenings were set aside for an open house. At these gatherings, Henri, other painters, and his students met to discuss art and liberal politics.

### 15 Gramercy Park South +

*National Arts Club*   Samuel J. Tilden, the governor of New York, purchased this town house in 1863; later he purchased the house next door at No. 14. In 1881 he asked Calvert Vaux, of Central Park design fame, to combine the two structures with a unified Gothic façade. Tilden, a political reformer who had made some enemies, was concerned with

Former New York Governor Samuel Tilden is serenaded by his political supporters outside his 15 Gramercy Park home on October 27, 1877. This address is now the National Arts Club. (*Harper's Weekly*, November 17, 1877)

his personal safety. His remodeling plans included a secret escape tunnel to East 19th Street. After his death in 1886, his estate was combined with the Lenox and Astor libraries to create the New York Public Library. The National Arts Club bought the double-sized house in 1906. The club, founded eight years earlier, was the first arts club to have both women and men as members. The membership included non-artists, too; both Theodore Roosevelt and Woodrow Wilson were active in club activities. It was here that member Paul Manship, the sculptor of *Prometheus* at Rockefeller Center, died of a heart attack on January 31, 1966.

### 16 Gramercy Park South ✚
*The Players Club*   In 1888 the great thespian Edwin Booth bought this town house and had it remodeled by Stanford White as a clubhouse for actors and other friends of the drama. Booth founded The Players Club in hopes of creating a cultured atmosphere for his fellow actors, who were considered coarse bohemians by much of society. Appropriately theatrical, Booth died here in his room on June 7, 1893, during a tempestuous thunderstorm that had blacked out the entire club. His bedroom has been preserved just as it was that night.

On the evening of December 22, 1890, five of the greatest architects of the Gilded Age met for dinner to discuss the upcoming World's Columbian Exposition. Chicagoan Daniel Burnham, the chief of construction, was here, hoping to persuade George B. Post, Charles McKim, Robert Peabody, and Richard Morris Hunt to help design the fair. The East Coast architects eventually agreed, and the "White City," as the Chicago fair became known, became a benchmark in American architecture. Club members, all male until as late as May 31, 1989, have included Mark Twain, Booth Tarkington, Sir Laurence Olivier, and Irving Berlin.

### 19 Gramercy Park South ✦

Purchased in 1887 by Stuyvesant Fish and his wife, Mamie, this corner town house was a major battleground in nineteenth-century society wars. The flamboyant Mrs. Fish was determined to unseat the stodgy, aristocratic Mrs. William Astor as New York's reigning society hostess. She nearly succeeded. She gave lively and less formal parties and is credited with shortening the traditional 10-course dinner to a mere 50 minutes. By the turn of the twentieth century, both Mrs. Astor and Mrs. Fish had moved to more fashionable digs on the Upper East Side.

In the 1950s and '60s, this house again became a society mecca when it was the home of Benjamin Sonnenberg Sr., the public relations wizard. It was Sonnenberg who had thought up the idea of having John D. Rockefeller give away dimes to children. He lavishly entertained his clients and celebrity, artist, and politician friends in this house.

### 21 Gramercy Park South ✦

This house was the winter home of writer and diplomat John Bigelow from 1881 until his death in 1911. Bigelow, who was the U.S. minister to France during the Civil War, persuaded the French government not to recognize the Confederacy.

## GRAMERCY PARK WEST

### 1 Gramercy Park West ✦

This town house was once the home of Dr. Valentine Mott, a famous surgeon during the Civil War, who helped to reorganize Bellevue Hospital.

### 2 Gramercy Park West ✦

The wedding reception for former President Benjamin Harrison and his bride, Mrs. Mary Scott Lord Dimmick, was held here at the home of Gifford Pinchot, America's first professional forester, on April 6, 1896.

Actor Edwin Booth as Hamlet, one of his signature roles, about 1879. A contemporary critic, Laurence Hutton, wrote, "In many minds, Booth is Hamlet and Hamlet is Booth." Booth posed again as the Prince of Denmark for his statue in the center of Gramercy Park.

## 4 Gramercy Park West ✦

James Harper Sr. bought this house in 1847. Harper was the eldest of the four brothers who founded the publishing firm of Harper and Brothers in 1817, later Harper & Row and now HarperCollins. He moved in with his second wife shortly after finishing a term as the sixty-fifth mayor of the city. The two iron street lamps still mark the home as a mayoral residence.

## IRVING PLACE

### 24 Irving Place

Italian patriot Guiseppe Garibaldi was a house guest of Michele Pastacaldi in August 1850. He stayed at this address for about two months before moving on to Staten Island, where he worked as a candlemaker. He became a naturalized citizen and stayed in the United States until 1854. Returning to Italy, he was instrumental in the unification of the country.

### 46 Irving Place

This was once the home of Helena Petrovna Blavatsky, an author and visionary who was instrumental in introducing Eastern religion and spiritual thinking into Western culture. It was here on the evening of September 8, 1875, that HPB, as she was often called, along with Henry Steel Olcott and William Q. Judge, founded the Theosophical Society.

### 55 Irving Place +

Author O. Henry lived in this house from 1903 to 1907. Legend has it that it was here that a looming deadline pressed Henry into writing his beloved Christmas short story, "The Gift of the Magi," in a three-hour drunken haze.

### 71 Irving Place +

Norman Thomas, the socialist politician and thinker, lived here in 1945. His wife, Violet, owned the building and opened a tea room here 10 years before they moved upstairs. Thomas was the Socialist Party candidate for President of the United States in every election from 1928 to 1948.

## LEXINGTON AVENUE

### 1 Lexington Avenue

Cyrus Field built in 1851 and lived in a brownstone that once stood at this corner. Field was a financier who dedicated his life and fortune to laying the first submarine telegraph cable between America and Europe. Despite the loss of his personal fortune in the depression of 1857, he found the needed capital to complete the project in 1858. He was also instrumental in building the elevated railroad system in New York City in the late 1870s.

### 9 Lexington Avenue

One of the most influential figures in New York during the nineteenth century was Peter Cooper, whose home stood on this site. He designed and built the first successful American steam locomotive, the *Tom Thumb*, and produced the first steel rails. Because of his invention, he became very wealthy and used his fortune to improve the lives of working-class citizens. His greatest gift was the founding of Cooper Union for the Advancement of Science and Art. After he died here on April 4, 1883, his son-in-law Abram S. Hewitt and his family lived in the house. Hewitt, a reform mayor of New York City from 1887 to 1888 and U.S. congressman, was instrumental in overthrowing the Tweed Ring's control of the city's government. He also spearheaded the fight for New York City's subway system.

Hewitt's daughters, Eleanor and Sarah, began collecting and storing examples of decorative arts in this house as teenagers. Their collection of lace, glass, buttons, drawings and prints, furniture, and countless forms of decoration and ornament became the core of the Cooper-Hewitt Museum. It was first displayed at their grandfather's Cooper Union and moved uptown to Andrew Carnegie's mansion in 1967.

### Lexington Avenue at East 23rd Street, southeast corner

*The Free Academy*   One hundred and forty-nine teenage boys attended their first day of school here on January 29, 1849. Chartered by the state legislature just a year and a half earlier, this was the first municipal system created for higher education in the United States. The Free Academy, renamed the College of the City of New York in 1866, was the beginning of the City University of New York. In 1907 it moved to the main campus at West 138th Street.

### 68 Lexington Avenue

*69th Regiment Armory* ✚   The famous Armory Show, officially called the International Exhibition of Modern Art, opened here on February 17 and ran until March 15, 1913. Some 1,300 works of art were displayed in the great drill hall of this building. The best-known and most influential exhibition in the United States, it introduced a provincial American public to modern art. In addition to the impressionists, post-impressionists, Fauves, and Cubists from Europe, half the show was made up of works by America's emerging modernists. Fueled by the popular press, close to 70,000 visitors came to view and judge the controversial works. Caricatured and praised, the most talked about painting of the show was Marcel Duchamp's Cubist/futurist *Nude Descending a Staircase, No. 2.*

### 123 Lexington Avenue ✚

Vice President Chester A. Arthur took the oath of office as President of the United States in this modest brownstone on September 20, 1881, at 2:00 A.M. upon learning of the death of President James A. Garfield, who had been shot by an assassin two months earlier. The oath was administered by New York State Supreme Court Justice John R. Brady.

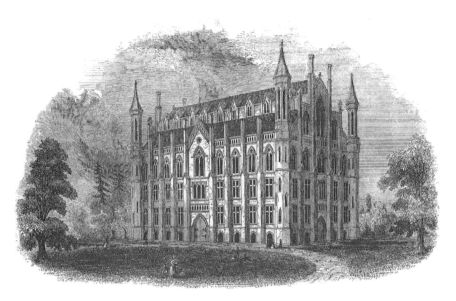

James Renwick Jr. designed the first home of the Free Academy on Lexington Avenue at East 23rd Street in 1848. Baruch College, part of the City University of New York (CUNY) system, now occupies the corner site. (Author's collection)

Other than George Washington, Arthur was the only president to take the oath in New York City. He later died at this house on November 18, 1886, a year after leaving Washington, D.C. Another famous resident of this house was William Randolph Hearst from 1900 to 1905.

## 405 Lexington Avenue

*Chrysler Building* ✦ Everyone's favorite Art Deco skyscraper was the tallest building in the world for a few months in late 1930 before the completion of the Empire State Building. But this 1,048-foot-high spire has another claim to fame: It was from here that the first color television broadcast in history was transmitted. CBS station W2XAB held a press preview for its high-definition, electronically scanned color broadcast on September 3, 1940.

## 511 Lexington Avenue

*LQ Nightclub* ✦ On November 29, 2008, New York Giants and Super Bowl star wide receiver Plaxico Burress accidentally shot himself in the thigh with a pistol hidden in his pants while at this nightclub. Faced with New York's tough mandatory sentencing for unlawful possession of a handgun, he pleaded to a lesser charge and was sentenced to two years in prison.

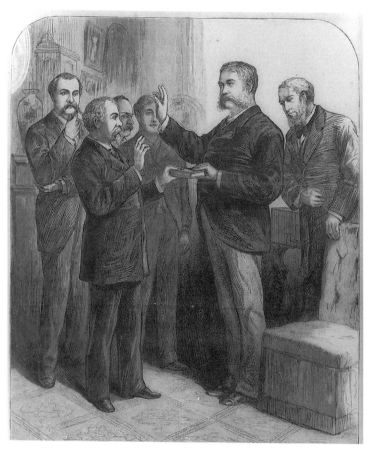

Vice President Chester A. Arthur was sworn in as President in his front parlor at his home at 123 Lexington Avenue on September 20, 1881. Arthur's elevation to the presidency had been anticipated. President James A. Garfield never recovered from his wounds inflicted by an assassin two months earlier. (*Frank Leslie's Illustrated Newspaper*, October 8, 1881)

## 525 Lexington Avenue

*Shelton Towers Hotel*  The tallest hotel in the world when built, the Shelton Towers was home to Alfred Stieglitz and Georgia O'Keeffe from 1925 to 1935. Their thirtieth-floor view was subject matter for his photographs and her paintings. Another famous art couple also lived here in 1941, Peggy Guggenheim and Max Ernst.

This is architect's William Van Allen final design in 1929 for the Chrysler Building on Lexington Avenue at 42nd Street. The upper floors of the tower underwent several design changes before becoming the familiar sunburst-tapered top.

*New York Marriott East Side* ✦ In a second-floor conference room of this hotel on November 5, 1990, Rabbi Meir Kahane was assassinated shortly after addressing a group of his supporters. The Brooklyn-born rabbi was the founder of the Jewish Defense League and a leader of a militant anti-Arab movement in Israel. El-Sayyid A. Nosair was acquitted of murder charges but was convicted on a lesser charge and imprisoned. Several of Nosair's followers were later implicated in the 1993 World Trade Center bombing and a terrorist plot to blow up the United Nations and the Holland and Lincoln tunnels.

## 541 Lexington Avenue +

*Hotel Montclair*   A 75-cent lunchtime concert on January 4, 1935, was Leadbelly's introduction to the New York City music world. He was born Huddie Ledbetter, and his appearance was the beginning of a musical career that would influence the blues, modern folk, and rock 'n' roll music. Library of Congress folklorist John Lomax, who first recorded Leadbelly while he was in prison, arranged the concert and invited the critics and the press. Leadbelly's "Goodnight, Irene" and "Midnight Special" are American folk song classics.

## 586 Lexington Avenue at East 52nd Street, northwest corner

*Trans-Lux Theater*   Early on the morning of September 15, 1954, Marilyn Monroe was posing over the subway grate outside this now gone movie theater. This publicity shot for her film *The Seven Year Itch* with her skirt blown up to her waist is now an icon in our popular culture. This very public shoot was also the final breaking point in her marriage to baseball great Joe DiMaggio. Egged on by gossip columnist Walter Winchell, an angry DiMaggio watched from across the street along with a thousand jeering spectators. That night the couple spent one of their last nights together fighting in their St. Regis Hotel suite.

## 600 Lexington Avenue

*Young Women's Christian Association Headquarters* +   Begun as the prayer group the Ladies' Christian Union in 1858, the "Y" started helping rural young women adjust to modern city life with employment, education, housing, and health services. The First International Conference of Women Physicians representing doctors from 32 countries was financed by the "Y" beginning on September 16, 1919. One of the goals of the six-week conference was "to cultivate an attitude of honest, open scientific interest in the subject of sex."

## 601 Lexington Avenue

*Citicorp Center* +   In 1977, Citicorp's innovative use of the air rights above St. Peter's Lutheran Church produced this radical design for their headquarters. Four giant stilt-like columns positioned at the center of each side, rather than the corners, freed up the corner site for a new church. But a year after the opening, a disastrous design flaw was discovered. The chief structural engineer, William LeMessurier, realized much to his horror that the bolted joints were too weak to withstand 70-mile-per-hour winds. Almost immediately nighttime crews began the necessary adustments, just as the hurricane season was approaching. Fortunately, Hurricane Ella veered away from the city in time to prevent a potential collapse of the 59-story tower. The near-crisis was hidden from the public for more than 18 years. These same massive supports were again strengthened in 2002, this time because of security concerns after the terrorist attacks of September 11, 2001.

## MADISON AVENUE

### 1 Madison Avenue at East 23rd Street

This was the home of Samuel Barlow, a lawyer and minor player in "the Great Diamond Hoax." In October 1871, jeweler Charles Lewis Tiffany, publisher Horace Greeley, and two Union generals, George B. McClellan (father of the future New York City mayor of the same name) and Benjamin F. Butler, all met here and were duped into lending credence to one of the greatest swindles in American history. A year later, it was revealed that two Kentucky cousins and con artists, Philip Arnold and John Slack, made off with more than $660,000 from selling worthless mining rights in Wyoming to hundreds of investors.

### Madison Avenue at East 24th Street, southeast corner

*Madison Square Presbyterian Church* Nicknamed "Dr. Parkhurst's Church," after its fiery minister, the Reverend Charles H. Parkhurst, this church was the scene of his blistering 1892 St. Valentine's Day sermon against citywide crime and police corruption. The city's Tammany Hall politicians denied Parkhurst's allegations, and the reverend was accused of making unsubstantiated accusations to a grand jury. At this point, the good doctor, along with a detective, took it upon himself to make a personal excursion into the city's underworld. This unlikely duo visited the worst gambling dens, saloons, and brothels and learned of the police payoffs that kept them in business. Now armed with proof, Parkhurst reported back to his congregation and to the press. This time, his revelations resulted in another grand jury investigation and the appointment of Theodore Roosevelt to the Board of Commissioners. The reverend's guide that night, detective Charles W. Gardner, later

Firebrand Reverend Charles H. Parkhurst of the Madison Square Presbyterian Church was a nineteenth-century reformer, unafraid to expose police corruption. His sterling reputation even survived his enemies' scheme to discredit him by sending prostitutes to his home. His wife invited the women in and served them tea.

wrote an account of the underworld visit, called *The Doctor and the Devil, or the Midnight Adventures of Dr. Parkhurst.*

## Madison Avenue between East 26th and East 27th streets, east side

*Madison Square Garden*    This lavish exhibition hall was erected on the site of the original terminal of the New York and Harlem Railroad, the Union Depot, and an even earlier version of a hall called Gilmore Gardens. Designed by Stanford White in 1890, the structure contained a huge amphitheater, two theaters, and a 332-foot tower topped with the scandalous nude statue *Diana* by Augustus Saint-Gaudens. It was on the roof garden cabaret on the night of June 25, 1906, that Stanford White was fatally shot by Harry K. Thaw, husband of showgirl Evelyn Nesbit, White's former mistress. Madison Square Garden was the site of the country's first artificial ice rink, on February 12, 1879; the first auto show, on November 3, 1900; the Paterson Strike Pageant on June 7, 1913; and the opening ceremonies for the first International Convention of the Negro Peoples of the World, beginning on August 1, 1920. The Democrats met here for their longest national convention on June 24, 1924, and stayed for 17 days until they agreed on John W. Davis for President and Charles W. Bryan (brother of the orator and frequent presidential candidate William Jennings Bryan) for Vice President. As the hotels and restaurants moved uptown, the Garden, which was never very successful, had an even harder time attracting crowds and making a profit. The advent of legalized professional boxing in New York state helped extend the life of the complex until it was demolished in 1925 to build the current headquarters for the New York Life Insurance Company.

### Madison Avenue at East 27th Street

Although there are many myths about the origins of baseball, it is well documented that New York City played an important role in the evolution of a child's ball game called rounders into organized baseball as early as the spring or summer of 1842. These first games, just as was later baseball, were played on a diamond-shaped infield with two teams, one "at bat" and the other in the field. A pioneer in the development of the "New York game," as it was called, was the Knickerbocker Base Ball Club, which played its games in a lot at this intersection. The club was formally established on September 23, 1845, with 28 young men who played the game "for health and recreation merely," but did set about improving and standardizing the rules. Their first organized game using the modern rules took place across the Hudson River at Elysian Fields in Hoboken, New Jersey, on June 19, 1846.

### 83 Madison Avenue

*Women's Hospital*   Dr. James Sims was one of the founders of this hospital and a pioneer in research into female reproduction. While in practice here during the 1860s, he was the first to artificially inseminate a woman to conception. He had numerous failed attempts. His low success rate was not the fault of his procedures, but poor timing and the lack of understanding of the menstrual cycle.

This poster of the second Madison Square Garden presents an unobstructed view of the Moorish-style entertainment venue. The Leonard Jerome mansion at 26th Street is at the right.

### 219 Madison Avenue

The nation's most famous banker, J. P. Morgan, bought a brownstone at this site in 1882. An early financial backer of Thomas Edison, Morgan soon commissioned the inventor to install his new invention, electric lighting, in his home. In spite of some mishaps, Morgan was pleased and his residence became the first in the world to be electrically lighted throughout. The power was supplied by a specially built generator located in a cellar under his stable. Morgan built his famous library to house his art and rare books, next door, on East 36th Street in 1906.

### 383 Madison Avenue

On March 6, 1944, William Patrick Hitler, nephew of Adolf Hitler, was sworn in as an apprentice seaman at a naval recruiting office once housed here. The new recruit spent two years trying to join the fight against the Third Reich. He was turned down by the British and Canadian armed services, but the U.S. Navy decided his enlistment was useful in the propaganda war. William Patrick Hitler and his family moved to Long Island after the war and went into hiding.

## Madison Avenue between East 46th and East 47th streets, west side

*Ritz-Carlton Hotel*   This hotel, popular with New York society, was the location of Castle House, a dancing school run by Vernon and Irene Castle in the years before World War I. The Castles, America's favorite dancing team, were the originators of the one-step and the Castle Walk. Another original was born here during the summer of 1917. Louis Diat, the great French chef, created vichyssoise. Working from his mother's recipe for potato-and-leek soup, Diat added milk and chilled his new soup before serving it at the hotel's rooftop restaurant.

Two of café society's biggest coming-out parties were held here in the Depression-racked 1930s. "Poor Little Rich Girl" Barbara Hutton, granddaughter of dimestore king F. W. Woolworth, had her $60,000 party on December 21, 1930. Brenda Frazier, "Glamour Girl Number One," came out on December 27, 1938. The hotel, which gave us the slang terms "ritzy" and "puttin' on the Ritz," was razed and passed into memory in 1957.

## 451 Madison Avenue

*Whitelaw Reid Mansion*   An art show organized by exiled European artists for the benefit of French relief, "First Papers of Surrealism," was held here from October 14 to November 7, 1942. The title of the show was an allusion to the first papers of immigrants to the United States. Marcel Duchamp, the designer of the show, used more than 16 miles of string to create a giant web covering the galleries. He wanted "to force the viewer to involve himself with his surrounding."

## 485 Madison Avenue +

Once called the Columbia Broadcasting Building, this was home to CBS from 1929 to 1965. On the top five floors were the early radio studios where Edward R. Murrow and Eric Sevareid broadcast the news and set the standards for broadcast journalism. It was also from here that Orson Welles broadcast his famous and frightening adaptation of H. G. Wells's *War of the Worlds* Halloween program on October 30, 1938. The show, which realistically documented a Martian invasion, provoked hundreds of call to local police and radio stations. Less than two weeks later, on November 11, Armistice Day, Kate Smith created another sensation by singing "God Bless America." The song by Irving Berlin was an instant hit and became an unofficial national anthem. Both these broadcasts confirmed the power of radio to touch the American psyche, particularly on the eve of World War II.

Vernon and Irene Castle, performing the tango, were world-famous celebrities, who influenced dance, clothing, and hairstyles. Vernon died tragically in 1918 while training American World War I airplane pilots.

These same studios were also landmarks in the history of television, beginning with the inauguration of the first regular schedule of TV broadcasting in the country. These daily test broadcasts from 2:00 to 6:00 A.M. and from 8:00 to 11:00 P.M. on station W2XAB were largely without sound. The first of these telecasts was on July 21, 1931. It was hosted by Mayor Jimmy Walker and featured Kate Smith, George Gershwin, and the "Columbia Television Girl."

## Madison Avenue at East 54th Street

*Club Monte Carlo*   On December 10, 1946, real estate developer William Zeckendorf Sr. and his wife were celebrating their wedding anniversary. At 2:00 A.M. his party was interrupted by a visit from Wallace Harrison, his architect. Harrison had come to ask if Zeckendorf would sell a piece of property along the East River at East 42nd Street to John D. Rockefeller Jr., who in turn would donate the land to the fledgling United Nations. The developer agreed to the $8.5 million deal on the spot. Four days later the UN General Assembly voted to accept the offer and stay in New York. This late-night negotiation and Rockefeller's generosity kept the UN in town.

## 625 Madison Avenue

Jacqueline Kennedy Onassis reported for work here at Viking Press in September 1975. Not surprisingly, her foray into the workaday world as a consulting editor was a media circus. The former First Lady's previous job was as the "Inquiring Camera Girl" in 1953.

## 647 Madison Avenue

This was the last home of William Magear Tweed. On December 4, 1875, while on a furlough from jail to visit his sick wife, he escaped from his guard. He slipped out the front door of this house after dark. The disgraced former political boss fled to Cuba and then sailed for Spain, where he was arrested upon arrival the following September. The fugitive was identified by means of one of his old nemesis Thomas Nast's political cartoons from *Harper's Weekly*. He was extradited to the United States the following year.

## MADISON SQUARE PARK

As was often the case with New York City parks, this land was first used as a potter's field. In 1807, the U.S. Arsenal was built to defend the city at this strategic junction of the Eastern Post Road and Bloomingdale Road, now Broadway. By 1824, the Arsenal had been converted into the House of Refuge of the Society for the Reformation of Juvenile Delinquents, the nation's first institution for delinquent children that segregated them from adult criminals. Named in honor of President James Madison, the park was opened in the 1840s. On November 11, 1877, the right arm of the Statue of Liberty holding her torch was forlornly planted here, where it remained for seven years as a scheme to help raise money for the pedestal in the harbor.

Visitors were permitted to climb into the disembodied arm of the Statue of Liberty for a view of the surrounding Madison Square Park. The admission fees were used to build the statue's pedestal on Bedloes (later Liberty) Island.

## PARK AVENUE

### Park Avenue between East 32nd and East 33rd streets, west side

*The Woman's Home*   Opened on April 2, 1878, this lavish hotel was built with funds bequeathed by the late "Merchant Prince" A. T. Stewart as a social experiment. It was intended to provide a supervised, wholesome

The Park Avenue Hotel on Park Avenue at East 32nd Street rises above its rustic neighbors in this photograph from about 1890. (Author's collection)

environment for the new emerging class of urban female workers. The strict house rules did not permit gentleman visitors, pets, sewing machines, pianos, or personal memorabilia. The "Home" closed after only two months; it proved to be too expensive and too restrictive even for Victorian women of the times. It soon reopened as the Park Avenue Hotel and supplied rooms for both sexes. The hotel was torn down in 1927 for the present office building.

### 35 Park Avenue ✦

Just after midnight on October 20, 1964, Joseph "Joe Bananas" Bonanno claimed, he was abducted here in front of his lawyer's apartment house. A founding member in 1931 of the "Commission," the Mafia's ruling body, Bonanno was scheduled to testify the next day before a grand jury. He was missing for 19 months. Authorities doubted his kidnapping story and believed he had gone into hiding to arrange a truce with his Mafia rivals. The once-powerful mobster relinquished his share of the action and retired to Arizona. He lived to the age of 97.

### 91 Park Avenue

This address was once the home of Andrew Haswell Green, who was called the "father of Greater New York" because of his work on the commission to consolidate Manhattan and the surrounding municipalities into the present-day city with five boroughs in the 1890s. Green, a city comptroller, was also a major force in establishing Central Park, the Metropolitan Museum of Art, and the New York Public Library. He was shot three times and killed by an insane man here on the sidewalk in front of his house on November 13, 1903. The killer and his victim did not know each other.

### Park Avenue at East 41st Street

On January 27, 1902, the roar of the city was humbled by a blast whose force was the equivalent of that of several bombs at this construction site for the new subway stop at this intersection. Moses Epps, a workman for the subway, had foolishly lit a candle to warm his hands within a few feet of 548 pounds of dynamite. The blast blew out the clocks in Grand Central Terminal and shattered glass for blocks. Epps managed to survive with just a few scratches, but five people died and 180 were injured. Most of those injured were guests at the nearby Murray Hill Hotel.

### 200 Park Avenue +

*Pan Am Building*   The fifty-ninth-floor rooftop heliport here was the site of a tragic accident on May 16, 1977. An idling helicopter keeled over, killing four people on the landing pad and a woman walking on Madison Avenue, who was hit by a piece of the rotor blade. The Metropolitan Life Insurance Company renamed this building the MET Building, after the airline, Pan Am, went out of business.

### 301 Park Avenue

*Waldorf-Astoria Hotel* +   This second address of the famous hotel was once the site of the Women's Hospital, a 150-bed institution opened just after the Civil War. When the hotel opened on September 30, 1931, the first meal was served to the king of Siam. The first Tony Awards ceremony took place in the Grand Ballroom on Easter Sunday, April 6, 1947. The awards, presented by the American Theatre Wing (whose cofounder Antoinette Perry the award is named for), were created to recognize distinguished achievement in the American theater. Among those first winners were Helen Hayes, José Ferrer, and Fredric March. The hotel has been host to every U.S. President since Franklin D. Roosevelt, who arrived by private railroad car on tracks buried beneath Park Avenue. The hotel was the meeting place between President Lyndon B. Johnson and the first pope to travel to America, Paul VI, on October 4, 1965.

## Park Avenue between East 50th and East 51st streets, east side

*St. Bartholomew's Church*　Beginning in 1983, this church was the focus of a protracted legal battle over whether owners of landmarked property could overturn their protected status in the face of financial hardship. The church wanted to demolish its community house and sell the land to an office developer. Refused twice by the Landmarks Preservation Commission, the church took its case to the U.S. Supreme Court, which upheld the commission's denial in March 1991.

## 390 Park Avenue

*Lever House* ✚　Completed in 1952, this international-style skyscraper was the first building to break the "street wall" of Park Avenue. The Lever House marked the transformation of the Avenue from a residential block to the premier address for postwar corporate America. Sleek, airy, and dramatic, this building presented a striking contrast with its old-fashioned stone neighbors. Threatened with the wrecker's ball for a bigger tower, it was saved just in time when it became eligible for landmark status on its thirtieth birthday. It was designated a New York City landmark on November 9, 1982.

## Park Avenue at East 56th Street

The railroad tunnel leading to Grand Central Terminal beneath this intersection was the scene of one of the city's worst train accidents. At 8:20 A.M. on January 8, 1902, a commuter train steam engine rammed into the last car of another, standing commuter train. The crash, which killed 15 passengers on the standing train, was the result of poor visibility in the tunnel, which was filled with steam, fog, and smoke. The accident prompted legislation prohibiting steam-powered trains on the island of Manhattan, which led to the exclusive use of cleaner electric locomotives. Without the soot and fumes, Park Avenue developed into a very desirable residential district, lined with apartment houses for the wealthy. Since World War II, office buildings have replaced all but one apartment house below 59th Street.

## PARK AVENUE SOUTH

### 213 Park Avenue South ✚

*Max's Kansas City*　Within a few weeks of its opening on December 6, 1965, the bar and restaurant that once occupied this building became a hangout for Andy Warhol and his "mod" entourage. The back room became a meeting place for his rock band, The Velvet Underground,

In 1911, this was Fourth Avenue north of the future site of Grand Central Terminal during construction of the underground train tunnels. The project, which took more than 10 years to complete, transformed a dangerous and unsightly train yard into Park Avenue, one of the city's most prestigious addresses.

and his counterculture, movie-star, and artist friends. Patti Smith, Bruce Springsteen, Philip Glass, and the band Devo have also performed here.

### Park Avenue South at East 18th Street, southeast corner

*Clarendon Hotel* This hotel, now gone, was the site of a meeting in March 1854 between Cyrus Field, Peter Cooper, and other investors to raise money for the transatlantic underwater telegraph cable. In 1871, the Grand Duke Alexis of Russia, the first member of the czar's family to visit the United States, was a guest here. The grand duke had stopped in New York on his way to hunt bison on the frontier.

### Park Avenue South at East 19th Street, southwest corner

*Parker Building* ✦ In 1907, Lee De Forest, a pioneer and inventor in the field of early radio, began fairly regular radio broadcasts from his top-floor laboratory here. De Forest promoted and expanded the idea of public broadcasting.

## 287 Park Avenue South at East 22nd Street, northeast corner

*United Charities Building* ✦ In hopes of improving race relations, the National Negro Conference and W. E. B. Du Bois's Niagara Movement Group met here on May 31, 1909. They joined to form the National Association for the Advancement of Colored People (NAACP), in the year of the one hundredth anniversary of the birth of Abraham Lincoln. The conference passed resolutions calling for equal civil, political, and educational rights and to demand the enforcement of the Fourteenth and Fifteenth amendments to the Constitution.

## Park Avenue South at East 26th Street, southeast corner ✦

Now a cooperative apartment complex, these three nineteenth-century buildings were once the headquarters of Louis Comfort Tiffany. Tiffany, the son of the jewelry founder, was a master of late-nineteenth-century design. His firm designed and manufactured his opulent stained-glass windows, mosaics, and glasswork here from 1881 to 1905.

## Park Avenue South at East 28th Street

*28th Street IRT Subway Station* On the opening day of the new subway, October 27, 1904, Henry Barrett entered this station and rode on one of the first trains. Shortly into his ride, he looked down and realized that his $500 diamond horseshoe stickpin was missing. Barrett thereby became the first recorded subway crime victim.

## ROCKEFELLER PLAZA

### 30 Rockefeller Plaza

*RCA Building* ✦ The focal point of Rockefeller Center and its highest building is the 70-story RCA Building, home of the National Broadcasting Company. This Art Deco landmark has been home to many milestones in the history of radio and television. Arturo Toscanini and the NBC Symphony Orchestra radio broadcasts originated from studio 8-H on Christmas Day 1937. Early television broadcasting began from studio 3-H in 1935. Studio 6-B, beginning on September 21, 1948, was home to Milton Berle's "Texaco Star Theater," the medium's first smash hit. As the show's popularity skyrocketed, so did the sales of television sets. When Berle's comedy/variety show first aired, there were about 500,000 sets in the country; within two years, the number reached 6 million. Studio 8-H has been the home of "Saturday Night Live" (originally titled "NBC's Saturday Night") since 1975.

The studio for the show "Twenty-One," the focal point of the quiz-show scandals, a low point in the history of television, was located here. On the December 5, 1956, show, a contestant, Professor Charles Van Doren, beat Herbert Stempel. This show, watched by millions, set in motion the public's eventual realization that this extremely popular quiz program and others had been rigged as a result of the contestants' being supplied with the correct answers.

The famous Christmas trees in Rockefeller Plaza pre-date the completed complex. The first such tree was put up and decorated in 1931 by construction workers grateful to have jobs during the Depression.

## 50 Rockefeller Plaza

*Associated Press Building* ✦ Antiwar and civil rights activist Allard K. Lowenstein was assassinated at his law office in this building on March 14, 1980. Lowenstein, a former one-term congressman from Long Island, was shot by a longtime acquaintance, Dennis Sweeney, who was deemed mentally ill. Lowenstein died later that evening at St. Clair's hospital.

On December 10, 1991, Terry Anderson, the Associated Press's chief Middle East correspondent and America's longest-held hostage, returned here for a sentimental visit. A quick tour of the fourth-floor newsroom was a highlight of Anderson's first day back in the United States. Showered with yellow rose petals from his emotional colleagues, the understandably crowd-shy Anderson had been given a hero's welcome from the time of his arrival at Kennedy Airport earlier in the day. The last of America's 18 hostages held in the Middle East, he was released after 2,455 days, almost seven years, in captivity.

## RUTHERFORD PLACE

### Rutherford Place at East 16th Street, northwest corner

*St. George's Church* ✦ Nicknamed "Morgan's Church," this house of worship built with contributions from financier J. P. Morgan was the site of his funeral on April 14, 1913. His son, John Pierpont Morgan Jr., narrowly missed being killed here on Sunday, April 18, 1920. Thomas W. Simpkin, an escaped mental patient, shot at Morgan Jr.; he missed Morgan but struck Dr. James Markoe, who was the Morgans' family friend and physician. The doctor had treated Morgan the elder when he himself was the victim of an earlier murder attempt. The dying Markoe was rushed to the Lying-in Hospital across Stuyvesant Square Park. The hospital, which had been built by Morgan at Markoe's urging, was where the doctor died.

## SUTTON PLACE

### 13 Sutton Place ✦

Seventy-seven-year-old Elizabeth Marbury died here in her home of a heart attack on January 22, 1933. The unconventional Marbury, who was the American literary agent for Oscar Wilde and George Bernard Shaw, was also the lesbian lover of Elsie de Wolf, a society leader and a National Democratic Party committeewoman.

## SUTTON SQUARE

### 14 Sutton Square ✦

Artist Robert Henri moved into this four-story brownstone after he returned from Europe in 1900. The river views from these windows became the subject of several of his paintings.

## UNION SQUARE EAST

### 18 Union Square East

*Union Square Hotel*   Henry George, the economist who formulated the single-tax theory, died on October 29, 1897, at the hotel that used to stand at this address. He was campaigning for the office of mayor of New York City at the time.

### 32 Union Square East ✦

Now united by one street address, this hodgepodge of buildings has been home to artist's studios, radical groups, capitalist corporations, and the Klein's department store annex. With a front-row seat for Union Square's mass meetings and protests, several left-wing political organizations were based here, including the communist newspapers the *Daily Worker* and *Freiheit* (German for "freedom"). In January 1968, Abbie Hoffman's new Yippies (members of his Youth International Party) set up headquarters here. Hoffman explained the party's literal open door policy, saying, "We did open an office. We left the door unlocked so that anybody could wander in and answer the phone and be a Yippie spokesman."

### Union Square East at East 17th Street, southeast corner

*Westmoreland Apartments*   Uncompromising abolitionist and publisher of the *Liberator* for 35 years, William Lloyd Garrison died here at the home of his daughter on May 24, 1879.

## UNION SQUARE PARK

At what was then just a crossing of two country roads, General George Washington assembled here a military unit and a committee of citizens to accompany him on his march into the city to take formal possession of New York from the British after the Revolutionary War. The equestrian statue of Washington, now near the center of the park, used to stand on the small traffic island at the intersection of 14th Street and Fourth Avenue. This was said to be the exact spot where Washington was welcomed by grateful New Yorkers. That date, November 25, 1783, later called Evacuation Day, was annually observed as a major city holiday well into the twentieth century.

Laid out as a residential square in 1831, the park became the focal point of the emerging theatrical district after the Academy of Music opened in 1854. The park became the place to mark the triumphs and tragedies of the Civil War. On April 20, 1861, the first huge rally to support the Union cause was held shortly after the shelling of Fort Sumter. Four years later almost to the day, on April 25, 1865, the denizens of Union Square Park paid their respects as the funeral procession of President Abraham Lincoln passed by. The park continued to be a popular location for rallies and protests, particularly labor demonstrations, well into the 1940s. On August 22, 1927, some 5,000 people converged on the square to demonstrate and keep vigil until the time of Ferdinando Sacco and Bartolomeo Vanzetti's execution. The immigrant pair were put to death after what most agreed (then and now) was an unfair trial.

It is fitting that Union Square is linked with the formation of another holiday, this one commemorating America's workforce. On September 5, 1882, the park was the final destination of 10,000 marchers who had left City Hall on what would be known as the country's first observation of Labor Day, 12 years before Congress made it a national holiday in 1894. Peter J. Maguire, a marcher that day and a union labor leader, was the originator of the idea.

*Union Square Park Subway Station, N & R Train Platform*    Willie Sutton, the legendary bank robber, boarded a downtown subway here the afternoon of February 18, 1952. It was his last ride as a free man for a long time. He was spotted by a fellow passenger, 24-year-old Arnold Schuster, who followed the fugitive to his Brooklyn home and then so advised the police. The police and Schuster were treated like heroes. Less than a month later, on March 8, Schuster was shot and killed on a street near his home. Sutton claimed he had nothing do to with the

This well-attended antiwar rally was held on August 8, 1914, at the north end of Union Square Park. Five days earlier, Germany had declared war on France. The United States didn't enter World War I until April 6, 1917.

killing, and the murderer was never caught. Sutton was convicted of robbery and sent to Attica prison until 1969.

*Union Square Park Subway Station, 4, 5, and 6 Train Platform* On August 28, 1991, at 10 minutes after midnight, this section of the station became the horrifying scene of the subway system's worst accident in 63 years. The crash occurred 200 feet north of Union Square Station when a drunken motorman, Robert E. Ray, fell asleep and rammed the speeding train into a dozen steel beams supporting the tunnel. The accident killed five riders and injured 200 others. It took six days to remove the wreckage of the train and repair the damaged station. Mass transit was in chaos as thousands of commuters were unable to use Manhattan's only East Side subway line.

## UNION SQUARE WEST

### 33 Union Square West

*Decker Building* ✦ Artist Andy Warhol moved his "factory" to the sixth floor of this building in early 1968. It was here on June 3, 1968, that he

This orderly procession around Union Square Park on September 5, 1882, marked the nation's first Labor Day celebration. The originator of the holiday, Peter J. McGuire, envisioned a parade to "show the strength and espirt de corps of the trade and labor organizations." (*Frank Leslie's Illustrated Newspaper*, September 16, 1882)

was shot by Valerie Solanas, the founder and sole member of S.C.U.M. (Society for Cutting Up Men). A disgruntled hanger-on, Solanas had wanted Warhol to film a screenplay of hers. The already eccentric Warhol survived the attack but became even more remote and lost his interest in making movies.

## FIRST AVENUE

### First Avenue between West 42nd and West 48th streets

*United Nations Secretariat Building* ✦ Even before the UN had its permanent headquarters along the East River (completed in 1952), delegates were already meeting at several locations around the city to plan the development of the new international organization. John D. Rockefeller Jr. donated the First Avenue site to help keep the organization from moving to either San Francisco or Philadelphia. For 60 years leaders from every nation have used the United Nations as a stage to capture the world's attention. None was more colorful than Soviet Premier

Nikita Khrushchev, who delivered his shoe-thumping tirade in September 1960.

## SECOND AVENUE

### Second Avenue at East 20th Street, northwest corner
A lamp post here was the longtime "office" of Tammany boss Charlie "Silent" Murphy in the early years of the twentieth century. One of the city's most powerful machine politicians, he orchestrated the careers of Governor Alfred E. Smith and Senator Robert F. Wagner.

## THIRD AVENUE

### 633 Third Avenue +
New York state Governor Eliot Spitzer addressed a packed briefing room here at his Manhattan office on March 10, 2008. In a statement

Tammany Hall boss Charles Murphy (*left*) never held an elective office, but he was one of the most powerful political leaders in the city's history. Here he is in 1914 conducting the people's business on the streets of New York.

lasting just over a minute, he confessed to being caught on a federal wiretap arranging a rendezvous with an expensive prostitute at a Washington, D.C., hotel. Spitzer hoped to survive the scandal, but two days later he returned to announce his resignation. In office less than 15 months, the aggressive former state attorney general had been known as "The Sheriff of Wall Street" and had campaigned to improve ethics in government.

### Third Avenue at East 46th Street, northeast corner

*United States Provost Marshal's Office*   The infamous New York City Draft Riots began on this spot when a mob burned down this building on July 13, 1863. Two days earlier, on Saturday, the first names in the military draft lottery were chosen under Congress's recent Conscription Act mandating military service in the Union Army during the Civil War. The draft was especially unpopular with the working class and with Irish immigrants, who were indignant over the stipulation that a $300 payment or the procurement of a substitute enabled the wealthy to evade service. The riot spread from this corner and engulfed much of the city, the violence and destruction lasting for three days. President Abraham Lincoln ordered Union troops back from the recent engagement at Gettysburg to restore order. The number of dead has never been known exactly, but estimates place the number of killed and wounded at more than 1,000. Known abolitionists and African Americans were the preferred targets. As many as 70 African Americans were lynched.

### 922 Third Avenue ✚

*Clancy's Bar*   On June 25, 1983, federal agents captured Joseph "Joe" Patrick Thomas Doherty while he was tending bar here. Doherty, a one-time Irish Republican Army guerrilla, was wanted in Britain for his part in killing a British soldier in Belfast in 1980. He escaped from a British prison while on trial and fled to New York. Doherty and his eight-year legal struggle in this country to prevent his extradition to Britain became a cause célèbre for opponents of British rule of Northern Ireland. After a U.S. Supreme Court ruling, Doherty was eventually deported on February 19, 1992.

## FIFTH AVENUE

### Fifth Avenue at West 14th Street, northwest corner

On February 20, 1861, President-elect Abraham Lincoln had a breakfast meeting here at the home of Moses Hicks Grinnell, a Republican supporter, with 100 prosperous merchants. This same house became the

The Civil War draft lottery began on July 11, 1863, at the Provost Marshal's Office on Third Avenue at East 46th Street. This site was the flashpoint for the worst riot in New York City history. The first American conscripted into the Union Army was New Yorker William Jones.

third home of Delmonico's restaurant two years later. The Sorosis Club, the first organized women's club, held its first official meeting on April 20, 1868, in a private dining room here. The club's founders included Phoebe Cary, Ann Lynch Botta, and Jenny June. Elaborate banquets were held here for Samuel F.B. Morse in honor of his invention of the telegraph, the Grand Duke Alexis Alexandrovitch of Russia, and Charles Dickens.

### 79 Fifth Avenue
This address was once the home of Mayor George Opdyke. During the four days of the Draft Riots in July 1863, his house was attacked twice. The house was saved, the first time by about 50 neighbors who helped turn back a mob intent on burning it down. The second time, the city police kept the rioters at bay.

### Fifth Avenue at West 15th Street, northwest corner
Carlo Tresca, radical writer and leader, was assassinated on this corner on January 11, 1943, at 9:40 P.M. in the darkness of the wartime blackout. He had just left the offices at 96 Fifth Avenue of the Italian anti-fascist newspaper *Il Martello* ("The Hammer"), of which he was the

editor. Tresca, a friend of Mayor Fiorello La Guardia's, had many enemies across the political spectrum. His killer was never captured.

### Fifth Avenue at East 16th Street, northeast corner
The home of Levi Parsons Morton once stood at this corner. Morton,
who was a U.S. congressman and New York governor, lived here for
three years until he was elected Vice President (serving with President
Benjamin Harrison) and moved to Washington, D.C., in 1889.

### Fifth Avenue at East 18th Street, northeast corner
August Belmont's elegant mansion and art gallery stood on this corner
site in the second half of the nineteenth century. This house was the
first in the city to have a private ballroom. Belmont, a society leader,
was a leading financier in the development of the subways.

### 130 Fifth Avenue
*Chickering Hall*   An auditorium, named for the piano makers, was once
at this site. It was here on May 17, 1877, that Alexander Graham Bell
made the first interstate telephone call over telegraph wires, to Thomas
Watson in New Brunswick, New Jersey. The attentive listeners heard
Watson not only speak but also sing. On January 9, 1882, Oscar Wilde
gave his first American lecture, entitled "The English Renaissance," to a
sold-out, standing-room-only audience. Another Englishman, Matthew
Arnold, also made his lecture debut at this hall a year later. In addition
to writers, Chickering was also a showplace for music: The Russian pianist Vladimir de Pachmann performed for his first American audience
here.

### 149 Fifth Avenue
*Lotos Club*   A reception here was given in honor of the newly arrived
team of W. S. Gilbert and Arthur Sullivan, the composers of light opera,
on November 8, 1879. Somewhat later, this club held a dinner for Henry
Morton Stanley to celebrate his successful search for Dr. David Livingstone in Africa.

### 162 Fifth Avenue
*Union Club*   The front steps of this club served as the stage for James
Gordon Bennett Jr.'s fall from grace as well as from New York society
on January 2, 1877. Bennett, heir of the founder and editor of the *New
York Herald*, James Bennett Sr., was, like his father, a brilliant newspaper

man. He was a great sportsman, and a celebrated drunk. He had appeared to be on the road to reform after he fell in love with and became engaged to the socialite Caroline May, but he regressed and embarrassed his future in-laws by publicly urinating in their fireplace at a New Year's Day reception. The next day, at high noon, Caroline's brother Frederick horsewhipped Bennett here at the Union Club. Bennett challenged the other man to a duel; a duel ensued, but no one was injured. This scandal destroyed Bennett's reputation and he left the country for France, where he established the *Paris Herald*.

## 175 Fifth Avenue
*St. Germain Hotel*   The first flicker of the Great White Way can be traced to an early electric sign that was on the Madison Square Park side of this hotel in July 1892. It was a manually synchronized flashing sign of blue, green, red, and frosted white lights. The sole function of this primitive spectacle was an advertisement for the new homes at Manhattan Beach on Long Island. This same triangle-shaped block would become home to the Fuller Building, now known as the Flatiron Building.

*Flatiron Building* ✦ Even before the innovative steel-skeleton frame had reached the full 21 stories, many New Yorkers were convinced that a strong wind would bring down this early skyscraper, built just after the turn of the twentieth century. Their fears and jokes about the highrise were tragically reinforced by a real-life accident only a year after the building was completed. On the evening of February 5, 1903, a powerful wind from a thunderstorm blew John McTaggart into Fifth Avenue, where he was run over by an automobile. The 14-year-old messenger from Brooklyn was on his third attempt to round the corner of the building when he was swept up by the powerful gust. He died that night of internal bleeding.

## Fifth Avenue at 23rd Street
On April 19, 1866, at this intersection, Henry Bergh reprimanded and threatened to have arrested a wagon driver for beating his exhausted horse. Bergh, the guiding spirit of the Society for the Prevention of Cruelty to Animals, informed the man that a new law that he had fathered and that had been passed earlier that day in the state legislature now prohibited cruelty to animals. Bergh had previously helped establish the Society for the Prevention of Cruelty to Children, in 1875.

### 200 Fifth Avenue, between West 23rd and West 24th streets

*Franconi's Hippodrome*   This corner was the site of the Hippodrome, a huge two-story brick amphitheater with a tented roof that had replaced a long-popular tavern called Madison Cottage. The highly publicized arena opened on May 2, 1853. In spite of the rather daring and innovative performances, including chariot races and gladiatorial contests, among other fare, the Hippodrome was a complete financial failure and was abandoned within two years.

*Fifth Avenue Hotel*   This hotel, the next structure on the site, opened on August 23, 1859. It was famous for its early elevator, described as a "perpendicular railway intersecting each story," and as a gathering place for political powerbrokers of the era. The term "amen corner" originated here; it referred to Sunday meetings of New York boss Senator Thomas C. Platt and his subordinates, who always agreed with him. The hotel dining room was the setting for an infamous Republican campaign dinner for presidential candidate James G. Blaine on October 30, 1884. A partisan speaker described the Democrats as the party of "rum, Romanism, and rebellion." Candidate Blaine's failure to disavow this insult cost him needed Irish votes in the city. Five days later, the Democratic Party candidate, Grover Cleveland, carried New York state and won the election.

*Toy Center*   The current office building, which dates from 1909, was the longtime home of the International Toy Center. It was in a fifth-floor showroom of Mattel Toys that the first Barbie doll was introduced to the world during the Annual Toy Fair on March 9, 1959. Ruth Handler, whose husband, Elliott, had started Mattel, created Barbie, naming her after their daughter Barbara.

### Fifth Avenue between 24th and 25th streets

A massive wood-and-plaster triumphal arch once spanned Fifth Avenue at this spot. The arch was built to commemorate Admiral George Dewey's victory over the Spanish fleet in Manila Bay during the Spanish–American War. On September 30, 1899, the returning hero was received with a huge procession that passed beneath the arch. Another tribute from the city was a sign hung from the Brooklyn Bridge, written out in electric lights, "WELCOME DEWEY." Dewey's fame was almost as short-lived as his decisive naval victory. Within a few months, as the full-scale-model arch began to crumble, plans for a more robust marble version were abandoned as a result of a lack of both interest and donations.

For much of the nineteenth century, the Fifth Avenue Hotel was the most fashionable hotel in New York. Located on the northwest corner of Fifth Avenue and West 23rd Street, in the heart of the entertainment district, centered on Madison Square Park. (*Harper's Weekly*, October 1, 1959)

### Fifth Avenue at West 24th Street

On May 15, 1920, at the annual Police Parade, dignitaries and honored guests seated on a reviewing platform here at this traffic island shared with the Worth monument were embarrassed by an interloper in their parade. Waving to the assembled leaders of New York's Finest was Nicky Arnstein, a small-time gambler and wanted fugitive. He was also the husband of Fanny Brice, the comedian and Ziegfeld Follies star, who was with him during his surprise appearance. The couple and their lawyer had joined the parade and drove past on their way downtown to surrender to the assistant district attorney. Arnstein had disappeared three months earlier and was wanted for his part in a plot to steal Wall Street bonds. He was later convicted and sent to jail. Fanny, after much soul-searching, divorced him.

### Fifth Avenue at 28th Street

Underworld crime figure Louis "Lepke" Buchalter surrendered to FBI director J. Edgar Hoover and columnist Walter Winchell in a parked car at this intersection on August 24, 1939. "Lepke," the head of Murder, Inc., the syndicate's professional hit squad, was wanted on narcotic charges. He believed he would get more lenient treatment from the

Topped with a statue of Victory, the Dewey Arch stood at Fifth Avenue and West 24th Street in 1899. A national hero on his return from the Spanish–American War, Admiral George Dewey was so popular that there was talk of his running for President of the United States. These aspirations were quickly dismissed after several embarrassing statements by the admiral.

federal authorities than from the Manhattan D.A., Thomas E. "Gang-buster" Dewey, who was also looking for him. As it turned out, he was convicted on federal narcotic charges, and then in a later trial Dewey won another conviction on murder charges. He was executed in the electric chair on March 4, 1944.

## Fifth Avenue at West 29th Street, northwest corner

*Marble Collegiate Church* ✚ On August 20, 1918, opera tenor Enrico Caruso married his American bride, Dorothy Benjamin, here. This church later became the pulpit for the influential Reverend Dr. Norman Vincent Peale from 1932 until his retirement more than 50 years later. It was here that Peale refined and preached his message that a proper state of mind, induced by simple prayer, could produce spiritual and material success on earth, ideas he presented in his bestselling book *The Power of Positive Thinking*. Richard M. Nixon was a member of this congregation in the mid-1960s and a follower of Dr. Peale. The reverend officiated at the wedding, here, of President-elect Nixon's daughter Julie to Dwight David Eisenhower II (known as David), the grandson of President Dwight Eisenhower, on December 22, 1968. The elder Eisenhower, a patient in Walter Reed Hospital at the time, watched the ceremony on closed-circuit television.

Another memorable wedding here on March 16, 2002, united actress Liza Minnelli and producer David Gest. More than 1,100 celebrity guests were players in this media extravaganza featuring Elizabeth Taylor, Mia Farrow, and Michael Jackson as part of the 36-member wedding party. The messy divorce only 16 months later also received extensive media coverage.

## Fifth Avenue at West 30th Street, southwest corner

*Holland House* Thomas Gainsborough's masterpiece *The Duchess of Devonshire*, the most famous stolen painting of its time, spent the night of March 29, 1901, at this hotel before returning to England and its rightful owners. The painting, recovered the day before, had been stolen by American-born Adam Worth in London in 1876. Worth was the greatest criminal mastermind of the nineteenth century and the prototype for the villain Professor Moriarty in the Sherlock Holmes mysteries. Frustrated in negotiations to ransom the painting, Worth kept it for more than 25 years, often carrying it in the false bottom of his luggage or rolled up in an umbrella.

In the early morning hours of July 26, 1903, the hotel's night porter awoke to the rare sound of an automobile horn. It came from a 1903 Winton, nicknamed the "Vermont," that had just completed the first transcontinental auto trip. The car's two occupants, Horatio Nelson Jackson and Sewall K. Crocker, were eager to get to their room and into bed. The duo finished the trip from San Francisco in 63 days, 12 hours, and 30 minutes and won a $50 bet.

## 291 and 293 Fifth Avenue

*The Little Galleries of the Photo-Secession* Both these address served as an innovative art and photography gallery founded by Alfred Stieglitz and Edward Steichen in 1905. Henri Mattisse's work was first shown in America in 1908 at "291," as the gallery was later named; so were the works of Henri Rousseau and Paul Cézanne in 1910, and those of Pablo Picasso in 1911. The Photo-Secession, a group of avant-garde photographers, was exhibited here. It was also the headquarters for *Camera Work*, the journal founded by Stieglitz to showcase the relatively new medium of photography.

## Fifth Avenue between West 33rd and West 34th streets, southwest corner

A stately mansion once here was the home of *the* Mrs. William Astor, the leading society hostess of the Gilded Age. It was here, at her annual party in the ballroom, that Caroline Astor presided over New York society. Shortly before the 1892 ball, her publicist, Ward McAllister, released to the press the list of the invited guests, the celebrated "Four Hundred." This privileged clique took up the physical capacity of Mrs. Astor's ballroom. Next door to the south, her nephew William Waldorf Astor tore down his mansion in 1893 to build an 11-story hotel, the Waldorf.

*Waldorf-Astoria Hotel*　By the time her nephew built his hotel, Mrs. Astor had decided to move uptown. Her mansion was torn down for a connecting hotel, the Astoria. The new hyphenated hotel, the Waldorf-Astoria, became an instant landmark. It was here at the hotel's inaugural dinner in 1896 that chop suey, unknown in China at the time, was invented in honor of the visiting Chinese ambassador. This Waldorf-Astoria was also the site of another famous society party, the Bradley Martin costume charity ball, reputed to be the most expensive party of modern times, held on the evening of February 10, 1897. Mrs. Cornelia Martin, whose jewels were valued at more than $60,000, was dressed as Mary Queen of Scots and her husband as Louis XV. The newspapers ridiculed and satirized the extravaganza as wasteful.

In room 1162, beginning on September 24, 1903, Philippe Bunau-Villa held several clandestine meetings planning a Panamanian revolt against Colombia. Within hours of the successful revolt, the U.S. government recognized a free Panama in exchange for building the Canal.

The hotel was the site of the National Broadcasting Company's first radio broadcast on November 15, 1926. More than 2 million listeners in 21 cities over 25 stations heard this historic broadcast. This was the beginning of the concept of a radio network.

During Ambassador Li Hung-chang's visit to the United States, his personal chef prepared all his meals. Here he is in the kitchen of the Waldorf-Astoria Hotel, the legendary birthplace of chop suey in September 1896. (*Harper's Weekly*)

*Empire State Building* ✦ The hotel, which moved to Park Avenue, gave way in 1931 to what was then the world's tallest building. A grand monument to capitalistic optimism in the face of the Great Depression, it was topped off with a mooring mast for the latest in air travel, the dirigible. But only one blimp ever docked, on September 16, 1931, before the idea was given up as too dangerous. The office tower was later the scene of a tragic air accident on the foggy morning of July 28, 1945. A B-25 Mitchell bomber crashed into the seventy-ninth floor on the 34th Street side. The pilot, Lieutenant Colonel William F. Smith, his two passengers, and eight people inside the building died.

### Fifth Avenue at East 39th Street, northeast corner

*Dickel's Riding Academy* After attending several polo games in England, newspaper publisher James Gordon Bennett Jr. arranged for an indoor version of the game to be played here in 1876. This was the first recorded polo game played in America and perhaps the first polo match to be played indoors. The game was a hit with Bennett and his wealthy circle. They continued to play indoors and within a few years moved their matches uptown and outside to what became known as the Polo Grounds north of Central Park.

## 450 Fifth Avenue

*Macbeth Gallery* The exhibition of "The Eight," including the painters John Sloan, Robert Henri, and Maurice Prendergast, opened here on February 3, 1908, competing with the prestigious but stodgy National Academy of Design's spring show. Panned by the critics and later called the "Ash-can school," these artists' works consisted of bold and realistic portrayals of urban life. Despite the reservations of the art establishment, the show drew in large crowds, and seven pictures were sold. Four of them were bought by Gertrude Vanderbilt Whitney for $2,225. These daring purchases marked the heiress's first foray into collecting modern art and would become the core of the future Whitney Museum of American Art.

## Fifth Avenue between West 40th and West 42nd streets

*Croton Reservoir* A milestone in the physical development of the city, this five-acre reservoir was begun in 1837 and filled, amid great fanfare, on July 4, 1842. The entire system of reservoirs, aqueducts, and tunnels that began 35 miles north of the city and supplied this 20-million-gallon distributing reservoir was a marvel of nineteenth-century engineering. The growing metropolis now had an abundant and potable supply of water. The thick Egyptian-style walls were topped by a popular promenade. Much of the infrastructure is still in use today.

*New York Public Library, Center for the Humanities* ✦ The Beaux Arts palace of knowledge that replaced the reservoir in 1898 was completed 13 years later. The creation of the New York Public Library, one of the world's greatest, involved a consolidation of the Astor and Lenox libraries and a bequest of former New York Governor Samuel J. Tilden. President William Howard Taft and the library's greatest living benefactor, Andrew Carnegie, were among the famous who attended the opening ceremonies on May 23, 1911. The knowledge stored here has contributed to the birth of the Polaroid camera, xerography (photocopying), the atomic bomb, *Reader's Digest*, "Ripley's Believe It or Not!" and countless other books, ideas, and inventions.

## 509 Fifth Avenue

A storefront shared with a milliner in 1909, this address was the first shop of Elizabeth Arden, the cosmetic entrepreneur. Arden, who

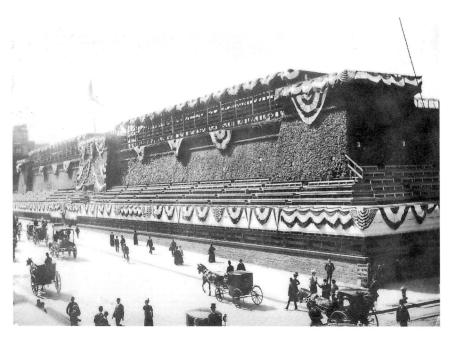

The Croton Reservoir is covered with bleachers and reviewing stand for a long-ago Fifth Avenue parade. The Egyptian-style reservoir was replaced by the current New York Public Library Research Building in 1911. (Author's collection)

changed her name from Florence Nightingale Graham, had arrived from Canada the year before. In what may have been a case of nominative determinism, she studied nursing but discovered she "didn't really like looking at sick people" and turned to a career in cosmetics.

## Fifth Avenue between West 43rd and West 44th streets

*Colored Orphan Asylum*  Much of the fury of the Draft Riots was directed at African Americans, who were seen as the cause of the Civil War and its resultant hated conscription. On the first afternoon of the riot, July 13, 1863, the rioters zeroed in on this target, a home for about 200 African American orphans under the age of 12. The superintendent barricaded the front door and quickly helped his charges to safety out a back door. Once inside, the mob ravaged everything. When they found a little girl left behind and hiding under a bed, they killed her. They set fire to the building and attacked the firemen brave enough to try to save it. The orphanage and three other buildings on the block burned to the ground.

## 522 Fifth Avenue +

*Sherry's Hotel*  Beneath three renovations is the 99-year-old core designed by McKim, Mead and White that was once the upper-crust hotel and restaurant Sherry's. It was the scene of two exorbitant Gilded Age dinner parties. The first, on March 28, 1903, was hosted by C. K. G. Billings to celebrate the opening of his new stables. All the guests sat astride 36 horses that had been brought up to the ballroom in the freight elevator. The other, on January 31, 1905, was a costume party given by James Hazen Hyde, Equitable Life Assurance's first vice president and son of its founder. This imaginative host spent more than $200,000—in policyholders' money—to re-create Versailles for his guests. His fate was not unlike that of the residents of Versailles. Soon after the public's indignation over the extravagance, he lost his job at the insurance (assurance) company and was forced to leave the country. His party also sparked a probe of the insurance giants by the state. Charles Evan Hughes, chief counsel to the legislative committee conducting the investigtion (and later a Supreme Court associate justice,

An early target of the mob during the Draft Riots was the Colored Orphan Asylum on Fifth Avenue at West 43rd Street. On Monday, July 13, 1863, rioters ransacked and burned the orphanage and left hundreds of children homeless. A new facility was built in 1867 on West 143rd Street at Amsterdam Avenue. (*Harper's Weekly*, August 1, 1863)

presidential candidate, U.S. Secretary of State, and Chief Justice of the United States), held 57 public hearings that prompted the state legislature to reform the insurance industry.

### Fifth Avenue between East 46th and East 47th streets

*Windsor Hotel*   At the end of the nineteenth century this fashionable hotel was home to two of America's wealthiest capitalists, John D. Rockefeller and Andrew Carnegie, and a way station for King Kalakaua of the Sandwich Islands and authors Matthew Arnold and Oscar Wilde. But on St. Patrick's Day 1899, it was the site of a tragic fire that took the lives of 33 people. Firefighters, hindered by the parade out front, were unable to save frantic guests, many of whom jumped from windows. One famous survivor was Isadora Duncan, who was teaching a dance class at the time of the blaze. She helped lead her young pupils to safety. The day before the fire, astrologer Evangeline Adams checked into the hotel and claimed later she had warned the proprietor, Warren Leland, that a "disaster" might happen the next day. Adams's prediction clinched her reputation as America's foremost astrologer. For the next 33 years until her own self-predicted death, she wrote bestsellers and a newspaper column, hosted several radio shows, and consulted her famous clients, among them J. P. Morgan, Tallulah Bankhead, and Enrico Caruso.

### 579 Fifth Avenue

The four-story brownstone that once stood here was the last address of the financier Jay Gould. His family had moved here in 1882 from across the street at 578 Fifth Avenue. Gould died in a second-floor bedroom here on December 2, 1892. His funeral was also held here, three days later.

### Fifth Avenue between East 50th and East 51st streets

*St. Patrick's Cathedral* ✚ Begun in 1858 on Fifth Avenue, the avenue of choice for the city's Protestant ruling elite, the new St. Patrick's Cathedral of the archdiocese of New York was a prominent symbol of the increasing Roman Catholic presence in the city in the middle of the nineteenth century. Waves of Irish immigrants, beginning in the 1830s, were changing the social fabric of the growing city and the nation. By 1855 a quarter of the population of Manhattan and Brooklyn had been born in Ireland. The new cathedral, the country's largest, was a fitting stage for the emerging power of the new immigrants in American life. St. Patrick's, delayed because of the Civil War, was dedicated on May 25, 1879, and has been the center of Roman Catholic New York life ever since. Pope Paul VI, the first pontiff to visit the Western Hemisphere, officiated at a Mass here on

October 4, 1965. Popes John Paul II and Benedict XVI have also offered Mass here. F. Scott Fitzgerald and Zelda Sayre were married here on Easter Sunday, April 3, 1920. Wakes were held here for General William T. Sherman on February 19, 1891; Arturo Toscanini on January 19, 1957; former Governor Alfred E. Smith on October 7, 1944; Babe Ruth on August 19, 1948; and Senator Robert F. Kennedy on June 8, 1968.

### 653 Fifth Avenue

*Cartier* ✦ Railroad tycoon Morton Plant built this corner limestone mansion in 1905. Soon after, the avenue began to change from residential to commercial and he decided to sell. His opportunity came in 1917 from Cartier Jewelers. Plant traded this house in exchange for $100 and a million-dollar two-strand necklace of 128 perfect natural pearls that his much-younger wife had admired. Clearly, Cartier got the better deal. Within a decade cultured pearls became widely available and natural pearls lost their value, while a mansion on Fifth Avenue is a still a mansion on Fifth Avenue.

This is the Easter parade on Fifth Avenue in 1900. The annual rite began in the 1870s as well-dressed parishioners left Easter Sunday services in the churches along Fifth Avenue: St. Thomas Episcopal Church, St. Patrick's Cathedral (pictured), and Trinity Episcopal Church.

## Fifth Avenue at East 52nd Street, northeast corner

This was once the site of the mansion of the city's leading abortionist, Ann Lohman, the notorious Madame Restell, as she was known. Business had been so brisk that by 1864 she was able to move her practice to this fashionable address, much to the horror of her new neighbors. Public opposition to abortion had curbed her practice, but she still continued to sell her "preventive powders" and pills from her basement office. She made the mistake of selling these dubious concoctions to a disguised Anthony Comstock, the moral crusader and chairman of the New York Society for the Suppression of Vice. He had her arrested and taken to the Tombs. Shortly afterward, while out on bail and back home, she committed suicide by slitting her throat in the bathtub on April 1, 1878, the day her trial was to begin. She left an estate of more than a million dollars.

## 660 Fifth Avenue

This was the site of William K. and Alva Smith Vanderbilt's "Petit Château." The French Renaissance–style château designed by Richard Morris Hunt set a new standard for palatial homes and started the trend for even larger "cottages" in Newport and castles on upper Fifth Avenue. A lavish housewarming costume ball was planned for March 26, 1883. More than 1,200 invitations were sent out, but none to the hostess's social rival, *the* Mrs. William Astor. Mrs. Vanderbilt explained that she could not invite a total stranger to her new home. The mountain came to Mohammed. Mrs. Astor swallowed her pride and called on the social upstart to garner a coveted invitation for herself and her daughter. At the party, Alva, costumed as "The Electric Light," and Caroline Astor, dressed as a Venetian princess, jointly reigned over New York society.

## Fifth Avenue at West 53rd Street, northwest corner

*St. Thomas Church* ✚ An earlier St. Thomas Church destroyed by fire in 1905 on this same site became *the* place for many society weddings after the marriage here of Charles John, Ninth Duke of Marlborough, and Consuelo Vanderbilt on November 6, 1895. This ultimately unhappy union marked the peak in the rage to have New York society daughters married off to foreign nobility. The 18-year-old Consuelo loved another, but her mother, Alva, was determined to have a titled daughter. The duke received close to $15 million as a dowry. Former President Benjamin Harrison was also married here, to Mary Scott Lord Dimmick, on April 6, 1896. Almost-President Thomas E. Dewey was married to Frances Hutt in the current church on June 16, 1928.

Designed by architect Richard Morris Hunt, the French Renaissance–style "Petit Châ-teau" at 660 Fifth Avenue was a tourist attraction in its day. It was a delicate version of the "Biltmore," the mansion Hunt later built for George Washington Vanderbilt in Ashville, North Carolina, the largest home in America.

### 725 Fifth Avenue

*Bonwit Teller Department Store*   A furious Salvador Dalí smashed the glass in a display window here on March 15, 1939. He threw a tub through the plate glass, narrowly missing a passer-by. The artist was upset that the store management had changed his Surrealist design without consult-ing him. He was arrested but given a suspended sentence. The depart-ment store was torn down to make room for Trump Tower.

*Trump Tower* ✚ Master builder and self-promoter Donald Trump's mixed-use apartment and office building served as the honeymoon re-treat for King of Pop Michael Jackson and Daughter of the King Lisa Marie Presley in the summer of 1994. The newlyweds stayed in a $10,000-a-month penthouse apartment here after their secret Domini-can Republic wedding on May 26. Seemingly mismatched from the start, the couple divorced 19 months later.

### 730 Fifth Avenue

*Crown Building* ✚ Originally named the Heckscher, this office building was the first home of the Museum of Modern Art, in 1929. The museum rented six rooms on the twelfth floor. Its first architecture show, the famed Modern Architecture International Exhibition, opened on February 9, 1932. The show, curated by Philip Johnson, MoMA's first director of the Architecture and Design department, and the architecture historian Henry-Russell Hitchcock established the "International Style" as the predominant mode of architecture in America for the next 40 years. This same building was involved in years of legal battles and international intrigue when it was discovered that Philippine President Ferdinand Marcos had secretly bought it in 1981. After the dictator was deposed, the Philippine government hoped to claim the profits from the sale of the building. In a compromise, the courts decided that the proceeds would be split among all the competing parties.

*Festival Theater*   On September 19, 1968, an usher in a movie theater that once occupied the ground floor of the Crown Building found Chester Carlson slumped over in his seat. Carlson, who invented xerography in a rented room in Astoria, Queens, in 1938, died that evening at Bellevue Hospital. He had sold a license to his photocopier to the Haloid Photographic Company, which later changed its name to the Xerox Corporation. Carlson earned a great deal of money, much of which he gave away to charity.

### Fifth Avenue at Central Park South, southwest corner
*The Plaza Hotel* ✦ The current castle-like Plaza Hotel, which had replaced an earlier version deemed too small, opened on October 1, 1907. The occasion was marked with a round of parties attended by the celebrities of the day: the Vanderbilts, James Buchanan "Diamond Jim" Brady, and Lillian Russell. The well-publicized parties proved a bonanza for the promoter of the city's first gas-driven metered taxis. He had the shining new cabs all parked in a neat little row in front of the hotel. Roughly 60 years later, "The party of the decade," Truman Capote's Black and White Ball, was held here on November 28, 1966. Capote decided to top off his recent success with his book *In Cold Blood* with a party for 500 friends in honor of *Washington Post* and *Newsweek* publisher Katherine Graham. The masked ball's guest list reflected Capote's passions, mixing society (Barbara "Babe" Paley), Hollywood (Frank Sinatra and Henry Fonda), and literary (Arthur Schlesinger Jr.) types.

### Fifth Avenue at 59th Street
This intersection was the assembly point for 10,000 African American marchers in a silent protest down Fifth Avenue on July 28, 1917. To the

The Plaza Hotel on Fifth Avenue with a line of taxis parked at the entrance in 1915. The newly completed Pulitzer fountain is in the foreground. (Author's collection)

accompaniment of muffled drums, 300 children dressed in white led this country's first African American civil rights march. The novel protest, organized under the auspices of the National Association for the Advancement of Colored People (NAACP), was prompted by recent race riots. The parade's message was communicated through placards

Ten thousand African American protesters marched silently down Fifth Avenue in a powerful and innovative show of solidarity on July 28, 1917. Several of the placards carried by the marchers questioned why African American troops fighting in Europe to make the world "safe for democracy" were denied basic civil rights at home.

and flyers handed out to spectators by African American Boy Scouts. The protesters marched to 23rd Street.

## SIXTH AVENUE

### 616–632 Sixth Avenue ✦

*Siegel-Cooper Department Store*   An estimated 150,000 people jammed this new store on Saturday night, September 12, 1896. Proclaimed "The Big Store" in its advertising, the 15.5-acre building occupied the entire block. There was once a telegraph office, a nursery, a florist, a hospital, a drugstore, a bank, a photography gallery, and an aviary all inside the store. The store had "all that is between a tenpenny nail and a roast rib of beef to a diamond bracelet and a velvet cape," according to the *New York Times*. After department stores started moving uptown in the beginning of the new century, Siegel-Cooper closed its doors in 1917. Shortly afterward, the building was used by the federal government as a United States Debarkation Hospital for World War I soldiers.

Shoppers crowd in front of Siegel-Cooper on Sixth Avenue between in West 18th and West 19th streets in 1903. The Sixth Avenue elevated, on the left, delivered trainloads of customers to the world's largest department store.

### 641–643 Sixth Avenue ✦

*Simpson, Crawford and Simpson Department Store*   Another dinosaur of a department store left over from the turn of the twentieth century "Ladies' Mile" glory days, this one, which opened in 1900, had one of the first escalators in New York City. The mammoth space came to life again in the early 1990s as this stretch of Sixth Avenue again became a shopping district.

### Sixth Avenue at West 23rd Street, southeast corner

*Edwin Booth's Theater*   America's great thespian Edwin Booth invested his much of his own fortune in this lavish theater, which cost more than a million dollars to build. When it opened in 1869, it was declared the most beautiful playhouse in the city, in addition to being the most modern. The innovative design of the auditorium included an early use of a sunken orchestra pit to improve the view of the stage from all seats. The cost of the theater and early productions forced Booth to declare bankruptcy after just five years. He did stay on as manager and occasional star. Sarah Bernhardt made her American debut here in the play *Adrienne Lecouvreur* on November 8, 1880. Later that month she created her signature role, that of Marguerite Gauthier in *La Dame aux Camelias*, a role she played more than 3,000 times over the next 43 years.

## Sixth Avenue at West 43rd Street, southwest corner

*Hanover House*  In a seedy hotel room on February 23, 1940, folk singer and composer Woody Guthrie wrote his greatest hit, "This Land Is Your Land." In the city for only a few days, Guthrie had worn out his welcome with friends, among them Burl Ives, and was forced to rent a room here. The song was Guthrie's response to Irving Berlin's "God Bless America."

## Sixth Avenue between West 43rd and West 44th streets, east side

*Hippodrome*  New York City's answer to the Roman Colosseum, the Hippodrome, with seating for 5,697 funseekers, opened on April 12, 1905. Frederick Thompson and Elmer Dundy, the creators of the magical Luna Park in Coney Island, built this huge theater. Cary Grant made his American debut on this giant stage in *Good Times* on August 8, 1920. The extravaganzas presented here with hundreds in the cast became expensive and unfashionable, forcing the theater to close in 1939.

## Sixth Avenue between West 47th and West 51st streets, east side

*Elgin Botanical Gardens*  Dr. David Hosack bought 12 acres of land for $4,807.36 at this site in 1802 and established his botanical garden. The doctor, a professor of botany and medicine at Columbia College, used the garden for teaching and raising plants for medicinal purposes. Unable to maintain the garden, he sold the land to New York state, which in turn gave it to Columbia College in 1814. In 1928, this same site, still owned by what had become Columbia University, was leased and developed into a masterpiece of urban planning, Rockefeller Center. In 1985, the university finally sold the 11.7-acre plot on which the center stands to the Rockefeller Group, the family's investment company, for $400 million.

## Sixth Avenue at West 50th Street

*Elevated Platform of the IRT Broadway Local*  On a warm Saturday afternoon, July 23, 1915, while riding the elevated train, Dr. Heinrich Albert, a German attaché, was dozing as he approached this corner, his stop. He jumped up and hurried off. Once on the platform, he realized he had left his briefcase behind. The doctor wasn't the only person interested in that briefcase. So was Frank Burke, a Secret Service agent

"Inside the Earth" was playing at the Hippodrome on Sixth Avenue between West 43rd and 44th streets when this photograph was taken in 1909. The performance featured a boat loaded with travelers sinking to the bottom of the theater's giant water tank. You could view this spectacle from the best seat in the house for a dollar and a half.

who had been following him. Burke picked up the case and took it to his superiors. Inside were details on planned German sabotage strikes against American military installations. After viewing the plans, Secretary of State Robert Lansing weighed the potential threat against the ethically dubious act of having stolen documents from a foreign diplomat. Rather than register a formal government complaint, he had the documents sent to the *New York World*. The resulting embarrassing stories helped edge the American public closer to siding with the Allies against Germany in World War I.

### Sixth Avenue at West 54th Street

Long before there was performance art, there was Moondog. Born Louis T. Hardin and blind since his teens, he was a unique and gifted musician who stood at this and nearby intersections dressed in a robe,

THE ELGIN BOTANIC GARDEN,
between 50th & 51st Sts. and 5th & 6th Aves, 1825

A.Weingartner's Lith. N.Y.                                    for D. T. Valentine's Manual 1859.

Today's Rockefeller Center's Channel Gardens occupies the same location as the earlier Elgin Botanical Gardens. This engraving from about 1811 is of the greenhouse and gardens where Dr. David Hosack grew plants for possible commercial use and herbal remedies. (Author's collection)

sandals, and horned Viking helmet for more than three decades. He was widely admired by a spectrum of musicians for his jazz-like compositions. *All Is Loneliness*, his best-known song, was a melancholy, dirge-like hit recorded by Janis Joplin. After 1974, "the Viking of Sixth Avenue" disappeared and it was assumed he had died, but he had accepted an offer to perform in West Germany and decided to stay there.

## 1335 Sixth Avenue
*New York Hilton Hotel* ✦ On April 3, 1973, outside this hotel, Martin Cooper dialed a phone number into a bulky 2.5-pound box and held it up to his ear. Cooper, a Motorola Company engineer, had just made the first public telephone call placed on a portable cellular phone. His call to a rival at AT&T Bell Laboratories was the beginning of a new era in personal telecommunications; no longer were calls from place to place, but from person to person. After "hanging up" (a term that actually no longer applied), he joined a press conference in the Hilton to introduce the phone.

The NAACP held its centennial convention here in July 2009 in the city where it was founded, a celebration of the organization's contribution to African Americans' strivings for racial equality. They were also justly proud of their guest of honor, President Barack Obama. The President related his personal trials as a black man and exhorted the members of the audience not to excuse any failures to achieve.

## SEVENTH AVENUE

### Seventh Avenue at West 23rd Street

*Subway Station* ✛ Standing among the rush-hour commuters here on June 6, 1966, was a group of undercover U.S. Army technicians conducting secret germ warfare tests. The agents dropped lightbulbs filled with 175 grams of Bacillus subtilis variant Niger on the tracks. Over the next five days, they measured the spread of these relatively harmless bacteria to determine the extent to which a similar biowarfare agent could circulate within the subway system. The report, eventually made public, determined that the dark and windy tunnels were an almost perfect setting for the survival and dissemination of germ agents such as anthrax.

### Seventh Avenue between West 23rd and West 25th streets

Shortly after 8:00 on the morning of September 22, 1915, this stretch of Seventh Avenue was the scene of an accident that killed 25 people. During work on the subway excavation for the construction of the new IRT, an explosion opened up a 30-foot pit in the street that swallowed a crowded trolley car and a brewery truck. The death and injury toll would have been higher but for the fact that the wooden-planked structure gave way slowly, allowing hundreds of people on the street to scramble to solid ground.

### 371 Seventh Avenue ✛

*Hotel Governor Clinton*   On the foggy night of June 12, 1942, four men exited the hatch of a U-202 German submarine 500 yards off the coast of Amagansett, paddled ashore, and took the Long Island Railroad into Manhattan. George Dasch and Ernest Burger checked in to this hotel, now called the Affinia Manhattan. These Nazi would-be saboteurs, along with another cell from a second submarine off the coast of Florida, planned to attack U.S. civilian and military targets. The next day, the two men here decided to abort their mission and confessed to the FBI. All eight conspirators were rounded up, tried, and convicted. Six were executed in the electric chair on August 8, 1942; Dasch and Burger

On September 22, 1915, the wreckage of a trolley car lies in the center of a subway excavation on Seventh Avenue between West 23rd and West 25th streets. This photograph graphically illustrates the "cut and cover" method used to construct the city's subways. A trench was dug down the street, then covered with a temporary wooden platform, which carried the normal street traffic while the construction continued underneath. When the subway was finished, the platform was replaced with a concrete roadway.

were given prison terms. President Harry S. Truman ordered their release in 1948, and they were deported.

## Seventh Avenue between West 31st and West 33rd streets, west side

*Pennsylvania Station* These two blocks were once the site of McKim, Mead and White's greatest masterpiece, Pennsylvania Station. The vast railroad station was modeled on the Roman baths of Caracalla and completed in 1910. In 1963, this impressive gateway to the city was torn down in the interest of modern architecture and greed. Pennsylvania Station died so that other beautiful historical buildings might live: The loss of this monument so galvanized the public that the New York City Landmarks Preservation Commission was created within two years.

*Madison Square Garden Center* ✦ Pennsylvania Station was replaced with a high-rise box accompanied by an equally banal hat box for the Garden's arena, with the railroad station stashed in the basement. The

This was the main waiting room of the old Pennsylvania Station. This magnificent station, the predecessor to the current Penn Station, stood at Seventh Avenue between West 31st and West 33rd streets for only 51 years.

arena was the site for three Democratic Party national conventions, in 1976, 1980, and 1992. The first two nominated Jimmy Carter for President and Walter Mondale for Vice President. The July 1992 convention nominated Bill Clinton for President and Al Gore for Vice President. The Republican Party held its first national party convention in New York City, here, in August 2004. The GOP nominated George W. Bush for President and Dick Cheney for Vice President.

A sad epilogue to the story of architectural loss was the death at this site of Louis I. Kahn. The famous architect died here of a heart attack in the "new" underground station on March 17, 1974. His body was taken to the city morgue, where he remained unidentified for several days. The world learned of this loss only after his wife, in Philadelphia, contacted the New York City police after becoming concerned because he had failed to return home.

### 401 Seventh Avenue ✦

*Hotel Pennsylvania*   The Manhattan Room in this hotel was a favorite with the Big Bands of the 1930s and '40s. The hotel's phone number was immortalized by Glenn Miller in his song "Pennsylvania 6–5000."

Edwin H. Land publicly demonstrated his "instant" picture camera—what eventually became the Polaroid—on February 21, 1947, at the winter meeting of the Optical Society of America here. The sad-eyed inventor was his own subject in an 8-by-10-inch print developed just 50 seconds after it had been exposed.

On November 19, 1953, this hotel was the site of a mysterious tragedy not fully explained for 22 years. On that night Frank Olson, a U.S. Army scientist and germ warfare specialist, jumped through a glass window and fell 10 stories to his death. It was reported as a suicide. In 1975 it was finally revealed that Olson's death was the result of a CIA experiment to study the effects of the drug LSD. The scientist, who was working on the project, codenamed MKULTRA, was an unwitting guinea pig after the drug was slipped into his drink. It was also revealed that the spy agency used prisoners and patrons of brothels set up and run by the agency to test the drug's effects.

## 753 Seventh Avenue

*Earl Carroll Theater*   This was the first of showman Carroll's theaters and the site of a notorious party that resulted in Carroll's serving jail time. At midnight on February 23, 1926, several hundred guests, including Condé Nast and Countess Vera Cathcart, were invited up on stage to fill their glasses from a bathtub filled with champagne and a nude model. Carroll was convicted of perjury (he testified that the tub was full of ginger ale) and spent four months in prison.

## 777 Seventh Avenue +

*Taft Hotel*   Jimmie C. Rodgers, the "father of country music," died at this hotel on May 26, 1933, while in town for a recording session. Rodgers was the first "hillbilly singer" to become a nationwide star as a result of the phenomenal growth of the radio audience in the 1920s.

The Taft was also the site of the death of another entertainer, on September 2, 1955. Actor Philip Loeb was found here, dead from an overdose of sleeping pills. Loeb, a victim of McCarthy-era blacklisting, was broke and despondent after losing his role on the popular television show "The Goldbergs" three years earlier. His career was finished after his name appeared in "Red Channels," a tattle sheet used to rout out possible communists in the entertainment industry. The building is now a cooperative apartment house.

## 787 Seventh Avenue +

*Equitable Center*   The thirty-fifth floor of this high-rise was the scene of a major battle of man versus machine. Garry Kasparov, the world chess champion, played a match with IBM's RS/6000 SP supercomputer, alias Deep Blue. On May 11, 1997, Deep Blue won the sixth and final game to win the match, 3½ to 2½. Advancing technology had finally made the victory inevitable. Deep Blue, with a total of 512 microprocessors working simultaneously, was able to consider 200 million moves per second. Kasparov was only human.

## 834 Seventh Avenue

*Stage Deli* ✦ This longtime home of celebrity sandwiches was also home to three New York Yankees players—Hank Bauer, Johnny Hopp, and Mickey Mantle—in the early 1950s. Their bachelor pad above the deli had just one bedroom with two twin beds and a cot for "the Mick."

## 870 Seventh Avenue

*Park Central Hotel* ✦ This hotel has been the scene of two mob shootouts, almost 30 years apart, neither ever solved. Arnold Rothstein, a gambler and the inspiration for F. Scott Fitzgerald's gangster Meyer Wolfsheim in *The Great Gatsby*, was shot in room 349 on November 4, 1928. Albert Anastasia was murdered in the barber shop of this hotel—then named the Park Sheraton—on October 25, 1957. Anastasia had been a hit man for the mob. A more peaceful demise happened in this hotel on June 29, 1933, when silent-screen comic Roscoe "Fatty" Arbuckle died of a heart attack in his sleep. Arbuckle, the first Hollywood star to make more than a million dollars a year, is infamous for a sex scandal that prompted the "Hays Code" to censor the movies. In spite of his being acquitted of the death of an actress at a party, Arbuckle's career was destroyed.

## 881 Seventh Avenue

*Carnegie Hall Studios* ✦ For more than 100 years, this building has been home and studios for many artists, including John Philip Sousa, Charles Dana Gibson, Isadora Duncan, Agnes De Mille, and Marlon Brando. Enrico Caruso made his first American recordings for the Victor Talking Machine Company in studio 826. The opera star, with a piano accompaniment, recorded 10 sides in a single afternoon on February 1, 1904.

## EIGHTH AVENUE

### Eighth Avenue at West 23rd Street, northwest corner

*Grand Opera House* On January 9, 1869, the opera *Il trovatore* was the opening performance at this theater, originally called Pike's Opera House. New owners Jay Gould and Jim Fisk, infamous stock market

As depicted shortly after its opening in 1868, the lavish Pike's Opera House once stood on the corner of Eighth Avenue and West 23rd Street. After 92 years, it was one of the longest-continuing venues in New York theater history. Built to perform operas, it was also a stage, vaudeville, and motion picture theater. (*Harper's Weekly*, January 25, 1868)

manipulators, changed the name the following year and used the upper floors for their offices. Fisk's funeral was held in his office in 1872 after he was shot by a jealous rival. In 1904 this same building housed a dancing school attended by five-year-old Fred Austerlitz, later known as Fred Astaire. The building burned down in 1960.

### Eighth Avenue at West 24th Street

In spite of threats of violence, the annual Orange Society Parade marched on Eighth Avenue on July 12, 1871. The parade celebrated the anniversary of the 1690 Battle of Boyne, when the Irish Protestants triumphed over the Irish Catholics. Understandably, this parade was unpopular with the city's large population of Irish Catholic immigrants. More than 800 policemen and 2,200 state militiamen were assigned to protect the marchers. As the procession passed West 24th Street, snipers from tenement windows fired into the crowd. Regiments within the

Based on an eyewitness account, this newspaper engraving recorded the gunfire during the Orange Society Parade on Eighth Avenue between West 23rd and West 24th streets. On July 12, 1871, the ensuing riot between Catholics and Protestant Irish immigrants and the police resulted in 47 deaths and many injuries (*Harper's Weekly*, July 29, 1871)

parade, the police, and the militia returned fire. When the shooting stopped, there were 47 casualties. The *Irish World* newspaper called the debacle the "SLAUGHTER ON EIGHTH AVENUE."

### Eighth Avenue between West 31st and West 33rd streets, west side

*General Post Office* ✦ Opened on Labor Day 1914, this formidable edifice designed by McKim, Mead and White has never once shut its doors. On April 29, 1919, while reading a newspaper story about a package bomb on his subway ride home, postal clerk Charles Caplan realized he had set aside several similar packages earlier that day. He rushed back, found them, and notified his supervisors. His timely intervention prevented bombs from being delivered to 16 new victims, including several presidential cabinet members, J. P. Morgan, John D. Rockefeller, and Supreme Court Justice Oliver Wendell Holmes Jr. The unknown terrorist, most likely an alien radical, had mailed a total of 36 bombs.

A far happier mail diversion takes place here every Christmas season. In the 1920s, several employees rescued a few "Dear Santa" letters from the dead letter office and used their own money to answer as many needy requests as possible. Now called "Operation Santa," run by volunteers, and financed by donations, the program receives more than 150,000 letters during the holidays.

Plans for transforming this grand building into a new station, to be named for the late Senator Daniel Patrick Moynihan, have been delayed for more than 20 years.

### 481 Eighth Avenue ✦

*Hotel New Yorker*  One of America's most memorable advertising slogans was born in the lobby of this hotel in April 1933. Ad man Milton Biow "discovered" bellhop Johnny Roventini, an ideal cigarette spokesperson. The Brooklyn-born Roventini's perfect B-flat pitch yell "Call for Philip Morris" was an immediate hit with radio listeners. His diminutive stature (43 inches tall at age 22) and black pillbox hat along with his spiffy scarlet jacket with brass buttons were perfect for print advertisements and later television commercials.

Master inventor Nikola Tesla was found dead in room 3327 here on January 7, 1943. Tesla, the holder of 700 patents, invented the first practical application of alternating electrical current. The 86-year-old inventor died an impoverished eccentric, a hermit who spent the last years of his life feeding the pigeons on the steps of the New York Public Library and at St. Patrick's Cathedral.

### 782 Eighth Avenue

New York City society was shocked by the murder of Civil War hero Major General Franz Sigel's granddaughter. The body of 22-year-old Elsie Sigel was found here in a trunk in a furnished room above Sun Leung's chop suey restaurant on June 18, 1909. She had been murdered by her Chinese lover, Leon Ling; the two had met while Elsie was active in missionary work in Chinatown. The case and the ensuing publicity inflamed "Yellow peril" bigotry. Ling disappeared and was never brought to trial, but the police, under public pressure, did crack down on the violent tongs, the Chinatown gangs.

### Eighth Avenue between West 49th and West 50th streets

*Madison Square Garden*  This was the site of the second, grittier Madison Square Garden, from 1925 to 1966, home to many smoky boxing matches and New York Rangers hockey games. On May 19, 1962, President John F. Kennedy's forty-fifth-birthday party was held here as part

On June 18, 1909, the strangled body of Elsie Sigel was found in a trunk in the top-floor apartment of Leon Ling at 782 Eighth Avenue. The police also discovered 35 love letters from Sigel to Ling.

of a Democratic Party fundraiser. More than 20,000 guests paid $1,000 a ticket to celebrate and see entertainers Harry Belafonte, Jimmy Durante, and Ella Fitzgerald. The unexpected highlight of the evening was Marilyn Monroe's breathy version of "Happy Birthday" to the President.

### 829 Eighth Avenue

Here were the offices for the *New York Morning Telegraph*. The one-time sheriff of Dodge City, William "Bat" Masterson, died at his desk of a heart attack on October 26, 1921. The lawman-turned-sportswriter had worked for this paper for more than 10 years.

## 851 Eighth Avenue ✦

*Howard Johnson Motor Lodge*   The FBI arrested fugitive Angela Davis outside her room on the seventh floor of this hotel on October 13, 1970, where she had been hiding for more than two months. She was wanted on kidnapping and murder charges.

## 987 Eighth Avenue

*Reisenweber's Restaurant*   The restaurant and dance club that long ago stood at Columbus Circle has earned an illustrious footnote in the history of jazz. Jazz, America's uniquely native music form, developed and nurtured by African Americans in the South during the latter half of the nineteenth century, was new to Northern white audiences until The Original Dixieland Jass Band debuted here on January 26, 1917. This unlikely all-white band named with an early spelling of the word "jazz" created a musical frenzy. Within a matter of days, Columbia had the group record "Darktown Strutter's Ball" and "Indiana," the first phonograph recording of a jazz band. The ODJB, as they were later called, also made a record for Columbia's rival, the Victor Company, in February. That recording of "Livery Stable Blues," led by cornet player Nick LaRocca, had the distinction of outselling Columbia's record and earned the claim of the first jazz band record to be released.

## NINTH AVENUE

## 75 Ninth Avenue ✦

*National Biscuit Company*   This block-long bakery was the 1912 birthplace of the first Oreo, the bestselling cookie in the United States. Nabisco moved to New Jersey in 1958. In 1997, the building became home to the Chelsea Market and several television studios.

## 280 Ninth Avenue ✦

Civil rights leader A. Philip Randolph, a founder of the first all–African American union, the Brotherhood of Sleeping Car Porters, lived here. In 1937, his union's collective bargaining agreement with the powerful Pullman Company was a significant turning point not only for the union's railroad porters, maids, and cooks but also for the entire African American community. Randolph died here at the age of 90 on May 16, 1979.

**Ninth Avenue between West 33rd and West 34th streets, east side**

*New York Institution for the Blind*   A 17-year-old Grover Cleveland accepted a position as assistant teacher at this school in the fall of 1853. The future President taught the younger students reading, writing, arithmetic, and geography here for one year.

## TENTH AVENUE

### Tenth Avenue at West 30th Street

*Hudson River Railway Depot*   On August 26, 1871, the corpse of a woman was found by the railway baggage master at this long-ago station. A few days later, the body was identified as that of Alice Augusta Bowlsby, an unmarried dressmaker from New Jersey who had died during a botched abortion performed by Jacob Rosenszweig, alias Dr. Ascher. Reported in sensational detail by the press, his subsequent trial and the public outrage led New York state to make causing the death of a woman or a fetus a felony. The rest of the country followed suit and these laws remained unchanged until abortion was decriminalized.

## EAST 15TH STREET

### 109 East 15th Street

*Century Club*   Auguste Bartholdi spoke here on January 2, 1877, to raise money for erecting the pedestal for his *Liberty Enlightening the World*, popularly known as the Statue of Liberty. The statue was a gift to the United States from the people of France, but the base was not included.

### 234 East 15th Street

Artist William Merritt Chase died here at his home on October 25, 1916, at the age of 68.

## WEST 15TH STREET

### 123 West 15th Street +

Martha Held, who rented this brownstone in 1912, was a popular German opera singer. The house was also a hotbed of German sabotage in the years before World War I. German sea captains, spies, and even the German ambassador to the United States, Count Johann von Bernstorff, visited here to exchange information and plot against U.S. involvement in the war. Plans were hatched here to blow up the Black Tom

Island munitions plant, the greatest act of foreign sabotage ever perpetrated on American soil up to that time.

### 308 West 15th Street

Around 1895, two rooms at this residence were home to painter Albert P. Ryder. The reclusive and eccentric symbolist artist lived here in squalor for 15 years.

## EAST 16TH STREET

### East 16th Street at Irving Place, northwest corner

*Westminster Hotel*  In 1876, a group of dog lovers met at the hotel that once stood on this corner to form the Westminster Kennel Club. Since that first dog show in May 1877 at Gilmore's Gardens, the club has had more than 130 annual shows. The Westminster show, named in honor of the hotel, is second only to the Kentucky Derby as the oldest continuously held sporting event in America.

### East 16th Street east of Avenue C

*Willard Parker Hospital for Contagious Diseases*  Typhoid Mary, the infamous chronic typhoid carrier, born Mary Mallon, was forcibly taken here by police for tests on March 19, 1907. Mary, once called "the most dangerous woman in America," was eventually quarantined by the health authorities for causing at least 53 cases of typhoid and three deaths. Dr. George Soper, an epidemiologist responsible for tracing the illness to Mary, later identified her as the most likely cause of more than 1,400 cases in Ithaca, New York, four years earlier. While working as a cook she had inadvertently infected her employers and their families. She was kept in almost complete quarantine for the next 30 years until her death on November 11, 1938. She died in a little cottage the city provided for her on North Brother Island, near Rikers Island.

## WEST 16TH STREET

### 17 West 16th Street ✦

From 1930 to 1973 this New York City–landmarked Greek Revival–style town house with the unusual bowed front was the famed Margaret Sanger Clinic for family planning. The house sits on land that was part of the seventeenth-century farm owned by Simon Congo, a free African American.

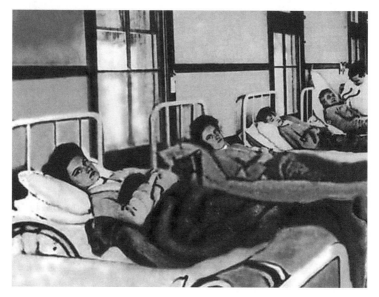

Mary Mallon, aka Typhoid Mary (*left*), lies in her hospital bed while quarantined for the first time in 1907. She was released on the condition she would not return to work as a cook. After breaking her promise, she was quarantined for the rest of her life.

### 24 West 16th Street ✛

Poet and editor William Cullen Bryant died here at his home on June 12, 1878. Margaret Anderson, the editor of the *Little Review*, lived in this same house in 1917.

### 41 West 16th Street ✛

A one-bedroom apartment on the ground floor of this building was home to songwriter Joni Mitchell in the mid-1960s, and it was here that she wrote her ode to the neighborhood, "Chelsea Morning." The country's first Baby Boomer President, Bill Clinton, a Mitchell fan, was inspired by the song to name his only daughter Chelsea.

### 51 West 16th Street ✛

On January 20, 1920, the American Civil Liberties Union was formed here to preserve and extend individual rights granted in the U.S. Constitution, specifically those enumerated in the Bill of Rights. The ACLU, the successor to a group opposed to U.S. entry into World War I, has been involved in many influential legal cases: the Sacco and Vanzetti, Scopes, and "Scottsboro Boys" trials; *Brown v. Board of Education*; and their most controversial effort, defending the right of a neo-Nazi group to march in Skokie, Illinois, home to a significant number of Jews. Their first director was Roger Baldwin, whose devotion to pacifism and human rights earned him the Presidential Medal of Freedom in 1981. He died that same year at age 97.

## EAST 17TH STREET

### East 17th Street at Park Avenue South, northwest corner

*Everett House Hotel*   This hotel was popular with entertainers employed in the Union Square theater district. But on election night of November 7, 1876, it was filled with Democratic Party politicians, here to celebrate the election as President of Samuel J. Tilden, New York governor and Gramercy Park neighbor. It was not to be. In an election widely regarded as having been stolen, Tilden won 250,000 more popular votes than his Republican opponent, Ohio Governor Rutherford B. Hayes, but he lost in the Electoral College. A commission with a majority of Republican members declared Hayes the winner. This was the closest presidential election in U.S. history until the election of 2000.

### 122 East 17th Street ✦

Erroneously called the "Washington Irving House," this corner house was home to Elsie de Wolf from 1894 to 1911. This one-time actress, with help from Stanford White and her society friends, became America's first modern interior decorator. Famous for her simple white interiors, she offered a radical design alternative to the busy Victorian clutter of the period. De Wolf lived and worked here with her longtime companion, Bessie Marbury, one of America's first literary agents. Marbury's most famous client, Oscar Wilde, lived in the house next door during an American tour. De Wolf and Marbury were notorious for their grand parties where society and the arts met.

### 327 East 17th Street

A four-story town house that once stood here was home to Antonín Dvořák from 1892 to 1895. The conductor had come to America to be the director of the National Conservatory of Music. While at this address he wrote his "New World Symphony." After an extended battle to save the house, including an appeal from Václav Havel, then the president of the Czech Republic, Beth Israel Medical Center razed the building for the Robert Mapplethorpe Residence, an AIDS hospice built with the help of the late photographer's foundation.

## WEST 17TH STREET

### 194 West 17th Street

Lola Montez, a performer who was the one-time mistress of Ludwig I of Bavaria, spent the last few months of her life in a barely furnished room at this address. She had suffered a stroke and died here on January 17, 1861. The once-great beauty was just 42 years old.

### 305 West 17th Street

This was the home of Charles Murphy, master machine politician and head of Tammany Hall. A power to be reckoned with, he orchestrated the election of several mayors, senators, and governors, including Alfred E. Smith. He also managed to destroy several political careers. His Tammany machine used fraudulent ballots to defeat newspaper mogul William Randolph Hearst's mayoral candidacy in 1905. Murphy died here on April 25, 1924.

ENTHUSIASTIC RECEPTION OF LOLA BY AN AMERICAN AUDIENCE.

Preceded by her reputation, Lola Montez scandalized New Yorkers with her erotic "spider" dance. Irish-born Eliza Rosanna Gilbert was given the title Countess of Landsfeld by her lover Ludwig I of Bavaria but used her stage name Lola Montez for her mediocre act.

## EAST 18TH STREET

### 78 East 18th Street
E. P. Christy, the founder of Christy's Minstrels, the popular forerunner of early minstrel shows, died here at his home on May 21, 1862, as a result of injuries he sustained in a suicidal jump from a second-story window into the back yard earlier in the month.

### 129 East 18th Street
*Pete's Tavern* ✦ Opened in 1864, this neighborhood institution bills itself as the oldest continuously operating bar in New York City. During Prohibition it was a speakeasy pretending to be a florist shop; thirsty customers would enter through a refrigerator in the back. Two beloved writers spent time here. A plaque above the front booth identifies the spot where O. Henry spent a great deal of time drinking while writing some of his short stories at the beginning of the twentieth century. Ludwig Bemelmans wrote the first lines of *Madeline*, his children's story, on the back of a menu one evening in 1938.

### 136 East 18th Street
One of the city's greatest treasures, Central Park, was conceived and planned in the parlor of a town house that once stood at this address. It was the home of Calvert Vaux, the landscape designer, who with his friend and partner Frederick Law Olmsted mapped out their design for the park during the fall and winter of 1857. The team's winning "Greensward Plan" almost missed the April 1, 1858, deadline and was the last entrant submitted to the judges.

### 142 East 18th Street
*Stuyvesant Apartments* The five-story building designed by architect Richard Morris Hunt that once stood at this address was considered the first true apartment house in the United States. Called "French flats" at the time it was built in 1869, the Stuyvesant helped make apartment living acceptable to middle-class Americans, particularly widows and young couples. Up to this time, multiple-family housing was considered shocking by polite society because it offered no more privacy or propriety than the tenements occupied by the poor.

## EAST 19TH STREET

### 28 East 19th Street
Actor Edwin Booth lived at this address from 1862 to 1865. His brother John Wilkes Booth, the assassin of Abraham Lincoln, often stayed here while visiting New York.

### 35 East 19th Street ✦

This altered town house was the home of journalist Horace Greeley from 1850 to 1853. He was the editor and publisher of the *New York Tribune* while living at this address.

### 132 East 19th Street ✦

This address has been home to many of America's greatest actresses. Mrs. Patrick Campbell, Theda Bara, Helen Hayes, Ethel Barrymore, and the Gish sisters, Dorothy and Lillian, all lived here (at different times) in this seven-story studio building.

### 139 East 19th Street ✦

Frederick Sterner, an English-born architect, bought this plain brick house and transformed it and eventually the rest of the block into a charming enclave of Mediterranean-style homes. Between Irving Place and Third Avenue, 19th Street is the New York City–landmarked "block beautiful" because of Sterner's efforts early in the twentieth century. After decorating his house with stucco, tiles, and ironwork, he bought other houses and did the same. A sanctuary for picturesque architecture, the block has also attracted writers and actors.

### 146 East 19th Street ✦

Artist George Bellows bought this house in 1910 and lived here until his death in 1925. Bellows, who learned carpentry and bricklaying from his father, raised the roof of this house eight feet and made improvements to his studio here. Bellows and his wife, Emma, often entertained friends, such as playwright Eugene O'Neill, radical Emma Goldman, and writer John Reed, here.

### 151 East 19th Street ✦

*Gramercy Park Apartments* ✦ Carl Van Vechten, music critic for the *New York Times*–turned–novelist, lived in the top-floor apartment of this building, beginning in 1914. A leader in the Harlem Renaissance movement, he was also a legendary Jazz Age giver of parties. Among his guests were music greats George Gershwin and Bessie Smith.

## EAST 20TH STREET

### 28 East 20th Street ✦

Theodore Roosevelt, the only New York City native to be elected President, was born at this address on October 27, 1858, and lived here until the age of 15. The original Gothic Revival four-story town house was demolished in 1916. Six years later, the building was replicated by Theodate Pope Riddle, the first woman architect in the United States and a survivor of the sinking of the *Lusitania*. Roosevelt's sisters and his widow (who had known him as a child) furnished the rooms to represent his boyhood home.

In 1922, three years after Theodore Roosevelt's death, his birthplace was reconstructed on its original site at 28 East 20th Street. As a child, the future President exercised in a top-floor gym to strengthen his lungs and overcome his asthma. (Author's collection)

### 52 East 20th Street

In 1855, this address was the home of Alice and Phoebe Cary. These sisters, both poets, held Sunday evening receptions for literary figures and social reformers of the day. John Greenleaf Whittier, Susan B. Anthony, and Horace Greeley all joined in the animated discussions.

### 235 East 20th Street

*New York Police Academy* ✦ After the evacuation of the city's emergency command center at 7 World Trade Center on the morning of September 11, 2001, officials were desperate to find a new base of operations from which to respond to the disaster. Beginning at Ground Zero, Mayor Rudolph W. Giuliani rushed on foot uptown, rejecting several possible sites along the way, including the Tribeca Grand Hotel and a fire station. By noon, it was decided to set up operations here at the Academy. For the next three days, authorities coordinated the city, state, and federal aid, evacuated lower Manhattan, and began the search and recovery effort at the World Trade Center site.

## WEST 20TH STREET

### 20–22 West 20th Street

This was the home of Bradley Martin, a wealthy businessman, and his society-leader wife, who gave what was reputed to be the most lavish party in modern times. After the Martins' much-criticized ball at the Waldorf Hotel on February 10, 1897, the city reassessed the value of this home and doubled the taxes. The embarrassed family moved to England.

### 42 West 20th Street

Two-time president of Venezuela and later dictator General José Antonio Páez died here at his home on May 6, 1873.

### 333 West 20th Street ✦

On November 5, 1938, painter Thomas Wilmer Dewing died here at his home at the age of 87. His paintings of solitary women lost in thought were popular in the early years of the twentieth century.

### West 20th Street at the Hudson River

*Chelsea Piers* ✦ Now home to a huge sports and entertainment complex, these piers were originally designed to dock the White Star Line's transatlantic ocean liners. The *Titanic*, the world's most famous ship, never arrived as scheduled on April 17, 1912. Instead, desperate crowds gathered here hoping for any news of their friends and family aboard the lost ship.

## EAST 21ST STREET

### 41 East 21st Street
In 1901 this address was a movie studio for Thomas Edison's early film company. The interior scenes for the 1903 classic *The Great Train Robbery* were filmed in this sky-lighted brownstone, the country's first indoor motion picture studio. This 12-minute action Western was the fledgling movie industry's first hit; it remained the most famous and profitable film until *The Birth of a Nation* in 1915. Edwin Stanton Porter, the director of *The Great Train Robbery* and many other pioneer films, recruited his movie stars at nearby Union Square, which was a popular hangout for unemployed stage actors. New York City was the center of the American film industry until early studios moved to the West Coast around the time of World War I.

## WEST 21ST STREET

### 30 West 21st Street ✛
*Danceteria*   Pop star Madonna's big break into show business happened at this one-time disco in the winter of 1982. Her then-boyfriend, club disc jockey Mark Karmin, played her demo recording of *Everybody* to an enthusiastic crowd, which led to a recording contract. Four years earlier, the 19-year-old Midwesterner had arrived in New York with very little money but a great deal of ambition.

## WEST 22ND STREET

### 5 West 22nd Street
This address was the last home of Samuel F.B. Morse, painter and inventor of the telegraph. As he lay dying, his doctor tapped him on the chest. "This is how we doctors telegraph," he said. "Very good," said Morse, speaking his last words. He died here on April 2, 1872.

## EAST 23RD STREET

### East 23rd Street at Park Avenue South
After coming ashore during the Revolutionary War Battle of Kips Bay, the advancing British forces chased the retreating revolutionaries inland toward this spot. It was roughly at the site of this present-day intersection that one detachment of Hessians captured 300 soldiers.

### East 23rd Street at Lexington Avenue

On May 20, 1899, Jacob German became the first person in the United States arrested for speeding in an automobile. Traveling along at 12 miles per hour, he was stopped by a bicycle-riding police officer. The 26-year-old German was the first in a long line of New York City taxi drivers in a hurry.

### 145 East 23rd Street

*Kenmore Hall Hotel* ✛ This hotel, a haven for drug dealers and prostitutes, was seized by federal agents and New York City police in a morning raid on June 8, 1994. The takeover by authorities represented the largest seizure ever made by the government of a building being used to sell narcotics. In 1926, writer Nathanael West worked here as a night manager, often supplying free rooms to his friends Dashiell Hammett and Maxwell Bodenheim and West's brother-in-law S. J. Perelman.

## WEST 23RD STREET

### 14 West 23rd Street ✛

This address was the birthplace of novelist Edith Wharton in January 1862. The present structure has been greatly altered.

### 165 West 23rd Street ✛

Writer Stephen Crane lived on the top floor of this brownstone from 1895 to 1896. The top floor was also the first New York City home of painter John Sloan from September 1904 to 1911. He used his expansive view of the city as subject matter for many of his paintings.

### 206 West 23rd Street ✛

Singer Patti Smith and artist Robert Mapplethorpe rented studio space in a loft at this address to work on their nascent art careers. By the spring of 1970, they were also living here. Smith and Mapplethorpe stayed here together for about two years.

### 222 West 23rd Street

*Chelsea Hotel* ✛ From its opening in 1884 as a pioneering cooperative apartment house to its present status as a hotel for the aspiring avant-garde, this imposing edifice has always been popular with actors, authors, artists, and musicians. A favorite with Sarah Bernhardt, the Victorian Gothic–style hotel has also been home to Thomas Wolfe, Dylan Thomas, Arthur Miller, William Burroughs, Jefferson Airplane, Bob Dylan, Patti Smith, Robert Mapplethorpe, and others. It was the setting for Andy Warhol's underground movie *Chelsea Girls* in 1966. On October 12, 1978, it was also the setting for the murder of Nancy Spungen. The 20-year-old was stabbed once in the stomach by her British musician boyfriend, Sid Vicious (né John Simon Ritchie).

## West 23rd Street between Ninth and Tenth avenues

*Chelsea Mansion*　Just south of present-day West 23rd Street was once the site of the ancestral home and birthplace, on July 15, 1781, of Clement Clarke Moore. Moore, a professor of Greek and Oriental literature at the nearby General Theological Seminary and author of the nineteenth century's primary Hebrew dictionary, is now known chiefly as the poet of "A Visit from St. Nicholas," later called "The Night Before Christmas," recited here for the first time during the holidays in 1822. The cherished poem, created for his six children, initiated the timing of Santa's nocturnal visit on December 24—not December 5, the eve of St. Nicholas's Day, as had been the tradition. It also helped improve Santa's image from a stern saint into a jolly old soul. The estate was subdivided and the mansion was demolished in 1854. Moore moved to a house, also now gone, on the southwest corner of West 23rd Street and Ninth Avenue that he shared with his daughter.

## 450 West 23rd Street +

James B. Moore, grandson of Clement Clarke Moore, once owned this house. A wealthy lawyer and patron of the arts, he befriended artists John Sloan, Everett Shinn, and George Luks at the turn of the twentieth century. Moore was the subject of William Glacken's 1905 *Chez Mouguin*, now at the Art Institute of Chicago. Moore's generosity extended to poet Edwin Arlington Robinson, who lived here from 1901 to 1905. The poet, who described his attic room as "my old cell," was living here when "Captain Craig" was published.

## 465 West 23rd Street

*The New School for Social Reseach*　This address was one of six rented brownstones that were the first home of the New School. In 1919, several members of Columbia University, among them Charles Beard, Thorstein Veblen, and John Dewey, founded the New School as an alternative to more traditional college education. In the 1930s it became a haven for the intelligentsia fleeing Nazi Germany, a "university in exile." Some of America's greatest minds have taught or lectured here over the years, among them W. E. B. Du Bois, Margaret Mead, John Maynard Keynes, Edward Albee, W. H. Auden, Robert Frost, Aaron

Copland, Lewis Mumford, Maya Angelou, Arthur Miller, Isaac Bashevis Singer, and Susan Sontag.

## EAST 24TH STREET

### 155 East 24th Street

*RCA Victor Studios*  Offices for RCA's record division moved to this address in 1929. Musical performers as varied as John McCormack, Marian Anderson, Harry Belafonte, and Perry Como have used recording studios here. Elvis Presley recorded some of his biggest hits, including "Don't Be Cruel" and "Hound Dog," here on July 2, 1956. The building was replaced by Baruch College's academic complex in 1998.

## WEST 24TH STREET

### 22 West 24th Street

This address was once Stanford White's favorite hideaway for his legendary trysts, complete with a room entirely covered with mirrors and another with a red velvet swing. It was here that the architect brought the 16-year-old Evelyn Nesbit for the first time, in 1901. This affair with the beautiful showgirl would cost White his life. Five years later, he was shot by Nesbit's crazed husband, Harry K. Thaw, who had married her well after her relationship with White had ended. In the trial, it was revealed that White would suggest that his guests "see [his] drawings and etchings," kept here. This mock-seductive invitation "to come up and see my etchings" became a popular line with aspiring playboys for decades after this revelation.

### 47 West 24th Street

*Martz Hotel*  This hotel, now gone, was the first New York City home of William Sydney Porter, in 1902. He had just been released from an Ohio prison, serving time for bank fraud, which accounts for his taking a pseudonym—O. Henry. It was here in his beloved adopted home, the city he called "Baghdad on the Subway," that he began his tremendously successful career as a writer of short stories.

## EAST 25TH STREET

### East 25th Street at Madison Avenue, northeast corner

*Appellate Division Courthouse* ✦ Fittingly, this exuberant gem of a courthouse was the site of a great legal victory in historic preservation. On December 16, 1975, the Appellate Division of the Supreme Court of

Before she was a chorus girl and Gilded Age celebrity, Evelyn Nesbit was a favorite model of artists and photographers. This portrait was taken by Gertrude Kasebier around 1900.

New York State, First Judicial Department, upheld the constitutionality of the state's law on the preservation of landmarks. The Penn Central railroad had argued that the New York City Landmarks Preservation Commission did not have the authority to deny the railroad the right to build a skyscraper over Grand Central Terminal and lost. The case went to the U.S. Supreme Court, which upheld the Appellate Court's decision, a decisive victory for the nation's historic properties.

## WEST 25TH STREET

### 1 West 25th Street

*New York Club* On the night of March 12, 1888, an exhausted Roscoe Conkling collapsed in the lobby of this club after an arduous trek from his Wall Street office during the Blizzard of 1888, the worst snowstorm in New York's history. The former U.S. congressman, senator, and White House aspirant reached this address after a three-hour ordeal that included his being trapped for 20 minutes in a Union Square snow drift. He died several weeks later, on April 18, as a result of exposure. He became the most famous victim of the blizzard, which claimed an estimated 400 lives in the Northeast. A statue of Conkling was to be placed in Union Square near the spot where he struggled in the snow, but it was placed instead at the southeast corner of Madison Square Park.

### 49 West 25th Street

General John Charles Frémont died here in a boarding house he owned, on July 13, 1890. Frémont, also known as the "Pathfinder" because of his

The front page of *Frank Leslie's Illustrated Newspaper* depicts people struggling in Printing-House Square during the Blizzard of 1888. The freakish spring storm, which lasted about 24 hours, generated 60-miles-per-hour winds, 21 inches of snow, and 5-degree temperatures.

Western surveys, was the Republican Party's first presidential candidate, in 1856, and a Union general during the Civil War.

## 57 West 25th Street

*Chimney Corner Hall* A house that once stood on this corner was a gathering place for Puerto Rican exiles. The group, attached to the Cuban Revolutionary Party, advocated for Puerto Rico's and Cuba's independence from Spain. What is now the official flag of Puerto Rico was unveiled here on December 22, 1895.

## EAST 26TH STREET

### 32 East 26th Street

This southwest-corner site was once the home of Leonard Jerome, the financier and society leader, who built his palatial six-story Second Empire–style mansion here in 1859. The huge second-floor ballroom was the scene of many of the era's most elegant parties. Around the corner on 26th Street, Jerome built a 600-seat private theater for his guests. Jennie Jerome, his daughter, who lived in this house from 1860 to 1867, married Randolph Churchill and was the mother of British Prime Minister Winston Churchill. In 1868, it became the home of the Union League Club, which had been formed to help raise troops for the Union Army in the early years of the Civil War.

### 104 East 26th Street

This armory, built in 1906, replaced a yellow brick house that was once the home of Herman Melville. Long forgotten and misunderstood by the readers of his day, Melville's last popular novel was *Typee*, written in 1846. He finished his manuscript of *Billy Budd* three months before dying here just after midnight on September 28, 1891. His wife, Elizabeth, considering *Typee* unfinished, packed it away. It wasn't discovered and published until 1924.

## WEST 26TH STREET

### 37–41 West 26th Street

*Miller's Hotel* A physically and mentally deteriorating Mary Todd Lincoln checked into this spa/hotel in October 1882. The former First Lady hoped to relieve her back problems. The hotel offered Turkish, electric, and Roman baths to relieve aches and pains. Louisa May Alcott also visited here, in the fall of 1875, when the spa was named the Bath Hotel.

Leonard Jerome built the mansion at the corner of Madison Avenue and East 25th Street just before the Civil War. Jerome, the "King of Wall Street," made his fortune as a stock speculator.

## EAST 28TH STREET

### 4 East 28th Street

*Hotel Latham* ✚ Ninety-nine-year-old photographer William Henry Jackson was living here when he fell and injured himself on June 26, 1942. His photographs, shown to members of Congress in 1872, were vital in the creation of Yellowstone, the country's first national park. The "grand old man of the National Parks" died four days later at Midtown Hospital and was buried in the National Cemetery in Arlington, Virginia.

On June 21, 1957, the FBI arrested the guest in room 839. William Fischer, alias Rudolf Abel, was a Soviet spy. He was tried and sentenced to life in prison. On February 10, 1962, he was exchanged for captured American Francis Gary Powers, the U-2 pilot shot down over the Soviet Union.

### 149 East 28th Street

*Church of St. Stephen Roman Catholic*   The funeral Mass of Louis Moreau Gottschalk was held at this church on October 3, 1870. An overflowing crowd of mourners was here to pay respects to the concert pianist, who had died the previous year on December 18, 1869, while on tour in Rio de Janeiro, Brazil. Gottschalk was the first American composer to achieve international recognition. Later that afternoon his body made its final journey to Brooklyn's Green-Wood Cemetery.

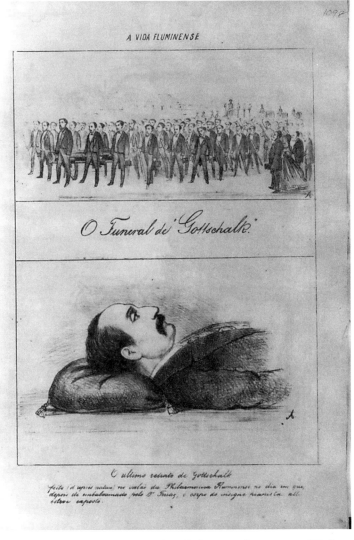

Largely forgotten today, Louis Moreau Gottschalk was a major composer of his time. Here he lies in state in Brazil before his return to New York ten months later for funeral services at Church of the Transfiguration on October 3, 1870.

## WEST 28TH STREET

### West 28th Street between Fifth Avenue and Broadway
This block of West 28th Street is known as the legendary Tin Pan Alley, the turn-of-the-twentieth-century's center of the sheet music business. Many of America's great composers, including Jerome Kern, George Gershwin, and Irving Berlin, began their illustrious careers creating popular songs on this block. Tin Pan Alley reached the peak of its influence around 1917; during that year more than 2 million copies of sheet music were sold. Soon after, the development of radio and the movies radically changed how songs were produced, and New York's share of the music business moved uptown to 46th Street and Broadway.

### 27–31 West 28th Street
*Fifth Avenue Theater*   The world premiere of Gilbert and Sullivan's *The Pirates of Penzance* was held at this theater on New Year's Eve 1879. A single performance had been staged the day before in England. The two "openings" were designed to prevent the opera from being pirated, a common occurrence because of lax international copyright laws. Arthur Sullivan conducted the orchestra and William S. Gilbert was in the audience for the sold-out performance here. An office building now occupies the site.

## EAST 29TH STREET

### 1 East 29th Street
*Church of the Transfiguration* ✦ In 1870, while searching for a church at which to conduct the funeral services for actor George Holland, his friend and fellow actor Joseph Jefferson was turned away by a pastor from a tony congregation who suggested they try "the little church around the corner where the matter might be arranged." Known since as the Little Church Around the Corner, it become a favorite of New York thespians. In addition to Holland's funeral, the church was the site of services for actors Edwin Booth, James William Wallack and his son John Lester Wallack, and Richard Mansfield.

## EAST 30TH STREET

### 323 East 30th Street
The home of sculptor Louise Nevelson was at this site from 1943 to 1959. In the garden she created sculptures of painted wood scraps and

found objects which she called "farm" assemblages. She sold the four-story town house to the developers of the current buildings, the Kips Bay Plaza apartment complex.

## WEST 30TH STREET

### 137 West 30th Street
*29th Precinct Police Station*   Station Commander Alexander Williams originated the term "Tenderloin" for this neighborhood in 1876. After he learned of his transfer here, he exclaimed: "Ah, fine, my boy, fine. It's been chuck steak for me; it'll be tenderloin now." Williams was anticipating his share of graft from prostitution and gambling in the neighborhood.

On December 14, 1882, a humiliated Oscar Wilde rushed into this police station, asking to see the captain on duty. He explained that he had just been swindled out of $1,000. The English author, on an American lecture tour, had been approached on Broadway by a young man who suggested lunch and a game of dice. Before he realized it, he was deeply in debt to the other players. Later, Wilde was unable to locate the town house where the gambling took place, but he did manage to identify, with the help of mug shots, one of the men involved, a notorious con artist known as "Hungry Joe" Sellick. The Board of Health eventually condemned the building, and the station moved across the street to the current New York City–landmarked building in 1908.

## WEST 32ND STREET

### 38 West 32nd Street
This address was once home to Commodore Matthew C. Perry, the naval officer who opened Japan to Western trade. In 1855 he moved into the house that once stood here and died here three years later on March 4, 1858, at age 63.

## WEST 33RD STREET

### 35 West 33rd Street
*Major's Cabin Grill*   While dining in this restaurant, New York lawyer Frank X. McNamara realized he was short of cash and unable to pay his bill. His embarrassment led to his creation of a new enterprise, the Diner's Club. His new company, allowing members to pay for meals on credit, gave birth to the modern credit card. A few months after the

founding in February 1950, McNamara returned here for a congratulatory meal and executed the company's first transaction.

## EAST 34TH STREET

### East 34th Street between First and Second avenues
Here was once the original shoreline of the East River in the eighteenth century, and on Sunday morning, September 15, 1776, it was the site of the Battle of Kips Bay. In a ditch above that rocky beach, a contingent of American troops waited for the British troops to begin their attack. Offshore in the East River were five British ships and about 80 flatboats loaded with more than 4,000 Redcoats. About 11:00, the ships' guns opened fire on the beach. After two hours of bombardment, the British landed and overpowered the remaining Americans defenders. Generals George Washington and Israel Putnam tried to rally their troops, but the patriots were forced to flee before the oncoming British.

## WEST 34TH STREET

### 1 West 34th Street
After tearing down the showplace of the "Sarsaparilla King," Dr. J. C. Townsend, department store magnate A. T. Stewart built his fabled palace on this corner site for his wife, Cornelia. After it was completed in 1867, he filled it with paintings—a Titian, a Rembrandt, and a Gilbert Stuart portrait of George Washington—and sculpture: *The Blind Girl of Pompeii* and *The Greek Slave*. But the Stewarts' marble museum wasn't a happy home. Stewart was ostracized by Knickerbocker society as a common tradesman, and the couple, who never had children, lived a lonely life in the shadow of their disapproving and aristocratic neighbor across the street, Mrs. William Astor. After Stewart died here on April 10, 1876, he left the bulk of his $40 million estate to Cornelia. He also bequeathed to Judge Henry Hilton, his friend and former assistant, $1 million. *Harper's Weekly* reported that the bequest was "the largest sum ever given by one man to another, not a relative, either in the United States or Europe."

### 147 West 34th Street
*Koster and Bial's Music Hall*   The first official public showing of a projected moving picture for a paying audience took place at this address on April 23, 1896. It was here as part of a vaudeville show that Thomas Edison's Vitascope was demonstrated to an enthusiastic crowd. The audience was treated to several short filmstrips, including one of two dancers performing the "umbrella" dance and another of a boxing

This was the home of Alexander T. Stewart on the corner of West 34th Street and Fifth Avenue. The *American Architect* reported that the $2 million five-story marble mansion "has caused more surmise and gossip than any other house ever erected in American." (*Harper's Weekly,* August 14, 1869)

match. One of the films, *The Beach at Dover,* appeared so real to these early filmgoers that several are said to have jumped up from their seats, afraid they were about to be drenched. This landmark in movie history was replaced in 1902 by the present R. H. Macy's department store.

### 311 West 34th Street

*Manhattan Center* ✦ On April 23, 1941, aviation hero Charles A. Lindbergh gave his first New York City speech at a rally held by the America First Committee, a short-lived isolationist group hoping to keep the United States out of World War II. Lindbergh, already perceived as friendly to the Germans, suggested among other things that England had already lost the war against Adolf Hitler. Two days later, President Franklin D. Roosevelt, asked his views on Lindbergh's speech, compared the aviator to those "sunshine patriots" at Valley Forge who had wanted General Washington to surrender. Lindbergh took offense at Roosevelt's remarks and resigned his commission in the U.S. Army Air Corps reserves. The American pacifist movement died after the Japanese bombing of Pearl Harbor on December 7 of that year.

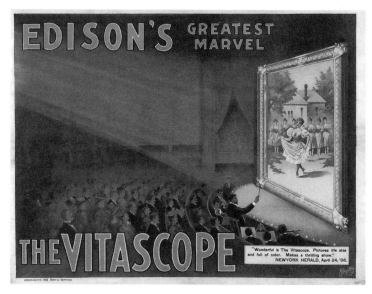

An early poster advertising Thomas Edison's motion picture invention the Vitascope. The first paying audience to see these moving pictures was at Koster and Bial's Music Hall on West 34th Street on April 23, 1896.

## WEST 35TH STREET

### 63–67 West 35th Street
*Garrick Theater*   As with most opening nights in the theater, the premiere of the play *Mrs. Warren's Profession* on October 30, 1905, was full of anticipation. But it was especially so on this night, because Anthony Comstock, the president of the New York Society for the Suppression of Vice, had threatened to stop the show. The comedy by George Bernard Shaw was about life in a brothel. Comstock, the ever-vigilant crusader, did manage to have the production closed for one performance, thereby providing priceless publicity for the play. The English language was enriched when Shaw coined the term "Comstockery" to describe misguided, prudish censorship.

## EAST 36TH STREET

### 125 East 36th Street ✛
After returning from their European honeymoon, Franklin and Eleanor Roosevelt moved into the house that still stands at this address. The couple lived in this rented house from 1905 to 1908. Their first child, Anna Eleanor, was born here on May 3, 1906.

## WEST 36TH STREET

### 16 West 36th Street
The home of social arbiter Ward McAllister was once at this address. Dubbed by contemporary wags as "Make-a-Lister," Mrs. William Astor's master party planner was famous for his list of New York society's "the Four Hundred." He committed the ultimate faux pas by writing an unflattering book, *Society as I Have Found It*, in 1890 and found himself ostracized by his former patrons.

## WEST 37TH STREET

### 11 West 37th Street
Nine-year-old Eleanor Roosevelt moved into this house, her maternal grandparents', in 1893, after her mother, Anna, died. The future First Lady lived here until shortly before her marriage to future President Franklin D. Roosevelt, her fifth cousin once removed, in 1905.

### 15 West 37th Street
This address was once the home of investigative reporter Nellie Bly, who moved here into the brownstone home of her new husband,

"The" New York social arbiter for more than 25 years, Ward McAllister ruled over an insecure newly moneyed class. This *Judge* cover lampoons McAllister with the ears of an ass, as he lectures Uncle Sam on proper behavior with the aid of a British gentleman.

industrialist Robert Livingston Seaman, in April 1895. Already famous at 28 years old, Nellie had married a 72-year-old millionaire bachelor.

### 226 West 37th Street

Long Island–born Catherine Devine was found strangled at this address on January 5, 1908. Working as a prostitute, the once-famous beauty was the belly dancer who had prompted a police raid on Herbert Barnum Seeley's bachelor's party at Sherry's Hotel. She named herself "Little Egypt," as did many exotic dancers, after the mythical dancer from the World's Columbian Exposition in Chicago in 1893.

## EAST 38TH STREET

### 3 East 38th Street

*Code Compilation Company*   A brownstone once at this address housed a firm that supposedly supplied commercial codes for businesses. It was also a front for the federal government's first peacetime cryptanalytic agency, Military Intelligence Section 8 or MI-8, also known by the more sinister-sounding nickname "the Black Chamber." It operated for 10 years until November 1929, when it was shut down by Secretary of State Henry L. Stimson, who reportedly said, "Gentlemen do not read each other's mail."

## WEST 41ST STREET

### 315 West 41st Street

On April 9, 1874, the police arrived at this Hell's Kitchen tenement and removed a battered nine-year-old girl. "Little Mary Ellen," as she became known in the press, was a Civil War orphan who had been repeatedly beaten and burned by her foster mother, Mary Connolly. Henry Bergh, the recent founder of the American Society for the Prevention of Cruelty to Animals, was instrumental in protecting Mary Ellen from her guardian. The child's unprecedented rescue, along with the subsequent child-abuse trial, marked the beginning of child-protection laws in America.

## EAST 42ND STREET

### 19 East 42nd Street

*Hotel Manhattan*   Sigmund Freud stayed in the hotel that once stood at this address while on his first and only trip to the United States, in August 1909. The "father of psychoanalysis" had left Vienna to give a

Nan Britton's bestseller, *The President's Daughter*, published in 1927, is considered one of the first "tell-all" books. The author, here posed with her daughter, Elizabeth Ann, met Warren Harding while she was still in high school.

series of lectures at Clark University in Worcester, Massachusetts. While in New York, he went sightseeing to Central Park, the Metropolitan Museum of Art, and Coney Island. One highlight of his trip to the city was his first visit to a motion picture show.

Seven years later, in May 1916, another guest, Senator Warren G. Harding of Ohio, began a love affair with Nan Britton at this same hotel. Their clandestine affair continued even after he was elected President in 1920. Their romance became public knowledge in 1927 after Britton wrote her book, *The President's Daughter*, about her child, Elizabeth Ann, whose father she claimed had been the late President.

### East 42nd Street between Park and Lexington avenues

An 87-year-old 20-inch water main a few feet below the pavement of 42nd Street ruptured and gushed million of gallons of water on October 17, 1991, a Thursday. The early morning deluge created chaos and paralyzed one of the most congested traffic spots in the world. Below ground, the area's three subway tunnels filled with water and were closed to thousands of rush-hour commuters. At street level, automobiles were diverted around the buckled artery, and nearby streets were closed. In the neighborhood's high-rises, offices and stores were forced to close because they lacked water and therefore lavatory facilities. The disaster served as a nagging reminder of the city's vulnerability to its aging and neglected infrastructure.

On July 18, 2007, one block south on East 41st Street, there was another disruptive and deadly infrastructure failure. A steam pipe exploded into a geyser of scalding steam and mud. The blast, which created a 40-foot crater, killed one and injured 30 people.

### 109 East 42nd Street +

*Commodore Hotel*   In 1980, this recently renovated hotel, with a new, glitzy facelift of reflective glass and a new name, the Grand Hyatt Hotel, became a symbol of the city's renewal after the fiscal crises of the 1970s.

In an earlier incarnation, it was the site of a nervous meeting between Whittaker Chambers and Alger Hiss, the key players in a spy case that propelled Richard M. Nixon into the national limelight and eventually to the presidency. Chambers testified before the House Committee on Un-American Activities that he knew Hiss, a former State Department official, was a communist. On August 17, 1948, in room 1400 of this hotel, freshman Congressman Nixon and the committee members watched Hiss confront Chambers. Hiss, who had earlier denied knowing Chambers, now admitted that his accuser was a man he had known nine years earlier as "George Crosley." Hiss denied spying and claimed he was being framed. But a jury believed Chambers, and Hiss was sent to prison for perjury.

## WEST 42ND STREET

### 33 West 42nd Street +

*Aeolian Hall*   George Gershwin introduced his "Rhapsody in Blue" in the third-floor concert hall of this building on February 12, 1924. Paul Whiteman's orchestra, with Gershwin as the piano soloist, performed the symphonic jazz piece.

### West 42nd Street between Fifth and Sixth avenues, north side

*Latting Observatory*   Built as an added attraction for the crowds attending the Exposition of 1853 across 42nd Street, this 350-foot wooden observation tower opened on June 30, 1853. The novelty of riding one of the first steam elevators in the country was capped with a visit to an ice cream parlor at the very top. The observatory was destroyed by fire on August 30, 1856.

At 350 feet, the Latting Observatory on West 42nd Street at Sixth Avenue towered over midtown in 1853. It was the city's first skyscraper. The wooden tourist attraction and the Crystal Palace across West 42nd Street were both destroyed in separate spectacular fires.

## 120 West 42nd Street

*Wurlitzer Building*   The Mine-Cine theater, located on the second floor of a building once at this address, had the dubious distinction of being the site of the first public live sex show, in the fall of 1970. It was advertised as a "studio tour" to circumvent the shifting obscenity laws of the time. For a fee of $5, members of the audience could watch the "filming" of a pornographic movie. This milestone was a turning point in West 42nd Street's transition from naughty postwar playground to hardcore location of the sex trade.

## 214 West 42nd Street

*New Amsterdam Theater* ✦ This 1903 Art Nouveau gem was the home of the famous Ziegfeld Follies. Beginning in 1913, Florenz Ziegfeld used this theater as his showcase for America's premier vaudeville talent. The stars of his elaborate musical revues were Fanny Brice, W. C. Fields, Marilyn Miller, Eddie Cantor, and Will Rogers. His composers included Irving Berlin, Victor Herbert, and Jerome Kern. In 1997, the Walt Disney Company's $34 million restoration and reopening of this theater spurred the rebirth of West 42nd Street. Doris Eaton Travis, the last surviving Ziegfeld Girl, died on May 11, 2010, at the age of 106.

## 234 West 42nd Street

*Liberty Theater* ✦ This movie theater is a landmark in the history of motion pictures. It was here that D. W. Griffith's film *The Birth of a Nation* had its East Coast premiere, on March 3, 1915. The film was shown to capacity audiences, despite a then-hefty admission price of $2. Still controversial after almost a century, Griffith's epic with its racial stereotyping and historical distortions of the Civil War and its aftermath was nonetheless a masterpiece of film making. *The Birth of a Nation* provoked protests and riots at some showings, yet it is often credited with having inspired African Americans to organize for their civil rights.

## 236 West 42nd Street ✦

*Empire Theater* This theater was originally named the Eltinge for female impersonator Julian Eltinge. In addition to a name and venue change from vaudeville to movies, this building has changed its location. When built in 1912, it was 168 feet closer to Broadway. Beginning on Sunday, March 1, 1998, as a test, the 3,700-ton theater was gently lifted off its foundation and moved on steel tracks equipped with rollers. Three weeks and six hours later, it was moved the final 140 feet to its current spot. Once the ornate lobby was restored and cleaned, historians realized that the beautiful muses painted on the dome were modeled on Eltinge, who interestingly enough never performed here. The lobby now serves as the entrance to a multiplex with 25 movie screens.

## 558 West 42nd Street

*Moynihan's Bar* New York Senator Daniel Patrick Moynihan's mother, Margaret, owned a bar at this address in the late 1940s. Abandoned by her husband, she raised her three children alone next door at No. 556. Future diplomat and presidential advisor Pat tended bar in the summer and on school holidays.

### West 42nd Street at the Hudson River

*Weekhawken Ferry Station*   A ragtag parade of 55 exhausted runners limped off the ferry here on May 26, 1928. They were on the last leg of a cross-continental marathon that began 84 days earlier in Los Angeles. The winner, Andy Payne, completed the "Bunion Derby" with a total elapsed time of 573 hours, 4 minutes, and 34 seconds. He claimed his $25,000 first prize at the Madison Square Garden finish line.

## EAST 43RD STREET

### 43 East 43rd Street +

*Hotel Biltmore*   The fifth floor of this one-time hotel was the frantic headquarters in the fall of 1915 for Henry Ford's ill-fated peace mission to end World War I. The industrialist, who hoped to have the troops "out of the trenches by Christmas," bankrolled an international delegation to travel to Europe aboard his "Peace Ship" and stop the war. Ford, along with 120 other pacifists, set sail on December 4, 1915, and arrived in Stockholm, Sweden, three weeks later. The idealistic and quixotic venture failed almost immediately and Ford returned to the United States within a week, having fallen ill.

The lobby of this hotel was a favorite meeting place for the co-ed set. "Meet me under the clock" became college campus buzzwords. This was where F. Scott Fitzgerald, also a favorite on campus, and his new wife, Zelda, spent part of their honeymoon, in room 2109 in April 1920. The clock is still here, but now it watches over a stark atrium created when the entire structure was remodeled into a glass-clad office building in the early 1980s.

## WEST 43RD STREET

### 108 West 43rd Street

*Hotel Diplomat*   On August 28, 1973, political activist Abbie Hoffman was arrested in a hotel room here for selling 2.5 pounds of cocaine to undercover drug agents. He spent the next six weeks in prison before being released on bail. While awaiting trial and a likely mandatory life sentence, he vanished. He spent the next six years in hiding, including stretches in Mexico and Canada. He also had plastic surgery to avoid being identified. The fugitive surrendered on September 4, 1980,

Henry Ford (*right*) discusses his plans to end World War I with William Jennings Bryan at the Biltmore Hotel on December 3, 1915. Former Secretary of State Bryan had resigned in protest in June over President Woodrow Wilson's handling of the aftermath of Germany's sinking of the *Lusitanna*.

pleaded guilty to a lesser charge, and served one year in prison before being released on parole.

### 229 West 43rd Street ✦
New York Times *Building*  On June 13, 1971, the *Times* ran the first installment of what became known as the Pentagon Papers, a secret study of policy decisions that drew the United States into the Vietnam War. Two days later the Nixon administration obtained a court order halting the publication on grounds of national security. The U.S. Supreme Court on June 30 upheld the right of the *Times* and the *Washington Post* to print the articles. The next year, the Pulitzer Prize in journalism was awarded to the *Times* and to investigative reporter Jack Anderson.

### 255 West 43rd Street
*Times Square Hotel* ✦ Here on June 13, 1962, the assassin of President John F. Kennedy, Lee Harvey Oswald; his Russian wife, Marina; and their baby spent their first night back in the United States after leaving the Soviet Union. It was here that Marina learned her first words of English—"hot" and "cold," from the bathroom faucets. They stayed only

that one night; the next day Oswald's brother wired him money to return to Texas.

## EAST 44TH STREET

### 5 East 44th Street

*Canfield's Gambling House*   This illegal but well-known gambling casino was popular with New York society's "Four Hundred" and millionaires such as John "Bet-a-Million" Gates. Richard Canfield, an art lover and bibliophile, operated this establishment along with clubs in Saratoga and Newport, the two resorts popular with New York society in the Gilded Age. In a gentlemen's club atmosphere, patrons wagered thousands of dollars on baccarat, roulette, and faro, a card game. During one rare raid, the police discovered $300,000 in IOUs from playboy Reginald Vanderbilt.

## WEST 44TH STREET

### 59 West 44th Street

*Algonquin Hotel* ✦ Famous for the Round Table wits of the 1920s, this hotel was initially made well known by Alexander Woollcott. In 1919, he was working as a newspaper reporter on assignment to write a piece on the hotel and fell in love with the apple pie served there. He kept coming back, each time bringing along friends such as Harold Ross, Heywood Broun, and Franklin Pierce Adams. The number of luncheon partners grew to include Robert Benchley, Dorothy Parker, and Robert Sherwood. The Algonquin has also been home over the years to John Barrymore, Douglas Fairbanks, and James Thurber.

### 145 West 44th Street

*Hudson Theater* ✦ Now part of the Broadway Millennium Hotel, this theater was the home of "The Steve Allen Show." Premiering on July 27, 1953, the pioneering late-night television talk show was broadcast only locally, on WNBT-TV (an earlier incarnation of the current WNBC-TV). It proved very popular, and beginning on September 27, 1954, with guests Wally Cox and Willie Mays, it was broadcast nationally. Retitled "The Tonight Show," the program became the longest-running talk show in history and the yardstick against which all other talk shows would be measured.

### 216 West 44th Street

*44th Street Theater*   The American Theatre Wing Stage Door Canteen was in the basement of this theater during World War II. The canteen opened on March 1, 1942, and operated until the end of the war. The combination soup kitchen/nightclub was host to more than 2,000 servicemen on busy nights.

### West 44th Street at the Hudson River
*Pier 84* This is now a beautiful park, but on April 4, 1956, this pier was packed with well-wishers and the press saying their goodbyes to Oscar-winning actress Grace Kelly. The Philadelphia native and her entourage of 80 relatives and friends were sailing aboard the *SS Constitution* for Europe. Two weeks later, she became Princess Grace after her marriage to Prince Rainier III of Monaco.

## EAST 45TH STREET

### 45 East 45th Street
*Roosevelt Hotel* ✦ Guy Lombardo and his orchestra, the Royal Canadians, made their New York debut in the Roosevelt Grill of this hotel, named for President Theodore Roosevelt. Beginning on December 31, 1929, Lombardo played "the sweetest music this side of heaven" here for the next 34 New Year's Eves before moving to the Waldorf-Astoria in 1963.

### East 45th Street, east of First Avenue
Near the East River there once stood a small stone house used by the British as an armory. In April 1775 it was the target of a daring midnight raid by Marinus Willett and a band of "Liberty Boys." The patriots had sailed down from Greenwich, Connecticut, ambushed the guards, and made off with arms and ammunition for the new Continental Army. Willett later served as mayor of New York City. This site is now part of the 17-acre United Nations complex.

## WEST 45TH STREET

### 75 West 45th Street
Women's rights leader Elizabeth Cady Stanton lived in a brownstone at this address during the Draft Riots of July 1863. Fearful of being a mob target because of her anti-slavery stance, she rushed her family to the fourth floor and escaped to the roof. In the melee, her son Neil was seized by the rioters. The quick-thinking teenager rescued himself by inviting his captors into a saloon "to drink to Jeff Davis."

## 105 West 45th Street

*El Fey* Opened on May 1, 1924, this famous speakeasy helped put the roar in the Roaring Twenties. Patrons, who were required to make it past the obligatory unmarked second-floor entrance, were often met by Texas Guinan and her signature greeting, "Hello, suckers." "Tex," a former silent-screen actress, entertained her celebrity revelers, such as Rudolph Valentino and Tom Mix, with her famous wisecracks, overpriced bootleg liquor, and chorus girls. The raucous scene, duly recorded by journalists Walter Winchell, Heywood Broun, and Ed Sullivan, made Tex a national personality. The party moved to several locations throughout the decade, even returning here, in the routine cycle of openings and police raids.

## 128 West 45th Street

*Peppermint Lounge* Officially recorded as the birthplace of the Twist in the summer of 1961, in reality it was the nightclub where mainstream culture was introduced to the swiveling fad. Chubby Checker had popularized the dance on "American Bandstand" a year earlier, and most teenagers were already tired of it when it became an overnight sensation here. Popular celebrities like Judy Garland, Tallulah Bankhead, the Beatles, and the Duke and Dutchess of Windsor, along with the accompanying press, flocked to this club to "do the Twist."

## West 45th Street, west of Broadway

On Saturday night, May 1, 2010, a T-shirt vendor alerted a mounted police officer to an idling smoke-filled SUV. The 1993 Pathfinder, abandoned only moments before, was packed with gasoline, canisters of propane, and a jury-rigged detonator. A combination of the vendor's vigilance, the would-be bomber's ineptitude, and quick police work enabled the FBI to arrest a suspect two days later in his seat aboard a flight that was about to depart for Dubai from Kennedy Airport. The would-be terrorist was Faisal Shahzad, a 30-year-old Pakistani-born American citizen.

## 332 West 45th Street

*Billy Haas' Restaurant* New York State Supreme Court Judge and legendary missing person Joseph F. Crater waved goodbye to his dinner companions outside this chophouse and got into a cab at 9:15 P.M. on August 6, 1930. The dapper six-foot judge was never seen again. The search continued well beyond Crater's being declared legally dead in

1937. Investigators were digging up back yards in Yonkers as late as 1964, based on visions of an alleged clairvoyant.

## EAST 46TH STREET

### East 46th Street between Lexington and Third avenues
In one of the first acts of violence by the mob during the Draft Riots, Metropolitan Police Superintendent John A. Kennedy was beaten unconscious on this block early on the morning of July 13, 1863. He would have been killed but for a Good Samaritan who convinced the mob that the superintendent was dead and took him to police headquarters.

### 210 East 46th Street
*Sparks Steak House* ✦ Mob boss Constantino Paul "Big Paul" Castellano and his bodyguard Thomas Bilotti were gunned down outside this restaurant on December 16, 1985. The killings, long denied by rival mobster John Gotti, resulted in Gotti's becoming head of the powerful Gambino crime family. It wasn't until Gotti's fourth racketeering trial that Salvatore "Sammy the Bull" Gravano, a former underboss–turned–government witness, testified that Gotti had indeed authorized the murders. Gravano also testified that he and his boss waited together down the block from the murder scene in their Lincoln sedan at the northwest corner of 46th Street and Third Avenue, directing the assassination. It was Gravano's courtroom revelations that finally convinced a jury to convict Gotti of murder and racketeering on April 2, 1992.

## WEST 46TH STREET

### 70 West 46th Strreet
*Columbia Hotel*  Here, on July 11, 1966, in his seedy fourth-floor room, Delmore Schwartz died of a heart attack. The once-brilliant poet, the youngest to win the Bollingen Prize, spent the last years of his life in a downward spiral of drug and alcohol abuse. His body lay unclaimed for two days at the morgue.

## EAST 47TH STREET

### 231 East 47th Street
Now Dag Hammarskjöld Plaza, this address was the site of Andy Warhol's first "factory," his studio in 1963. The silver-painted and aluminum foil–covered walls were the sets of his early films *Kiss*, *Haircut*, and *Eat*. The "50 Most Beautiful People" party was held in his loft here in the

spring of 1965. Judy Garland, Tennessee Williams, Allen Ginsberg, and other celebrities attended the party, which lasted until five o'clock the following afternoon.

## WEST 47TH STREET

### 41 West 47th Street ✦
*Gotham Book Mart*   Once marked by the sign "Wise Men Fish Here" designed by John Held Jr., this bookstore was the spiritual heart of literary New York from its opening in 1920. In addition to famous literary customers, the shop employed Allen Ginsberg, Everett LeRoi Jones, and even Tennessee Williams as sales clerks. The store has since moved to 16 East 47th Street.

### 412 West 47th Street ✦
Editor Harold Ross and his wife, Jane Grant, bought this town house in 1922. His friend Alexander Woollcott moved in shortly after and the house became a meeting place for the writers of the 1920s. It was here that Ross founded *The New Yorker* in 1925.

## EAST 48TH STREET

### 229 East 48th Street ✦
E. B. White wrote the classic children's story *Charlotte's Web* here in 1949. He and his wife, editor Katharine White, who summered in Maine, lived here for 11 years until moving out in 1957.

## WEST 48TH STREET

### 150 West 48th Street
*Billy Lahiff's Tavern*   Midway between the lights of Broadway and the old Madison Square Garden, this bar was the place for the theater crowd to hob-nob with the sports world. It was also fertile ground for two celebrated columnists, Damon Runyon and Walter Winchell, who occasionally stayed in the furnished rooms upstairs.

### 157 West 48th Street
*48th Street Theater*   The theater that once was at this address was the scene on April 18, 1926, of the first major dance concert of Martha Graham. This concert helped establish Graham as the leading exponent of modern dance in America.

### West 48th Street at the Hudson River

Early in 1942, while berthed at Pier 88, the French ocean liner *SS Normandie* was being transformed into a troop ship for the Allied war effort. On February 9, she caught fire. The blaze was confined to the upper decks and was pretty much under control in a few hours, but all the water pumped into the ship from fireboats and the fire engines on the pier caused the ship to list to port. Eventually the luxury liner rolled over into the icy Hudson. The lifeless hulk spent the remainder of the war in New York and was then sold for scrap. Possible explanations for the destruction ranged from Nazi sabotage to mob blackmail to just plain carelessness.

### Off West 48th Street in the Hudson River

US Airways Flight 1549 splashed down in the middle of the Hudson River at 3:30 P.M. on a bitter cold January 15, 2009. Only minutes after taking off from La Guardia Airport, the plane lost power after a bird strike disabled two engines. Miraculously, the crew landed the airbus without injuries, only the second such safe water landing by a commercial jet. All 155 on board were evacuated onto the wings before boarding a flotilla of ferries, fireboats, and tugboats that came to their rescue. Captain Chesley B. "Sully" Sullenberger III, the last person off, twice checked the sinking cabin for any remaining passengers.

## EAST 49TH STREET

### 244 East 49th Street ✦

Actress Katharine Hepburn first rented this town house in 1932. She later bought the house and lived here for more than 60 years.

## WEST 49TH STREET

### 239 West 49th Street

*St. Malachy's Roman Catholic Church* ✦ This neo-Gothic church and its separate "actors' chapel" has been a spiritual sanctuary for the Broadway community since 1903. The funeral mass for silent-screen star Rudolph Valentino was held here on August 30, 1926. Mary Pickford, Gloria Swanson, and Pola Negri attended the service. Fred Allen was married here, as were Jimmy Durante and Joan Crawford (but not to each other).

### West 49th Street Pier

On September 17, 1952, film great Charlie Chaplin stepped aboard the *Queen Elizabeth* bound for Europe accompanied by his wife, Oona, the daughter of Eugene O'Neill, and their four children. It would be 20 years before he returned. The second day at sea Chaplin received a telegram informing him that he was being barred from reentering the United States until he answered to charges of "moral and political turpitude" before an Immigration Board of Inquiry. The English-born comedian, who lived in the United States for 40 years but never became a citizen, had long been targeted by J. Edgar Hoover's FBI for his left-wing political views. The "Little Tramp" returned to the United States to receive a special Academy Award on April 16, 1972.

## EAST 50TH STREET

### 100 East 50th Street
*Waldorf-Astoria Towers* + This twin-towered annex to the famed hotel is reserved for residential suites. The list of residents reads like a *Who's Who in America*: Adlai Stevenson, General Douglas MacArthur, and Cole Porter. Former President Herbert Hoover, who had the longest post-presidency of any U.S. President, lived here for almost 30 years. He died in suite 31A on October 20, 1964, at the age of 90 from a massive internal hemorrhage. European royalty, including the Duke and Duchess of Windsor and Prince Rainier and Princess Grace of Monaco, used the hotel as their home while in New York.

### 305 East 50th Street
A four-story town house once at this address was crushed in one of the city's worst construction accidents. On March 15, 2008, a crane being used to build a high-rise at 303 East 50th Street toppled, demolishing parts of several buildings as it fell. The 22-story crane snapped its anchors, killing six construction workers and a tenant of 305 East 50th Street. On May 31, 2008, another crane collapsed on East 91st Street, killing two workers.

## WEST 50TH STREET

### West 50th Street at Seventh Avenue, north side
*Roxy Theater* Built by theater entrepreneur S. L. Rothafel and christened with his nickname, this 5,920-seat movie "palace" was one of the most elaborate of the Roaring Twenties. The opening on March 11, 1927, featured the gala premiere of the film *The Love of Sunya*. The distinguished guests included His Honor the mayor, Jimmy Walker; the governor of New Jersey; and four U.S. senators. Hollywood was represented by Charlie Chaplin, Harold Lloyd, and the star of the picture, Gloria

Swanson. Swanson was also on hand to bid a final farewell on March 9, 1960, when the theater was demolished.

### 345 West 50th Street
*New York Polyclinic Hospital*   The writer O. Henry died at this hospital on June 5, 1910. Silent-screen idol Rudolph Valentino also died here, of peritonitis, on August 23, 1926.

### West 50th Street at the Hudson River
The *Queen Mary* docked here at Pier 90 on June 20, 1945. The former luxury liner, still doing war duty as a deep gray–painted troop carrier, brought home the first shipload of American troops from Europe after V-E Day. The waterfronts of Staten Island, Brooklyn, and Manhattan along the Hudson River were lined with well-wishers. New York harbor was filled with a flotilla of boats, and the dock was crowded with wives and sweethearts. Many of those 14,526 servicemen and servicewomen aboard, though, were on only a short furlough and soon left to fight the war in the Pacific. The *Queen Mary* would later help reunite English war brides with their American husbands. The ship is now permanently docked in Long Beach, California, as a floating hotel.

## EAST 51ST STREET

### 22 East 51st Street
The four-story brownstone that once stood at this address was the home of railroad magnate Edward Henry Harriman. It was here on November 15, 1891, that his son William Averell was born. Averell was governor of New York and advisor to several U.S. Presidents.

### East 51st Street at First Avenue, northwest corner
*Mount Pleasant*   James Beekman's mansion was here from 1763 to 1874. This house, with the first greenhouse in America, served as the headquarters of General William Howe of the British Army during the Revolutionary War. It was here that patriot Nathan Hale, America's first spy, was hanged for espionage on September 22, 1776.

## WEST 51ST STREET

### 51 West 51st Street
*Toots Shor's Restaurant*   Opened in 1940 by former BVD underwear salesman and speakeasy bouncer Toots Shor, this was the site of his

On June 20, 1945, the *Queen Mary* sails up the Hudson River to Pier 90 at West 50th Street, her decks crammed with the first returning troops from Europe after V-E Day. (National Archives)

first restaurant. Shor, a brassy host, lorded over the assembled "crumb bums"—sports figures, sportswriters, and celebrities—who gathered here. In 1958, he sold his lease for $1.5 million. This address became home to the Sperry-Rand Building, and Shor moved on to several other locations.

### West 51st Street west of Broadway, north side

A vicious mob attack on journalist Victor Riesel took place here in the shadows near the Mark Hellinger Theater at about 3:00 A.M. on April 5, 1956. After leaving Lindy's restaurant, Riesel was confronted by a small-time hood who threw acid in his face, permanently blinding him. Riesel, an outspoken critic of corruption, had spoken earlier on mob racketeering in the labor unions. The mob had the attacker, Abraham Telvi, killed two weeks later. Despite his blindness, Riesel continued his crusade in his newspaper column. He died in 1995.

### 332 West 51st Street ✦

Just steps from his apartment at this address, Alvin "Shipwreck" Kelly collapsed and died of a heart attack on October 11, 1952. The flagpole sitter's stunts epitomized the "era of wonderful nonsense" of the 1920s. He once spent 49 days atop a flagpole in Atlantic City. He was holding a scrapbook of his exploits when he died.

## EAST 52ND STREET

### 435 East 52nd Street

*River House* ✦ Edwin Howard Armstrong, the inventor of FM radio, plunged to his death from his thirteenth-story apartment on the night of January 31, 1954. He was despondent over his failing relationship with his wife and protracted legal battles concerning his radio-related patents. Other tenants in this building were Henry and Clare Boothe Luce, who lived here from 1936 to 1960.

### 450 East 52nd Street

*The Campanile* ✦ When screen actress Greta Garbo wanted to be alone, she came here, her home for more than 40 years. In addition to the famous recluse, this last building on the block before the East River was home to Noel Coward and Alexander Woollcott. Dorothy Parker, Woollcott's friend and Algonquin Round Table lunch partner, nicknamed the place "Wit's End."

## WEST 52ND STREET

### West 52nd Street between Fifth and Sixth avenues

Nicknamed "Swing Street," this block was once lined with run-down brownstones that housed small jazz clubs. Dizzy Gillespie, Charlie Parker, Miles Davis, Sarah Vaughan, Count Basie, Buddy Rich, and many more great musicians played here during the block's heyday in the 1930s and '40s. The first club to open was the Onyx, later called "the Cradle of Swing." Other clubs included the Famous Door (first at 35 West 52nd Street), the Three Deuces (75 West 52nd Street), and the Downbeat (66 West 52nd Street).

### 46 West 52nd Street

*Commodore Record Shop* This popular hangout for jazz musicians was also a small recording company. On April 20, 1939, Billie Holiday recorded one of her signature songs, "Strange Fruit," about the lynching of African Americans in the South. In spite of the fact that Holiday's own label, Columbia, refused to record it and some radio stations banned it, the song became an early and potent anthem of the civil rights movement.

## EAST 53RD STREET

### 3 East 53rd Street

*Stork Club*  It was at this locale on the evening of October 16, 1951, in one of the city's choicest nightspots, that America was again painfully reminded of the country's racial bigotry. The American-born black dancer and French sensation Josephine Baker was badly treated and refused service here during her U.S. tour. The unpleasantness escalated the next day when Baker denounced the club and another diner, powerful columnist Walter Winchell, for not coming to her aid. Winchell's initial embarrassment soon turned to wrath and he used his gossip column to smear Baker. Baker lost club engagements and returned to France embittered by her homeland's intolerance. Today, this site is the serene Samuel Paley Park.

Newly married Ronald and Nancy Reagan at the Stork Club in the early 1950s. The nightclub at 3 East 53rd Street was an essential stop on any publicity tour. (Courtesy of the Ronald Reagan Presidential Library)

## EAST 54TH STREET

### 60 East 54th Street

*Hotel Elysee* ✦ One of America's preeminent playwrights, Tennessee Williams died in his suite at this hotel on February 25, 1983, at the age of 71. Long addicted to drugs and alcohol, Williams didn't die of an overdose but was asphyxiated by a medicine-bottle cap lodged in his throat.

## WEST 54TH STREET

### 4 West 54th Street

At this site was the New York City home of John D. Rockefeller, founder of the family oil empire. Built in 1865, it was one of the first town houses in this newly fashionable section of upper Fifth Avenue. In 1884, Rockefeller, forever frugal, bought the modest four-story brownstone, rather than build a European-style mansion like those of many of the other robber barons of the era. He and his wife, Laura, made very few decorating changes and split their time after he retired in the 1890s between this house and the family's Pocantico Hills estate. After Rockefeller died in 1937, the house was torn down to make room for the sculpture garden of the Museum of Modern Art, a leading beneficiary of the family's charity.

### 13 West 54th Street ✦

This brownstone was the childhood home of Nelson A. Rockefeller, elected governor of New York four times and the second U.S. Vice President to be appointed to office, across the street from his grandfather John D. Rockefeller's house. It was here that the former Vice President had his fatal heart attack on the night of January 26, 1979.

### 37 West 54th Street ✦

This was the home and music studio of Léon Theremin, a pioneer in electronic music and the inventor of the tereminvox (commonly known as the theremin). A Russian immigrant, he had moved to New York in 1927 to promote his new instrument. On September 15, 1938, he mysteriously disappeared. Long rumored to be dead, even by his American wife, he was sighted in Moscow in 1962. He had allegedly been kidnapped by Soviet secret police and spent time in a labor camp. He earned his freedom by working on sophisticated listening devices used to bug Premier Joseph Stalin's private apartment and the American embassy.

**254 West 54th Street** ✦

*Studio 54* Built originally as the Gallo Opera House in 1927, this cavernous space became the high temple of the disco culture of the late 1970s. Patrons like Truman Capote, Bianca Jagger, Andy Warhol, and the designer Halston mingled with other celebrities and politicos long into the night under the spell of drugs, flashing lights, and blaring music. The club closed in 1980 after its owners, Steve Rubell and Ian Schrager, were convicted of tax evasion.

## EAST 55TH STREET

**30 East 55th Street**

A lavish apartment in a building once at this address was one of many "floating" brothels operated by Polly Adler, the city's most notorious madam. A police raid here on March 5, 1935, resulted in the only jail time Adler ever served: 24 days. She ran her high-class operation for more than 20 years protected by the mob and her influential customers. After retiring, she wrote her bestseller, *A House Is Not a Home*.

**152 East 55th Street**

*The Atkins Center* ✦ Dr. Robert C. Atkins, the cardiologist and diet guru, slipped on the ice and suffered a fatal head injury on the sidewalk in front of his clinic and residence on April 8, 2003. He died 10 days later at the age of 72. His 1972 book, *Dr. Atkins' Diet Revolution*, which has sold a record 15 million copies, describes a controversial weight loss program advocating the intake of fats over that of carbohydrates. Ten months after his death, Atkins's secretly released autopsy report continued to fuel the debate over the doctor's own health and the merits of the diet.

## WEST 55TH STREET

**108 West 55th Street**

*Chemists Club* At a meeting here on January 8, 1909, Leo Baekeland presented his new compound to the New York chapter of the American Chemical Society. He called it Bakelite, the world's first fully synthetic plastic. He made his discovery while searching for a replacement for shellac in his Yonkers laboratory. His fellow chemists immediately realized the potential uses for the new substance, but few people in 1909 could have imagined that plastics would become the building blocks of the modern age.

## EAST 56TH STREET

### 330 East 56th Street ✦

*Sutton Club* In the fall of 1930, writer Nathanael West worked as a night manager at this hotel, just as he had a few years earlier at another family property, the Kenmore Hall Hotel on East 23rd Street. Again he supplied cheap or free rooms to fellow writers. But it was here that his experience with the hotel guests, many defeated and embittered by the Great Depression, provided inspiration for characters in his famous novel *Miss Lonelyhearts*.

### 353 East 56th Street

Forced to flee his native Holland for England in 1939, artist Piet Mondrian fled again after the Nazis started bombing London. He moved to this address, his first New York apartment and studio. It was here that he completed his last painting, *Broadway Boogie Woogie*, a lively variation on his grid designs as an homage to his adopted city's street patterns.

## EAST 57TH STREET

### 109 East 57th Street

*Ritz Tower* ✦ Once owned by William Randolph Hearst, this building was home to television personality Arlene Francis, and also the site of a freak accident. On June 23, 1960, a barbell fell out of Francis's eighth-floor apartment window and struck and killed a tourist. The victim had just left the ground-floor French restaurant Le Pavilion, where he had celebrated his sixtieth birthday.

### 115 East 57th Street

*Galleria* ✦ On the morning of March 20, 1991, four-year-old Conor Clapton fell to his death from a window of his mother's fifty-third-story apartment here. His father, guitarist Eric Clapton, coped with his grief by writing his mournful "Tears in Heaven," a song that won the 1993 Grammy Award for song of the year.

## WEST 57TH STREET

### 2 West 57th Street

On August 29, 1896, President Grover Cleveland and members of his cabinet met with Li Hung, the Chinese viceroy, at this address. Li was the first representative of the Chinese government to visit the United

States. This was the home of W. C. Whitney, a former Secretary of the Navy.

### 4–6 West 57th Street

A teenage Theodore Roosevelt moved to this address with his family in 1873. He later returned here, in 1880, with his bride, Alice Lee, to live in an apartment made for them on the third floor. But this address would hold unbearable memories for the future President. It was in this house that both his wife and his mother would die on the same day, February 14, 1884. Alice, who had just delivered the couple's first child, died of Bright's disease; his mother, Martha, known as Mittie, died of typhoid fever. This house was eventually replaced by the current office building (730 Fifth Avenue).

### 30 West 57th Street

*Art of This Century Gallery*   Heiress and high priestess of modern art Peggy Guggenheim and her new husband, artist Max Ernst, opened her

Theodore Roosevelt wrote his book *The Naval War of 1812* in the library of his home that stood at 6 West 57th Street. His first wife, Alice, and his mother, Mittie, both died here on St. Valentine's Day, 1884. (Theodore Roosevelt Collection, Harvard College Library)

gallery here on October 21, 1942. It quickly became a showcase for abstract expressionism and Surrealism. Artists Jackson Pollock, Robert Motherwell, Hans Hofmann, Adolph Gottlieb, and Mark Rothko are all promoted and exhibited here. Guggenheim is quoted as hoping the gallery "serves its purpose only if it succeeds in serving the future instead of recording the past." The gallery stayed open until 1947, when Guggenheim moved to Venice.

## 60 West 57th Street

*Hemisphere House* ✦ Novelist Jerzy Kosinski had an apartment here. Sometime after midnight on May 3, 1991, the author committed suicide with a combination of alcohol, barbiturates, and a plastic bag, the same method detailed in his most recent novel, *The Hermit of 69th Street*.

## 101 West 57th Street

*Buckingham Hotel* ✦ Ignacy Paderewski, pianist and statesman, died of pneumonia in this hotel on June 29, 1941. Paderewski, who had been the prime minister of Poland after World War I, was in America working for the Polish cause since the German occupation of Poland in 1939. Broadway chronicler Damon Runyon also lived here for several years before his death in 1946. Per a request in the writer's will, his friend Captain Eddie Rickenbacker, the World War I flying ace and head of Eastern Airlines, scattered Runyon's ashes over Manhattan from a small plane on December 18, 1946.

## 120 West 57th Street ✦

*Hotel St. Hubert* A leading figure in the evolution of American literature, William Dean Howells lived in this building, then a hotel, from 1910 until his death on May 11, 1920. The 84-year-old author had caught a cold three weeks earlier and died in his sleep.

## 154 West 57th Street

*Carnegie Hall* ✦ Peter Ilyich Tchaikovsky, on his only trip to America, formally opened the hall directing his *Marche Solennelle* on May 5, 1891, while donor Andrew Carnegie sat in box number 33. For more than 100 years, great entertainers have performed here: Ignacy Paderewski, Antonín Dvořák, and Vladimir Horowitz. Leonard Bernstein made a triumphal appearance on November 14, 1943, as a replacement for conductor Bruno Walter, who was ill. Not only a showcase for classical music, the auditorium has heard the sounds of Benny Goodman, Duke Ellington, and the Beatles. The hall has also served as a lecture platform for Mark Twain, Woodrow Wilson, Winston Churchill, and Martin Luther King Jr.

### 205 West 57th Street

*The Osborne* ✦ Leonard Bernstein wrote the music for *West Side Story* while he lived in this building. On October 19, 1978, it was the site of murder and suicide: Oscar-winning actor Gig Young shot his bride and then shot himself in their bedroom.

### 215 West 57th Street

*Art Students' League* ✦ Anthony Comstock, founder and special agent of the New York Society for the Suppression of Vice and U.S. postal inspector, raided this famous art school on August 2, 1906. This overzealous reformer confiscated the recent issue of the league's magazine, *The American Art Student*. The issue, which Comstock found "indecent," contained illustrations of nudes drawn by some of the students. A list of the faculty of this school reads like a *Who's Who of American Art*: William Merritt Chase, Thomas Hart Benton, Thomas Eakins, Augustus Saint-Gaudens, Robert Henri, George Bellows, Edward Hopper, John Sloan, and Jackson Pollock.

### 309 West 57th Street

A small two-room furnished apartment at this address was the last home of exiled Hungarian composer Béla Bartók. In New York since October 1940, he was given a post as an ethnomusicologist at Columbia University, where he gave concerts. He died on September 26, 1945, at West Side Hospital at 57 West 57th Street and was buried in Hartsdale, New York. His remains were removed to Hungary with great pomp in the summer of 1988.

### 340 West 57th Street

*Park Vendome* ✦ James Montgomery Flagg, one of America's most famous illustrators, died here in his apartment on May 27, 1960. The 82-year-old artist created the World War I recruiting poster of Uncle Sam with the caption "I WANT YOU FOR U.S. ARMY."

## WEST 58TH STREET

### 202 West 58th Street

*Elysee Theater* Longtime health food guru and publisher Jerome Irving Rodale was at this theater for a taping of "The Dick Cavett Show" on June 7, 1971. After his interview, the 72-year-old author quietly

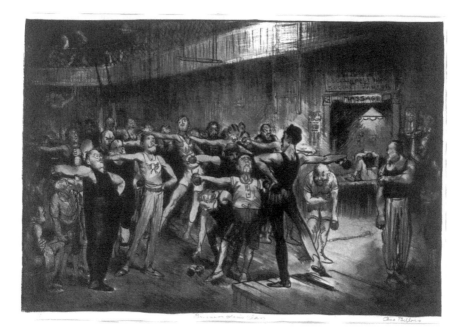

George Bellows' print of 1909 *Business Men's Class* was done while he was a member at the "Y" that once stood at 318 West 57th Street. Bellows, a natural athlete, gave up a potential baseball career with the Cincinnati Reds to be an artist.

slumped over in his chair and died of a heart attack. The show was never broadcast.

### 352 West 58th Street

For almost two years, painter George Bellows rented a room at a house at this address for $7.50 a week. From 1904 to 1906, he shared his small room with another aspiring artist, where they both lived and worked.

## EAST 59TH STREET

### 5 East 59th Street ✦

*Playboy Club*   On February 5, 1963, a newly trained Playboy waitress ostensibly named Marie Catherine Ochs reported for work here at this fading bastion of male supremacy. This particular Playboy Bunny on her first day was actually Gloria Steinem, the 28-year-old budding feminist author, who had infiltrated the club to write "A Bunny's Tale," an article that originally appeared in *Show* magazine. Steinem's tale helped establish her as a voice of the newly emerging women's movement. Deborah Harry was also a Bunny here, before becoming the lead singer of the band Blondie.

## WEST 59TH STREET

### 447 West 59th Street
*Sloane Hospital for Women*   Anne Frances Robbins, who later became First Lady Nancy Reagan, was born at this hospital on July 6, 1921.

# ABOVE 59TH STREET

## ADAM CLAYTON POWELL JR. BOULEVARD

### 2090 Adam Clayton Powell Jr. Boulevard ✦

*Hotel Theresa* Once called the Waldorf of Harlem, this landmark in African American history didn't even begin admitting blacks as hotel guests until it was purchased by African American businessman Love B. Woods in 1937. From that time on, it was the premier social hub for African American celebrities and entertainers. Famous guests have included Joe Louis, Jimi Hendrix (room 406), and Malcolm X (suite 128). Premier Fidel Castro of Cuba in a gesture of egalitarianism insisted on staying in this hotel while attending meetings at the United Nations in September 1960. It was here that he met with Nikita Khrushchev of the Soviet Union, Gamal Abdel Nasser of Egypt, and Jawaharlal Nehru of India. Now called the Theresa Towers, it is an office building.

### 2225 Adam Clayton Powell Jr. Boulevard ✦

*Lafayette Theater* Segregated when it opened in 1912, this theater became home to Harlem's first African American professional stock company, the Lafayette Players. Stage actors Paul Robeson and Charles Gilpin performed here, as did musicians Leadbelly, Duke Ellington, Bessie Smith, Ethel Waters, and Fletcher Henderson. On April 14, 1936, 20-year-old Orson Welles directed the first all–African American production of *Macbeth* here. The façade was destroyed in 1990 by the current church.

### 2305 Adam Clayton Powell Jr. Boulevard ✦

A second-floor office here was the site of Dr. Elizabeth "Bessie" Delany's first dental practice. She earned her degree in dentistry from Columbia University in 1923 and was the second African American woman licensed to practice in New York City. In 1994, she and her sister, Sadie, both over 100 years old, were the authors and subjects of a bestselling book based on their long lives, *Having Our Say*, later turned into a play with the same title.

### 2588 Adam Clayton Powell Jr. Boulevard

*Paul Laurence Dunbar Apartments* ✦ This six-building complex, named for the African American poet, was developed by John D. Rockefeller Jr. as the first large cooperative project in the country built for African Americans. The innovative complex is built around a large interior garden court. One of the first tenants in 1928 was author and editor W. E. B. Du Bois, who lived here until 1934. Other celebrated tenants were Paul Robeson, singer and actor; A. Philip Randolph, labor leader; Matthew A. Henson, North Pole explorer; and Bill "Bojangles" Robinson, dancer.

## AMSTERDAM AVENUE

### 108 Amsterdam Avenue
This was the family home of 19-year-old Gertrude Ederle, the first woman to swim across the English Channel. On August 6, 1926, she completed her swim in a record-breaking time—14 hours and 31 minutes, two hours faster than the men's record. This favorite New York City daughter was honored with a ticker-tape parade down Broadway.

### 929 Amsterdam Avenue
An apartment at this address was the center of a controversy that by today's standards seems quaint but in the spring of 1968 was a landmark in the battle for women's rights. A 20-year-old Barnard College sophomore, Linda LeClair, was living here with her boyfriend, Peter Behr, a 20-year-old Columbia University student, in violation of Barnard's strict housing policy for unwed female students. Her threatened expulsion

Gertrude "Trudy" Ederle prepared for her English Channel swim by swimming 21 miles from lower Manhattan to Sandy Hook, New Jersey.

prompted student protests and extensive media coverage, including a front-page article in the *New York Times*. Barnard eventually compromised: LeClair could stay in school, but she would be banned from the college cafeteria and social activities.

## Amsterdam Avenue between West 110th and West 112th streets, east side

*Cathedral of St. John the Divine*   The cornerstone was laid on December 27, 1892, the feast day of St. John, for what is intended to become the largest Gothic cathedral in the world. It is the principal church of the Episcopal diocese of New York. Nicknamed "St. John the Unfinished," this cathedral has endured more than a century of starts and stops and several major design changes. Such major league players as J. P. Morgan, John D. Rockefeller, and Franklin Delano Roosevelt have helped with the constant fundraising needed to build the landmark.

## Amsterdam Avenue at West 114th Street, northeast corner

*St. Luke's Hospital* ✦ On November 5, 1915, Booker T. Washington was admitted to a private room here. The 59-year-old civil rights leader and educator was dying of hypertension and kidney failure. Determined to

Over 100 years in the making, St. John the Divine Cathedral, the world's largest Gothic cathedral, is still unfinished today. This aerial photograph was taken in 1917.

return to the South, he was placed on a train and died four hours after arriving at his Tuskegee Institute in Alabama nine days later.

In the initial days of the (then unrecognized and unnamed) Acquired Immune Deficiency Syndrome (AIDS) epidemic, a patient with a strange new disease underwent a brain biopsy here and was diagnosed with toxoplasmosis. This opportunistic infection later became commonly recognized as an early sign of AIDS. The young man who died here on January 15, 1981, is now considered one of the earliest AIDS-related deaths in the United States.

### 1150 Amsterdam Avenue

*Philosophy Hall, Columbia University* ✦ In 1913, in a basement laboratory, Edwin Howard Armstrong, a recent Columbia graduate, was demonstrating his new invention, the regenerative circuit, which greatly improved the reception of wireless messages. One of the witnesses to this demonstration was David Sarnoff, the future chairman of Radio Corporation of America, or RCA. These two radio visionaries had another meeting in this same laboratory 20 years later, in 1933, this time so that Sarnoff could witness another of Armstrong's inventions, frequency modulation, or FM.

### Amsterdam Avenue between West 138th and West 141st streets, east side

*Shepard Hall, The City College of the City University of New York* ✦ The Great Hall, a cathedral-style auditorium, has long been a center for academic discourse. Speakers here have included three Roosevelts: Theodore, Franklin, and Eleanor. On April 5, 1940, some 2,000 students met here to protest a court decision to rescind the City College professorship offered to renowned philosopher Bertrand Russell. The Russell appointment created a firestorm, pitting opponents of academic freedom against religious leaders and conservatives. Within the year, the New York state legislature condemned the Russell appointment and formed a committee to investigate alleged subversives and communists in the public schools. The committee and its tactics were a harbinger of McCarthyism in the 1950s.

New Yorkers were justly proud of "the poor man's Harvard" and thrilled that their hometown CUNY basketball team was the only one to win both the NCAA and NIT championships in the same year, 1950. But on February 18, 1951, pride changed to shame after three star players were arrested for taking bribes from gamblers to fix games over a three-year period. College basketball's worst betting scandal spread from there to other schools.

## BROADWAY

### 1883 Broadway

*Colonial Theatre*   Two early film comedic greats, Charlie Chaplin and Stan Laurel, made their American debuts together in a vaudeville skit at this theater called "The Wow-wows, or a night in a London Secret Society" on October 3, 1910. Also introduced here at the Colonial in the play *Runnin' Wild* on October 29, 1923, was a dance craze, the Charleston. The snappy dance, created on the docks in Charleston, South Carolina, came to epitomize the abandon of the Roaring Twenties. The comedy team of George Burns and Gracie Allen also appeared on the Colonial's stage.

### Broadway between West 62nd and West 66th streets, west side

*Lincoln Center, Vivian Beaumont Theater* ✛ One of the biggest flops in corporate marketing history was announced on this theater's stage on April 2, 1985. The Coca-Cola Company held a press conference to announce plans to replace its century-old soft-drink formula with "New Coke." There was an immediate outcry, and within three months the company reversed itself: It would sell "Classic" Coke, along with the new, sweeter version. In spite of theories to the contrary and an eventual increase of soft-drink market shares, the company claims it made a mistake.

### Broadway at West 63rd Street, northwest corner

*Lincoln Arcade Building*   This building was a popular site for artist's studios in the early part of the twentieth century. George Bellows, Thomas Hart Benton, Rockwell Kent, and Marcel Duchamp all had space to work here. This was also home to Robert Henri's School of Art from 1909 to 1912. Some of Henri's students were Yasuo Kuniyoshi, Edward Hopper, and Stuart Davis. Another artist with space here was Pat Sullivan, the creator of Felix the Cat, America's first successful animated cartoon character. The arcade was destroyed in a three-hour blaze on January 29, 1931.

### 1970 Broadway

*Frank E. Campbell's Funeral Chapel*   From August 24 to 30, 1926, this address was the scene of a near-riot among mourners waiting to view the body of silent-screen idol Rudolph Valentino. Mounted police had to be called to control the frenzied crowd. More than 100 people were injured, some after crashing through the funeral home's front window. Eventually 90,000 fans filed through the Gold Room to see Valentino, laid out in a silver coffin with a glass cover. An honor guard, supposedly sent by Italian dictator Benito Mussolini, supplied additional protection from inconsolable fans.

## 2107 Broadway

*The Ansonia* ✦ An old friend rising above Broadway, this landmark apartment house has been home to many musical artists, such as Enrico Caruso, Arturo Toscanini, Ezio Pinza, Lily Pons, and Igor Stravinsky. In the basement, Plato's Retreat was at different times a straight and a gay sex club. The club closed its doors in the mid-1980s because of changing sexual attitudes and the fear of AIDS.

## Broadway at West 75th Street, northwest corner

*Somerindyke House* Hessians occupied the house that once stood just north of this intersection during the Revolutionary War. Later, in the 1790s, Louis-Philippe, citizen-king of France from 1830 to 1848, lived and taught school here for a short time while in exile during the Napoleonic regime.

## 2745 Broadway

This address was once the summer home of Isidor Straus, a co-owner of R. H. Macy's department store. Both he and his wife, Ida, lost their lives on the *Titanic* on April 14, 1912. The family sold the Victorian house, and within a year the Clebourne apartment house was built on the site. A memorial to the Strauses is located in a small park nearby, at West End Avenue and 106th Street.

## Broadway at West 106th Street

Once a buckwheat field on the Jones farm, this present-day intersection was the site of the Battle of Harlem Heights on September 16, 1776, during the Revolutionary War. More of a skirmish than a battle, the shooting began shortly after patriot Lieutenant Colonel Thomas Knowlton engaged the British Light Infantry. By the time the fighting was finished, the action had moved to Broadway near today's West 120th Street. In spite of the death of Knowlton, it was considered an American victory and a needed boost to the rebels' low morale.

## Broadway at West 114th Street to West 120th Street, east side

*Bloomingdale Insane Asylum* Opened in 1821, this was the first mental hospital in New York state. It moved to White Plains, New York, in the 1890s.

The Battle of Harlem Heights was fought on what is now on Columbia University's campus on September 16, 1776. The American forces, who had recently lost the Battle of Long Island and a skirmish at Kips Bay, were in danger of losing control of all of Manhattan. General George Washington and his troops won the battle by chasing the British off the heights south into what is now Central Park.

*Columbia University Campus* ✛ This hilltop location became the third and current home of Columbia University in 1897. Charles F. McKim, who was also the architect of many of the initial buildings, designed the uncompleted master plan of the campus. McKim's masterpiece is the monumental Low Memorial Library. The sculpture *Alma Mater* by Daniel Chester French on the surrounding terrace in front of the library became a focal point for the student protest movement of the late 1960s. A student sit-in at several university buildings led to the closing of the school on April 26, 1968. Four days later, 1,000 riot police officers stormed the campus and began dragging away the student protesters in the five closed buildings. Many students were arrested and injured. They were opposed to the new gymnasium planned for Morningside Park and the university's affiliation with a consortium that did military research for the federal government.

### 3030 Broadway
*Pupin Physics Hall, Columbia University* ✛ Enrico Fermi and John R. Dunning started their final experiment with a cyclotron to split a

For much of the nineteenth century, the area around Broadway and West 114th Street was the tranquil setting of the Bloomingdale Village Asylum. The hospital was an early advocate of "moral treatment," a humane and enlightened approach to mental illness.

uranium atom in a basement laboratory of this building on January 25, 1939. The atomic age began with this research, which led to the development of atomic power and the bomb. Fermi had become a professor of physics here at Columbia University after fleeing fascist Italy.

### 3032 Broadway

*Horace Mann School, Columbia University* ✦ In the auditorium of this building, Albert Einstein, lecturing on his theory of relativity, introduced "time" as the fourth dimension on April 15, 1921. Einstein, speaking in German, explained one of most revolutionary theories of twentieth-century science to a room packed with students and faculty.

### Broadway at West 120th Street to West 122nd Street

On September 16, 1776, a wheat field once here was the site of the heaviest fighting of the Battle of Harlem Heights during the Revolutionary War. A British force of about 5,000 men faced off against about 2,000 patriots. After the battle ended later that day, the Americans losses were about 30 soldiers killed while the British had 14 casualties.

*Union Theological Seminary* ✦ October 16, 1940, was registration day for the first peacetime draft in U.S. history. The Selective Service system, created by Congress in response to Adolf Hitler's invasion of France, required 15 million American men to sign up for possible military service. But eight Union Theological Seminary students, although already exempt from the draft, refused and were arrested. Called the "Union 8," these pacifists were tried and sentenced to a year in prison. By December, the Civilian Public Service was established for conscientious objectors as an alternative to combat duty.

### 3755 Broadway ✦

*American Geographical Society*   It was here, during the late summer of 1917 in the midst of World War I, that a group called the "Inquiry" met to discuss a possible permanent international association to preserve peace. Under secret orders from President Woodrow Wilson, his trusted advisor Edward M. "Colonel" House, Walter Lippmann, and others met to plan for the postwar age and to draft a constitution for the President's cherished League of Nations, forerunner to today's United Nations. The building, part of the Audubon Terrace complex, now houses Boricua College.

### Broadway at West 165th Street to West 168th Street

*Hilltop Park*   Once solid rock, this site was carved out of the ramparts of Washington Heights to build this all-wood baseball stadium. One of the highest spots in Manhattan, the ballpark was the first home of the New York Yankees, then called the Highlanders. Their first game was on April 30, 1903, when the Highlanders beat the Washington team 6–2. The Yankees played their last game here in 1912, and the stadium was torn down two years later. The hilltop was then chosen as the site of a tabernacle where Billy Sunday, a baseball player–turned–evangelist, preached to the faithful. At his most successful revival here, in 1917, he tallied up 98,264 conversions. Columbia-Presbyterian Medical Center replaced the tabernacle in 1925.

### 3950 Broadway at West 165th Street, southeast corner

Audubon Ballroom ✦ Built in 1912 by Thomas Lamb, this was the site of the nation's first dance marathon, which began on March 30, 1923. Alma Cummings won the contest by dancing continuously for more than 24 hours. Popular jazz and Big Bands played here in the 1930s, '40s, and early '50s. It was here on February 21, 1965, that Malcolm X was assassinated. The charismatic African American leader was about to address his audience when he was shot and killed on stage. The motive for the killing and the identity of the assassins are still in question, but three men were convicted of the murder and given life sentences. A year earlier, Malcolm X had broken away from his mentor Elijah Muhammad and his Nation of Islam and formed his own group of followers. The ballroom is now part of Columbia University's Audubon Biomedical Science and Technology Park.

## CENTRAL PARK

Political leaders and reformers, including William Cullen Bryant, realized in the 1840s the need for a public park for the rapidly growing city. Concerned about the influx of immigrants forced to live in crowded

One week after his home in Elmhurst, Queens, was firebombed, Malcolm X was fatally shot while speaking on this stage at the Audubon Ballroom at 3950 Broadway on February 21, 1965. The two arrows show the path used by the gunmen as they fled.

urban neighborhoods, they envisioned a "rural" park setting as a release valve for the new social tensions. Their most idealistic goal was that of a park as a democratic meeting ground, where all classes of people could relax in a pastoral setting.

In 1856 land was acquired and the Central Park Commission created. A design contest for the park was established, and Frederick Law Olmsted and Calvert Vaux won with their joint "Greensward" based on English landscape principles. Central Park became the first landscaped public park in the United States. Some 1,600 residents of small settlements, including Seneca Village on what is now the west side of the park near the Great Lawn, were removed. More than 20,000 workers labored in the age of horsepower to transform the natural glacier-formed setting into a park. The bedrock was blasted away, mountains of dirt and rocks were moved, streams were diverted, and lawns and meadows were formed to create the bucolic vistas. More than 270,000 trees and shrubs were planted. In the midst of this picturesque landscape, a formal area, The Mall was created for promenading, a popular pastime for those early Victorian visitors. One of the Olmsted/Vaux team's most innovative ideas was to separate the crosstown traffic from the park in four sunken transverse roads, a vision created long before the automobile age.

Central Park has served as the city's back yard, witnessing the joys and tragedies of urban life for more than 150 years. It can be experienced collectively in any of the park's gathering points or virtually alone in the remote or isolated areas. One private moment took place on June 13, 1859, when Frederick Law Olmsted married Mary Olmsted, his brother's widow, in the park. It has been home to the homeless, most visibly during the Great Depression in so-called "Hoovervilles" on the Great Lawn. The park has been the site of rallies, concerts, protests, and a few well-publicized murders. Yet it is incredibly safe, still the tranquil retreat envisioned by its designers. The changing seasons in the park help keep the city in touch with nature. Each season brings its own fitting activity, whether ice skating on the pond or sunbathing on the Great Lawn. Each fall is marked by the New York City Marathon, first run entirely in the park on September 13, 1970.

Central Park is remarkably resilient, given the increasing number of visitors over the years. What was considered a large crowd of 20,000 attended the unveiling of Cleopatra's Needle, an ancient Egyptian obelisk, in February 1881. But that number seems small compared with the 800,000 visitors during the Statue of Liberty centennial weekend, July 5, 1986, which is believed to be the largest crowd ever.

The park has fought off many inappropriate encroachments over the years, including a proposal to situate Grant's Tomb here, an amusement park, numerous parking lots, and even an airport. One such encroachment, not fought off by the park or by the environment of the North American continent for that matter, was the introduction of non-native species of the European starling. On March 6, 1890, Eugene Scheifflin released 80 of the birds here. His well-intentioned plan to introduce all the birds mentioned in the works of Shakespeare to America was an ecological disaster. In 1998 the American Museum of Natural History discovered a brand-new park inhabitant, an unusual tiny centipede that lives in the leaf litter. It turned out to be not only a new species never before seen but a new genus, now named *Nannarrup hoffmani*.

A National Historic Landmark since 1964, the park has dramatically improved since the work done by the Central Park Conservancy, founded in 1980. With a host of donors and volunteers, the Conservancy has helped restore and maintain Olmsted and Vaux's vision.

CENTRAL PARK.
NEW YORK CITY
Looking South from the Observatory.

In this 1859 bird's-eye view of Central Park looking south, Bethesda Terrace, in the center, is pictured without "The Angel of the Waters," which was erected in 1873. The spires of St. Patrick's Cathedral can be seen in the background.

## CENTRAL PARK NORTH

### Central Park North between Fifth and Lenox avenues, north side

*The First Polo Grounds* Publisher James Gordon Bennett Jr. once owned this block and as far north as 112th Street, using the land to play polo, a game he and other New York sportsmen had recently introduced to America. Baseball games shared the field as early as 1880. The first National League game, here, on May 1, 1883, was between the Gothams, later renamed the New York Giants, and Boston. More than 15,000 fans, including former President Ulysses S. Grant—the largest crowd in New York baseball history up to that time—came out to root for the home team. Another footnote in the history of baseball took place here on October 23, 1884—the beginning of a three-game series began for "the championship of the United States." The Providence Grays of the National League and the New York Metropolitans of the American Association met in the sport's first post-season championship games, a forerunner to the first World Series, begun 19 years later in 1903.

## CENTRAL PARK WEST

### 115 Central Park West

*Majestic Apartments* ✛ A carpenter named Richard Bruno Hauptmann was hired to work on the construction of this building. Hauptmann was later tried and executed for the kidnapping and death of the baby son of aviator Charles A. Lindbergh. The prosecution used Hauptmann's altered time sheet for the day of the kidnapping, March 1, 1932, supposedly showing he was not at work, to help convict him during the sensational trial.

Twenty-five years later, on May 2, 1957, another footnote in the history of crime took place in this lobby. Gangster Frank Costello was returning to his seven-room penthouse when he was shot in the head by a mob hit man. Costello survived his wound and lived to the ripe old age of 80.

### Central Park West at West 67th Street

This Central Park playground marks the spot of city planner Robert Moses' first public defeat. Dismissing neighborhood concerns, he wanted to expand the parking for his Tavern on the Green restaurant.

This is an 1887 home game schedule for the New York Giants. The team played their games at the first Polo Grounds stadium on Central Park North between Fifth and Lenox avenues.

But this time the master builder met his match, underestimating the determination of the well-heeled, media-savvy mothers who lived in the nearby buildings. They blocked his bulldozers on April 17, 1956, and ensured that the incident was covered in the city's newspapers. Moses had the land cleared after dark, but by then the battle had been lost. He backed down and created a second playground, which he claimed had been his plan from the beginning. Tavern on the Green thrived for many more years before closing at the end of 2009.

## Central Park West at West 72nd Street, northeast corner

On a windy November 27, 1997, the Cat in the Hat balloon float in the Macy's Thanksgiving Day Parade blew out of control and bumped into a lamp post, knocking several parts of the metal frame down onto the crowd below. The most seriously hurt was Kathleen Caronna. She was in a coma for nearly a month and endured months of physical therapy.

The accident prompted stricter guidelines for the use of floats during high-wind conditions. This wasn't the first accident with one of the balloons. After the 1933 parade, one of the intentionally released balloons collided with a small biplane over Queens. The plane went into a 5,000-foot dive but recovered.

## Central Park West at West 74th Street

At age 68, real estate broker Henry H. Bliss became the country's first automobile fatality at this intersection on September 13, 1899. He had just gotten off a southbound trolley when he was knocked down and run over by an electric cab driven by Arthur Smith. Bliss died later in a hospital.

## Central Park West between West 77th and West 81st streets

*American Museum of Natural History* ✦ Home to more than 32 million scientific specimens, this museum also once "displayed" two human specimens. Minik and his father, two of seven Inuit tribesmen brought to New York by Robert E. Peary on his return from his 1897 Greenland expedition, lived here. After Minik's father died of tuberculosis and the boy was abandoned by Peary, the seven-year-old was raised by a museum curator. Minik fought for years to claim and bury the bones of his father, which the museum had placed on display. The other human exhibit was Ota Benga, a Congolese pygmy. Benga, first brought to the United States and exhibited at the 1904 St. Louis World's Fair, lived at the museum in the summer of 1906. His visit was short-lived, but his next stop was even more degrading: the Bronx Zoo. Unthinkable today, Minik and Benga's exploitation was an early nineteenth-century racist interpretation of Darwinian evolutionary theory. Both had sad, short lives, unable to adapt to America or return to their native lands.

## 211 Central Park West

*Beresford Hotel*  A hotel that once stood at this corner of 81st Street was the birthplace of Henry Morgenthau Jr. on May 11, 1891. He was Secretary of the Treasury from 1934 to 1945 during much of Franklin D. Roosevelt's administration, a period of tumultuous financial history that included the Great Depression and World War II. His son, Robert M. Morgenthau, was Manhattan district attorney from 1975 until his retirement at age 90 in 2009.

*The Beresford* ✦ The current apartment house, named after the hotel, was home to famed anthropologist Margaret Mead from 1966 to 1978.

She worked across the street at the American Museum of Natural History.

### 293 Central Park West
*Towns Hospital*   On December 11, 1934, a drunken Bill Wilson staggered into this small hospital for the treatment of drug and alcohol abuse. It wasn't his first time, but it was his last. Wilson, a once-successful Wall Street broker, stopped his drinking with the help of Dr. William Silkworth and a spiritual awakening he had here. He applied his experience and new sobriety to co-found Alcoholics Anonymous.

## COLUMBUS AVENUE

### Columbus Avenue between West 65th and West 66th streets, east side
*Sharkey's*   A saloon that once stood on this site was run by an ex-boxer named Sailor Tom. In the days when boxing was illegal in New York state, a loophole in the law permitted athletic clubs to stage fights. On nights there was a fight here, the saloon became an athletic club. Sharkey's was immortalized in the paintings and prints of artist George Bellows. Begun in 1907, his "boxing" paintings are full of energy and color and have become iconic.

### 490 Columbus Avenue
*Hellmann's Delicatessen*   Hellmann's Blue Ribbon Mayonnaise was introduced by German American Richard Hellmann, the owner of this delicatessen, in 1912. His dressing was so popular that within three years he gave up his store to devote his attention to his new mayonnaise plant in Astoria, Queens.

## COLUMBUS CIRCLE

The reputed head of the Brooklyn mafia, Joe Colombo Sr., was fatally shot in the head at an Italian American civil rights rally here on June 28, 1971. Colombo, the organizer of the event, died after seven years in a coma. Jerome Johnson, the assailant, was killed at the scene. Johnson's reason for the attack was never known, but it is believed he was hired by a rival gang.

## DYCKMAN STREET

### Dyckman Street at Payson Avenue
The jawbone of a mastodon was unearthed near this intersection on March 24, 1925. These prehistoric giants inhabited the entire Hudson

River Valley during the last ice age, about 18,000 years ago. The discovery, now in the collection of the American Museum of Natural History, is the remains of the oldest known inhabitant of Manhattan.

## EAST END AVENUE

### East End Avenue at East 88th Street

*Gracie Mansion*   Archibald Gracie built this charming house overlooking the East River in 1799 as a summer home. A successful merchant and ship owner, he entertained Louis-Philippe (later king of France), Alexander Hamilton, Washington Irving, and the Marquis de Lafayette here until he was forced to sell in 1823. It remained a private home until 1896, when it was purchased by the city's Parks Department. It was the first home of the Museum of the City of New York in 1924 before becoming the official mayoral residence. Fiorello La Guardia moved in on August 1, 1942. The mansion has been the site of many weddings, but only one former mayor was married here. On May 24, 2003, Rudolph W. Giuliani wed Judith Nathan, with his successor, Mayor Michael R. Bloomberg, officiating. Late in his second term Giuliani had separated from his second wife, TV personality and actress Donna Hanover, and moved in with friends, leaving Gracie Mansion to the First Lady and their children. Bloomberg, a billionaire, has never lived here, preferring his own town house on East 79th Street.

## EDGECOMB AVENUE

### 409 Edgecomb Avenue

*Colonial Parkway Apartments* ✦ This 13-story apartment house was the heart of Harlem's exclusive Sugar Hill section, so named because life was "so sweet" for those celebrated African American residents who could afford to live here from the 1930s to the 1950s. Tenants who have lived here include W. E. B. Du Bois, Roy Wilkins, William Stanley Braithwaite, and Thurgood Marshall, the first African American Supreme Court justice.

## FORT TRYON PARK

The Battle of Fort Washington during the Revolutionary War was fought on this ridge on November 16, 1776. An American, John Corbin, was killed while firing his cannon. His wife, Margaret, took his place. After the Americans were soundedly defeated, a wounded Margaret

Gracie Mansion was part of Carl Schurz Park before becoming the official home to New York City mayors.

was released by the British victors. She was the first woman to receive a pension from the U.S. government as a disabled soldier.

## FORT WASHINGTON AVENUE

### 177 Fort Washington Avenue
*Milstein Hospital* ✦ For more than 15 years, Martha Sharp Crawford von Bülow, known as Sunny, was a patient here in a ninth-floor room with a panoramic view of the Hudson River. The wealthy heiress was the tranquil eye of a legal hurricane since slipping into an irreversible coma the night of December 21, 1980, in Newport, Rhode Island. Her husband, Claus, was tried twice for and eventually acquitted of her attempted murder. The prosecution claimed he'd tried to kill her with a lethal injection of insulin that induced her coma. She never regained consciousness and died on December 6, 2008. Former President Bill Clinton underwent cardiac bypass surgery here on September 6, 2004.

## GRACIE SQUARE

### 10 Gracie Square ✦
Unfazed by the Great Depression, this luxury building was completed in 1931 and included East River dockage to ferry the wealthy to their

country homes in Connecticut and Long Island. Longtime resident Madame Chiang Kai-shek died in her sleep here in her 18-room apartment on October 23, 2003, at the age of 105.

## HIGHBRIDGE PARK

Named for the oldest bridge in Manhattan, this park was the setting of the most famous political commercial ever filmed. The "Daisy" ad, created for Lyndon B. Johnson's 1964 presidential campaign, showed a little girl counting petals replaced by a nuclear countdown and a mushroom blast. Johnson's Republican opponent, Barry Goldwater, was not mentioned, but the implication was clear: He would lead the nation into nuclear war. Broadcast only once, on September 7, 1964, it helped ensure Johnson's landslide victory and heralded the birth of political attack ads.

## LENOX AVENUE

### 596 Lenox Avenue, between West 140th and West 141st streets

*Savoy Ballroom* Billed as "the world's most beautiful ballroom," the Savoy was also one of the largest. On busy nights it accommodated crowds of up to 5,000. The second-level dance floor extended the length of the entire block. After opening on March 12, 1926, and for the next two decades, this spot became *the* place to dance. Many new dances originated and were popularized here, including the Black Bottom and the Lindy Hop. Drummer and bandleader Chick Webb, the "King of the Savoy," challenged other bands in the popular "battle of the bands." Benny Goodman's hit rendition of "Stompin' at the Savoy" in 1936 served as a tribute to and advertisement for the ballroom.

### 644 Lenox Avenue

*Cotton Club* First opened and owned by former heavyweight boxing champion Jack Johnson in 1920 as the Club Deluxe, it was reopened for white customers only in 1923 as the Cotton Club. The "Old South" decor, complete with slaves' cabins and cotton plants, was the stage set for such entertainers as Duke Ellington, Cab Calloway, Bill "Bojangles" Robinson, Ethel Waters, and the Nicholas Brothers. The club was popular with the adventurous set looking for new thrills, including the city's "Night Mayor," Jimmy Walker. After a race riot on March 19, 1935, whites stopped coming uptown and the club moved to the Times Square area.

## MADISON AVENUE

### 689 Madison Avenue

Theodore Roosevelt's residency here became the focus of an effort to disqualify him as the Republican nominee for governor in 1898. His opponents claimed he didn't fulfill the New York state gubernatorial requirement of having lived five continuous years in the state because he had spent part of that time in Washington, D.C., while Assistant Secretary of the Navy in 1897. As part of a political deal, the issue was dropped and Roosevelt won the nomination and the governorship.

### 816 Madison Avenue

In 1886 Grover Cleveland was the first, and only, President to marry in the White House. Two years later he and his bride, Frances, moved into a four-story town house that once stood at this address. The President had just lost his reelection bid to Benjamin Harrison. While Cleveland was in "retirement" in New York, his daughter Ruth was born, on October 3, 1891. The following year Cleveland made a comeback in a rematch with Harrison. He won the presidency and returned to Washington, D.C., with his new family, thereby achieving another first as the only President to serve two nonconsecutive terms.

### 1018 Madison Avenue ✦

*Light Gallery*   Robert Mapplethorpe had his first photography exhibition at this address in one of the first art galleries devoted to contemporary photographs. His small Polaroids of flowers and nude men were displayed in a space at the back of the gallery used for new, experimental works. The show's invitation, a nude self-portrait with a strategically placed adhesive dot, elicited a good turnout for the opening on January 6, 1973.

### 1111 Madison Avenue ✦

In September 1898, newlyweds Alfred and Emmeline Stieglitz returned from their extended honeymoon and moved into a top-floor 12-room luxury apartment here paid for by the wealthy bride. On July 8, 1918, Emmeline unexpectedly returned home to find Stieglitz and Georgia O'Keeffe engaged in a compromising photo session. Outraged, she gave Stieglitz an ultimatum: He must either stop seeing O'Keeffe or move out. He left and returned only for his possessions. Some of his most beautiful photographs are of O'Keeffe, whom he married in 1924. The building is now the consulate of the Czech Republic.

## MORNINGSIDE DRIVE

### 60 Morningside Drive

*President's House, Columbia University* ✦ Before he became the thirty-fourth President of the United States, Dwight D. Eisenhower was the president of Columbia University. He was reluctant to take the position but felt pressured by the university trustees, who were determined to have the World War II hero as president. Eisenhower was released from his Pentagon duties and moved to this house in June 1948. It was an unhappy match from the start, as the general and the faculty were not very compatible. After just two years, Eisenhower gladly took on the job of advising the first Secretary of Defense, James Forrestal, in his newly created cabinet post, and shortly thereafter Eisenhower was made the commander of the North Atlantic Treaty Organization (NATO).

## PARK AVENUE

### Park Avenue between East 66th and East 67th streets, east side

*Seventh Regimental Armory* ✦ When built, this cavernous structure was the model for all future armories; it is now used for antique shows, for military units, and as a women's homeless shelter. Erected for the New York state militia's elite soldiers, the "Silk Stocking" regiment, it was home to the largest volunteer militia in the nineteenth century. On November 17, 1879, President Rutherford B. Hayes opened a combination world's fair, shopping mall, and sideshow in the huge drill hall to raise $140,000 to furnish the building. The result was a lavish smorgasbord of Victorian design, the best by Louis Comfort Tiffany. Some 35,000 New Yorkers paid their respects here to General Douglas MacArthur, who lay in state in the Clark Room on April 8, 1964.

### 730 Park Avenue ✦

Writer Edna Ferber died here at her home on April 16, 1968, at the age of 82. She wrote *Giant* and *Ice Palace* while in this building. This address was also home to songwriter Richard Rodgers from 1945 to 1971.

### 740 Park Avenue ✦

This was the childhood home of Jacqueline Kennedy Onassis from ages three to nine. Her maternal grandfather, James T. Lee, who also lived here, was a successful developer who had built this luxury apartment house in 1929. The year before, Jacqueline's mother, Janet Lee, had married John Vernou Bouvier III. Bouvier, a handsome free-spender, lived here because of his father-in-law's charity. The marriage ended in divorce the year they moved out, 1938.

## 820 Park Avenue +

This address was home to Herbert Henry Lehman, governor of New York from 1932 to 1942. He died in his apartment on December 5, 1963, the day he was to leave for Washington, D.C., to receive the Presidential Medal of Freedom from President Lyndon B. Johnson. This was also the last home of another New York governor, Alfred E. Smith. He lived here from the late 1930s until his death in 1944.

## 890 Park Avenue

*St. Ignatius Loyola* + This Catholic church was the site of Jacqueline Kennedy Onassis's funeral on the morning of May 23, 1994—the same neighborhood church where she was baptized as an infant and confirmed as a teenager. After the private service, the family accompanied the body aboard a chartered plane to Washington, D.C., where they were met by President Bill Clinton for the journey to Arlington National Cemetery. The former First Lady was buried next to her first husband, President John F. Kennedy.

## 895 Park Avenue +

Some 90 well-heeled guests attended a party here at the duplex apartment of composer Leonard Bernstein on January 14, 1970. The gathering was a fundraiser for the Black Panthers. In addition to the $10,000 raised for the militant left-wing group, the party aroused the interest of the FBI and the media. Tom Wolfe satirized the party in an article for *New York* magazine, labeling it "radical chic."

## Park Avenue at East 88th Street

CBS television news anchorman Dan Rather was beaten here by a man yelling, inscrutably, "Kenneth, what is the frequency?" on the evening of October 4, 1986. The assailant was not caught and the slightly surreal crime passed into legend, with the bizarre interrogative becoming a pop culture catchphrase and even a hit song by the rock band R.E.M. Eleven years later, a *Daily News* reporter connected the Rather attack with William Tager, who had been convicted of the fatal shooting, on August 31, 1994, of Campbell Montgomery, an NBC technician, outside the "Today" show studio. Tager, who said he believed the television networks were monitoring him and beaming messages into his head, plea-bargained a charge of first-degree murder down to one of first-degree manslaughter and was sent to Sing Sing prison.

## RIVERSIDE DRIVE

### 137 Riverside Drive
*Clarendon Apartments* ✦ William Randolph Hearst lived here in one of the city's largest apartments from 1908 to 1926. Five years after moving in, he bought the entire building in order to expand his already huge apartment. Over the years his palatial home grew to include the top five floors of the 12-story building. The 30-room apartment contained the "English Room," the "Gothic Room," and a "Tapestry Gallery" that was two stories high and ran the entire length of the building.

### 490 Riverside Drive
*Riverside Church* ✦ On April 4, 1967, the Reverend Dr. Martin Luther King Jr. spoke here in favor of merging the civil rights and anti–Vietnam

After his landlord denied a request to remodel his already huge apartment, William Randolph Hearst bought the building at 137 Riverside Drive. This is the vaulted banquet hall used to display the publisher's tapestries and medieval armor collections.

War movements, saying that the war threatened African Americans' struggle for equal rights. His speech, which encouraged draft evasion, called the U.S. government "the greatest purveyor of violence in the world today." Eleven days later, King helped lead the largest antiwar demonstration to date—consisting of more than 100,000 people—from Central Park to United Nations headquarters. Desmond Tutu, Nelson Mandela, César Chávez, and Fidel Castro have also spoken here.

### Riverside Drive at West 122nd Street

*Grant's Tomb* ✦ The city's most popular tourist attraction at the turn of the twentieth century, the tomb is largely overlooked today. Built not only to house the remains of the eighteenth President and Civil War hero and those of his wife, it was conceived as a grand monument, in the age of monuments, to the growing self-assurance of America's standing in the modern world. On August 8, 1885, the gathering of mourners along the funeral route from City Hall was the largest ever seen in the city. Twelve years later on "Grant Day," April 27, 1897, the seventy-fifth anniversary of his birth, the crowds were even larger for the formal dedication of the finished edifice. Millions of spectators, along with President William McKinley, Vice President Garret A. Hobart, and 13 governors, watched 60,000 marching troops and a parade of ships in the Hudson during the ceremonies. The pomp and significance of the event were compared by contemporary observers to the transfer of Napoleon's remains from St. Helena to Paris.

Grant's tomb was also a focal point in the fall of 1909 for the Hudson–Fulton celebration, which saluted the anniversaries of Henry Hudson's discoveries in 1609 and Robert Fulton's successful development of the steamboat in 1809. Many of these events were staged along the banks of the Hudson River. One of the highlights was Wilbur Wright's flight in an airplane over Grant's Tomb on October 4, 1909. The pioneer aviator took off from Governors Island, flew up the Hudson, circled the monument, and returned to Governors Island. The plane was outfitted with a red canoe in case a water landing proved necessary. This historic 33-minute trip included the first airplane flight over the island of Manhattan.

### 765 Riverside Drive

This address marks the spot where the home of John James Audubon stood until 1930. In 1841, the painter and naturalist bought 24 acres and built a home he called "Minnie's Land," in honor of his wife. He died

On August 8, 1885, the body of former President Ulysses S. Grant was first laid to rest in this temporary hillside tomb in Riverside Park. Today's grandiose tomb was built with donations from over 90,000 people, the largest fundraising operation up to that time.

here on January 27, 1851. He is buried in nearby Trinity Cemetery, which was once part of the Audubon farm.

## ST. NICHOLAS AVENUE

### St. Nicholas Avenue at 145th Street

The single worst accident during the construction of the subway took place 60 feet below this intersection on October 24, 1903. This cut of the subway system, the second-longest two-track rock tunnel ever built in the United States and the deepest in the entire New York City system, was a complicated engineering endeavor. A crew of subway workers, having just heard the all-clear call from their foreman, returned to the recent blast site. A 44-foot boulder dropped from the roof of the tunnel, killing six men instantly and seriously injuring eight more. The foreman and nine of the workers, mainly immigrant Italian laborers, died.

On October 28, 1943, W. C. Handy, the famous blues composer, fractured his skull after falling off this subway platform. The accident left him completely blind.

### 935 St. Nicholas Avenue +

Musician Duke Ellington lived at this address for 22 years, from 1939 to 1961, in apartment 4A. Not far from here is the "A" subway line, which opened while Ellington lived here. This subway was the inspiration for one of his most popular songs, "Take the A Train."

## ST. NICHOLAS PARK

*Hamilton Grange National Memorial* + The Grange was the country home of Alexander Hamilton, author of many of the *Federalist Papers* and the nation's first Secretary of the Treasury, when this area of northern Manhattan was considered "the country." The only home Hamilton ever owned, the two-story Federal-style house was built for him in 1802 by architect John McComb. The 35-acre estate had a grove of 13 gum trees, representing the original colonies, given to Hamilton by George Washington. He was very happy here and once wrote of his beloved retreat, "I am always sure to find a sweet asylum from care and pain." Unfortunately, he was able to enjoy only two years here before he was killed by Vice President Aaron Burr in their famous duel. This is the third site for the house. Originally located on 143rd Street west of Convent Avenue, it was moved two blocks south to a cramped site on Convent Avenue in 1889 to escape demolition. It was moved to the park on June 7, 2008.

## ST. NICHOLAS PLACE

### 10 St. Nicholas Place +

Built in 1888, this New York City–landmarked Romanesque Revival mansion was home to James Anthony Bailey, partner in the famous Ringling Brothers and Barnum and Bailey Circus. The 30-room limestone residence—one of the few surviving freestanding mansions in Manhattan—is now a funeral parlor.

## WEST END AVENUE

### 128 West End Avenue

*Consolidated Edison Company's Energy Control Center* At 5:15 P.M. on November 9, 1965, the first indication of serious trouble for the city's

This fanciful illustration depicts Alexander Hamilton's Grange at its original location near West 143rd Street. In its new, larger park site all four side porches were restored to their historical appearance.

The Grange being moved to its new location in St. Nicholas Park. (National Park Service)

power supply appeared on the instruments here. Within minutes, the lights in the room flickered and the city slipped into darkness. This was the beginning of the nation's worst blackout. The power failure, which spread across nine states and three Canadian provinces, affected 30 million people. Power was not fully restored to the city until 13 hours later.

## YORK AVENUE

### 1270 York Avenue
*Rockefeller Institute for Medical Research* ✦ It was here, in the early 1940s, that biologist Oswald Avery and his colleagues discovered that the substance responsible for recording hereditary information in cells is deoxyribonucleic acid, better known as DNA.

## FIRST AVENUE

### 1152 First Avenue
*T.G.I. Friday's* A landmark in the dating scene, this address was the birthplace of the modern singles bar. Alan N. Stillman bought the run-down Good Tavern for $10,000 and redecorated, creating a clean, cheerful, woman-friendly meeting place for the neighborhood's young urban professionals long before they were called yuppies. Opened on March 15, 1965, the bar was a tremendous success. By that summer, police barricades had to be used to control the crowds of thirsty singles, and within a year Stillman's enterprise earned a million dollars. The formula, along with the Tiffany-style lamps and potted ferns, was quickly imitated by Maxwell's Plum, Mister Laffs, and a thousand other bars across the country.

### First Avenue between East 70th and East 75th streets, east side
*Jones Woods* A beautiful wooded tract of land that swept down to the shore of the East River, Jones Woods was considered a likely candidate for the city's new park in 1851, but it was rejected in favor of what became Central Park. On September 17, 1860, Stephen A. Douglas, the Illinois senator and Democratic Party candidate for the presidency, was the guest of honor at a campaign rally and barbecue here. Some 3,000 loyal supporters attended and listened to the senator offer them solutions to the crisis of slavery and possible secession of the Southern states. On election day, Douglas received an almost two-to-one plurality in the city, but Abraham Lincoln, whom Douglas had defeated in a

1152 First Avenue was the first location of the popular T.G.I. Friday's bar. Today there are more than 1,000 restaurants in 60 countries. (Courtesy of T.G.I. Friday's)

Senate race two years before, carried the state's 35 electoral votes and won the presidency.

### 1901 First Avenue

*Metropolitan Hospital* ✚ Legendary jazz great Billie Holiday ended her long-running battle with drug addiction and the police at this hospital. While here, she was placed under arrest for heroin possession after a nurse reported finding the drug in a silver foil package in her room. Holiday died here on July 17, 1959.

**2242 First Avenue ✚**

*New York Mortuary Services*   After famed British broadcaster Alistair Cooke died of cancer in his Manhattan home on March 30, 2004, his body was brought here for cremation. A year later, his family learned that Cooke's bones had been harvested and sold. The company removed body parts, some possibly diseased, from the corpse and then sold them as transplants for the living. At least two of those involved in the crime plea-bargained and were imprisoned.

## THIRD AVENUE

### Third Avenue at East 66th Street, northwest corner
*Sign of the Dove Tavern*   Nathan Hale, the Connecticut schoolteacher–turned–American spy, was captured by the British at this tavern on September 21, 1776. Legend has it that he said his famous last words, "I only regret that I have but one life to lose for my country," and was hanged nearby the next day.

## FIFTH AVENUE

### 781 Fifth Avenue
*Sherry Netherland Hotel* ✚ Jesse Livermore, infamous stock market operator, shot and killed himself outside the men's room of this hotel on November 28, 1940. Livermore, nicknamed the "Boy Plunger of Wall Street," was a speculator often singled out for contributing to the crash of 1929.

### 810 Fifth Avenue ✚
After losing his race for the presidency in 1960 and a subsequent race for the governorship of California in 1962, Richard M. Nixon left his native state and moved to this corner building in 1963. In spite of his "last press conference" vow that he was leaving politics and "you [the press] won't have Nixon to kick around anymore," he began campaigning for Republican candidates and resurrecting his political career. One Republican he did not help was New York Governor Nelson A. Rockefeller, who had owned an apartment here since 1937. Rockefeller and Nixon, rivals for their party's 1968 nomination, used different elevators to their respective homes to avoid each other. Nixon was elected President in 1968 and was forced to resign in 1974 under threat of certain impeachment and removal from office. His successor, Gerald R. Ford, appointed Rockefeller his Vice President.

## Fifth Avenue at 67th Street

Winston Churchill, forgetting that Americans drive on the right-hand side of the road, stepped in front of an oncoming car at this intersection on December 13, 1931. He was dragged several feet and fractured two ribs. The future British prime minister was taken to Lenox Hill Hospital, where King George telephoned to ask about his condition.

## 962 Fifth Avenue

The world's costliest residence, when built, was on this corner. Built by millionaire Montana Senator William Andrews Clark, it stood only 24 years, from 1903 until it was torn down in 1927. This proud monument was celebrated in 1904 in a poem by Wallace Irwin:

> Senator Copper of Tonapah Ditch
> Made a clean billion in minin' and sich
> Hiked for Noo York, where his money he blew
> Buildin' a palace on Fift' Avenoo
> "How," sez the Senator, "can I look proudest?
> Build me a house that'll holler the loudest."

## Fifth Avenue between East 80th and East 84th streets

*Metropolitan Museum of Art* ✦ The museum's most famous visitor was *La Giaconda*, more popularly known as the *Mona Lisa*, by Leonardo da Vinci, which went on exhibit beginning on February 7, 1963. The lady with the enigmatic smile was displayed behind bulletproof glass and given Secret Service protection. Some 16,000 visitors waited on line to see her that first day.

## 995 Fifth Avenue

*Stanhope Hotel* ✦ Charlie "Bird" Parker, the jazz alto-saxophone musician, died here in the suite of his friend and jazz maven Baroness "Nica" de Koeningswarter, an heiress to the Rothschild fortune. Parker, a longtime abuser of drugs and alcohol, had refused to be taken to the hospital and died of a heart attack on March 12, 1955, at the age of 34.

## 1040 Fifth Avenue ✦

In 1964, Jacqueline Kennedy, the widow of President John F. Kennedy, moved to this apartment building hoping to find some privacy for herself and her children, Caroline and John Jr. She lived here in her fifteenth-floor apartment until her death on the night of May 19, 1994, of cancer of the lymphatic system at the age of 64.

The Fifth Avenue mansion of Senator William Andrews Clark of Montana, "The Copper King," was this French Empire–style towered concoction made of white granite. The 130-room palace was a testament to what money could buy at the beginning of the twentieth century.

## 1107 Fifth Avenue +

This site was once the town house of society leader Marjorie Merriweather Post Hutton, heir to the Post cereal fortune. In 1924, she was persuaded by a builder to tear down her home and allow him to re-create her 54-room mansion atop the current apartment house. A separate entrance and elevator allowed for her privacy. She lived in her triplex here until 1941. She was unable to rent out her spacious home, and it was eventually divided into six different apartments.

## 1130 Fifth Avenue +

Built in 1915, this mansion was one of the last grand private homes completed on Fifth Avenue. Federal income tax (instituted in the 1860s), the difficulties of running a large house, and the gradual acceptance of apartment living by the rich were changing the avenue into a row of apartment buildings. One man who could still afford the luxury was Elbert Gary, a founder and longtime chairman of U.S. Steel. When he died here on August 15, 1927, his company was the largest industrial corporation in the world. It was widely speculated that the news of his death was delayed until after the close of the stock market for fear of the effect on the company's stock. As was the case with many of the remaining mansions, they became homes to societies or institutions. In 1953, the Audubon Society moved in, and in 1974 it was home to the International Center of Photography. In 1999, ICP sold the property to Bruce Kovner, who spent several years and a great deal of money to convert it back to a private residence.

## 1489 Fifth Avenue

Dressmaker and entrepreneur Lena Bryant opened a shop at this address in 1904. While here, she created her well-known design for a modern, stylish maternity dress. The success of this dress enabled her company, Lane (an early misspelling) Bryant, to grow into today's clothing retail giant.

## 2078 Fifth Avenue

The country's ultimate pack rats, Homer and Langley Collyer, lived at this address for 38 years. The brothers—Homer, a lawyer, and Langley, a concert pianist—moved here in 1909. On March 21, 1947, the police were summoned to look for the reclusive brothers. What they found, after a day of burrowing through tons of refuse, was the emaciated body of Homer. It took another three weeks to find Langley's body. He, like his older sibling, apparently starved to death, ensnared in his own burglar booby-trap. The brothers had filled the house with more than 120 tons of junk, including five pianos and a Model T Ford automobile. They also left an estate worth $300,000.

## EAST 60TH STREET

### 14 East 60th Street

*Hotel Fourteen* ✦ Still located at this address, this residential apartment house was the headquarters in June 1945 for David Ben-Gurion and other emissaries from Palestine—so many, in fact, that it was nicknamed "Kibbutz 14." They were making plans for a future British withdrawal from Palestine and the establishment of a Jewish state. Ben-Gurion, the future first prime minister of Israel, was in New York to find American Jews willing to bankroll and support the fight for independence.

The ground level was home to the Copacabana. Opened in 1940, this famed nightclub headlined Frank Sinatra, Tony Bennett, and Sammy Davis Jr. On July 24, 1956, Dean Martin and Jerry Lewis made their last public appearance together as an act. That last audience was filled with comic greats, among them Milton Berle, Eddie Cantor, Jackie Gleason, and Jack Benny.

## EAST 61ST STREET

### 6 East 61st Street

*Hotel Pierre* ✦ Built by famed chef Charles Pierre, this hotel opened for business one year after the stock market crash of 1929. Wealthy guests, seemingly unfazed by the Depression, dined on opening night (October 1, 1930) at a dinner prepared by another renowned epicurean, 85-year-old Auguste Escoffier, who was hired to set up the hotel's kitchen.

Many guests were decidedly upset on January 2, 1972, when the largest hotel jewel robbery in history took place here. Five burglars wearing masks and tuxedos stole an estimated $10 million in cash and precious gems from the hotel's safe-deposit boxes. The two-hour heist was never solved, but a million dollars' worth of the jewels were eventually recovered.

### 151 East 61st Street ✦

At 12:55 A.M. on June 2, 1919, a bomb rocked this address, the home of Judge Charles C. Nott Jr. The homemade bomb exploded prematurely, killing the man and the woman who were planting it on the front stoop. The judge was away in Connecticut and no one in the house was injured. This bombing was one of many that evening in what was believed to be a nationwide plot to retaliate against the U.S. Justice Department's crackdown on suspected radicals and anarchists. Bombs went off in Boston, Cleveland, and Pittsburgh. An explosion also damaged the home of Attorney General A. Mitchell Palmer in Washington, D.C. Again the bomber was killed by the blast, and his target escaped injury.

### 217 East 61st Street ✦

Still standing, this town house was a wedding present from President Theodore Roosevelt to his flamboyant daughter Alice in 1906. Alice married, in a White House ceremony, Congressman Nicholas Longworth of Ohio, who later became Speaker of the House. When another White House wedding took place 65 years later, that of Patricia Nixon to Edward F. Cox in 1971, Mrs. Longworth was in attendance. Critic Clifton Fadiman also lived in this house, as did actor Montgomery Clift, who died of a heart attack here on July 23, 1966.

## EAST 63RD STREET

### 16 East 63rd Street ✦

Edie Sedgwick, 1960s flower child and drug addict, lived in an apartment at this address during her "15 minutes" of fame. Daughter of wealthy parents, Edie was discovered by Andy Warhol and transformed into his companion, alter ego, and star of several of his movies.

### 120 East 63rd Street ✦

At 5:32 P.M. on December 5, 1933, the state of Utah ratified the Twenty-first amendment to the U.S. Constitution, officially repealing Prohibition and ending "The Noble Experiment." Three minutes later, on a sidewalk outside this address, Herbert Chase had the distinction of being the first post-repeal person to be arrested for public intoxication. The 26-year-old was arraigned in night court and given a suspended sentence.

### 154 East 63rd Street ✦

From 1927 to 1950, this address was home to Judge Samuel Seabury, a political reformer who spent much of his career fighting Tammany Hall corruption. After midnight on New Year's Day 1934, Fiorello La Guardia took the mayoral oath of office in the library of this town house. The new mayor wanted to honor Judge Seabury for his support and also felt that a fancy inauguration celebration in the midst of the Great Depression would be unseemly. The ceremony was repeated four years later on January 1, 1938, for the mayor's second term.

## WEST 63RD STREET

### 22 West 63rd Street

*Daley's 63rd Street Theater*   After playing here for more than 41 weeks, the universally panned but provocative play *Sex* was just about to close when a lucky thing happened. On February 9, 1927, the police raided the theater and arrested the star and playwright, Mae West, and the rest of the cast. The bawdy West was told that if she canceled the show, the officials would drop the charges. But West chose to fight instead. At her court date, April 19, 1927, she was found guilty of corrupting the morals of youth, sentenced to prison for 10 days, and fined $500. The publicity made West a celebrity.

## EAST 64TH STREET

### 29 East 64th Street +

Mary Scott Lord Dimmick Harrison, the widow of President Benjamin Harrison, died here in her apartment on January 5, 1948, at the age of 89. Mrs. Harrison, the President's second wife, married him after he left office and never lived in the White House. She was active in Republican politics well into her eighties.

### 133 East 64th Street +

On December 11, 2008, Bernard L. Madoff was arrested and charged with operating a $65 billion Ponzi scheme, wherein new investment money is used to pay existing investors. The scam, the largest in financial history, destroyed the financial security of thousands of Madoff's clients, including celebrities, a U.S. senator, and charities. Placed under 24-hour house arrest for three months, he lived here in his luxury penthouse. He was sentenced to 150 years on June 29, 2009.

### 210 East 64th Street

*Manhattan Eye, Ear and Throat Hospital* +   On October 29, 2001, this hospital was closed when it was learned that an employee, Kathy T. Nguyen, was dying of inhalation anthrax. She was the latest victim of a frightening new terrorist attack, adding to the national anxiety in the immediate wake of the attacks of September 11. Several anthrax-laced letters were sent to the news media and politicians, resulting in the deaths of five people, including Nguyen's. The hospital, which re-opened a week later, was free of any contamination, as was Nguyen's Bronx apartment. It is still a mystery how she came into contact with the deadly bacteria. Seven years later, the FBI announced that the biot-errorist was Bruce E. Ivins, a U.S. government microbiologist. Ivins committed suicide on July 29, 2008, just as the FBI was about to charge him with murder.

## WEST 64TH STREET

### 170 West 64th Street

*Con Edison*   On November 16, 1940, the discovery on a windowsill of a small wooden box was the beginning of a mystery unsolved for 17 years. Inside was a crude pipe bomb, the first of more than 37, left by "the Mad Bomber," as he was dubbed by the press. His bombs, along with tirades against the electric utility Consolidated Edison, were left all over the city: at the New York Public Library, Grand Central Terminal, and Radio City Music Hall. Fifteen people were injured before George Metesky, a disgruntled former Con Edison employee, was arrested at his Connecticut home on January 18, 1957. He was convicted and spent 17 years in a prison for the criminally insane. He was released in 1974.

## EAST 65TH STREET

### 47-49 East 65th Street +

These are two separate town houses with a shared neo-Georgian front entrance. One town house was a 1905 Christmas present from Sara Roosevelt to her only child, Franklin D. Roosevelt, and his bride, Eleanor; the other was a home for herself. The future President and his family lived in No. 49, and Sara lived in No. 47. This living arrangement reflected the close relationship between Roosevelt and his mother, and it also contributed to the often-strained relationship between Eleanor and her mother-in-law. Twice in his lifetime Franklin here returned here to recuperate, each time from one of the most frightening diseases of the twentieth century. On September 19, 1918, Roosevelt, who was then the Assistant Secretary of the Navy, had just landed on the troop ship *USS Leviathan*. He nearly died from the Spanish influenza of 1918, one of the world's worst epidemics, which killed more than 20 million people. His second recuperation began on October 28, 1921, when he returned from the hospital with polio. He never fully recovered but learned to overcome his disability. He resumed his political career and became New York governor in 1929 and President in 1933.

### 142 East 65th Street +

Former President Richard M. Nixon, who spent much of his political wilderness years between his vice presidency and his presidency in New

York City, returned to Manhattan following a few years of self-imposed exile in San Clemente, California, after his resignation because of the Watergate and related scandals. He and his wife, Pat, lived in this town house for about a year and a half until 1981. Nixon had tried to buy several cooperative apartments in the neighborhood but was rejected by the buildings' co-op boards on the grounds that his celebrity would be too disruptive to the other tenants. He and Pat later moved to Park Ridge, New Jersey; she died in 1993 and he died exactly 10 months later, in 1994, at the age of 81.

## EAST 66TH STREET

### 3 East 66th Street

A brownstone that once stood at this address was the home from 1881 to 1885 of former President Ulysses S. Grant. It was during this time in New York that Grant formed a brokerage partnership with his son and Ferdinand Ward. The venture was a financial disaster and bankrupted Grant, his friends, and several banks. He spent the last years of his life writing his bestselling *Memoirs* to provide for his family after his imminent death.

### 4 East 66th Street ✦

This was the home of Bernard Baruch, presidential advisor, financier, and the man for whom Baruch College is named. While visiting here on January 5, 1953, British Prime Minister Winston Churchill met with another World War II ally, President-elect Dwight D. Eisenhower. Baruch lived here from 1948 until his fatal heart attack on June 20, 1965.

### 57 East 66th Street ✦

Artist Andy Warhol bought this 1911 Georgian-style town house in 1974. Warhol, an eclectic collector, used the house as a combination art warehouse, flea market, and living quarters. After his death in 1987, his estate had Sotheby's auction off the contents of the house. The nearly 10,000 items in the 10-day sale raised $25.3 million. The treasures ranged from antique jewelry to Warhol's collection of cookie jars.

### 200 East 66th Street

*Manhattan House* ✦ Big Band musician Benny Goodman lived and died—of a heart attack, on June 13, 1986—in this apartment house. Found by his side were his clarinet and a music stand holding a Brahms composition.

Bernard Baruch visited with two old friends, General Dwight D. Eisenhower (*right*) and Winston Churchill (*left*), at his home at 4 East 66th Street on January 5, 1953. In two weeks, Eisenhower would be sworn in as President and in October Churchill would be reelected as British prime minister.

### 265 East 66th Street

*Solow Tower* ✦ Window washer brothers Alcides and Edgar Moreno and an improperly secured scaffold plummeted to the street from this skyscraper on December 7, 2007. Edgar died on impact, but, miraculously, Alcides survived the 47-floor fall. His survival was partially attributed to the fact that he clung to the scaffold like a surfboard, thus slowing and cushioning his record fall. He has recovered enough to walk and talk.

## WEST 66TH STREET

### 7 West 66th Street

*American Broadcasting Company* ✦   Once the site of a stable called Durland's Riding Academy, this television studio was the site of the fourth and final debate between Vice President Richard M. Nixon and Massachusetts Senator John F. Kennedy on October 21, 1960. These debates, which would forever change American presidential campaigns by establishing television as the definitive medium for reaching the voters, helped elect Kennedy two weeks later. The most heated of the debates, this one was devoted to foreign policy, particularly America's dealings with Fidel Castro.

### 57 West 66th Street

*St. Nicholas Skating Rink*   One of America's earliest indoor ice-skating rinks was built on this site in 1896. The building later became an arena important in the history of boxing. Jack Johnson, Jess Willard, Floyd Patterson, and Cassius Clay Jr. (later Muhammad Ali) all fought matches in the St. Nicholas Ring. It is now the site of the American Broadcasting Company's headquarters.

## EAST 67TH STREET

### 163 East 67th Street

*Park East Synagogue* ✛ An historic meeting took place here on April 18, 2008, when Benedict XVI, on his first visit to the United States as pope, visited a Jewish place of worship. It was only the third papal visit to a synagogue in the 2,000-year history of the Catholic church. The German-born pontiff, who had been conscripted into Hitler Youth as a 14-year-old, met with Rabbi Arthur Schneier, a Holocaust survivor.

## WEST 67TH STREET

### 1 West 67th Street

*Hotel Des Artistes* ✛ Harry Crosby, a tortured poet of the 1920s, killed himself and his girlfriend, Josephine Bigelow, here on December 10, 1929. These luxurious studio apartments have been home to Rudolph Valentino, Norman Rockwell, Isadora Duncan, Fannie Hurst, and Berenice Abbott. Another longtime resident was illustrator and portrait painter Howard Chandler Christy. His murals of wood nymphs decorate the walls of the street-level restaurant, Café des Artistes, which closed in 2009.

### 15 West 67th Street

*Central Park Studios* ✛ This was home and studio to artist Stuart Davis from 1955 to 1964. It was also home to poet Robert Lowell. The first issue of *The New York Review of Books* was born on Lowell's dining room table in 1963.

### 33 West 67th Street

*Atelier Building* ✛ From 1914 to 1920, apartment 2FE was the home of Walter and Louise Arensberg, two of the earliest and most important collectors of modern art in America. In addition to filling this soaring two-story space with art by Marcel Duchamp and Henri Matisse, the wealthy couple made their home a gathering place for the avant-garde. They donated their famous collection to the Philadelphia Museum of Art in 1950. Illustrator James Montgomery Flagg, creator of the "Uncle Sam Wants You" recruiting poster, also lived here.

## EAST 68TH STREET

### 39 East 68th Street ✦
This was the longtime home and office of Roy Cohn, a truly polarizing figure in American politics. Cohn first became a household name as Senator Joseph McCarthy's chief counsel during the televised Army hearings in 1954. After he and the Wisconsin senator were discredited, Cohn began a lucrative legal practice representing wealthy defendants from society matrons to crime bosses. He lived here until his death of complications resulting from AIDS in 1986.

### 525 East 68th Street
*New York Hospital–Cornell Medical Center* ✦ On October 23, 1979, the deposed shah of Iran was admitted to the seventeenth floor of the George Baker Pavilion under the assumed name of David Newsome. He had just entered the country secretly from Mexico for cancer treatment and a gall bladder operation. Within hours of his arrival the press broke the story. Two weeks later, "student" demonstrators in Tehran reacted to the news by occupying the U.S. embassy and capturing 52 Americans. In return for the hostages, the demonstrators demanded that the shah be returned to Iran for trial and execution. The U.S. government refused. The shah eventually left the United States in search of a country that would grant him sanctuary and died the following year in Egypt. The hostages were not released until January 20, 1981, moments after the inauguration of President Ronald Reagan, who had defeated incumbent President Jimmy Carter in part because of the hostage crisis.

Eight years later, another gall bladder operation at this same hospital would also have tragic repercussions. Pop artist and media star Andy Warhol died in his private room on the twelfth floor in the early morning hours of February 22, 1987, after complications from his gall bladder operation. The hospital settled a wrongful-death suit with the Warhol estate five years later.

Former President Richard M. Nixon died here on April 22, 1994. The 81-year-old Cold Warrior and Watergate "unindicted co-conspirator" had been brought here four days earlier after a suffering a stroke in his suburban Park Ridge, New Jersey, home.

## EAST 69TH STREET

### 157 East 69th Street ✝

The carriage houses along this block of East 69th Street were built in the 1880s for the mansions and town houses to the west toward Central Park. All have been restored and converted to modern use. No. 157 was the home and studio of abstract-expressionist painter Mark Rothko. The brilliant colorist killed himself here on the morning of February 25, 1970.

### 169 EAST 69TH STREET ✝

Reuben Lucius "Rube" Goldberg, the creator of cartoons of wonderfully absurd contraptions, died here at his home at the age of 87 on December 7, 1970. In 1948 Goldberg won a Pulitzer Prize for his editorial cartooning.

## WEST 69TH STREET

### 38 West 69th Street ✝

Exiled German expressionist painter Max Beckmann once lived at this address. On December 27, 1950, he told his wife he was going for a walk and maybe to the Metropolitan Museum of Art, which was exhibiting one of his self-portraits. He died of a heart attack on the corner of West 61st Street and Central Park West.

## WEST 71ST STREET

### 75 West 71st Street

After living in a large suite at the Fifth Avenue Hotel for two years, Civil War General William T. Sherman bought a four-story town house at this address in 1888. He died here on St. Valentine's Day 1891, a week after his seventy-first birthday. A large funeral was held at St. Patrick's Cathedral to mark the passing of one of the last of the Union generals.

### 160 West 71st Street ✝

*Alamac Hotel*  The International Grandmasters Tournament, better known as the "New York 1924," began on St. Patrick's Day of that year at this one-time hotel. Dr. Emmanuel Lasker, who had lost his World Chess Champion title in 1921 after a remarkable 27-year reign, won again, beating José Raúl Capablanca. Lasker, who was also a brilliant mathematician and philosopher, later fled Nazi Germany and immigrated to New York City in 1937.

## EAST 72ND STREET

### East 72nd Street at Madison Avenue, northwest corner
A fortress-like Romanesque mansion designed by Stanford White in 1882 was home to the Tiffany family. Father Charles Lewis Tiffany, founder of the jewelry store, had this eight-story home built for himself, although he never lived here, and his two children and their families, including artist Louis Comfort. It dominated this corner until it was torn down in 1936.

### 39 East 72nd Street ✦
The French Jesuit priest Pierre Teilhard de Chardin died suddenly while at this address visiting friends on Easter Sunday, April 10, 1955. He was a brilliant scholar in several fields of study: geology, paleontology, philosophy, and the evolution of early humankind. It was his writings on evolution that put him at odds with the teachings of his church. The Vatican censored many of his works.

### 141 East 72nd Street ✦
This was the last home of Thomas E. Dewey. He was governor of New York from 1942 to 1954 and twice nominated as the Republican presidential candidate, in 1944 and 1948. He lived here between 1955 and 1971.

### 155 East 72nd Street
The notorious Dr. Max Jacobson once had an office here. Also known as "Dr. Feelgood" and "Miracle Max," he administered amphetamine-laced injections of hormones, vitamins, and steroids during the 1960s, a period when dangerous and addictive drugs were less understood or controlled. His roster of celebrity patients included Winston Churchill, Alan Jay Lerner, Timothy Leary, Tennessee Williams, and Truman Capote. Another of Jacobson's patients was John F. Kennedy, who first had an appointment while a presidential candidate in the fall of 1960 for relief of his lifelong back pain. The doctor secretly continued giving injections to Kennedy even while he was President. In 1975, the New York State Board of Regents revoked Jacobson's medical license. He died in 1979.

### 190 East 72nd Street

*Tower East* ✦    Author John Steinbeck died here at his home on December 20, 1968. He had only just recently moved to this address from 206 East 72nd Street, where he had lived since 1951.

### 524 East 72nd Street

*Belaire* ✦    On October 11, 2006, Cory Fulton Lidle, a New York Yankees pitcher and novice pilot, slammed his Cirrus SR20 plane into the thirteenth floor on the north side of this condominium tower. Both Lidle and his flight instructor, Tyler Stanger, were killed. No one in the building was seriously injured. In a strange coincidence, the plane destroyed the apartment of another high-profile accident victim—Kathleen Caronna, who was injured in 1997 when a Thanksgiving Day Parade balloon knocked over a lamp post. She was not at home at the time of the crash.

## WEST 72ND STREET

### 1 West 72nd Street

*The Dakota* ✦ This apartment house, built by Singer sewing machine magnate Edward Severin Clark and designed by Henry J. Hardenbergh, was fully rented even before it opened on October 24, 1884. The Dakota quickly overcame two serious obstacles to success—first that it was too far from the center of town and that apartment buildings were not socially acceptable for the upper classes. In the present day, the building has always been popular with artists, and two of the greatest musicians of the twentieth century lived and died here. John Lennon was shot just inside the entrance gate on December 8, 1980, by Mark David Chapman, and Leonard Bernstein died in his apartment on October 14, 1990, of a heart attack.

### 201 West 72nd Street

*The Alexandria* ✦ In the spring of 2003, Elizabeth Gibson found a large painting in the garbage in front of this apartment house. After some research, she discovered that her find was *Three People*, painted by Mexican artist Rufino Tamayo in 1970. The Houston, Texas, owners and the FBI had been looking for it for 20 years. In 2007, the returned painting was sold at a Sotheby's auction for $1.049 million. Gibson received a $15,000 reward and a finder's fee from Sotheby's.

### 214 West 72nd Street ✦

Now multiple apartments, this brownstone was the childhood home of writer Dorothy Parker. The family lived here from the time Dottie Rothschild was born in 1893 until her mother, Eliza, died in 1898.

## 253 WEST 72ND STREET

*Westover Apartments* ✦ Roseann Quinn, a teacher of the deaf, was stabbed to death here in her apartment on January 2, 1973. Quinn's murder by a pickup in a singles bar became a symbol of the dangers of the sexual revolution. Her case became the basis for the novel and subsequent movie *Looking for Mr. Goodbar.*

## EAST 73RD STREET

### 11 East 73rd Street ✦

The prestigious firm of McKim, Mead and White designed and built this Venetian *palazzo*-style mansion to the specifications of ailing publisher Joseph Pulitzer in 1903. Pulitzer, who was nearly blind, had a wooden model of the façade made so that he could judge the design by touch. The publisher was also painfully sensitive to sound and dictated that the house be as soundproof as possible. After moving in, he was troubled by the noise of a pump needed to control a spring beneath the house. In frustration the millionaire had another architectural firm build him a bedroom at the rear of the mansion. This bedroom, supported on its own foundation, had soundproofed walls, heavy double doors, and windows with three panes of plate glass. The building was converted to apartments in 1934.

### 127 East 73rd Street ✦

Stanford White designed this Federal-style town house for illustrator Charles Dana Gibson, his close friend. Gibson moved into this house in 1903 with his beautiful wife, Irene, his frequent model and the prototype for the famous "Gibson Girl." The artist died here on December 23, 1944, at the age of 77.

## EAST 74TH STREET

### 4 East 74th Street ✦

Painter Marc Chagall and his wife moved to a top-floor apartment of this Beaux Arts town house. This was their first American home after they fled Nazi-occupied France in 1941.

### 23 East 74th Street

*The Volney* ✦ This former residential hotel was a one-time home of Richard Rodgers in the 1940s. It was also the last home of Dorothy Parker, who died at this hotel on December 7, 1967. She had been living here since 1963. She wrote the play *Ladies of the Corridor* based on her life and observations here.

### 55 East 74th Street ✦

Eleanor Roosevelt, the 78-year-old "First Lady of the World," died in her apartment here on November 7, 1962. She had lived in this building since 1959.

### East 74th Street at the East River

Captain William Kidd's farm, Saw Kill, was on this site in the 1690s. During the Revolutionary War, this bluff was a battery fortified by the American rebels before the British occupation.

## WEST 74TH STREET

### 54 West 74th Street ✦

This was the address of Raphael Soyer's studio. Five weeks after the artist died on November 4, 1987, a burglar broke in and stole between 400 and 500 prints valued at up to $200,000.

### 100 West 74th Street ✦

Dr. Zane Grey opened a dental practice in this building in 1900, advertising "all modern methods and latest appliances for painless dentistry." Grey was miserable and after five years left the profession to try something else. He married, moved to rural Pennsylvania, and became wildly successful writing Western novels.

### 307 West 74th Street ✦

On October 11, 1984, the police raided the apartment here of Sheila Devin, who was actually socialite Sydney Biddle Barrows. She was charged with running a high-class prostitution ring of 20 to 30 call girls. The 32-year-old Barrows, a descendant of a family that had crossed on the *Mayflower*, was quickly dubbed the "Mayflower Madam" by the tabloid press. She went on to become a celebrity and to write self-help books.

## EAST 75TH STREET

### 216 East 75th Street ✦

The basement cold-water flat in this building was artist Andy Warhol's first apartment of his own, in 1952. He wasn't alone here for too long; a few weeks after he moved in, his mother sold her home in Pittsburgh and joined him.

## EAST 76TH STREET

### 6 East 76th Street ✦
Franklin D. Roosevelt married Anna Eleanor Roosevelt, his fifth cousin once removed, on St. Patrick's Day, March 17, 1905, at this town house of the bride's aunt Mrs. E. Livingston Ludlow. President Theodore Roosevelt, Eleanor's uncle, gave away the bride. "Well, Franklin," the President told the groom, his fifth cousin, after the ceremony, "there's nothing like keeping the name in the family."

### 35 East 76th Street
*The Carlyle Hotel* ✦ President Harry S. Truman often stayed at this hotel. It was here, during the early days of live television, that reporters with their bulky cameras would play catch-up during the President's "constitutionals" around the neighborhood. President John F. Kennedy used his apartment, 34A, as his New York City White House. The hotel also has another Kennedy family connection: John F. Kennedy Jr. had his last breakfast here the day of his fatal plane crash.

### 215 East 76th Street
On the morning of July 16, 1964, off-duty police Lieutenant Thomas Gilligan shot and killed James Powell, a 15-year-old African American youth, at this address. The incident had escalated after an apartment house superintendent sprayed water on Powell and his companions. Powell's death provoked race riots in Harlem and Bedford-Stuyvesant in Brooklyn. There were 520 arrests over a five-day period.

## WEST 76TH STREET

### 42 West 76th Street ✦
*Wright-Humanson School for the Deaf* Helen Keller came to this address in October 1894, at age 14, to attend school for two years. Her devoted teacher and friend, Annie Sullivan, accompanied her. While here, she improved her speech and lip-reading skills and studied French and German.

### 306 West 76th Street ✦
Comedian and singer Fanny Brice and her husband, Nicky Arnstein, lived at this address during most of the 1920s. Fanny, the long-suffering

Not a conventional beauty, Fanny Brice nonetheless became a star in Florenz Ziegfeld's "Follies." She lived at 306 West 76th Street during most of the 1920s.

wife, was often alone while mobster Nicky was in prison. After he was released from Leavenworth, he showed no signs of reform, and Fanny divorced him in 1927.

## EAST 77TH STREET

### 37 East 77th Street ✦
Novelist and historian Paul Leicester Ford was shot and killed here by his brother, Malcolm Ford, who then committed suicide. The deaths, the tragic result of a long family feud, took place in the library of the writer's apartment on the morning of May 8, 1902.

### 57 East 77th Street ✦
Conductor Victor Herbert collapsed and died of a heart attack while climbing the stairs here to visit his physician, Dr. Emmanuel Baruch, on May 26, 1924.

### 63 East 77th Street
The funeral for Boss William Magear Tweed was held here at the home of his son-in-law, Frederick Douglas, on April 17, 1878. Many of the

mourners who lined the streets followed the funeral procession to the family plot in Brooklyn's Green-Wood Cemetery.

## WEST 77TH STREET

### 44 West 77th Street
*Manhattan Square Studios* ✛ In 1909, sculptor Karl Bitter moved into this newly built neo-Gothic apartment house. He lived here until his death in 1915.

## EAST 79TH STREET

### 2 East 79th Street ✛
Oilman Harry Sinclair, who lived in this French château–style mansion from 1921 to 1929, was involved in the Teapot Dome scandal of the 1920s. He refused to testify at U.S. Senate hearings on the government oil leases and was held in contempt of Congress. He went to jail on the contempt charges for three months from this house in 1927, but he was acquitted on charges of defrauding the government. Later it was home to Augustus van Horne Stuyvesant Jr. and his sister, Ann Stuyvesant, the last direct descendants of Governor Peter Stuyvesant.

### 17 East 79th Street ✛
This limestone town house is home to Democrat-turned-Republican-turned-Independent, businessman-turned-mayor, Michael R. Bloomberg. In 2009, he spent $102 million of his own money—about $174 per vote—on his successful campaign for a third term. Bloomberg, the wealthiest man in New York City, chose to live here rather than in the mayor's official residence, Gracie Mansion.

### 39 East 79th Street ✛
This address was the home of etiquette expert Emily Post, who had this stylish apartment house built in 1925 and encouraged her friends to be tenants. America's supreme arbiter of good taste lived here until 1960.

### 108 East 79th Street
On December 12, 1910, Dorothy Arnold, 25-year-old heiress and niece of the late U.S. Supreme Court Justice Rufus Peckham, left her parents' home to go shopping downtown along Fifth Avenue. She encountered a girlfriend at Brentano's bookstore on 27th Street and then she vanished. Arnold's disappearance launched one of America's greatest manhunts. She was never found.

## WEST 79TH STREET

### 168 West 79th Street
*Notre Dame Convent School* ✦ The future president of the Philippines and populist answer to the corrupt Ferdinand Marcos, Corazon Aquino attended this school from 1947 to 1949.

## EAST 80TH STREET

### 2 East 80th Street ✦
Built by her grandfather F. W. Woolworth as a gift for her mother, this mansion was the birthplace of dime-store heiress Barbara Hutton on November 14, 1912. Always popular with the gossip columnists, the "Poor Little Rich Girl" was married seven times.

## EAST 82ND STREET

### 63 East 82nd Street ✦
This brick town house was home to writer Lillian Hellman from 1944 to 1970. Her longtime lover, Dashiel Hammett, joined her in 1958 and spent his dying days in her care. He died at nearby Lenox Hill Hospital on January 10, 1961.

## WEST 82ND STREET

### 155 West 82nd Street ✦
Future Cuban dictator Fidel Castro and his bride, Mirta, spent their honeymoon in this brownstone in the fall of 1948. They stayed in the apartment of her brother, Rafael Diaz-Balart. Rafael's sons Lincoln and Mario both became U.S. congressmen representing Florida.

## EAST 84TH STREET

### 128 East 84th Street
*Shanley's Laundry Shop* Next door to this address, a cellar entrance stairway was the drop-off point for $20,000 in blackmail money on Saturday, November 7, 1992. Republican Party fundraiser and socialite Joy Silverman had been instructed to have her doorman deliver the money in an envelope in exchange for nude photographs. The FBI had been working on the case, and agents were watching the scene. Within moments of the appointed time, 10:30 A.M., a woman picked up the envelope. The woman was only a go-between for New York State Chief

Judge of the Court of Appeals Sol Wachtler. The judge, the highest-ranking jurist in the state and likely Republican candidate for the New York governorship, was arrested the same day for extortion. Wachtler, resentful after his affair with Silverman ended, had been threatening and harassing his ex-lover and her daughter for months. He served a 15-month sentence in a medium-security prison in North Carolina.

## EAST 85TH STREET

### 450 East 85th Street ✦
Henry Miller, author of the sometimes banned *Tropic of Cancer*, was born on the top floor here on December 26, 1891.

## EAST 86TH STREET

### 2 East 86th Street ✦
*Adams Hotel*   On May 20, 1942, Hector Guimard, the French architect and designer, died at this one-time hotel. In exile and hopelessly out of fashion, he had been the leading proponent of the Art Nouveau style. He is remembered for his iconic and fanciful Paris Metro entrances. The building is now a luxury condominium, and its official address is 1049 Fifth Avenue.

## WEST 86TH STREET

### 7 West 86th Street
In the summer of 1900, James Buchanan "Diamond Jim" Brady moved into this four-story brownstone. It was packed with *objets d'art* from a European trip, all arranged by a society interior decorator. The house also had a restaurant-style (i.e., huge) kitchen to match his appetite, huge closets for his clothes and diamond jewelry, and a rarely used exercise room.

### West 86th Street at the Hudson River
In the fall of 1919, Edward Albert, the Prince of Wales and later Edward VIII, made his official headquarters on the British warship *Renown* at anchor here. The prince was on his first visit to the United States and Canada. As King Edward VIII in 1937, he abdicated the throne to marry an American divorcée, Mrs. Wallis Simpson.

## EAST 88TH STREET

### 57 East 88th Street
On the morning of August 28, 1963, two young women, Janice Wylie and Emily Hoffert, were viciously murdered in their third-floor apartment here. The following spring, George Whitmore Jr. was arrested, beaten, and coerced into confessing to the crime. Eventually, Whitmore was exonerated and the real killer, Richard Robles, was caught and convicted. Tremendous publicity and two books on the case became major factors helping to abolish the death penalty in New York state in 1965. Whitmore's treatment at the hands of the police also influenced the U.S. Supreme Court's 1966 decision in *Miranda v. Arizona*, which requires the police to advise criminal suspects of their rights to remain silent and to have a lawyer present during questioning.

### East 88th Street between York and East End avenues, south side
This was the site of John Jacob Astor's summer home, known as "Hell Gate." The financier spent the summers of the 1830s and '40s here on the 13-acre estate. The house lasted until 1869.

## EAST 89TH STREET

### 59 East 89th Street
*Church of St. Thomas More (Roman Catholic)* ✦ A memorial for John F. Kennedy Jr. and his wife, Carolyn Bessette Kennedy, was held here on July 23, 1999. The service ended a week of enormous media attention since the son of the country's thirty-fifth President, his wife, and sister-in-law disappeared while in his small plane off the coast of Martha's Vineyard. Some 350 invited guests, including President Bill Clinton, Kennedy's uncle Senator Edward M. Kennedy, and his sister, Caroline Kennedy Schlossberg, attended the memorial. The police cordoned off the surrounding block to give the mourners some measure of privacy.

### East 89th Street at the East River
This jutting promontory was once known as Horn's Hook. It was fortified by the Americans in 1776 before the British occupation of the city. It was again fortified against the British in 1814 during the War of 1812.

## WEST 90TH STREET

### 5 West 90th Street
Hetty Green died at the age of 82 on July 3, 1916, in her son Edward's home, a modest red brick town house that was replaced by the current

Financier Hetty Green explained her money-making success to the *New York Times* in 1905: "I buy when things are low and nobody wants them. I keep them until they go up and people are anxious to buy them."

apartment building. She was reputed to be the richest woman in the world. Nicknamed "the Witch of Wall Street," she made her money with stocks and shrewd investments. A lifelong miser, she left an estate of more than $100 million.

### 303 West 90th Street ✦

A classic gangster-style shootout took place at this address on May 7, 1931. Francis "Two Gun" Crowley, 19, fled to the top floor of this five-story building two days after killing a policeman. "Two Gun" fought it out with about 300 policemen who surrounded the place. He finally surrendered after the police fired more than 700 rounds. His 16-year-old girlfriend, Helen, and his partner, Rudolph Duringer, also survived the siege, hiding under a bed.

### 317 West 90th Street

Patty Hearst, the kidnapped heiress–turned–revolutionary, spent several days in hiding in this brownstone in June 1974. Jack Scott, a fellow radical and owner of the apartment, helped Hearst, alias "Tania," drive across the country from San Francisco. Hearst was the object of one of the nation's biggest manhunts for a year and a half before being caught by the FBI. Defended by attorney F. Lee Bailey at her trail for her part in a Symbionese Liberation Army (SLA) bank robbery, she was convicted but had her sentence commuted after 21 months by President Jimmy Carter. Later, she received a full pardon from President Bill Clinton.

## EAST 91ST STREET

### 2 East 91st Street
*Cooper-Hewitt Museum* ✦ Steel magnate Andrew Carnegie built his mansion here in 1901. That same year, he retired and sold his interest in his companies for a personal profit of $300 million, which he vowed to give away. When he died 18 years later, he had managed to give away the astounding sum of $350 million, much of it on public libraries.

### 24 East 91st Street
This was once the home of Carl Schurz, Civil War general, editor, and namesake of the nearby park. He had bought this house from his friend and neighbor Andrew Carnegie in 1902. Schurz died here on May 14, 1906.

## WEST 91ST STREET

### West 91st Street west of Columbus Avenue
*Apthorpe House* This mansion, built in 1764 and demolished in 1892, was headquarters for the British during the Revolutionary War. It was jointly occupied by General Sir Henry Clinton and Lord Charles Cornwallis in September 1776.

## EAST 93RD STREET

### 56 East 93rd Street ✦
Completed in 1932, this elegant curving town house was one of last large private homes to be built in Manhattan. It was built by wealthy stockbroker William Goadby Loew and was later home to Billy Rose, the theatrical producer. For almost 30 years it was an alcoholism recovery center for Roosevelt Hospital, treating celebrities like writer John Cheever and baseball's Darryl Strawberry. In September 2003 it was converted into additional classroom space for the nearby Spence School for girls.

### 179 East 93rd Street ✦
This was the boyhood home of the Marx Brothers. The large family lived in a small flat here from 1895 to 1910.

## EAST 94TH STREET

### 14 East 94th Street +
From 1932 to 1942 this was the home of playwright George S. Kaufman. In 1944 Kaufman sold this white town house to pianist Vladimir Horowitz, who lived here until his death on November 5, 1989.

### 339 East 94th Street +
This building and the surrounding block, now gentrified, were considered dangerous in the early 1980s, when Barack Obama lived here. The future Illinois senator and President was attending graduate school at Columbia University.

## WEST 94TH STREET

### 250 West 94th Street
*Stuart Apartment House* + Women's suffrage leader Elizabeth Cady Stanton lived here at this address, her son's home, from 1892 until her death here on October 26, 1902. While here she was visited several times by her old friend and ally Susan B. Anthony. This address was also home to author Norman Mailer. It was here on November 19, 1960, that a drunken Mailer stabbed his wife, Adele, with a penknife after a party in their apartment. He was jailed and later released on probation. At a hearing in December, Adele refused to sign a complaint, so no charges were filed.

## WEST 95TH STREET

### 115 West 95th Street
Eight-year-old Virginia O'Hanlon lived in a Queen Anne–style town house that once stood at this address. In 1897, Virginia wrote a query letter to the editor of the *New York Sun*, whose reply has been immortalized as a part of American Christmas folklore. The reassuring editorial reply contained the famous line "Yes, Virginia, there is a Santa Claus." O'Hanlon grew up, married, and was regularly interviewed by the press, usually at Christmastime.

## EAST 96TH STREET

### 108 East 96th Street
*Park 96* + This apartment building is a rare example of a New York City high-rise that became shorter. Originally 31 stories tall, the building was reduced to 19 stories in the spring of 1993 as penalty for a zoning violation. After a seven-year court battle, the developer had been ordered by the city to demolish the top 12 floors. The builders attributed the error to a mistake on the city zoning map.

### 130 East 96th Street +

On April 2, 1934, Harold Giuliani, 26, was arrested for armed robbery of a milkman in this apartment house. The crime was interrupted by a tipped-off police officer, and the thief spent 16 months in Sing Sing. Giuliani was the father of the future federal prosecutor, New York City mayor, and presidential candidate Rudolph W. Giuliani. He never confessed his criminal past to his son.

## WEST 96TH STREET

### 204 West 96th Street +

A fire at this address on December 5, 1947, led the Secret Service to the country's longest-sought and most inept counterfeiter. Edward Mieller, 72, whose two-room flat was destroyed by the fire, was forced to move in with his daughter in Queens. Sometime later, two youths scavenging through the old man's belongings tossed outside by the firefighters found some of his homemade dollar bills. Their discovery led to Mieller's capture. He had started printing his primitive bills nine years earlier, first singles and then larger denominations. Years of practice had not improved his technique. For some time his $1 bills included the misspelling "Wahsington" for the name of the nation's first President.

### West 96th Street at the Hudson River

On September 30, 1880, this was the beginning of the last leg of a journey over the centuries and over 6,000 miles. It was from here that a 3,500-year-old Egyptian obelisk, a 224-ton granite shaft nicknamed "Cleopatra's Needle," was inched to its current site in Central Park behind the Metropolitan Museum of Art. This gift from Egypt arrived by the ship *Dessoug* and was tugged night and day over wooden tracks, with the aid of cannonballs, first up 96th Street to Broadway and then south to 86th Street. It continued across town to Fifth Avenue, where it again was turned south to 82nd Street before entering the park, a journey of 112 days.

## EAST 97TH STREET

### 60 East 97th Stree +

Fashion designer Calvin Klein rescued his daughter Marci at this address 10 hours after she was abducted on February 3, 1978. Eleven-year-old Marci, who was on her way to the Dalton School, was persuaded to follow her former babysitter Christine Ransay to her sixth-floor apartment here. Ransay and her half-brother Dominique called Klein, demanding a $100,000 ransom. After paying the ransom and learning of her whereabouts, the designer, accompanied by the FBI, rushed to

The obelisk in Central Park is the oldest human-made outdoor object in the city. One hundred and thirty years in New York City air has worn away the stone. The hieroglyphics are legible in this photograph from 1903.

this address. The kidnappers, apprehended within hours, received prison sentences.

## WEST 102ND STREET

### 313 West 102nd Street ✦
Elliott Roosevelt—younger brother of Theodore, the future President, and father of Eleanor, the future First Lady—died at this address on

Eleanor Roosevelt was an orphan by the age of 10 years old. Here she is posed with her father, Elliott, who died in 1894. Her mother, Anna, had died two years earlier of diphtheria. Eleanor was raised by her maternal grandmother. (Courtesy of the Franklin D. Roosevelt Library)

August 14, 1894. The widowed Elliott, an alcoholic and an embarrassment to his family, lived in this house with his mistress under the assumed name Mr. Elliott. He was knocked unconscious in a fall and died, at the age of 34.

## WEST 103RD STREET

### 245 West 103rd Street ✦
This brownstone was the childhood home of actor Humphrey Bogart at the turn of the twentieth century. His father, Dr. Belmont DeForest Bogart, a surgeon, used the first floor as his medical office, and his mother, Maude, a successful magazine illustrator, had her artist's studio upstairs. The roof was reserved for the doctor's pigeon coops.

## WEST 113th STREET

### 278 West 113th Street ✦
8Master magician and escape artist Harry Houdini (né Erich Weiss) and his wife, Bess, bought this house in 1904. The 26-room mansion was

large enough for his substantial library on magic, a basement workshop in which to perfect props, an oversized bathtub in which to practice underwater escapes, and even room for his beloved mother, Cecilia. After his mother died, the grief-stricken magician moved out to live at his brother's family home in Queens. Three years later he returned and the house became the scene of many séances—Houdini trying to contact his dead mother and later Bess hoping to hear from Houdini himself after his death on Halloween 1926.

## WEST 115TH STREET

### 601 West 115th Street

*The Regnor* ✦ On May 16, 1979, while walking on the sidewalk in front of this 1912 apartment house, Grace Gold, a Barnard College freshman, was struck on the head and killed by a piece of terra cotta. The seventh-floor lintel loosened by age fell from the Columbia University–owned building. The tragedy prompted Local Law 10 of 1980, which required owners to inspect their façades and cornices for repairs once every three years. The law has had mixed results. Some owners check and preserve their buildings, while others remove beautiful decorative stonework rather than repair it.

## EAST 116TH STREET

### 233 East 116th Street ✦

*East Harlem Presbyterian Church* Fresh from Union Theological Seminary, Norman Thomas became the minister at this church, passing up a wealthier parish, in 1911. While here, he helped found the National Civil Rights Bureau (later the American Civil Liberties Union) in 1917. Because of his opposition to U.S. involvement in World War I and membership in the Socialist Party, church administrators and parishioners pressured him to resign in 1918. He gave up the ministry and devoted the rest of his life to social causes, the peace movement, and many unsuccessful attempts to win elective office as a Socialist Party candidate.

## WEST 116TH STREET

### West 116th Street at Lenox Avenue

*Central Park Arena* In 1880, Angel Fernandez built Manhattan's only bullring. Over the summer, eight toreadors, led by the renowned Angel Valdemoro, performed three bullfights with untamed steers shipped from Texas. As a concession to the American audiences, the advertisements promised there would be no cruelty to the animals.

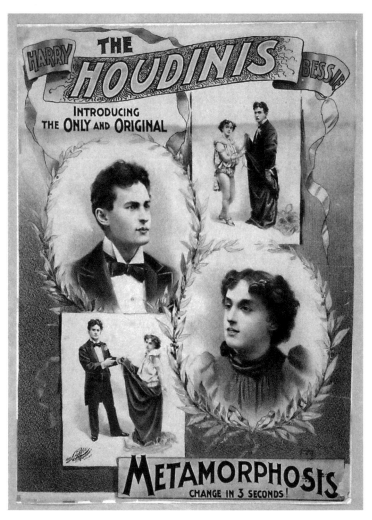

After their marriage in the summer of 1894, Bess Houdini joined Harry's magic act. At only five feet tall and under 90 pounds, her tiny frame, along with her agility, made her the perfect partner, particularly for their famous "Metamorphosis" trick, in which they changed places.

## WEST 118TH STREET

### 208 West 118th Street ✦

*Minton's Playhouse*   Opened in 1938 by saxophonist Henry Minton, this jazz club was the birthplace of bebop, a provocative style of jazz with an insistent beat and piercing dissonances ideal for small bands. During the club's peak in the early 1940s, lively jam sessions included such jazz greats as Charlie Parker, Dizzy Gillespie, and Miles Davis. Minton's also attracted the Beat writers Allen Ginsberg and Jack Kerouac, who would come here to listen to pianist Thelonious Monk.

## EAST 123RD STREET

### East 123rd Street at the Harlem River

A manhole on the end of this block was the site of a legendary sighting of a New York City sewer alligator on February 9, 1930. Three teenage boys shoveling snow discovered the reptile. The existence of Gotham's fabled but elusive creature was given credence by a report in the next day's *New York Times* headlined "ALLIGATOR FOUND IN UPTOWN SEWER."

## EAST 125TH STREET

### 41 East 125th Street

*Dapper Dan*   On May 20, 1986, Mike Tyson and Mitch "Blood" Green fought in the boxing ring at Madison Square Garden. Two years later, on August 23, 1988, at five o'clock in the morning, the two heavyweights met again in an infamous rematch here on the sidewalk. Tyson, who was leaving an all-night clothing store, encountered Green, and they started to argue. When the brawl ended, Tyson had fractured his hand and Green had a cut above his nose. Green sued for $25 million and eventually received $45,000 in damages for his injuries.

### 55 East 125th Street ✛

Former President Bill Clinton opened his post-presidential office in this building with much fanfare on July 30, 2001. Earlier, Clinton was stung by the furor over his last-minute pardons, especially the one of exiled Marc Rich, and the initial decision to locate his office in a posh building at 152 West 57th Street at taxpayers' expense. His move to Harlem was a public relations coup that helped restore his battered image. The friendship between Clinton—famously called by novelist Toni Morrison "the first black President"—and the neighborhood has benefited both parties.

## WEST 125TH STREET

### 5 West 125th Street

*Young Men's Christian Association, Harlem Branch*   On October 22, 1912, Dale Carnegie inaugurated his phenomenal career as the master guru of self-confidence by teaching his first public-speaking course here. The 24-year-old entrepreneur had persuaded a reluctant manager of the "Y" to allow him to teach his course—on a commission basis—to business-people. Carnegie's classes were a tremendous success, and he went on to write *How to Win Friends and Influence People*. The book became the biggest bestseller of a nonfiction work in modern times, second only to the Bible.

### West 125th Street between Adam Clayton Powell Jr. Boulevard and Lenox Avenue

This block on Harlem's main business artery was chosen as the spot for the city's first 25 parking meters—16 years after the first in the nation were put in use in Oklahoma City. Acting Mayor Joseph T. Sharkey borrowed a dime, much to the amusement of a crowd of dignitaries and onlookers, to activate the first meter at 12:57 P.M. on September 19, 1951. Ten cents enabled the driver to park here for an hour between the hours of 8:00 A.M. and 6:00 P.M.

### 230 West 125th Street ✦

*Blumstein's Department Store*　A longtime landmark in Harlem, this de-partment store opened in 1894. In June 1934, the store became the major target of the "Buy Where You Can Work" protest. The African American community, including leaders such as the Reverend Adam Clayton Powell Jr., boycotted and picketed the store for a month until management agreed to hire 35 African American clerks and salespeople. The successful protest forced other major businesses to end or not prac-tice discrimination against African Americans and served as a model for later boycotts. By 1943 the store was the first to feature African American models and mannequins and even the first African American Santa Claus.

On September 20, 1958, when Dr. Martin Luther King Jr., who was autographing copies of his new book, *Stride Toward Freedom*, here, he was stabbed by Izola Ware Curry, a mentally unstable African American woman. The 29-year-old King was rushed to Harlem Hospital and un-derwent three hours of surgery to remove a steel letter-opener. New York Governor W. Averell Harriman and Roy Wilkins of the NAACP both went to the hospital to check on his condition. Although his re-covery was slowed by pneumonia, he was released by the hospital two weeks later. In a characteristic act, King forgave Curry and said he bore her no ill will. Nonetheless, she was judged incompetent to stand trial and was committed to a hospital for the criminally insane.

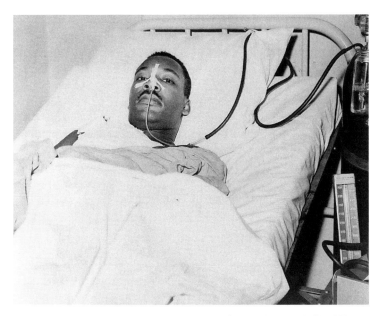

The Reverend Martin Luther King Jr. spent two weeks in Harlem Hospital in 1958 recovering from a stabbing during a book signing. His condition was complicated by pneumonia.

## 253 West 125th Street

*Apollo Theater* ✦ In addition to being the showcase for African American musical talent, the Apollo is also a Harlem institution. Its golden age began in 1934, when the new owners, Frank Schiffman and Leo Brechter, began a "colored revue." Over the years, entertainers from Bessie Smith to Ray Charles have performed here. On November 21, 1934, Ella Fitzgerald made her debut in the club's famous amateur contest, winning first prize. Other winners in the Wednesday night competitions have included "Godfather of Soul" James Brown, Sarah Vaughan, and the Jackson Five. The theater has also served as a gathering place for New York's African American community.

On the night of May 6, 1995, it was the site of an historic reconciliation between Dr. Betty Shabazz, the widow of Malcolm X, and Louis H. Farrakhan, the Nation of Islam leader. Shabazz had repeatedly and publicly declared Farrakhan partly responsible for her husband's murder. Called "A New Beginning," the event was part political rally and part fundraiser for Malcolm X and Dr. Shabazz's daughter Qubilah, who earlier in the week agreed to "accept responsibility" for her involvement in a plot to kill Farrakhan. Federal prosecutors had agreed not to take the case to trial if she sought psychiatric, drug, and alcohol treatment.

## EAST 126TH STREET

### 17 East 126th Street ✤
On assignment for *Esquire* magazine in August 1958, photographer Art Kane used this brownstone as a backdrop for his famous jazz musician portrait. Among the 57 jazz greats who spilled down the steps to the curb were Dizzy Gillespie, Gene Krupa, Thelonious Monk, and Count Basie. This address has become the place for a group photo for everyone from the local Little League baseball team to "gangsta rappers."

## WEST 126TH STREET

### West 126th Street near Frederick Douglass Boulevard
*Hotel Braddock*   What began as an argument between the hotel management and a female guest escalated into a full-fledged race riot on August 1, 1943. James Collins, a white police officer, was attempting to arrest the woman for disturbing the peace when Robert Bandy, an African American serviceman, came to the woman's aid. Bandy fought with the officer and hit him before fleeing the hotel. Collins chased and shot Bandy in the shoulder and marched him to nearby Sydenham Hospital. A crowd gathered and grew angry with each retelling of the story and each rumor. By the time it was over, six black people were dead, 500 had been injured, and more than 100 had been jailed.

## EAST 127TH STREET

### 20 East 127th Street ✤
This brownstone row house was home to poet Langston Hughes for some 20 years. He lived on the top floor of what was then a rooming house, beginning in 1947.

## WEST 129TH STREET

### 211 West 129th Street
*Salem United Methodist Church* ✤ On April 9, 1928, this church was the site of one of the social events of the 1920s, the wedding of Harlem Renaissance writer Countee Cullen and W. E. B. Du Bois's daughter Yolande. The African American community was delighted to celebrate this elite union, which lasted only two years. Langston Hughes and

Arna Bontemps were part of the wedding party, and the marriage was officiated by the groom's adoptive father, the pastor of the church.

## WEST 134TH STREET

### West 134th Street east of Lenox Avenue

The first apartment houses in Harlem that became available to African Americans are located on this block. In 1910 landlords, unable to find white tenants for their new buildings, permitted Philip A. Payton, an African American Realtor, to fill two apartment houses with black tenants. Several neighborhood white property owners panicked and bought the buildings in order to evict the African Americans. In response, Payton and his Afro-American Realty Company purchased several other buildings and made them available to African Americans. Later St. Philip's Episcopal Church, a black congregation, purchased several apartment houses on West 134th Street. The church paid more than a million dollars for the property, the largest real estate agreement involving African Americans up to that time. The racial economic warfare ended as whites abandoned Harlem. Long denied decent housing, African Americans who had been forced to live in the overcrowded ghetto centered on West 53rd Street, called San Juan Hill, flocked to Harlem. African Americans from the U.S. South, who came to the city during World War I for better wages and a better life, also moved to Harlem. By 1920, the African American population of New York City had grown four times larger in a decade, and most of this growth was in Harlem. Harlem was well on the way to becoming the heart and capital of black America.

### 210 West 134th Street

*St. Philip's Episcopal Church* ✦ The African American congregation at this church, one of the first to move to central Harlem, in 1909, was established in the early nineteenth century in lower Manhattan on Centre Street. It was instrumental in attracting blacks to the neighborhood. Two African American architects, George W. Foster Jr. and Vertner W. Tandy (the latter the first African American architect registered in New York state), designed the since–New York City–landmarked Gothic church.

## WEST 135TH STREET

### 103 West 135th Street

*The 135th Street Branch of the New York Public Library* ✦ This branch served as the meeting place for the writers of the Harlem Renaissance of the mid-1920s. These gifted African American authors began to depict African American life and culture realistically in their works, often written in African American dialect and reflecting a growing black pride. The group included Langston Hughes, Jean Toomer, and Countee Cullen. The basement was home to the American Negro Theater, where actors Harry Belafonte and Sidney Poitier made their debuts. This branch, still standing, served as the initial repository for Arthur Schomburg's extensive archive and history of African American life. The collection, now named in honor of Schomburg, is housed next door on Lenox Avenue.

### 180 West 135th Street
*The Harlem Young Men's Christian Association* ✦ After the organization outgrew the branch across the street at 181 West 135th Street, this structure was built in 1932. The "Y" served as a first home for many African American men moving to the city during the mass migration of African Americans from the U.S. South to Northern cities during the 1920s and 1930s. These two branches were the first New York homes to Langston Hughes, Ralph Ellison, and Claude McKay.

### 187 West 135th Street ✦
A National Historic Landmark, No. 187 was the last home of James Weldon Johnson, from 1925 until his death in 1938. Johnson was an author and poet during the Harlem Renaissance and a noted African American political leader. While attending Columbia University, he supported Theodore Roosevelt in the presidential election of 1904 and wrote a campaign song, "You're All Right Teddy." He was rewarded for his efforts with two consular posts in South America. His poem "Lift Every Voice and Sing" was later set to music and was known as the Negro National Anthem.

### West 135th Street at the Hudson River
On April 7, 1917, one day after Congress declared war on Germany, the collector of the Port of New York, Dudley Malone, and 600 of his Customs agents boarded the German passenger ship *Vaterland*, docked here. The ship was declared interned. This quiet drama performed with dignity and cooperation by both parties was the United States' first act of war against Germany and the beginning of American involvement in World War I.

Two years later, in September 1919, these piers anchored the *SS Yarmouth*, owned by the charismatic African American leader Marcus Garvey and his Black Star shipping line. This small steamship was intended to be the first link between his African American followers and the "African motherland." Garvey planned to use this and other ships for his "Back to Africa" campaign. This campaign proved to be his undoing. Garvey's financial dealings with the Black Star line led to a prison term for mail fraud and his deportation to Jamaica.

## WEST 136TH STREET

### 108 West 136th Street

This address was once the elegant home of Madam C. J. Walker, a very successful African American woman who sold hair-care products. The Georgian-style home was constructed from two existing town houses by African American architect Vertner W. Tandy in 1915, shortly after African Americans began buying Harlem real estate. After Walker's death in 1919, her daughter A'Lelia Walker Robinson lived in the house and created a lively literary salon for the Harlem Renaissance writers of the 1920s. She named it the Dark Tower Tea Club, after a monthly column, "The Dark Tower," written by her friend the poet Countee Cullen. The town house was demolished in 1941 for the Countee Cullen Branch of the New York Public Library, an addition to the branch on West 135th Street.

## WEST 138TH STREET

### 56 West 138th Street

Marcus Garvey was shot here in the *Negro World* office on October 14, 1919, by George Tyler, a disgruntled investor. Garvey was taken to Harlem Hospital, and Tyler was arrested. Two days later, Tyler committed suicide by jumping from a third-floor jail cell. Garvey recovered and became even more popular.

### 120 West 138th Street +

*Liberty Hall* This was the site of the first International Convention of Negro Peoples of the World. In August 1920, more than 3,000 delegates ratified a Declaration of Independence with 66 articles, a universal anthem, and the colors red, black, and green. Marcus Garvey was elected "provisional President of the Republic of Africa." Garvey and his powerful newspaper, *The Negro World*, were influential in furthering the cause of African American rights and African nationalism. The month-long convention culminated in a mass meeting at Madison Square Garden. The building later became the headquarters for the Universal Negro Improvement Association (UNIA).

### 132 West 138th Street

*Abyssinian Baptist Church* ✦ This neo-Gothic–style church was once the power base for the Reverend Adam Clayton Powell Jr., Harlem's controversial and flamboyant congressman from 1945 to 1970. Powell, a leading voice for African Americans in the civil rights era, built his major Harlem following here through his father's Abyssinian pulpit. The congregation, the largest black congregation in the United States, was founded in 1808 in lower Manhattan.

## WEST 139TH STREET

### 228 West 139th Street ✦

Fletch Henderson, jazz pianist and orchestra leader, bought this house in 1924. To help pay the mortgage, he rented rooms to fellow musicians who played in the nearby clubs. Cab Calloway was one of the boarders. He spent his first night in New York City here in September 1927.

## WEST 145TH STREET

### West 145th Street at Convent Avenue

This intersection at 9:00 A.M. on November 27, 1924, was the starting point for the first Macy's Thanksgiving Day Parade, then called the Christmas Parade. The guest of honor then, as now, was Santa Claus. But in this first parade, St. Nick was really given the royal treatment. After riding his sleigh float along the long and roundabout route, Santa was crowned "King of Kiddies" while seated on a gold throne on the marquee over the entrance to the 34th Street store. The Thanksgiving Day Parade has been a beloved New York City tradition for every year since, except for several years during World War II.

## WEST 155TH STREET

### West 155th Street between Frederick Douglass Boulevard and the Harlem River Drive

*Polo Grounds* After the stands at the old Polo Grounds on Central Park North were torn down in 1890, the Giants baseball team moved its games uptown to this location a year later. In addition to the Giants, who played here for six or seven years, this field was home to the New York Yankees for about a decade beginning in 1912 and also the first home to the New York Mets in 1962. In the 1890s Harry Magley Stevens, the director of catering, popularized (some say invented) the hot dog. He called them "red hots." On April 16, 1920, home plate was the site

In October 1913, the World Series was played at the Polo Grounds at West 155th Street, the home field for the New York Giants. The Philadelphia Athletics beat New York four games to one.

of the only Major League fatality during a game. Cleveland Indians shortstop Ray Chapman was killed by a spitball. The site is now a housing project of four towers over 30 stories.

## WEST 160TH STREET

### 555 West 160th Street ✦

On July 9, 1986, a sports car stopped here and its occupants stepped out to buy drugs from three dealers seated on the stoop. The passengers were U.S. Attorney and future mayor Rudolph W. Giuliani, wearing sunglasses and dressed in a Hell's Angels black leather vest, and New York Senator Alfonse D'Amato, disguised in an Army cap and windbreaker. The two "undercover" officials, city police, and no fewer than 30 conspicuous federal officers were on a mission to demonstrate to the public how easy it was to buy crack cocaine. The event was called an intelligence-gathering operation and no arrests were made. It also marked the beginning of D'Amato's reelection campaign.

# GENERAL INDEX

Edward VII, 96, 174, 178
Edward VIII, 299, 303, 369
Eight, The, 149, 242
"18 Happenings in 6 Parts," 156
Einstein, Albert, 326
Eisenhower, Dwight D., 239, 339, 356, 357
Eisenhower, Dwight David II, 239
Eisenhower, Julie Nixon, 239
electricity, 29, 43, 52, 57, 70, 79, 109, 164, 171, *172*, 183, 187, 193, 199, 209, 216, 223, 235, 236, 247, 263, 281, 308, 333, 355
Electric Lady Studios, 168
elephants, 4, *5*, 12
elevated railway, 37, *166*, 207
elevators, *18*, 69, 70, 91, *114*, 143, 202, 236, 244, 292, 348, 351
Elgin Botanical Garden, 253, *255*
Elizabeth II, 15, 38
Ellington, Duke, 196, 312, 319, 337, 344
Ellis Island, 3, 129
Ellison, Ralph, 384
Eltinge, Julian, 294
Embury, Philip, 40
Emerson, Ralph Waldo, 123
Emma, Queen of the Sandwich Islands, 159
Emmett, Dan, 84, 91
*Emperor Jones, The* (O'Neill), 128
Empire State Building, 209, 241
Equal Rights Party, 91
Equitable Life, 17, *18*, 244, 259
Ericsson, John, 79, 153
Erie Canal, 126
Ernst, Max, 210, 311
Escoffier, Auguste, 352
espionage, 46, 54, 78, 93, 99, 105, 118, 157, 253, 256, 259, 266, 282, 290, 292, 302, 304, 308, 348
Evacuation Day, 228
Evans, Walker, 121
Everett House Hotel, 269
Exchange Building, 11
Exhibition of 1853, 201

Fairbanks, Douglas, 297
Fall, Albert B., 41

FALN, 11
*Fantasticks, The*, 141
Farrakhan, Louis H., 381
Farren, George Percy, 85
Farrow, Mia, 239
*Faust*, 187
FBI, 70, 78, 118, 129, 131, 237, 256, 282, 299, 303, 340, 355, 362, 368, 372, 374
Federal Hall, 58, *59*, 61
Federal Reserve Board, 8, 41
*Federalist Papers*, 344
Federalist Party, 88
Feeks, John, 29
Felix the Cat, 323
Ferber, Edna, 339
Fermi, Enrico, 325
ferries, 34, 35, 36, 56, 67, 71, 114, 142, 295, 302
Field, Cyrus, 207, 224
Fields, W. C., 195, 294
Fifth Avenue Hotel, 236, *237*, 360
Fillmore, Millard, 20, 88, 90
Fillmore East, 152
Finkelstein, Isaac, 126
fires, 3, 9, 10, 15, *16*, 17, 18, 21, 36, 38, *39*, 42, 46, 60, 66, 68, 70, 71, 80, 85, 88, 93, 101, 106, 111, *113*, 123, 131, 143, *144*, 156, *157*, 166, 167, 175, 195, 199, 200, 243, 245, 247, 292, *293*, 302, *328*, 374
fireworks, 188
First Houses, 156
Fischer, Bobby, 85
Fischer, William, 282
Fish, Hamilton, 174
Fish, Mamie, 205
Fish, Stuyvesant, 140, 205
Fisk, Jim, 46, *47*, 97, 260
Fitch, John, 106
Fitzgerald, Ella, 264, 381
Fitzgerald, F. Scott, 246, 260, 295
Five Points, 150, *151*
Flagg, James Montgomery, 313, 359
Flatiron Building, 235, *238*
Fleischmann's Vienna Model Bakery, 101
Floradora Girls, 187
flu. *See* influenza

Seneca Village, 329

Sennett, Mack, 176

September 11 terrorist attacks, 4, 19, 20, 37, 38, 60, 68, *157*, 202, 213, 274, 354

Seton, Elizabeth Ann, 54, *55*

Sevareid, Eric, 217

*Seven Year Itch, The*, 212

Seventh Regimental NYSM, 154, *155*, 339

Seymour, Horatio, 93, 179

Shabazz, Betty, 381

Shah of Iran, 359

Shahzad, Faisal, 299

Shanksville, Pennsylvania, 71

Sharkey's, 334

Shaw, George Bernard, 227, 288

Shearing, George, 198

Shearith Israel Congregation, 54, 137, *138*

Shearith Israel Graveyard, *138*

Sheridan, Philip, *110*

Sherman, William T., *110*, 246, 360

Sherry Netherland Hotel, 348

Sherry's Hotel, 244

Sherwood, Robert, 297

Shinn, Everett, 149, 277

Sickles, Daniel, 161, *162*

Sigel, Elsie, 263

Sigel, Franz, 263

Siegel-Cooper Department Store, 251

Sign of the Dove Tavern, 348

Silverman, Joy, 368

Silverstein, Larry, 72

Simmon's Tavern, 57

Simon and Garfunkel, 158

Sims, James, 215

Sinatra, Frank, 196, 197, 249, 352

Sinclair, Harry, 41, 367

Sinclair, Upton, 80

Singer, Isaac Bashevis, 115, 278

Singer, Isaac Merritt, 120, 160

Singer Building, 18, *19*

Sinsheimer Café, 116

Sixty-ninth Regiment Armory, NYSM, 208

Slack, John, 213

slavery, 10, 34, 38, *40*, 42, 57, 63, 64, 79, 84, 85, 90, 101, 107, 111, 112, 125, 132, 136, 286, 298, 337, 346

Slide, The, 82

Sloan, John, 158, 165, 167, 242, 276, 277, 313

Smith, Albert E., 44

Smith, Alfred E., 54, 120, 132, 190, 231, 246, 270, 340

Smith, Bessie, 272, 319, 381

Smith, Francis Hopkinson, 172

Smith, Kate, 195, 217

Smith, Patti, 88, 224, 276

Smith, William F., 241

Smithsonian Institution, 6

Socialist Party, 207, 377

Society for the Prevention of Cruelty to Animals, 235, 290

Society for the Prevention of Cruelty to Children, 235

Society of Independent Artists, 173

soda fountain, 37

Sonic Youth, 87

Sonnenberg, Benjamin Sr., 205

Sons of Liberty, 17, 32, 40, 51

Soong May-ling. *See* Chiang Kai-shek, Madame

Soper, George, 267

Sousa, John Philip, 192, 260

Soviet Union, 68, 129, 175, 282, 296, 319

Soyer, Raphael, 364

Spanish–American War, 36, 45, 122, 236, *238*

Sparks Steakhouse, 300

speakeasies, 80, 128, 199, 271, 299, 304

Spitzer, Eliot, 72, 231

Spock, Benjamin, 65

Springsteen, Bruce, 81, 224

Spungen, Nancy, 277

Stadt Huys, 50

Stage Deli, 260

Stage Door Canteen, 297

Stamp Act, 6, 17, 32, 58

Stamp Act Congress, 58

stamps, 43, 77

Stanley, Henry Morton, 22, 234

Stanton, Elizabeth Cady, 90, 298, 373

Statue of Liberty, 219, 220, 266, 329

*Steamboat Willie*, 198

## MANHATTAN AND THE CIVIL WAR

## MANHATTAN MAYHEM

## MANHATTAN AND THE PRESIDENTS

## MANHATTAN AND THE REVOLUTIONARY WAR

**If *All Around the Town* has piqued your interest in New York history, check out the following related titles:**

*A Century of Subways: Celebrating 100 Years of New York's Underground Railways*
Brian J. Cudahy

*Civil Rights in New York City: From World War II to the Giuliani Era*
Clarence Taylor (ed.)

*Dutch New York: The Roots of Hudson Valley Culture*
Roger Panetta (ed.), with a Foreword by Russell Shorto

*Fifth Avenue Famous: The Extraordinary Story of Music at St. Patrick's Cathedral*
Salvatore Basile, with a Foreword by Most Reverend Timothy M. Dolan, Archbishop of New York

*Going Coastal New York City: Urban Waterfront Guide, Second Edition*
Barbara LaRocco

*The Hudson-Fulton Celebration: New York's River Festival of 1909 and the Making of a Metropolis*
Kathleen Eagen Johnson, with a Foreword by Kenneth T. Jackson and a Preface by Mark F. Rockefeller

*Lost Waterfront: The Decline and Rebirth of Manhattan's Western Shore*
Photographs by Shelley Seccombe, Introduction by Phillip Lopate, Foreword by Albert K. Butzel

*The Rose Man of Sing Sing: A True Tale of Life, Murder, and Redemption in the Age of Yellow Journalism*
James M. Morris

*A Short and Remarkable History of New York City*
Jane Mushabac and Angela Wigan

*The Street Book: An Encyclopedia of Manhattan's Street Names and Their Origins*
Henry Moscow

*Under the Sidewalks of New York: The Story of the Greatest Subway System in the World*
Brian J. Cudahy

*Victor Herbert: A Theatrical Life*
Neil Gould

**Available at www.fordhampress.com, independent and chain bookstores, and online resellers.**